WORD FOR WINDOWS DESIGN COMPANION

The Desktop Guide to Creating Great-Looking Brochures, Ads, Newsletters & More

◆　　◆　　◆　　◆　　◆　　◆　　◆　　◆　　◆

THROUGH VERSION 6

Katherine Shelly Pfeiffer

VENTANA
PRESS

Word for Windows Design Companion:
The Desktop Guide to Creating Great-Looking Brochures, Ads, Newsletters & More
Through Version 6, Second Edition

Library of Congress Cataloging-in-Publication Data

Pfeiffer, Katherine Shelly.
    Word for Windows design companion : the desktop guide to creating great-looking
  brochures, ads, newsletters & more through version 6 / Katherine Shelly Pfeiffer. -- 2nd ed.
       p. cm.
    Includes bibliographical references and index.
    ISBN 1-56604-075-2
    1. Microsoft Word for Windows.   2. Desktop publishing   I. Title.
  Z253.532.M53P47   1994
  686.2'2544536--dc20   93-43097
                                              CIP

Book design: Marcia Webb, Karen Wysocki
Cover design: Pam Belleville and Spring Davis-Charles, One-of-a-Kind Design;
  adaptation: Robert Harris
Illustrations: Katherine Shelly Pfeiffer (Chapter 5 through Chapter 9), Cassell Design,
  April Higgins, Susan Worsley
Index service: Dianne Bertsch, Answers Plus
Editorial consultant: Daniel Will-Harris, TypeStyle Ink
Technical review: Brian Little, The Imagination Workshop
Editorial staff: Diana Merelman, Pam Richardson, Jessica Ryan
Production staff: Brian Little, Terri March, Marcia Webb
Proofreader: Eric Edstam

Excerpt from David Rubin's article, "Sound for Multimedia," quoted by permission from New
  Media Research, Los Altos, CA, publisher of *New Media Products*.

Second Edition 9 8 7 6 5 4 3 2 1
Printed in the United States of America

Ventana Press, Inc.
P.O. Box 2468
Chapel Hill, NC 27515
919/942-0220; FAX 919/942-1140

TRADEMARKS

Trademarked names appear throughout this book. Rather than list the names and entities that own the trademarks or insert a trademark symbol with each mention of the trademarked name, the publisher states that it is using the names only for editorial purposes and to the benefit of the trademark owner with no intention of infringing upon that trademark.

LIMITS OF LIABILITY AND DISCLAIMER OF WARRANTY

The author and publisher of this book have used their best efforts in preparing the book and the programs contained in it. These efforts include the development, research and testing of the theories and programs to determine their effectiveness. The author and publisher make no warranty of any kind, expressed or implied, with regard to these programs or the documentation contained in this book.

The author and publisher shall not be liable in the event of incidental or consequential damages in connection with, or arising out of, the furnishing, performance or use of the programs, associated instructions and/or claims of productivity gains.

ABOUT THE AUTHOR

Katherine Shelly Pfeiffer is a Professor of Art at East Los Angeles College, where she teaches computer graphics, desktop publishing design and art history. In 1988, she was first-place winner in the Xerox Ventura Publisher Design for Excellence Contest; her winning entry was subsequently used on Ventura Publisher packaging. She is author of the *LaserJet Font Book* and a regular columnist for *Technique* magazine. Her articles have appeared in *Business Publishing* and *Desktop Communications*. She is an avid aquarist and has published articles in several aquarium magazines. She holds a Ph.D. in art history from UCLA. She lives in Los Angeles with her husband and son.

ACKNOWLEDGMENTS

The long journey of this book has brought me into contact with a great many generous and talented people. Among those whose help has been indispensable are

My husband, David, for his loving support.

Daniel Will-Harris (who seems to know more about most software than the people who designed it) for his excellent technical editing and his invaluable and incisive advice on matters too numerous to list.

Don Chipperfield, Professor of Art at East Los Angeles College, for critiquing my typography and encouraging me in this endeavor.

For fonts and information on typefaces: LaVon Collins and Kathy Mandel of Adobe Systems, Inc.; Stefan Wennick of Bitstream; Judith Frye at Casady & Greene; Bill Neuenschwander for Digital Typeface Corporation; Zuzana Licko of Emigre; Bob Hager of Linotype-Hell; and Steve Kuhlman of Monotype Typography.

For technical support: Peter Stamos at Microsoft; Bill Powell of LaserMaster; and the Word for Windows technical support staff at Microsoft.

Also at Microsoft Corporation: Christy Gersich, Kornel Marton and Tracy Van Hoof. And special thanks to Carol, Tonya, Lou-Ann and Carol for assistance above and beyond their job descriptions.

At LaserMaster Corporation: Bill Neuenschwander and Bill Dreis.

At Ventana Press: Brian Little, Joy Metelits, Pam Richardson, Jessica Ryan, Marcia Webb, Elizabeth Woodman and the dedicated staff at Ventana Press.

Dedication

Dedicated with love and gratitude to my parents:
Mary "Mimi" DeCoudres Pfeiffer &
Shelly Bernhardt Pfeiffer

Contents

Introduction   **xix**

Section I: **Looking at Word**

Chapter

1

From Word Processing to Desktop Publishing   **1**

The Word Screen Tour   3
    Tools of the Trade ◆ Formatting Toolbar

Custom Tailoring   6

Macro City   6

Everybody's Doing It: The Drag & Drop   7

Windows With a View   7

Help Is Close at Hand   8

A Program With Character(s)   9

Beautiful Pages With Formatting Options   9

Let's Get Graphic   12

Chart Your Future   14

Chapter 2

Desktop Publishing Features & Commands   17

Paragraphs & Paragraph Marks   20

Getting Word Ready   22

　　Saving ◆ Abandoning Changes & Using Undo

Coping With Multiple Files   23

Outlines   24

Editing Reminder & Aggravation Avoider   25

Installing New Fonts   25

　　Working Without Matching Screen Fonts

Macros   27

Customize Word's Interface   29

　　View ◆ General

Custom Toolbars   31

Section II: Looking at Design

Chapter 3

A Brief Introduction to Design   35

The Dynamic Duos   36

Typographics Elements   42

　　Typefaces ◆ Type Families ◆ Type Size ◆ Line Space
　　◆ Line Lengths & Column Widths ◆ Kerning, Letter
　　Spacing & Ligatures ◆ Type Alignment

Page Layout Basics   57

　　Grids: The Page Skeleton ◆ Attention-Getters

Chapter 4

Design Do's & Don'ts 65

Do Doodle ◆ Show Your Face(s) ◆ The Collection Box ◆ Double Up ◆ Big Is Best ◆ Consistency Counts ◆ What's Your Line? ◆ Heading Into Space ◆ Zap the Gaps ◆ Dam the Rivers ◆ The Hole Story ◆ Bar That Space Bar ◆ When in Rome ◆ Real Smart Quotes ◆ Help for Widows & Orphans ◆ The Bottom Line ◆ The Conservative Type ◆ Boxing Rules ◆ A Shady Background ◆ Stay Regular ◆ Crowd Control ◆ Lost in Space

Section III: **Looking Good With Word**

Chapter 5

Business & Personal Correspondence 83

Letterhead   83

Projecting the Sender's Image ◆ Choosing Type ◆ Incorporating Logos & Artwork

Business Cards   88
Fax Covers   89
Memos   90
Résumés   90
Typeset Business Letters & News Releases   91
Announcements, Invitations & Awards   92
Step-by-Step Illustrations   94

Chapter 6

Forms & Surveys 133

Forms Follow Function   133
Design Tips & Traps   135
Surveys   136
Step-by-Step Illustrations   138

Chapter 7

Promotional Materials: Ads, Flyers & Brochures   **165**

Advertisements   168
Flyers   168
Brochures   169
Step-by-Step Illustrations   172

Chapter 8

Newsletters   **211**

Anatomy of a Newsletter   211
Using a Grid   215
A Few Pitfalls to Avoid   215
Column Formats   216

> One-Column Format ◆ Two-Column Format
> ◆ Three-Column Format ◆ Four-Column Format ◆ Two-
> and-a-Half-Column Format

Step-by-Step Illustrations   222

Chapter 9

Books, Catalogs & Manuals   **247**

Front Matter   248
Main Text Section   249
Back Matter   251
Book Design   251

> Selecting a Typeface ◆ Traditional Versus Modern
> Book Design ◆ Pagination

Manuals   255
Catalogs   256
Step-by-Step Illustrations   258

Section IV: **A Closer Look**

Chapter 10

Character & Paragraph Formatting 303

Character Formatting 303

Applying Character Formatting ◆ Gray/Blank Boxes ◆ Copying Character Formatting ◆ To Undo Manual Character Formatting ◆ Replacing a Character ◆ Character Spacing ◆ Superscript & Subscript ◆ Using Special Characters

Paragraph Formatting 315

Displaying & Removing Paragraph Marks

The Paragraph Dialog Box 317

Line Spacing (Leading) Options ◆ Other Line-Spacing Options ◆ Using At Least & Exactly Line Spacing ◆ Spacing Before & After Paragraphs ◆ Creating Special Vertical Spacing ◆ Alignment ◆ Tabs & Tab Leaders

Removing, Repeating & Copying Paragraph Formatting 326

Other Ways to Alter Paragraph Formatting

Styles & Templates 328

Chapter 11

Frames, Borders & Tables 331

Frames 331

Creating a Frame Style ◆ Working Inside & Outside a Frame ◆ Frames for Special Purposes ◆ Positioning & Sizing Frames ◆ Getting Stuck in Frames

Borders & Shading 338

Border & Shading Basics ◆ Creating Rules

Tables   347

    Creating a Table ◆ Formatting Text in Tables ◆ Using
    Borders Inside Tables ◆ Borders Around Tables & Table
    Cells ◆ Margins in Tables ◆ Spacing Inside Cells
    ◆ Spacing Between Rows & Columns ◆ Potential
    Problems in Working With Tables

Chapter 12

Graphics   **357**

Clip Art   357

Windows Drawing Programs   358

    Word's Drawing Tools ◆ Windows Paint
    ◆ Microsoft Graph

Scanning   362

Type As Art   363

    Microsoft WordArt

Importing Graphics   366

    Importing Problems ◆ Embedded Objects

Working With Graphics   368

    A Note on Printing Graphics

Chapter 13

Tips & Trouble-Shooting   **375**

Page Setup   375

    Mirror-Image Pages ◆ To Make Uneven Columns
    ◆ Margins for Large Text & Graphics ◆ Changing Page
    Dimensions Inside a Document ◆ Test for Paper-Tray
    "Slop" ◆ Headers & Footers ◆ Frames vs. Tables vs.
    Text Boxes

Printing Tips   383

Trouble-Shooting   384

    Tortured Text ◆ Toolbar Trials ◆ Flying Objects
    ◆ Frame Frights ◆ Missing Pieces ◆ Stubborn
    Styles ◆ Flighty Fonts ◆ Pages Plus ◆ Memory
    Messages

Section V: **Appendices**

Appendix A

Type Selection Guide   **397**

Type Families   397

Simplified Type Classifications   400

Building a Type Library   411

Create a Type Specimen   413

Selecting Digital Typefaces   416

Font Managers   417

Recommended Font Developers   421

Typefaces Used in *Word for Windows Design Companion*   426

Appendix B

Font Library   **433**

Appendix C

A Few Words on Paper   **447**

Companion Disks Sneak Preview   451

Glossary   453

Bibliography   463

Notes on Hardware & Software   473

Index   475

Introduction

Not long ago, the typical Courier 10 document was an acceptable form of business communication. With the advent of the personal computer—followed by its democratization of the graphic arts—nearly everyone who produces printed materials should know at least the basics of desktop publishing and graphic design.

The good news is that many word processors now include graphics features that allow everyone to make their documents more attractive and persuasive.

Word for Windows is more than an exceptionally powerful word processor. It's a cornucopia of advanced text formatting, page layout, graphics handling and chart-making features and functions—tools that when properly used can make your word processed materials look their best.

Moreover, its capabilities surpass many desktop publishing program offerings; and its efficient use of the Windows interface, the Standard toolbar, the Formatting toolbar and the rulers, make the great power of this program accessible and fun to use.

WHO NEEDS THIS BOOK?

Word for Windows Design Companion, Second Edition, was written as a source of ideas and information for anyone who uses Word for Windows version 6 or 2, as well as anyone interested in switching from another word processor. No matter what type of documents you wish to produce—letters, reports, forms, books, brochures, manuals, advertisements, flyers—you'll find tips and examples to help you design them for optimal visual impact.

All the illustrated documents in Section III of this book were created in Word for Windows. The techniques used to produce each example are explained in detail so that you can create your own design using the same methods.

WHAT'S INSIDE

In Section I, "Looking at Word," I introduce and summarize the Word for Windows conventions, screen features, commands and menu structures that make the program ideal for document design. Section II, "Looking at Design," focuses on considerations you need to think about when designing any documents. To reinforce this information, you'll learn many of the tips, tricks and traps of basic design that can make the difference between a fair document and a great one.

Section III, "Looking Good With Word," presents a gallery of Word for Windows documents that demonstrate a wide variety of design styles. The introduction to each of these chapters discusses the artistic and technical issues involved in the designs.

Each document is accompanied by a complete explanation of the layout and design, typefaces and dimensions used to create it, and a step-by-step description of the

Word for Windows techniques used. The documents illustrated and discussed include letterhead stationery, business cards, résumés, invitations, announcements, brochures, advertisements, news releases, memos, order forms, purchase orders, award certificates, calendars, surveys, flyers, newsletters, reports, books and technical manuals.

Section IV, "A Closer Look," addresses Word's formatting features for text, frames, borders and tables. You'll also find a chapter devoted to importing graphics from other programs, using scanned images, and creating illustrations, charts and other art using Word's drawing tools, Microsoft Draw, Microsoft Graph and Microsoft WordArt.

The last chapter alerts you to problems you may encounter in your design work and offers solutions for dealing with them.

HOW TO USE THIS BOOK

I've tried to present the material in this book in a useful, logical fashion. However, before you start to read, please look at the sample documents—they're meant to inspire and encourage you. If you're familiar with Word already, you'll probably be able to utilize the samples immediately. If you need more information on design issues, read Chapters 3 and 4. For more technique and formatting information, see Chapters 10 and 11.

Note: This book does not contain step-by-step instructions for basic Word and Windows procedures. If you don't know how to open and close a document; or what cut, copy and paste mean; or how to select text—you need to read your *User's Guide* before you attempt to re-create the designs in Section III.

HARDWARE & SOFTWARE REQUIREMENTS

In order to create documents similar to the ones shown in this book, you'll need a PC using an 80286 (theoretically possible, but not recommended), 80386 or higher microprocessor, Word for Windows version 6 or 2 and Windows 3.0 or later. I also strongly recommend using a mouse; it's well suited to the tasks involved in page layout.

Two megabytes of memory (RAM) are recommended; 4 or more megabytes would be much better. You'll need a minimum of 5 megabytes of hard disk space, but you should plan on using 10 to 15 megabytes for the full program. (Buy the biggest hard disk you can afford. Windows likes lots of space for swap files when working in 386 Enhanced mode.)

SEIZE THE DAY!

While producing truly great design may take years of experience and formal training, the craft of making desktop published materials look crisp, clean and well designed is something anyone can master with some effort. If this book helps you save time and money over more expensive methods, and if along the way you pick up a few pointers on making your printed materials more attractive and persuasive, it will have achieved its purpose. Let's get started.

—Katherine Shelly Pfeiffer

I

Looking at Word

1
From Word Processing to Desktop Publishing

Why use a word processor for page layout? With a standard word processor you create pages in much the same way as the old-fashioned typewriter—but your computer is NOT a typewriter. Ordinary word processors use monospaced, monolined type, like Courier. Their interline spacing is rigid and crude, falling in single-line increments. Subtlety is impossible to achieve. And it's often impossible to include graphics. Furthermore, your word processed reports and newsletters look just like every other word processed document.

Word for Windows Version 6 crosses the frontier—from the drab world of word processing into the exciting world of desktop publishing. The new version features a cornucopia of page layout tools that are easy to learn and a delight to use. Now you can produce your own professional-looking business cards, letterheads, reports, newsletters and advertisements.

Word for Windows Design Companion, Second Edition, offers you the tools and inspiration that will let you take advantage of Word's graphics power. With a basic knowledge of the program and the ideas and information that fill this book, you can easily make the transition from word processing to desktop publishing.

In this section, we'll explore the powerful Word for Windows features and commands that help you translate your ideas into attractive document pages. This chapter presents a brief overview of the Word for Windows screen features. Chapter 2 summarizes the commands and options you'll need to create your desktop publishing projects.

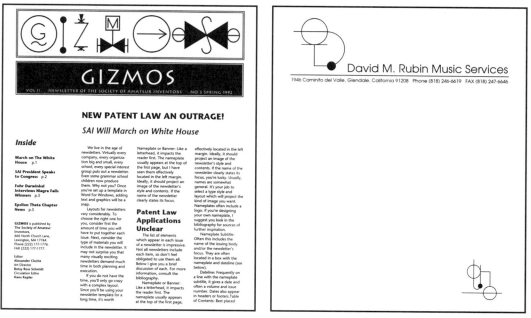

Figure 1-1: Have fun while designing exciting projects with Word for Windows.

Word's attractive and inviting document window provides a user-friendly environment. In addition to all the standard Windows 3.1 features, Word for Windows Version 6's document window provides a host of new features. The Standard toolbar is now accompanied by the Formatting toolbar (formerly the Ribbon) and a redesigned horizontal and vertical ruler. Let's take a tour of the Word screen.

Tools of the Trade

Version 6 has increased the number of predefined toolbars to 13. Toolbars can be dragged and dropped either as floating toolbars or anchored onto any edge of the screen. They can be reshaped merely by dragging their edges. The Standard toolbar includes many new icon buttons, as well as those available previously, noted below in Version 2. Among these are the Format Painter, Undo, Redo, AutoFormat, Column and Table insertion, drawing and graphing, in addition to Spell Checking, Open, Save, Print, Print Preview, Cut, Copy, Paste, etc. Don't fear being confused by all the new buttons. As your cursor points to a button, Word now produces a ToolTip that identifies the button's function.

In Version 2, the Toolbar (the top icon bar) gives you instant access to the most frequently used commands. These include new, open, save, print, cut, copy, paste, automatic bulleting and numbering of paragraphs, indenting, table and column creation, adding frames and zooming in and out of your page view. From here, too, you can instantly launch the integrated drawing and graphing programs, Microsoft Draw and Microsoft Graph.

Best of all, you can customize the toolbars to include the commands you use most often. And you can save a toolbar with a template; thus you can tailor the toolbars to every type of work you do.

Formatting Toolbar

Below the Standard toolbar, the Formatting toolbar allows virtually instant access to all your typefaces and type sizes. You can change to bold, italic or bold italic with a click of the mouse. You can also set paragraph and tab alignments left, centered, right or justified as well as choose bulleted and numbered lists, apply indents and open the new Borders toolbar. (The Ribbon [the second icon bar] in Version 2 allows access to all of the above except for the bulleted and numbered lists, and indents, which are located on the Toolbar. There is no Borders and Shading toolbar in Version 2.)

Golden Rulers

The rulers in Version 6 and the Ruler in Version 2, which can be set in inches, picas, points or centimeters, provide click-and-drag simplicity for setting all margins: columns, cells of tables, full-paragraph indents and negative indents (line/lines projected into the left or right margin), hanging indents (all lines indented under the first line) and first-line indents (first line of a paragraph indented), as well as all tab settings. The rulers are completely interactive, so you can see where you're moving as you go. Version 6's rulers are even easier to read and understand than those in Version 2 were. Further, the new vertical ruler makes accurate placement of graphics, headers, footers, top and bottom margins, and table row heights easier than ever.

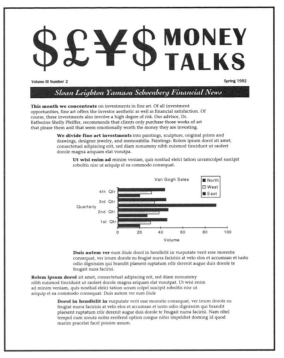

Figure 1-2: The rulers make it easier than ever to vary paragraph indents and position elements on the page.

The multiple paragraph indents used in Figure 1-2 are easy to accomplish using the Word for Windows horizontal ruler (Ruler). Creating and inserting the table from the Standard toolbar (Toolbar) are as easy as 1, 2, 3.

The combined features of the Standard toolbar, Formatting toolbar and rulers encourage you to experiment and have fun with your document. It should inspire you to be creative. And if you should make a mistake (heaven forbid!), don't worry; the Standard toolbar (Toolbar) also sports the Undo icon, which now keeps track of the last 100 actions!

CUSTOM TAILORING

To make your life easier, these onscreen aids are accompanied by total flexibility in the setup of your program preferences.

In other words, this program can work the way you work; you do not have to learn to work *its* way. You can display or not display scroll bars, the status bar, any and all of the other toolbars, including the Standard toolbar (Toolbar), Formatting toolbar (Ribbon) and rulers. You can display or not display virtually all nonprinting characters; you can display or not display pictures, text boundaries and table gridlines. Most of the frequently used commands have been or can be assigned shortcut keys. And Version 6 allows you to assign virtually any key combination to any command.

MACRO CITY

Macros can be added to your standard drop-down menus so that they're immediately accessible. Version 6 presents a new group of useful macros, among which the font sample generator, automatic organization chart maker and the find symbol macro are my favorites. (Version 2 comes with an excellent collection of typesetting macros, including drop caps and automatic Smart Quotes [proper quotation marks and apostrophes].) Virtually all of the excellent typesetting macros available in Version 2 have now become standard commands in Version 6.

EVERYBODY'S DOING IT: THE DRAG & DROP

All editing tasks have been greatly facilitated by the Drag and Drop feature, which lets you select text and then drag it to a new location. You can also move paragraph marks, graphics and tables in frames this way. Version 6 has expanded on Drag and Drop by allowing you to drop and drag across Windows and even compatible OLE applications. Further, Drag and Drop now automatically includes spaces before and after the text being moved so that it will mesh properly with the text it is moved into.

WINDOWS WITH A VIEW

If you want to see your work more clearly, you can zoom in on it anywhere from 25 to 200 percent. Speaking of views, the file finder provides a preview of both documents and graphics before you retrieve them. Dialog boxes for changing typefaces and styles, as well as page setup, character formatting, frame formatting, border formatting, etc., all have previews so that you can see what you're going to get before you apply it. Version 6 features more visual aids in dialog boxes, such as a preview of the view you'll see when selecting various Zoom increments. New tabbed dialog boxes make the variety of your options more obvious because they stand up and out. This saves an enormous amount of time and eliminates a lot of guesswork.

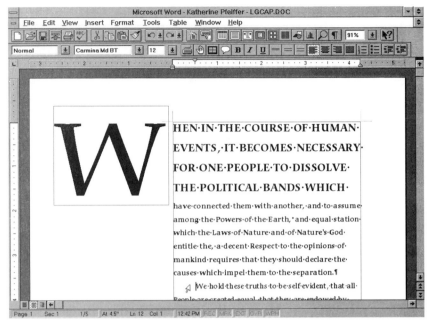

Figure 1-3: All the commands necessary to select the typefaces, initial capital and special margins for this layout are within easy reach in the document window.

Another time-saver is the one-step command that places page numbers where you want them on your document.

HELP IS CLOSE AT HAND

Version 6 has greatly extended Help features. Virtually all dialog boxes contain a Help button that takes you directly to the help you need. New Examples and Demos walk you through the many complex steps for various procedures. And you can get context-sensitive help at the touch of the F1 key. The Help feature even allows you to print the Help file you're reading. This has proven to be of great value to me, since I seem to forget what I read all too often! If you enable WordPerfect Help, F1 activates that handy feature. These are just a few of the many features that make the program easy and fun to use. (Version 2 doesn't include the Help button in dialog boxes or the Examples and Demos. You should rely on the F1 key—it works very well. You just need to remember to use it.)

A PROGRAM WITH CHARACTER(S)

A good example of how easy it is to use Word for Windows is in its handling of characters. Many features help format characters and paragraphs.

The program comes with some handsome predesigned templates you can use to format your documents. Templates contain page-setup information, such as margins, page orientation, etc. They also have styles for formatting paragraphs and characters, as well as borders, rules and boxes. Altering these predefined styles is simple. Merely format the characters from the Formatting toolbar (Ribbon) and click on the style name you wish to use (or type in your own). The program then asks if you want this to be the new format for the style.

BEAUTIFUL PAGES WITH FORMATTING OPTIONS

Good document design depends in large part on the accurate manipulation of type. Word for Windows gives you accurate control over character selection and placement, either as individual characters or in words and paragraphs.

Version 6 has broken many of the restrictions found in Version 2. The largest point size possible now is 1,637 points, or over 22 inches, which I would hardly call a limitation! Automatic pair kerning for most fonts above a certain size is now supported.

In the Format/Font (Format/Character) dialog box, you can make characters superscript, subscript, underlined, double underlined, all-caps and small caps; you can also change character color and expand or contract inter-character spacing. (*Note:* Word for Windows 2 does not support automatic kerning and neither version supports tracking [automatic addition of space between letters to create justified lines]. Because I find that both of these typesetting features are often misused and abused, I don't mourn their absence.) Type size in Version 2 can be specified in points from 4 to 127. You can overcome this limit, however, by using Microsoft Draw (see Chapter 12).

Paragraph formatting controls include left, center, right and justified alignment options, positive and negative indents, spacing before and after the paragraph and between lines. Indents can be as exact as you require—to the point. You can specify exact line spacing or let the program select an amount for you. The Single setting is often quite satisfactory and frees you from resetting line spacing if you change type size. A complete range of tab settings (plus decimal tabs) and tab leaders (leader characters are solid, dashed or dotted lines that fill the space created by the tab stop) are included.

All paragraphs, frames and tables support borders and background shading. The Borders and Shading toolbar, accessible from a button on the Borders toolbar, offers you a selection of 11 border styles and 16 colors, as well as 26 fill patterns. Two of the border styles are new in Version 6, one each of dashed and dotted lines. Version 2 does not have these options. Borders, or lines (known as *rules* in graphic design lingo), can be inserted above, below and to either or both sides of any paragraph, frame or table cell (each side can have a different type of border). You also can use plain or shadowed boxes as borders.

The Word for Windows shading option lets you create reversed type and horizontal rules of practically any depth using the techniques described later in this book.

Word's tables, frames and Text Box (new in Version 6) capabilities give you total control over placing such page elements as graphics, pull-quotes, picture captions, tabular material and forms. In working with long documents, the program allows for multiple page setups. For example, you might want to use different margins and column structures for technical documentation and the illustrations in a report. It also lets you change right and left headers and footers within the same document. This feature might come in handy for complex reports and manuals where headers/footers can contain page contents information. (See the 4 Seasons software instruction manual in Chapter 9.)

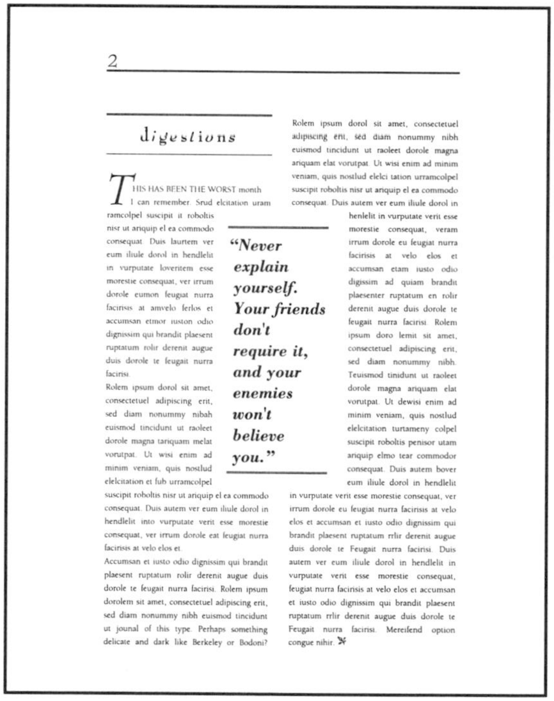

2

digestions

THIS HAS BEEN THE WORST month I can remember. Srud elcitation uram ramcolpel suscipit it roboltis nisr ut ariquip el ea commodo consequat. Duis laurtem ver eum iliule dorol in hendlelit in vurputate loveritem esse morestie consequat, ver irrum dorole eumon feugiat nurra facirisis at amvelo ferlos et accumsan etmor iuston odio dignissim qui brandit plaesent ruptatum rolir derenit augue duis dorole te feugait nurra facirisi.

Rolem ipsum dorol sit amet, consectetuel adipiscing erit, sed diam nonummy nibah euismod tincidunt ut raoleet dorole magna tariquam melat vorutpat. Ut wisi enim ad minim veniam, quis nostlud elelcitation et fub urramcolpel suscipit roboltis nisr ut ariquip el ea commodo consequat. Duis autem ver eum iliule dorol in hendlelit into vurputate verit esse morestie consequat, ver irrum dorole eat feugiat nurra facirisis at velo elos et.

Accumsan et iusto odio dignissim qui brandit plaesent ruptatum rolir derenit augue duis dorole te feugait nurra facirisi. Rolem ipsum dorolem sit amet, consectetuel adipiscing erit, sed diam nonummy nibh euismod tincidunt ut jounal of this type. Perhaps something delicate and dark like Berkeley or Bodoni?

"Never explain yourself. Your friends don't require it, and your enemies won't believe you."

Rolem ipsum dorol sit amet, consectetuel adipiscing erit, sed diam nonummy nibh euismod tincidunt ut raoleet dorole magna ariquam elat vorutpat. Ut wisi enim ad minim veniam, quis nostlud elelci tation urramcolpel suscipit roboltis nisr ut ariquip el ea commodo consequat. Duis autem ver eum iliule dorol in henlelit in vurputate verit esse morestie consequat, veram irrum dorole eu feugiat nurra facirisis at velo elos et accumsan etam iusto odio digissim ad quiam brandit plaesenter ruptatum en rolir derenit augue duis dorole te feugait nurra facirisi. Rolem ipsum doro lemit sit amet, consectetuel adipiscing erit, sed diam nonummy nibh. Teuismod tinidunt ut raoleet dorole magna ariquam elat vorutpat. Ut dewisi enim ad minim veniam, quis nostlud elelcitation turtameny colpel suscipit roboltis penisor utam ariquip elmo tear commodor consequat. Duis autem bover eum iliule dorol in hendlelit in vurputate verit esse morestie consequat, ver irrum dorole eu feugiat nurra facirisis at velo elos et accumsan et iusto odio dignissim qui brandit plaesent ruptatum rrlir derenit augue duis dorole te Feugait nurra facirisi. Duis autem ver eum iliule dorol in hendlelit in vurputate verit esse morestie consequat, feugiat nurra facirisis at velo elos et accumsan et iusto odio dignissim qui brandit plaesent ruptatum rrlir derenit augue duis dorole te Feugait nurra facirisi. Mereifend option congue nihir.

Figure 1-4: Frames make it easy to create and place a pull-quote.

Best of all, Word for Windows gives you plenty of incentive to experiment with different formatting specifications. Its preview window lets you see your choices before you change your entire document. Thus, you don't have to be afraid to make a mistake. You'll catch it early enough that changing it won't be such a headache.

LET'S GET GRAPHIC

Graphics, black and white as well as color, can be imported or created in Word for Windows. Version 6 has replaced Microsoft Draw (used in Version 2) with a totally integrated drawing program. A button on the Standard toolbar opens the Drawing toolbar. The drawing tools now allow the placement of text or graphics behind or in front of the basic text layer of the document. The new drawing tools incorporate the capabilities of the old Microsoft Draw (in Version 2), which let you create graphics with boxes, circles, round-cornered boxes and lines of various textures and thickness, as well as access all your fonts. Drawings in Version 6 are created as an integral part of the document. New alignment and snap to grid features make arranging artwork much easier, and a remarkable Callout tool lets you create callouts with ease. Further, Version 6 has greatly expanded over Version 2 the number of graphic file types that can be imported. Sixteen file types are now supported, including encapsulated PostScript or .EPS files. (In Version 2, using Draw, which is accessible from the Toolbar, graphics can be placed almost anywhere on a page, including under text. Draw offers an excellent way to make fancy heads, ornaments, etc. Because Draw is dynamically linked to your document, anything you create can be automatically inserted into it. However, it does not have the same number of alignment and special features as the drawing tools in Version 6. See more on this in Chapter 12.)

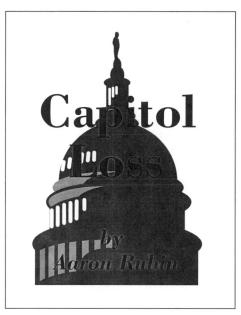

Figure 1-5: Word for Windows lets you place text over graphics.

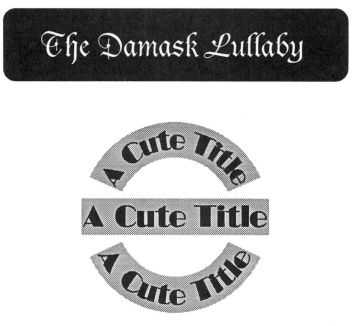

Figure 1-6: Word's drawing tools and WordArt help you add graphic accents to your titles and headings.

WordArt in Version 6 has been removed from the realm of tinker toys and made into a tool capable of quality output. Now all installed TrueType fonts can be used to create eye-catching text arrangements.(In Version 2, you can create whimsical graphics using the Microsoft WordArt feature, which allows you to rotate and slant text as well as to create text in a circle. Unfortunately, the typefaces that come with this feature are pretty crude.)

CHART YOUR FUTURE

Also accessible from the Standard toolbar (Toolbar) is Microsoft Graph, used for making charts. This integrated program lets you create your own charts by entering data and selecting a favorite chart type from its chart gallery. Virtually all aspects of your chart can be easily customized. Seventeen patterns and 16 colors are available. You may use any of your printer's typefaces.

Because Microsoft Graph (like Microsoft Draw in Version 2) is dynamically linked to your document, when you go back and alter figures, the chart is automatically updated. Charts can be fun to use; sections in the 3D pie chart, for instance, can be selected and dragged to any position you choose.

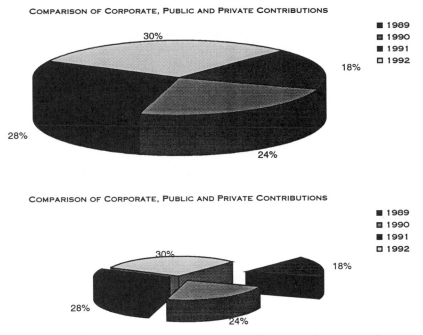

Figure 1-7: A 3D pie chart from Microsoft Graph before and after pie sections were repositioned.

MOVING ON

The features discussed above make page layout easier and more enjoyable than it's ever been before in a word processing program. With these time-saving features and the commands and options reviewed in the next chapter, you can really spread your wings and explore new territory in desktop publishing page layouts.

2

Desktop Publishing Features & Commands

Most of the tasks you'll encounter in creating desktop published documents can be accomplished using a handful of commands and their related dialog boxes. Here's a brief summary of the tasks you'll need to perform often and the commands you need to complete them. All of these commands can be made into buttons on the Standard toolbar (Toolbar). (See the discussion on customizing the Standard toolbar on page 31.)

The following table indicates the most commonly referred-to name changes in features and commands from Version 2 to Version 6.

Version 2	Version 6
Toolbar	Standard toolbar
Ribbon	Formatting toolbar
Format/Border	Format/Borders and Shading
Microsoft Draw	the drawing tools
Ruler	horizontal and vertical rulers

To make it easy for those of you who have not yet made the leap to Word for Windows Version 6, I have put all commands and instructions for Version 2 that differ from Version 6 in parenthesis.

To insert a frame. Use the Frame command on the Insert menu or the Frame button on the Standard toolbar. I refer to this as Insert/Frame or the Insert/Frame command.

To insert a table. Use the Insert Table command on the Table menu or the Insert Table command icon on the Standard toolbar. I refer to this as Table/Insert Table or simply the Insert/Table command.

To format characters. Use the Font (Character) dialog box, which is displayed when you click on the Font (Character) command in the Format menu. Many of the options in this box are also available on the Formatting toolbar, just below the Standard toolbar. I refer to this as the Format/Font command or the Format/Font dialog box. Also, while working in a paragraph, or with some characters, a click on the right mouse button will produce a short menu. This menu will give you direct access to the Font dialog box. (In Version 2, some of the options in this box are also available on the Ribbon. I refer to this as the Format/Character dialog box or simply the Character dialog box.)

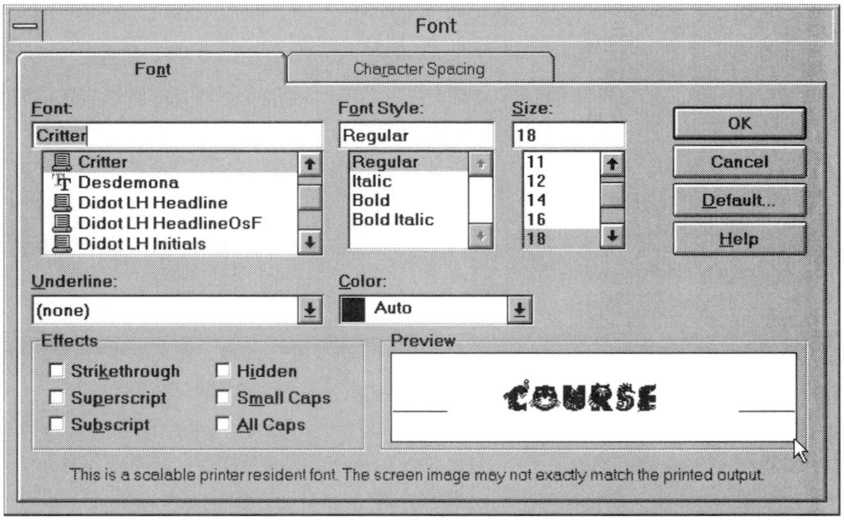

Figure 2-1: You can give your text special appearance effects using options in the Font dialog box.

To format paragraphs. Use the Paragraph dialog box, which is displayed when you click on the Paragraph command in the Format menu. I refer to this as Format/ Paragraph dialog box or simply the Paragraph dialog box. Some of these commands now appear on the Formatting toolbar. Also, while working in a paragraph, you can click on the right mouse button and a short menu will appear. This menu will give you access to the Paragraph dialog box.

To format borders. Use the Borders and Shading (Border) dialog box, which is displayed when you click on the Borders and Shading command in the Format menu. I refer to this as Format/Borders and Shading, Format/ Borders dialog box or the Borders dialog box. In Version 6 only, a button on the Formatting toolbar now accesses the Borders and Shading toolbar. This toolbar, like others that pop up in response to a click on an icon button, stays open until you click on the icon button again.

To format frames. Use the Frame dialog box, which is displayed when you click on the Frame command in the Format menu. I refer to this as Format/Frame or Frame dialog box.

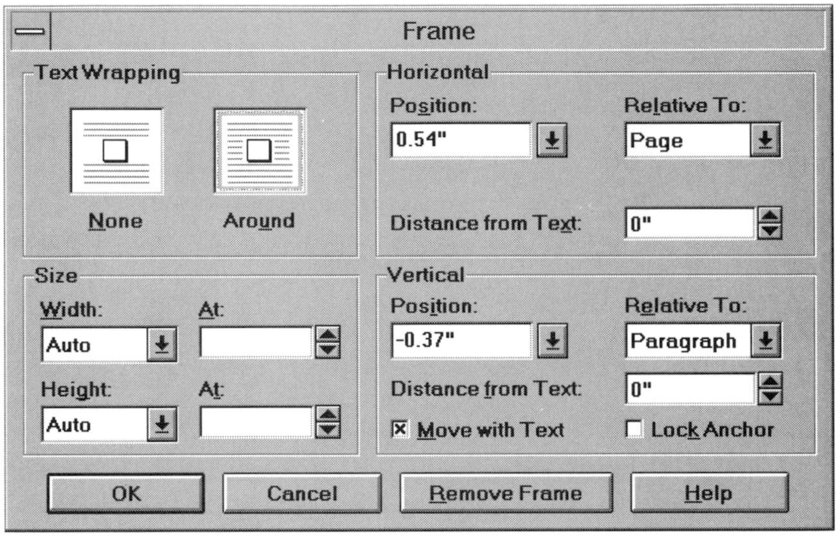

Figure 2-2: Using options in the Frame dialog box, you can place your frame exactly where you want it on the page.

I often identify other commands and dialog boxes opened from a menu simply by giving the menu name followed by a slash and then the command or dialog box name. Hence, File/Open refers to the Open dialog box that appears when you click on Open in the File menu.

PARAGRAPHS & PARAGRAPH MARKS

While the Word for Windows approach to paragraphs will be discussed at length in Chapter 10, it's important for you to have some idea of its significance from the beginning. Word treats anything—text, graphic, table, frame or blank line—followed by a paragraph mark (¶) as a paragraph. You produce one of these every time you press the Enter key alone. (If you press Enter+Shift, you get a line break but no paragraph mark. This situation is identified by a tiny right-angle arrow.)

Word relies on the paragraph mark to store most formatting instructions for the information preceding it. These include paragraph indents, alignment, line spacing inside, before and after the paragraph, tab information and all border settings. Inadvertent removal of a paragraph mark may cause major formatting mischief. This makes displaying paragraph marks while working highly desirable (see below).

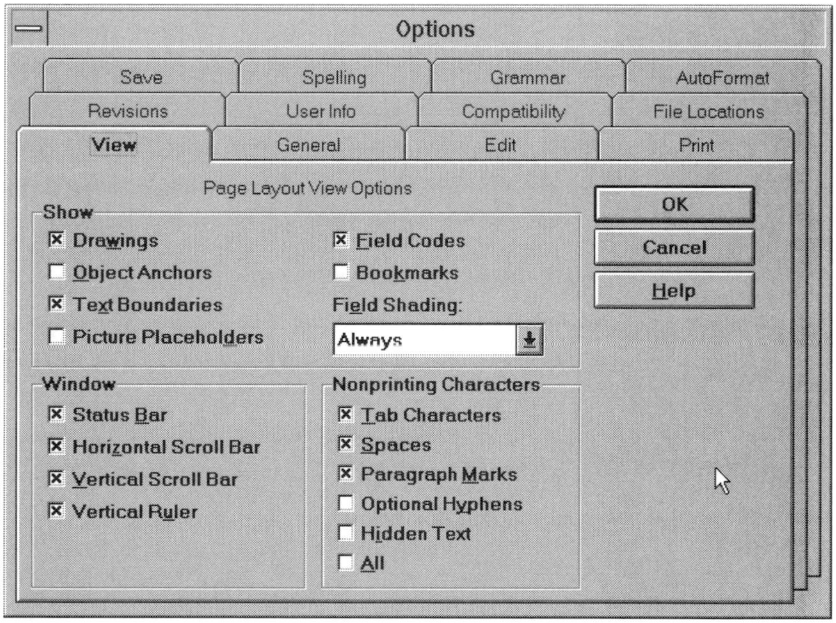

Figure 2-3: To display paragraph marks, use the Tools menu's Options dialog box.

In this book, I usually refer to "paragraphs," not "paragraph marks" as the manual often does. If a paragraph contains no text (merely a blank line or a blank line with border formatting), I often refer to it as an empty paragraph. It might also be called a line break, empty line or new line.

GETTING WORD READY

Before you begin your document layout, here are some tips for optimizing Word.

Saving

Save often and select Always Create Backup Copy and Automatic Save Every 5 Minutes in the Tools/Options/ Save Tab (Category). As with any other program, you'll avoid much grief by saving your work often. Also, when you save a document, it frees up memory. This is especially true with Version 6, because the Undo feature saves all your editing actions until you save.

Before saving a file with complex formatting, such as one with frames, tables, etc., always use View/Page Layout, View/Zoom, Zoom to Fit in Window and Whole Page View, and if relevant, Multi Page View (not available in Version 2). This will prevent you from saving a version in which you've accidentally caused frames or other elements to move to a location you don't want.

Along with saving your work to disk, save at least some of the rejected printouts. These will help you remember why you did what you did and why certain type styles or formatting options were rejected. I save mine in folders with clear plastic pocket-pages. (File N View by Lyon is inexpensive and popular. Itoya makes another.) These pages let you keep many rejects in a pocket under the final version.

Abandoning Changes & Using Undo

While Version 6's 100 levels of Undo is a tremendous feature, you can't always undo an action. Nor does Undo behave in a totally consistent manner. As the manual says, you can *usually* reverse your most recent action. (Italics mine.) So before making serious changes to formatting, headers and footers, charts or graphics, save your work. Then, if you cannot undo something you've done and wish to abandon the changes, simply close your document without saving changes and reopen it.

If you take my advice and use automatic backup copies, you can retrieve your work even after saving an incorrect version. (Undo cannot undo a Save command.) First, close the document, *but do not save it again.* Choose File/ Open. In the path box, change the file name to *.BAK. A list of all available backup files will appear. Your document name will be in the list if you saved it at any time prior to the current mishap. Open this document. Save it with a new name with the .DOC extension. (Word won't let you save the *.BAK copy with the name of its parent document.) Close the backup and then save the *.DOC file with the original name.

COPING WITH MULTIPLE FILES

Often you'll want to print, copy, search through or delete a group of files without opening each one. In the File/ Open dialog box, click on the Find File button. Once it scans your path for all files of the specified type, you can use Ctrl+click to select the multiple items you want to print, copy or delete.

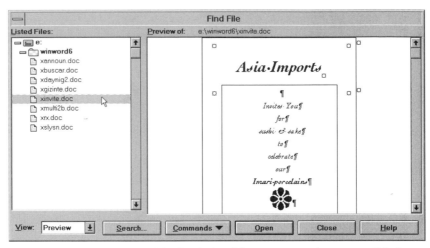

Figure 2-4: You can quickly find the file you want by using File/ Open/Find File.

The Find File button option also allows you to sort files in a variety of ways, view them in a small preview window and search for specific files and/or information.

OUTLINES

Word's outline feature is so easy to use and facilitates so many different activities, I strongly recommend that you explore it. In the View menu, click on Outline. You can ask it to display any level of headings—so that you can see the structure of even a long, complex document easily—and it allows you to move these headings with their attendant text by simply dragging them from one location to another. From this view, you can easily cut and paste sections of one document into another. You can also print the outline with any level of headings shown.

Further, using the promotion and demotion features, you can easily change heading styles from one to another. For instance, you might decide to create a new heading style for a group of existing heads. In the Outline View you can select just the ones you want to change and quickly promote or demote them to the new desired style. This is sometimes quicker than reformatting the style or searching the document to change the styles in the other views.

EDITING REMINDER & AGGRAVATION AVOIDER

Remember that once you've selected anything—text, graphic, etc.—the next keyboard entry you make will replace the selection, unless you've altered the default. This is great for speeding up editing, but it's terrible if you forget to *deselect* before forging ahead. Often, for example, you'll have text selected because you've moved it to a new location. The next action you take is to reflexively press the Enter key. Boink! Your text disappears. (Just hit Undo.) You must get used to deselecting anything you've moved before proceeding to the next operation. You can turn this feature off in the Tools/Options/Edit Tab (Tools/Options/General dialog box in Version 2), but once you're used to it, editing is much easier.

INSTALLING NEW FONTS

Word has a special relationship with printers. It actually works directly with them rather than going through the Windows interface. Because of this, after you add fonts through a Windows font manager (see Appendix A) or other installation process, you should go to the File/Print Setup dialog box and set up your printer again. When you close the box, Word searches for new fonts and installs them. If you do not do this, Word may not know you have installed new fonts. (This tip does not apply in Version 6.)

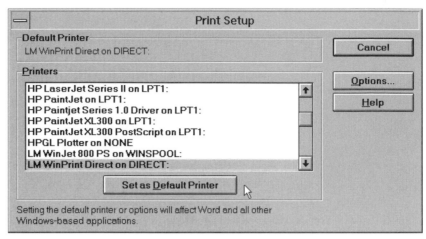

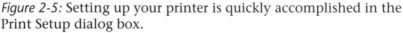

Figure 2-5: Setting up your printer is quickly accomplished in the Print Setup dialog box.

Working Without Matching Screen Fonts

For a variety of reasons you may be working without matching screen fonts. (Usually this happens because you're not working with scalable outline fonts managed by one of the popular Windows print managers. See Appendix A for a discussion of fonts and font managers.) If you do this, onscreen line lengths in Page Layout Views will seldom match those that print.

Version 6 automatically uses TrueType fonts to match your printer fonts as closely as possible if you don't have matching screen fonts. To get the most accurate information in Normal View, clear the Draft Font and Wrap to Window check boxes in Tool/Options/View tools. This may still not be accurate.

In Version 2, if you've set Line Breaks And Fonts As Printed in the Tools/Options/View category, word wrap remains consistent so that the number of onscreen and printed lines match. However, onscreen line lengths often extend beyond the right margin, where you won't be able to see or edit them. To edit such lines, you'll have to go back to Normal View or turn off Line Breaks And Fonts As Printed. I recommend the former option.

If the line disappears on the right and you want to stay in Page Layout View, you can still determine the end of a line. Continue to enter text until the line wraps, then back up one character. Your cursor will then be at the end of the line even if you can't see it.

I strongly recommend that you give up working without matching screen fonts and move to working with TrueType fonts as soon as possible. A basic collection ships with Windows 3.1, and many inexpensive collections of these fonts are available. They will make your life a lot easier and your documents look a lot better.

MACROS

Word comes with a useful collection of macros. To see them, read the instructions that come in the ReadMe file installed as an icon in the group with WinWord Version 6 (open NEWMACRO.DOC in Version 2) that was installed with the program. This document lets you watch the macro run and describes its purpose. Among the most useful macros are the font sample generator, the automatic organization chart maker and the find symbol macro. Popular macros in Version 2, such as Enable Smart Quotes, Smart Bullets, the Watermark, etc., have become standard features in Version 6.

When working in Version 2, I strongly recommend you install all macros related to Smart Quotes, Smart Bullets and Smart Numbering. If you have a PostScript printer, I also recommend installing the Watermark macro. Smart Quotes assures correct quotation marks and apostrophes; Smart Bullets and Smart Numbering facilitate making lists with consecutive bullets or numbers. The Watermark creates a repeating design under text on PostScript printers only. (But you can do this with your own printer using the method for repeating frames described in Chapter 11—if your printer supports such printing.) I have added all of these macros to my Edit menu so that they're readily available.

Using the Macro Record command in Version 2, I have created two simple macros that help me a lot. The first, which I call "Zoom200," immediately zooms to 200 percent. I have this represented on the Standard toolbar by the magnifying glass. My other macro immediately brings me into Print Preview with a double-page spread showing.

I know that macro recording frightens many computer users. Try making a few simple ones. You'll soon realize how handy they are and how simple they are to create. In Version 6, to record a macro, click on Tools/Macro. Enter a macro name and then click on Record. You can then add a description for your macro and choose whether to assign the macro to a toolbar, menu or keystroke combination. You can also decide whether to make the macro available to all templates (globally) or to only a specific template. Once these decisions are made, the macro dialog box closes and a small window appears with the buttons to stop or pause your macro recording. When you are finished, click the stop button on the Macro Record window and your macro will be fully functional.

In Version 2, don't be afraid to make a macro using the Macro Record command. In the Tools menu, click on Record Macro. Next, give your macro a name and a key combination, then turn on the recorder and perform the actions necessary to accomplish the desired task. Then, open the Tools menu and click on Stop Record, which has replaced Record Macro in the menu. Macros can be assigned to all your templates or just to a specific one.

CUSTOMIZE WORD'S INTERFACE

The ability to tailor its interface to suit your working style is one of Word's greatest attributes. The Standard toolbar (Toolbar) and other options parameters in the Options dialog box offer you a smorgasbord of interface features. To customize your working environment, choose Customize and Options in the Tools menu. (Just Tools/Options in Version 2.)

To give you some food for thought, the following are the settings I use.

View

Window: I use horizontal and vertical scroll bars. The status bar tells you which page you're on and reminds you of command options such as "Move Where?" for moving text, etc. I set the Style Area Width at .05 inch, which is helpful while working in Normal and Outline Views when you want to retag individual paragraphs (it identifies the name of each paragraph's style on the left).

Display All: As an aid to accuracy, I display nearly everything: Table Gridlines, Text Boundaries and Line Breaks. (In Version 2, show Fonts as Printed.) Depending on the document, I may display the actual pictures or the Placeholders, and I may or may not display field codes.

Tip: If you are working on a document that seems to behave in mysterious ways—say, for instance, line breaks occur in places you can't explain—try displaying field codes. You may have inadvertently inserted a code that is causing problems.

Nonprinting Characters: To ensure accuracy, select Display All to reveal Tabs, Spaces, Paragraph Marks, Optional Hyphens and Hidden Text (remember that none of these items will print). In page formatting, being able to see these nonprinting marks will help you avoid trouble. Paragraph marks carry all style formatting and are particularly important (see more in Chapter 10); also, seeing tabs and spaces takes the guesswork out of accurately placing words as well as individual characters.

But by all means turn off these visual identifiers if they're disconcerting when you're working on a tricky layout. You can also use Print Preview to see how the page will look without them.

General

All these seem to me to be quite personal, and I don't believe your choice will have any effect on your page layout.

Background Repagination: This one is a sticky wicket for me. I like to use Background Repagination because I find it bothersome to have to remind the program to repaginate. However, turning it off saves my hard disk a great deal of wear and tear. I recommend that you try both options. (You can put a button on the Standard toolbar to order Repagination.)

Measurement Units: For the default measurements units, I recommend either inches or picas. Remember that you can enter units in any measurement system no matter which system is the default one. The default measurement system will affect the rulers and all dialog boxes. While some authors are even beginning to speak of interline spacing in terms of inches, this isn't traditional. Try to think of type size and line spacing (leading) in points, because type is measured in points (see Chapter 3, "A Brief Introduction to Design").

CUSTOM TOOLBARS

Customizing your toolbars will make page layout faster and easier by giving you instant access to the commands and menu items you use most often. Remember, you can save different toolbars with different templates. Version 6 has made customizing the toolbars a great deal of fun. From the View menu select Toolbars and then click on the Customize button. You simply drag icons off that you don't want and drag on the ones you do want. You can also add commands to the Standard toolbar not previously assigned to buttons by selecting the All Commands option in the Categories list box after you click on the Customize button. I display both the Standard and Formatting toolbars, on which I have buttons for New, Open, Save, Close, Cut, Copy, Paste, Spell Check, Print, Print Preview, Undo, Format Painter, Undo and Redo, AutoFormat, Automatic Numbered List, Bulleted List, Insert Table, Indent and Un-indent, Column Formatting, Drawing toolbar, Microsoft Graph, Borders and Shading toolbar, Font, Paragraph and Frame Formatting, Page Layout View and Full Page Width View, Multi Page View, Zoom Control and Help.

(In Version 2, customizing the Toolbar takes some time and planning. Consult the *User's Guide* for detailed instructions. I use icons for New, Open, Save, Close, Cut, Copy, Paste [I like the paste bottle icon], Undo, Copy Format, Zoom to 200% [my macro], Automatic Numbered List, Bulleted List, Insert Table, Indent and Un-indent, Column Formatting, Insert Frame, Microsoft

Draw and Microsoft Graph, Character, Border, Paragraph and Frame Formatting, Print, Page Layout View and Full Page Width View.)

Unless you choose otherwise, all these custom choices will be saved with your NORMAL.DOT. When you exit the program after making these selections, the program will ask if you want to save global changes. Say Yes.

MOVING ON

These brief capsules are not meant to replace the excellent detailed guidance provided in the Word for Windows *User's Guide*. But they'll serve as quick references as you study the illustrated examples in Section III, "Looking Good With Word."

Before we see Word in action, however, let's focus on one of the most important ingredients in an effective desktop published document—good page design.

II

Looking at Design

3

A Brief Introduction to Design

Though a program like Word for Windows makes page layout a pleasure, it can't design a document for you. There are no substitutes for study and practice in any art form, but you can improve your work by paying close attention to the basic concepts.

You can also learn a lot by borrowing ideas from work that pleases you. If you haven't already done so, start a collection of inspirational design examples. (Also, see the Bibliography in the back of this book for further reading suggestions.)

If you're like me, you're eager to get started. But first, for those who need some orientation and have the patience to sit still for it, I'll give you a brief overview of publication design essentials.

Before you can design anything, you must be clear about the nature and purpose of your publication. As you start each project, write down the answers to the following questions:

◆ *What is the purpose of this document?* Consider how different a work of fiction, which will be read for pleasure, should be from a product or service advertisement or a technical manual. The more serious or difficult the material, the more skillful you must be in enticing the reader.

◆ *Who will read your pages*? The age, education, experience and sophistication levels of your audience should influence your design strategies. Older readers appreciate larger type. Some readers respond to elegance; others to an unpretentious look.

◆ *Are your readers busy people who want their information in bytes and blurbs, or are they looking for in-depth analysis?* If they're motivated to seek information, you can get by with small type and a simple page design. On the other hand, reaching out to "hook" your targets to sell a product calls for a bolder typographic approach.

Answering these questions will help you structure and design your document. In the chapters that follow, you'll see how specific design requirements are handled in various documents. But before focusing on particulars, let's look at some general principles that relate to arranging type and graphics.

THE DYNAMIC DUOS

When designing a document, pay attention to what I call the "dynamic duos." I refer to structure and order; style and tone; harmony and contrast; positive space and negative space; symmetry and asymmetry as dynamic duos because the members of each pair are dependent on each other.

Structure relates to the way a document is laid out (as a single sheet or two-page spread); page orientation (vertical or horizontal); margin and gutter sizes; and the placement of text blocks, lines, graphics and other elements.

Order organizes the document contents and guides the reader through the information with carefully designed headings, subheadings, indents, bullets, etc.

Style involves historical and cultural associations. You may wish to evoke a feeling of the Old West, the Gay Nineties or the Space Age. Ornamental graphics and distinctive typefaces contribute to style. *Tone*, on the other hand, establishes a mood: formality, informality, playfulness, elegance or sobriety. The type styles you choose and the way you compose the text communicate a tone, whether you're aware of it or not. Better to be aware and make these elements work *for* you rather than against you.

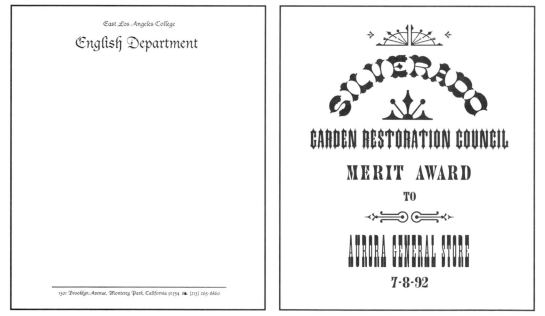

Figures 3-1 & 3-2: Ornamental typefaces and graphics can evoke the styles of other times and places.

Harmony and *contrast* depend totally on one another—they're absolutely relative, to use an oxymoron. A satisfying design must balance these two to fit the nature of your publication. Normally, an ad would require more contrast than a technical report. Using correct proportions among page elements is perhaps the major factor in achieving harmony. While harmony imparts comfort, familiarity and restfulness, too much of it—for example, long unbroken blocks of text—may bore the reader. Too much contrast, on the other hand, leads to distraction and interferes with comprehension. (Figures 3-3 and 3-4 show examples of contrast and harmony.) Everything you do on the page contributes to either harmony or contrast.

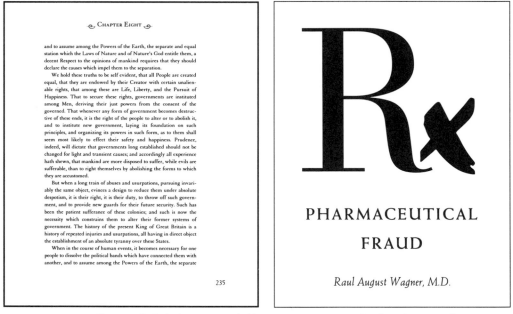

Figures 3-3 & 3-4: Two different strategies: the book page design stresses harmony; the title page stresses contrast.

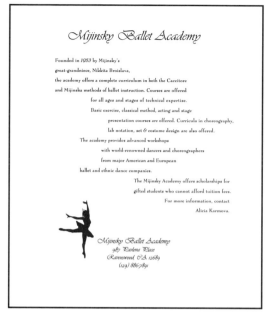

Figure 3-5: This ballet school ad balances contrast and harmony.

Positive space and *negative space* (commonly known as white space), which I think of as positive and negative *shape*, are as intimately connected as night and day. Positive space contains an image or text. Negative space is the area that is blank, or without images or text. They literally cannot exist without each other. The Asian yin/ yang symbol, shown in Figure 3-6, illustrates this clearly.

In the *Tao-te-ching*, Lao-Tzu wrote the following:

> Thirty spokes share the wheel's hub;
> It is the center hole that makes it useful.
> Shape clay into a vessel;
> It is the space within that makes it useful.
> Cut doors and windows for a room;
> It is the holes which make it useful.
> Therefore profit comes from what is there;
> Usefulness from what is not there.

Figure 3-6: Positive and negative space cannot exist without each other, as shown by the yin/yang symbol.

Western cultures tend to be more conscious of positive rather than negative space and shape. We focus on text, illustrations, rules (lines) and boxes on a page, and regard what's left over as "just holes." But it's important to remember that the negative space is just as important to the overall composition and overall comprehension.

When you create a block of text or insert an illustration, you also create outlines and shapes. To better see the contours and dynamics you've created, try squinting at your work or holding it backward against the light to see if the shapes form a harmonious, balanced composition.

Symmetry and *asymmetry* are your structure options for the placement of text and graphics on a page. Traditional symmetrical page design goes back to the beginning of printing; it works well for long texts meant to be read with a minimum of interruption. Its style is formal, dignified, logical. It's the essence of order over chaos. Strict symmetry must be handled carefully because the human eye picks up even minor imbalances.

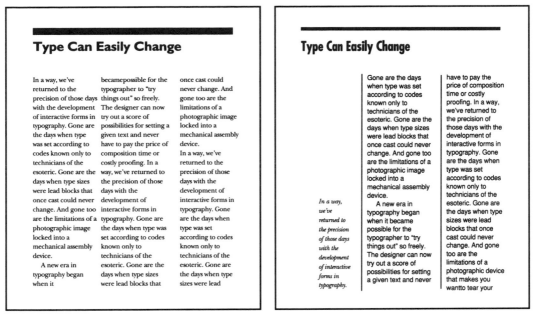

Figure 3-7: A symmetrical page structure is formal. An asymmetrical arrangement is informal.

An asymmetrical arrangement, which is nature's way, is informal, flexible and, I think, easier to work with. It can be elegantly austere or pleasingly playful. Combining symmetry and asymmetry can be difficult—I recommend against it.

When planning your layout, if you're having trouble deciding which style would be most effective, create one of each and choose the one that works best. One of the benefits of computer typesetting is being able to change your mind and try something else quickly.

Traditionally, publication design is called *typography*. The primary typographic design elements are blocks of text, headings, subheads and rules. Type terminology has evolved over centuries into a practical vocabulary for publishers, printers, typesetters, editors and proofreaders. Let's take a closer look at what these terms mean.

Typefaces

Type comes in many designs, called typefaces. While each typeface is unique, systems have been designed to help classify them into groups. Type can be classified according to its use and its appearance. Most typefaces fall into one of two major categories: serif and sans-serif. Letterforms in a serif typeface are designed with small ornamental finishing strokes at the ends of main character strokes. Sans-serif designs have no finishing strokes.

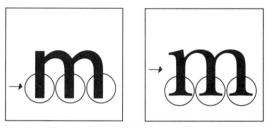

Figure 3-8: Sans-serif letterforms (left) are plain and unadorned. Serif letterforms (right) have small ornamental finishing strokes.

Serif shapes and sizes vary from one serif typeface to another. Also, the main strokes in serif faces vary in thin/ thick contrast and orientation. Garamond, Baskerville, Times and Palatino are perhaps the most common serif typefaces. Figure 3-9 shows some other popular but less well-known serif typefaces. These typefaces are easy to read; for this reason, they're often used for book text.

Matthew Carter designed the
beautiful ITC GALLIARD in 1978
for Mergenthaler Linotype.

ITC STONE SERIF was created
by Sumner Stone.

Lucien Bernhard created
BERNHARD MODERN
for the ATF in 1937.

Figure 3-9: Serif typefaces, often used for book text, are easy to read.

Sans-serif letterforms consist of unembellished straight and circular lines. In most sans-serif designs, there is little if any thick and thin contrast in character strokes. The result is type with clean lines, uniform "weight" and a functional look. Within the broad sans-serif classification, two design trends have emerged: the traditional forms, represented by Helvetica and Univers, and the geometric forms, such as Futura and Avant Garde Gothic. Figure 3-10 shows examples of sans-serif typefaces.

Paul Renner's geometrical sans-serif, FUTURA, is closely associated with the Bauhaus.

ITC AVANT GARDE GOTHIC was designed by Herb Lubalin and Tom Carnase.

HELVETICA, designed by Max Miedinger, is often called Swiss. Linotype owns the right to use the name Helvetica, which it licenses to other companies.

ITC STONE SANS was designed by Sumner Stone and works well with its cousin, ITC Stone Serif.

Figure 3-10: Sans-serif type has a clean, functional look.

In the United States, many typographers still rely on serif typefaces for long text settings. However, English and other European publishers commonly use sans-serif type for extensive text, including books. Make your type choices with your readers and your particular publication in mind. I have used both groups in the examples throughout this book.

Your typeface choices will depend on the nature of the project, your readers' expectations and experience, the overall tone you want to impart and the typefaces you have or plan to add to your collection. Other factors to consider are output and reproduction processes that will be used in the final product. Some typefaces survive low-resolution printing (standard 300 dpi laser printer output) better than others. (In Appendix A, I recommend typefaces suitable for various types of printing.)

Text Faces

Serif and sans-serif faces comprise the majority of what are called "text faces." Masses of text make up the largest positive shapes in a page layout. The way you handle text blocks determines to a great extent whether your page elements will work harmoniously together.

If you squint at pages that have blocks of type, you'll notice that some blocks are light gray and others dark gray. Some appear to have texture, while others look smooth. These "coloring" and texturing effects are created by the size, style, weight and other characteristics of the type used in the text blocks. Typefaces that set dark may be useful in ads, but I think they impart too much personality to be appropriate for publications such as technical reports, for instance.

Figure 3-11: Dark, heavy type that works well in an ad (left) would be inappropriate for book text (right).

In order to use your own type collection wisely, I suggest you make a type specimen template and then print samples of your typefaces to use as test blocks for designing your layouts. (See the specimen template in Appendix A.)

Display Faces
In contrast to the utilitarian type relied on for readable bodies of text is the more dramatic "display" type used for headlines, chapter titles, decorative initial caps, advertising slogans and other special applications. Display faces come in myriad designs and styles ranging from familial variations of serif and sans-serif text faces to

replications of handwritten script, period revivals and extravagant fanciful creations. Zapf Calligraphic and Cloister Black, an imitation of medieval lettering styles, are popular examples.

This is Aachen Bold from Adobe

THIS IS ITC BEESKNEES FROM DTC

This is Mariage from DTC

This is Mistral from DTC

THIS IS UMBRA FROM ADOBE

Figure 3-12: Decorative display typefaces draw attention.

In using display type, remember that once a typeface attracts attention, it's best to use it with great caution and never for long texts. Treat display faces like condiments in cooking.

Type Families

Typefaces designed for text generally come in "families"—groups of faces based on the same design. Family members vary in weight, width and style but work harmoniously together. Serif families normally include the standard roman (upright), italic (slanted), bold and bold italic versions. Some also include light, extra-bold and black weights, and a variety of widths, such as compressed, narrow, condensed, wide, extra-wide and expanded.

Serif Typeface Family

Palatino
Palatino Italic
Palatino Bold
Palatino Bold Italic

Sans-serif Typeface Family

Helvetica
Helvetica Italic
Helvetica Bold
Helvetica Bold Italic

Figure 3-13: Most typeface families include roman, italic, bold and bold italic. Many also include light, extra-bold and other versions.

There are fewer sans-serif typefaces, but some of the families are quite large. For example, the Univers typeface was designed with 21 closely knit family members. (Adrian Frutiger, the Swiss typographer who created the Univers family, originally developed a numbering system to describe its members rather than rely on imprecise descriptive names.) Faces in a single family work harmoniously together.

Type Size

Type size and line length are traditionally measured in points and picas, respectively. There are 72 points to the inch, 12 points to a pica and therefore 6 picas to the inch. (I find it easier to remember there are 36 points, or 3 picas, to the half-inch.) While the system seems odd at first, there's no use fighting it. If you can get used to it, you'll find document layout much easier because type is always measured in points.

The point size of a typeface is measured from baseline to baseline when the type is set solid—that is, without interline spacing. (The baseline is the invisible line on which the characters sit.) The size includes not only the height of the tallest ascender (usually the lowercase l) and the depth of the lowest descender (a lowercase y or g) but also a tiny amount of extra space. This space prevents ascenders on one line from touching descenders on another line when the type is set without interline spacing (leading).

12-point ITC Stone Serif with no leading

When in the Course of Human Events, it becomes necessary for one People to dissolve the Political Bands which have connected them with another, and to assume among the Powers of the Earth, the separate and equal Station to which the Laws of Nature and of Nature's God entitle them, a decent Respect to the Opinions of Mankind requires that they should declare the causes which impel them to the separation.

12-point Bernhard Fashion with no leading

When in the Course of Human Events, it becomes necessary for one People to dissolve the Political Bands which have connected them with another, and to assume among the Powers of the Earth, the separate and equal Station to which the Laws of Nature and of Nature's God entitle them, a decent Respect to the Opinions of Mankind requires that they should declare the causes which impel them to the separation.

Figure 3-14: The same point size can vary in appearance from typeface to typeface.

You might assume that all typefaces of the same point size appear to be the same size. Not so. Figure 3-14 shows how the same point size looks in different typefaces. Proportion plays a large part in the appearance of a typeface character: ascenders and descenders can be long or short; and body size, or x-height (determined by the size of the lowercase x), can vary considerably among typeface designs. Large-x-height typefaces need extra line spacing; or they can be set smaller without sacrificing legibility. The Helvetica and Stone type families have large x-heights. Centaur and Gill Sans have small x-heights.

high x-height   low x-height

Figure 3-15: Body size, or x-height, plays a role in determining the "visual size" of a typeface.

Line Space

Line space, or "leading" (a term carried over from the early days of metal typesetting, when strips of lead cast in specific point increments were placed between rows of type), is the amount of space between lines of text. Unlike the typewriter, modern desktop systems, including Word for Windows, allow you to set spacing in small, discrete increments to suit your typographic needs.

Selecting the correct amount of line space helps the reader move through a line of text and quickly find the beginning of the next line. Too little or too much leading impedes a reader's ability to move through the text. Long text lines need more leading than short lines. Also, smaller type sizes generally need less leading, unless the lines are very long (which is usually a bad mix anyway).

12-point ITC Stone Serif with no leading

When in the Course of Human Events, it becomes necessary for one People to dissolve the Political Bands which have connected them with another, and to assume among the Powers of the Earth, the separate and equal Station to which the Laws of Nature and of Nature's God entitle them, a decent Respect to the Opinions of Mankind requires that they should declare the causes which impel them to the separation.

12-point Bernhard Fashion with no leading

When in the Course of Human Events, it becomes necessary for one People to dissolve the Political Bands which have connected them with another, and to assume among the Powers of the Earth, the separate and equal Station to which the Laws of Nature and of Nature's God entitle them, a decent Respect to the Opinions of Mankind requires that they should declare the causes which impel them to the separation.

12-point ITC Stone Serif with 4 points leading and a longer line

When in the Course of Human Events, it becomes necessary for one People to dissolve the Political Bands which have connected them with another, and to assume among the Powers of the Earth, the separate and equal Station to which the Laws of Nature and of Nature's God entitle them, a decent Respect to the Opinions of Mankind requires that they should declare the causes which impel them to the separation.

12-point Bernhard Fashion with 4 points leading and a longer line

When in the Course of Human Events, it becomes necessary for one People to dissolve the Political Bands which have connected them with another, and to assume among the Powers of the Earth, the separate and equal Station to which the Laws of Nature and of Nature's God entitle them, a decent Respect to the Opinions of Mankind requires that they should declare the causes which impel them to the separation.

Figure 3-16: Short text lines need less line space; longer lines require more.

Line Lengths & Column Widths

Line length, type size and leading are intimately related. The right combination of the three produces the most inviting and most readable typography. It's hard to set up precise formulas that always work, but here are a few guidelines.

Most readers look at material from 12 to 14 inches away. Given this, studies show that type in the 9-point to 12-point range is the most legible. (Sizes over 12 points seem to slow reading down.) A line of 10 to 12 words comprising 60 to 70 characters (18 to 24 picas) is a manageable length. As mentioned before, when line length increases, line spacing must also increase.

Lines set without leading are more difficult to read. I always recommend leading unless there's some pressing space problem and the text is short and/or in a small point size. Of course, too much leading makes it difficult for the reader's eye to flow from line to line.

Here's how to translate these rules into specific numbers: in type sizes 9 through 12, one to four points of lead can be added to the point size of the type (depending on visual factors such as x-height and line length) to determine the appropriate amount of line space. For example, a short line of small-x-height 10-point type will probably need only one extra point of lead—in other words, 11-point line spacing. A longer line of 12-point, large-x-height type will easily take four points of leading; this is called 16-point line spacing (12/16 in type specimens). These suggestions also apply to text faces set in blocks. Line spacing for text faces used in large point sizes and for display faces will need to be worked out on an individual basis.

Manipulating spacing can be a little trickier than it first appears. Page programs handle leading in different ways, and maintaining alignment and getting the appearance right depend on where the additional space is placed. Usually it's added either below the type line or proportionately above and below. If you have a choice, consistently adding leading below	**M**anipulating spacing can be a little trickier than it first appears. Page programs handle leading in different ways, and maintaining alignment and getting the appearance right depend on where additional space is placed. Usually it's added either below the type line of proportional above and below. If you have a choice, consis	**M**anipulating spacing can be a little trickier than it first appears. Page programs handle leading in different ways, and maintaining alignment and getting the appearance right depend on where additional space is placed. Usually it's added either below the type
9-point type	9-point type	9-point type
9-point leading	10-point leading	12-point leading

Figure 3-17: Leading and line length affect the readability of a type block.

Kerning, Letter Spacing & Ligatures

From the time of Gutenberg to the invention of photo-typesetting, type characters were made of lead. Each letter was cast in relief on a rectangular block so that it could be set next to any other letter or character. The raised character image was inked and printed. When the printer set two letter blocks such as V and A next to each other, he was left with an unsightly gap. To remedy this, he *kerned* the letters—he filed down the lead blocks so that the letterforms themselves could fit closer together.

After such alteration, however, these characters were useless except for the particular letter combination for which they were modified. Soon, frequently kerned character combinations began to be cast as separate type pieces—hence the ligatures. The most common ligatures are ff, fi, fl, ffi and ffl. Most of these are available only in a few "expert" type fonts used for top-quality typography.

In contrast to contemporary typesetting practices, kerning was employed rarely in traditional printing. Instead, type was skillfully designed to fit well without kerning. I was trained using lead type, and I still prefer when possible to leave my characters with the original designed-in space around them.

However, when you're dealing with headlines, titles or any large or decorative letterforms, it's often necessary to use kerning to refine the letter spacing. In regular text, especially if you're going to output to laser printer resolution, use restraint with kerning so your body text won't look squashed and uneven.

Letter spacing is the opposite of kerning: adding, rather than subtracting, space between letters. Like kerning, use it sparingly. I like to use it to improve readability in headings with all-capitals. The goal is to achieve the appearance of an equal amount of space around each letter. Therefore, two adjacent capital I's can benefit from being spaced farther apart, while two capital O's placed next to each other may need no adjustment or some kerning.

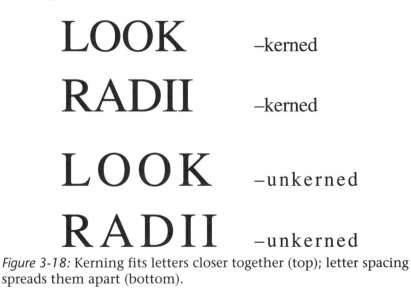

LOOK   –kerned

RADII   –kerned

LOOK   –unkerned

RADII   –unkerned

Figure 3-18: Kerning fits letters closer together (top); letter spacing spreads them apart (bottom).

Letter spacing and kerning can also be used to control gaps, or rivers, created by hyphenation and justification in text blocks. I recommend against it. You can ruin your text's overall integrity by destroying its even texture. It's much better to hyphenate manually or to edit the text.

Another problem results when consecutive hyphenated line endings create a string of hyphens along the right-hand margin. Convention demands no more than three consecutive right-margin hyphens; and if you get a bad row of them, you'll see the problem. This too must be repaired. Convention demands no more than three

Rivers.

Another problem results when consecutive hyphenated line endings create a string of hyphens along the right-hand margin. Convention demands no more than three consecutive right-margin hyphens; and if you get a bad row of them, you'll see the problem. This too must be repaired. Convention demands no more than three consecutive

Rivers repaired.

Figure 3-19: Manually hyphenate or edit text to correct "rivers" in justified type blocks.

Another problem results when consecutive hyphenated line endings create a string of hyphens along the right-hand margin. Convention demands no more than three consecutive right-margin hyphens; and if you get a bad row of them, you'll see the problem. This must be repaired. Convention demands no more than three consecutive right-margin hy-

Excessive hyphenation.

Another problem results when consecutive hyphenated line endings create a string of hyphens along the right-hand margin. Convention demands no more than three consecutive right-margin hyphens; and if you get a bad row of them, you'll see the problem. This too must be repaired. Convention will demand no more than three

Minimal hyphenation.

Figure 3-20: Use manual line breaks to avoid excessive hyphenation.

Type Alignment

The alignment of type plays a key role in communicating tone in your publication. Your four choices are left-aligned with ragged-right margin; centered with ragged-left and ragged-right margins; right-aligned with ragged-left margin; and justified (aligned on left and right margins, usually with considerable hyphenation). Centered and justified alignments project a formal tone. Left-aligned, ragged-right columns seem friendlier. Right alignment, of course, is so unnatural that it immediately attracts attention.

Manipulating spacing can be a little trickier than it first appears. Page programs handle leading in different ways, and maintaining alignment and getting the appearance right depend on where additional space is placed. No matter how your program deals with type, there is no substitute for careful proofing and close

flush-left/ragged right

Manipulating spacing can be a little trickier than it first appears. Page programs handle leading in different ways, and maintaining alignment and getting the appearance right depend on where additional space is placed. No matter how your program deals with type, there is no substitute for careful proofing and close

centered

Manipulating spacing can be a little trickier than it first appears. Page programs handle leading in different ways, and maintaining alignment and getting the appearance right depend on where additional space is placed. No matter how your program deals with type, there is no substitute for careful proofing and close

flush-right/ragged left

Manipulating spacing can be a little trickier than it first appears. Page programs handle leading in different ways, and maintaining alignment and getting the appearance right depend on where additional space is placed. No matter how your program deals with type, there is no substitute for careful proofing and close attention to detail.

justified

Figure 3-21: You can choose from four type-alignment schemes for text blocks.

In choosing alignment, bodies of text and headings should be considered separately, since their functions are different. Centered alignment, for instance, is disconcerting in long texts, but it can be just right for titles, heads, wedding invitations and other formal announcements.

In working with alignment, you must also consider line length and how much hyphenation to allow. Even when working with unjustified text, line endings often must be modified with hyphenation to keep them from looking too ragged.

PAGE LAYOUT BASICS

Most of your pages will consist of harmonious gray masses of text. Bringing order to the sea of gray makes the page not only more attractive but more functional.

Grids: The Page Skeleton

To begin a project, establish a basic structure and internal order. Many professional designers work with a grid. This geometric "skeleton" helps guide the designer in organizing the page elements and arranging the positive and negative spaces. A grid structure can be as simple as the top, bottom, left and right page margins. It can be complex enough to provide for locating all columns, gutters (the space between columns and between facing pages), headers, footers, notes, illustrations and page numbers. Complex publications like newsletters, brochures, forms and reports benefit from this type of approach. (For more information on grids, see the Bibliography in the back of this book.)

Figure 3-22: A grid helps organize page elements.

In laying out a multipage document, *always* design your pages in pairs as two-page spreads; your readers should be able to see and read each set of facing pages as a compositional unit. Structure the entire space as a whole, or the document will end up visually fragmented.

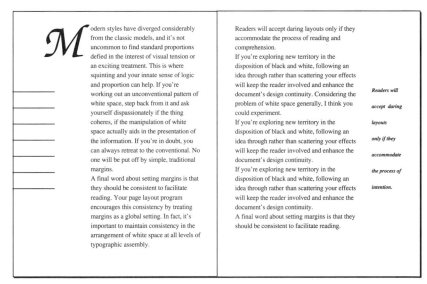

Figure 3-23: Always design your pages as two-page spreads.

Most designers recommend creating a full-size design on translucent paper that can be used to check against the finished product. My own method usually is to work it out in general on paper, then play with it on the computer until I'm satisfied with how it looks. I find working with the computer easier than working out dimensions with a ruler. Choose the method that works best for you.

It's not surprising that a skillful page designer carefully considers the following graphic elements and which to use as attention-getters (reader cues) to communicate most effectively. It's a balancing act: too many reader cues may fragment rather than focus attention; on the other hand, too much undifferentiated text can cause a reader to lose interest and miss valuable information.

Attention-Getters

Many methods and devices can be used to help you create order and get attention. Specific applications will come in later chapters, but I'll introduce the methods briefly here.

- Change type: Vary typeface, size, style. Use capitals and lowercase. Use all-capitals. Use a display-size initial for the first letter of the first word of a paragraph, page or document.

- Use white (negative) space: Use indents and extra line spacing above and/or below text; increase gutter space between columns; widen margins. White space draws immediate attention to an area and gives it added importance. Always proportion the space to suit its purpose—the more important, the more space.

◆ Change column structure for emphasis: Sometimes switching column formats can be an effective attention-getting device. For instance, use one large instead of two small columns, etc. A change in the number of columns immediately signals the reader that the topic has changed. This works especially well in newsletters and reports.

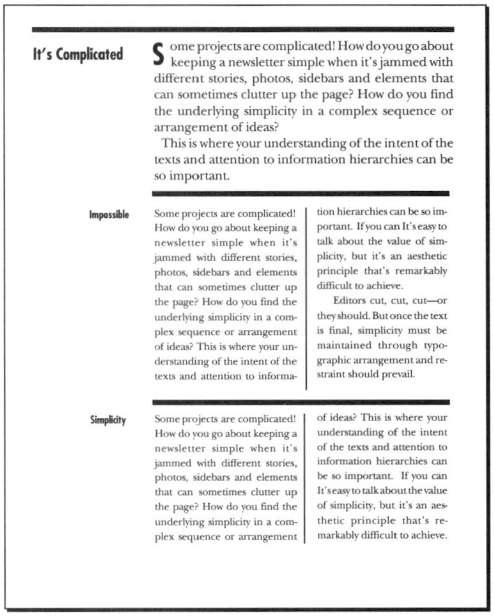

Figure 3-24: Design column layout to grab the reader's attention.

◆ Use graphic devices as reader cues: Dingbats, bullets, oversize quotation marks and numerals all grab attention. (A dingbat is a typographic ornament used to signify the end of a text section or to introduce list items. See Appendix B for more

examples of dingbats.) These nonalphabetic characters quickly draw the reader's eye. They add
visual excitement to your document. Their strong
typographic character makes them ideal compan-
ions for type. I often prefer them to illustrations.

Figure 3-25: Typographic symbols and ornaments add spice to your
presentations.

◈ Add rules and boxes: Rules are lines placed under
headlines for emphasis and separation. Rules and
boxes make dramatic statements; too many will
create confusion and visual distress. Rules add
substance and structure to headings. Be careful
when using them in text because they create barri-
ers. Always have a clear reason for stopping your
reader. Boxes should be reserved for text sections
that can be read both separately and in conjunction with the related text.

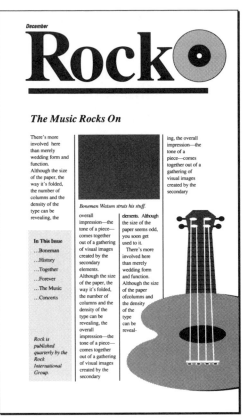

Figure 3-26: Restrained use of rules and shading adds visual interest to your pages.

◆ Work with shading: Graphic patterns can be used behind, above or under items to be emphasized. Much like boxes, shaded or tinted panels work to isolate sections of text from their surroundings. (A shaded area is known as a screen in printing terminology.) Be sure to use these graphic elements with restraint; too many will create confusion.

◆ Include illustrations and photographs: Artwork of any type will grab the reader's attention. Studies have shown that ideas accompanied by illustrations (including photographs) make a stronger and longer-lasting impression.

As with all other intuitive endeavors, there is no one correct way to approach the sequence of designing a document. When I work, I start with a definite concept or design for my document. If, after combining my concept with the actual text and graphics, it doesn't look "right," I change elements. Each such change either looks "right" or calls for another change.

I don't believe there's a neat and tidy way to create. It's an interactive process. You choose something that turns out to look good or bad and it leads you to try something else. And, fortunately, just as there are 50 ways to leave your lover, Word's plentiful features nearly always offer several ways to solve a problem. The suggestions I offer in this book on how to accomplish specific tasks are the ones I've found to work best for me. But don't be afraid to try others and work out your own best solutions.

Now that we've reviewed the basic concepts involved in typography and page layout, I recommend you start by doing the following:

- Answer the questions I posed at the beginning of the chapter regarding the nature of your publication and your readers.

- Study your collection of inspirational examples.

- Decide whether your document should be formal or informal. Work up several thumbnail (small) sketches of the document.

- Try symmetrical and asymmetrical layouts. Work your design out on paper before you set it up on the computer, and choose the scheme that works the best.

Have a good time designing your documents with Word for Windows. Its great flexibility and easy access to styles, fonts, alignment and line spacing make it easy to experiment with your typography and layouts.

Design Do's & Don'ts

Desktop publishing design requires weaving together many intricate details. With so many choices to make, we often become preoccupied with certain aspects and, caught off guard, we overlook others. The oversights are easier to spot when the document comes back from the printer: a missing letter in the title, an incorrect date, an extra line space below a heading. Here are some tips to help you avoid such unpleasant surprises.

Do Doodle

Don't rush into your document design. Before you begin working on your computer, do some doodling—it will save valuable time later on. Start with a series of thumbnail sketches. Once you've worked out some promising designs for your ideas, develop them in more detail on full-size sheets of paper. Create your grid at this stage.

This preliminary work might sound like a lot of trouble, but believe me, it will pay off in the long run.

Figure 4-1: Fresh ideas emerge as you sketch preliminary "thumbnail" sketches.

Show Your Face(s)

Make a set of type-specimen pages that show your typefaces in typical column settings with various amounts of line spacing, as in the sample I've provided. These will be helpful when you're trying to choose type styles and sizes for your page elements. (See more type-specimen examples in Appendices A and B.)

Figure 4-2: Create your own type-specimen pages to help bring your design together quickly.

The Collection Box

Don't feel obliged to be original. Plagiarize, plagiarize, plagiarize! Yes, imitation is the sincerest form of flattery, and it's one of the best ways to learn typography. But is this legal? It's illegal only if you copy the typography of another work so closely that yours could be mistaken for the original. When you're good enough to do that, you'll no longer be interested in imitating someone else's work.

Duplicate things from this book. But don't stop here. Start saving every document design that attracts you—business letters, brochures, forms, newsletters, logos, etc. I collect so many that I've had to organize them into separate file folders; but many people just store them all together in a box. When you need a design of your own, peruse your collection for inspiration.

Double Up

When you're creating multiple-page documents, think in terms of page pairs from the very beginning—in your thumbnail and full-page sketches. Then use the Word for Windows preview mode to display your double-page spreads before making final typographic adjustments.

Big Is Best

Don't be chicken. If you've decided to introduce a contrasting element, make the contrast BIG. If it's a box meant to separate one area of text from another, give it a serious border. Give it room. Make it stand out. If it's a headline or title, make it different from its surroundings. If it's a graphic, make it dramatic.

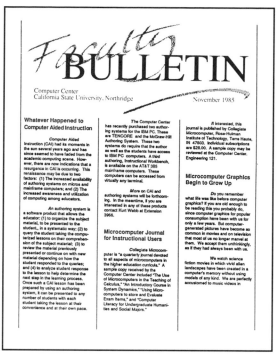

Figure 4-3: Bold contrast brings vitality to your design.

To create contrast, remember that we notice big before little, dark before light, things on top before things underneath, and deviations in structure before overall structure.

Consistency Counts

Multiple-page documents rely on visual consistency. Don't change page margins from one section to another. It's confusing and it looks dreadful.

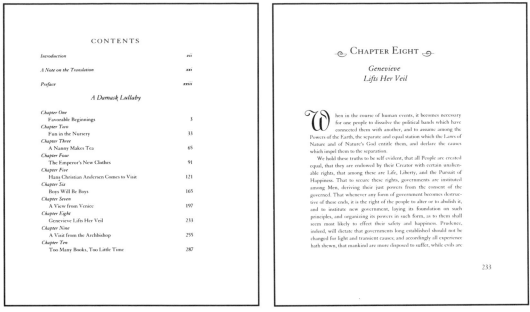

Figure 4-4: Give your design elements overall consistency in longer documents.

Wherever possible, use the same type size and style for headings and subheadings of equal importance within the same document. Also, maintain consistency in column widths, space between columns, page number placement and other reader cues—unless there's a clear, logical reason to make them different.

What's Your Line?

Don't set small type in long lines or large type in short lines. Maximum line length for comfortable reading is about 60 to 70 characters. For the most legible text, 9-point to 12-point type, set in line lengths between 18 and 24 picas, is recommended. In multicolumn pages, where lines must be shorter, use the smaller type sizes—9-point or 10-point.

Lines can be just about as long as you want them, if they have enough leading (or line spacing) between them so the reader can find the next line when returning to the left margin. However, there's a limit to the number of words the reader can comfortably

If you are having a lot of trouble getting justified columns to look good, the culprit may well be that lines are too short or type too large. There is an optimum average number of words to a line for smooth justification, and that number varies according to the typeface and the page program you're using. Try setting the type one point size smaller, retaining ample leading for ease of reading.

Figure 4-5: Type size, line length and leading are closely related.

Don't set long lines too close together or short lines too far apart (unless it's an advertisement). Space between lines of text must be proportional to line length; otherwise your reader will have a difficult time finding the beginning of each new line. The longer the line, the more line space needed. One to four points of leading (depending on point size) will work well for normal body text.

Heading Into Space

Don't confuse the reader by placing your headings and subheadings too close to the text above. The space between a heading (or subheading) and the text that follows should be noticeably less than the space between the heading (or subheading) and preceding text.

Aliquip ex ea com dolor in reprehenderit in volupatate nonumy.
Ipsum dolor sit amet, con.

Sensitivity to variations in spacing

Minimim venami quis nostrud.
Laboris nisi lorum ipsum dolor sit.
Aliquip ex ea com dolor in repre-
henderit in volupatate nonumy.

Com dolor in reprehenderit in volupatate nonumy. Minimim venami
quis nostrud.

Sensitivity to variations in spacing

Laboris nisi lorum ipsum dolor
sit. Aliquip ex ea com dolor in
reprehenderit in volupatate.

Figure 4-6: Headings should be closer to the text they introduce than to the preceding text.

Avoid widely spaced letters and lines in headings and subheadings, unless you're using these devices deliberately as design elements (in an advertisement, for example). Headings and subheadings not only give the reader information, their contrasting sizes and weights provide visual interest on the page. However, in order to work effectively, a heading and its text need to be seen as one unit.

As type size increases, space between letters appears disproportionately large. Also, depending on type size and paragraph settings, Word for Windows may insert more line space than you need. Feel free to reduce intercharacter and interline space when necessary when you're using a large type size.

Zap the Gaps

You've heard it before, but it's worth repeating: stop using two spaces at the end of a sentence. When your document is typeset, the two spaces make unsightly gaps in your beautiful, evenly spaced bodies of text.

Dam the Rivers

Empty white areas that the eye links together vertically in a text block are referred to as "rivers." Rivers most often occur in justified text set with minimum hyphenation. This effect can be exaggerated if you're inserting two spaces, instead of one, between sentences. Always look over your document for rivers. (It helps to view the page upside down.)

feugait nulla facilisi. Lorem ipsum dolor sit amet, consectetuer adipiscing elit, sed diam nonummy nibh   euismod tincidunt ut laoreet dolore magna aliquam erat volutpat. Ut wisi enim ad minim veniam, quis nostrud exerci tation   ullamcorper suscipit lobortis nisl ut aliquip ex ea commodo consequat.

Figure 4-7: "Rivers" of white space in your text can be distracting.

The Hole Story

Avoid unsightly holes between page layout elements in your documents. These may occur because your material doesn't quite fill the space allotted. Try an accent graphic. Try large quotation marks around a pull-quote. Put an anecdote in a box. Do anything, but don't leave that gaping hole!

Figure 4-8: "Holes" of trapped white space can ruin an otherwise good design.

Figure 4-9: Rework the surrounding design elements to solve the problem.

Bar That Space Bar

Eschew the habit of using the space bar to form indents. Why? First, in justified text, the space allowed for each character varies, so your indent depths will be irregular.

Second, indents and other text-formatting specifications should all be incorporated into your paragraph styles. Allow Word for Windows to do all that spacing for you automatically.

When in Rome

If you've decided you need to do what the Romans do (did) and use Roman numerals (for example, in page and section numbers or other reference elements), don't use them with numbers larger than VII (some say V). They're too hard to count!

Real Smart Quotes

Use real quotation marks and apostrophes instead of the inch and foot marks (typewriter quotes). Word for Windows provides the Enable Smart Quotes macro. USE IT!

"Smart Quotes" outclass "Typewriter Quotes"

Figure 4-10: "Smart Quotes" outclass "typewriter quotes," thanks to a special Word for Windows feature.

Help for Widows & Orphans

With Widow Control on, Word for Windows automatically prevents "widows" (the last line of a paragraph printed alone at the top of the next column or page). It also prevents "orphans" (the first line of a paragraph printed alone at the bottom of a page). Widow Control is found in the Format/Document dialog box. If you have a paragraph with three lines or fewer, Widow Control will *not* work. To keep the lines of a small paragraph from being separated, select Keep Paragraph Together in the Format/Paragraph dialog box. *Note:* At times you might be disconcerted to find parts of a paragraph moved to a new column or page. If this disturbs your design, turn Widow Control off or rewrite your text.

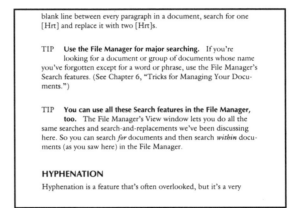

blank line between every paragraph in a document, search for one [Hrt] and replace it with two [Hrt]s.

TIP   **Use the File Manager for major searching.**   If you're looking for a document or group of documents whose name you've forgotten except for a word or phrase, use the File Manager's Search features. (See Chapter 6, "Tricks for Managing Your Documents.")

TIP   **You can use all these Search features in the File Manager, too.**   The File Manager's View window lets you do all the same searches and search-and-replacements we've been discussing here. So you can search *for* documents and then search *within* documents (as you saw here) in the File Manager.

HYPHENATION
Hyphenation is a feature that's often overlooked, but it's a very

Figure 4-11: The Word for Windows "Widow Control" feature also prevents "orphans."

The Bottom Line

Avoid headings and subheadings that fall at the bottom of a page or column. In single-column layouts, selecting Keep Paragraph With Next in the Format/Paragraph dialog box will prevent this problem. (Be sure Widow Control is on for all paragraph styles.) In multiple-column layouts, you may have to tolerate uneven column bottoms or edit the text.

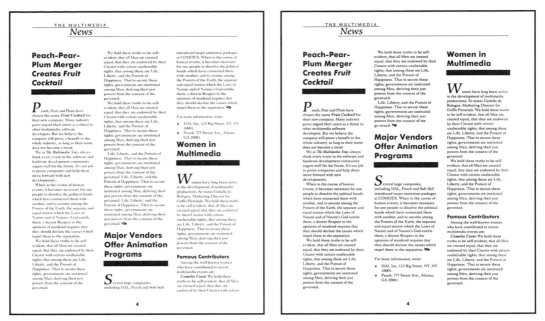

Figures 4-12 & 4-13: Don't strand subheadings at the bottom of a column. With Word for Windows, you can easily relocate headings.

The Conservative Type

Don't set long text in all-capitals, italics, very large or very small type sizes or reversed type. These are all difficult to read.

Boxing Rules

Boxes and rules should be used with restraint. Reserve them for items that need separation from other page elements.

In general, avoid boxes around headings and subheadings if you've already placed vertical rules between columns and/or put a frame around the page. Excessive horizontal and vertical rules can make the page look too busy. As Hamlet said to the players, "With all, gently."

Figure 4-14: Overuse of rules and boxes makes a page "busy."

A Shady Background

If you use shaded backgrounds in tables or boxes, be sure you have enough contrast between text and background. For black text, background gray shading should be no more than 30 percent. If you're using white type, black makes the best background.

Stay Regular

Avoid erratic spacing between elements in a layout. Complex documents depend on a constant, unvarying underlying structure. Irregular spaces create visual havoc. It's much easier than you think for an extra blank line to appear at the beginning or end of a paragraph. Working with View Preferences Paragraph Marks set to On should eliminate this. You'll quickly see other anomalies if you look at your pages upside down.

Crowd Control

Don't create claustrophobia. A page with insufficient white space has the same effect as a crowded room—the reader's first instinct is to get away. Be sure that outer margins provide a generous frame for page contents and that boxed text and graphics have internal white space to set them apart from surrounding text.

Figure 4-15: Avoid claustrophobia by giving your page breathing room.

Lost in Space

Avoid visual fragmentation caused by too much white space. If spacing between paragraphs, graphics, headings and subheadings is too great, the page appears to have no integrated structure. This space, alas, cannot be prescribed by mathematical formulas. You'll have to experiment until you get the page elements to look like a group rather than unrelated parts.

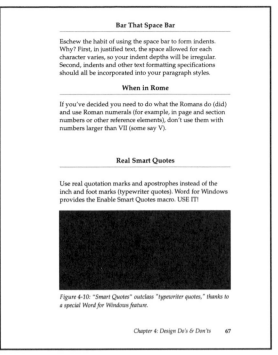

Bar That Space Bar

Eschew the habit of using the space bar to form indents. Why? First, in justified text, the space allowed for each character varies, so your indent depths will be irregular. Second, indents and other text formatting specifications should all be incorporated into your paragraph styles.

When in Rome

If you've decided you need to do what the Romans do (did) and use Roman numerals (for example, in page and section numbers or other reference elements), don't use them with numbers larger than VII (some say V).

Real Smart Quotes

Use real quotation marks and apostrophes instead of the inch and foot marks (typewriter quotes). Word for Windows provides the Enable Smart Quotes macro. USE IT!

Figure 4-10: "Smart Quotes" outclass "typewriter quotes," thanks to a special Word for Windows feature.

Chapter 4: Design Do's & Don'ts 67

Figure 4-16: Inconsistent spacing among design elements can give your page an amateurish look.

Except for the outer page margins, any white shape that appears more prominent than the page contents is probably too large. Look at your layout in Print Preview and then study the printed page from several feet away.

MOVING ON

Now that we've spent some time thinking about design issues and features, we can move on to examples that illustrate how to use them in your documents.

III

Looking Good
With Word

5

Business & Personal Correspondence

In demonstrating the versatility of Word for Windows, I use the term "correspondence" to cover a wide range of documents, including letterheads, business cards, fax covers, memos, résumés, news releases, announcements and invitations. Because we all use these forms of communication from time to time, designing them is personally meaningful. Also, they're usually single-page documents, so the designs should be relatively straightforward—which makes this a good place for us to start our Word for Windows design tour.

The chapters in Section IV provide detailed instruction on all techniques used in this section.

LETTERHEAD

The letterhead is the single most important document we use, in my opinion. So rather than choosing a pre-designed style from your local printer, why not design your own?

A good letterhead performs three critical functions: it provides the name, address, phone numbers, etc., of the sender; it carries a message; and it graphically projects the sender's image and purpose. These specifics focus your design, and the small amount of fixed information involved gives you maximum creativity in placing it.

You can put your letterhead just about anywhere on the page (except in the middle!), but first take into account the kind of correspondence you'll be using it for. Will it be typewritten, word processed or handwritten? Will it be legal or full of complex numerical data? Do you need a special-size sheet and envelope? A careful review of your typical correspondence will help you avoid creating a nonfunctional letterhead.

The structure of your design will be established by the placement of the letterhead itself and the correspondence block that will occupy the bulk of the page. In setting your hierarchies for the letterhead information, be sure to make the sender's name or logo the focal point. For some reason, many beginning designers make the name and address close to the same size; aesthetically and logically, this makes no sense. (An exception to this might be when numbers are used as a design element.) Finally, fold your design as it will be placed in the envelope so that your letterhead shows.

Projecting the Sender's Image

If you want to play it safe, centering your letterhead is always acceptable. This communicates a stable, traditional tone. If you want the numbers immediately under the name, I usually suggest inserting a rule between the two, as in the David M. Rubin Music Services example (see page 97). You can also separate them with a distinct space or a radical change in typeface as in my Writer-Designer stationery (page 107) or the Cogent Books news release (page 115).

Another alternative is to put the numbers at the bottom, with or without a rule. This can prevent the visual distraction of lots of numbers lessening the impact of the image projected by the name and/or logo.

With a centered letterhead, you might try justifying the lines, spreading the information across the top or bottom. But you'll need to add considerable character spacing to make this look good. Widely spaced letters can give a contemporary, elegant look. I used this technique in the WJR (page 103) and David Rubin examples.

Flush-left alignment is less formal than centered alignment. It imparts some dynamism to the page and makes it easy to work with a logo-text combination. It does, however, make placement of the phone and fax numbers more difficult because when set flush-left, they form a long string that usually projects out beyond the name/logo. In the WJR example, therefore, I put the numbers at the bottom of the page.

Alternative arrangements can be seen in the Films International (page 99) and sans-serif ELAC English Department (Chapter 3) letterheads.

Less traditional alignments for letterhead include flush-right, stacked-right, stacked-left, lower left or right corner. These arrangements will require formatting your correspondence in unusual ways. I like the design of my stationery with the flower motif (page 105) because the open text area forms a compact column on the left. I find these proportions more pleasing than those of a traditional page, and I don't mind projecting an unconventional image. But you'll have to consider whether you (and your readers) would be comfortable with this kind of style.

Choosing Type

The type style you choose for your letterhead makes a strong statement about you. Here, the image-evoking properties of type are at their most potent because there's little else on the page (assuming you're not including complex artwork). It's the type style that makes the initial impact on your reader—and we all understand the significance of first impressions. (See Appendix A for information on selecting a typeface.)

It's not necessary to print all information in the same typeface. Sans-serif faces are excellent for the small type often used for addresses and phone numbers. They tend to project a modern, businesslike image.

Serif faces will give your stationery a traditional look; note, however, that they may be less legible in small sizes if output by a laser printer.

Incorporating Logos & Artwork

Logos and ornaments are welcome inclusions, adding character and a personal touch to your correspondence. While this isn't the place for a discourse on logo design, I would like to suggest a number of possibilities for enhancing your letterhead:

◆ Set your initials in a large point size (36 points and up). This makes a positive personal statement. And initials will fit with the other type on your page in an aesthetically pleasing way. (See the WJR example on page 103.) To find the best arrangement, experiment.

◆ Try setting initials in several styles so you can select the one that makes the most interesting shapes—both positive and negative. Try all-caps, lowercase and combinations. Try different typefaces.

◆ Excellent ornaments can be found in the Windows TrueType Wingdings, ITC Zapf Dingbats, Linotype Pi fonts, the international symbol set and the Carta typefaces as well as the Arts & Letters and Corel-DRAW drawing programs (Dingbats are discussed in Chapter 12 and Appendix A). I used these in the David M. Rubin (page 97), Hana Hotel (page 95) and WJR designs (page 103) and for my own stationery. Clip art can be adapted too, as in the Films International letterhead (page 99).

Figure 5-1: Dingbats can add zest and personality to an otherwise bland design.

◆ Unless you're going to print in color, I think black-and-white images look best, because they use positive and negative shapes in the same fundamental way that type does. Images with multiple gray tones introduce a totally different feel—one that demands aesthetic judgment in evaluating visual impact. Because of their 3D illusions, photographs and illustrations introduce new complexities in terms of creating contrast and balance.

◆ You can scan in a company logo and use it as a bitmap, or convert it to an object, using the trace function in drawing programs like Harvard Draw or Micrografx Designer.

BUSINESS CARDS

Business cards present quite a challenge. How is one to get all that information, composed attractively and in a way that projects a company's image, in a mere 2 by 3 1/2 inches? Not an easy job, but a fun one. (See the Films International card on page 109.) Limitations such as these make your choices easier and focus the design challenge. After all, there are fewer decisions to make.

It makes sense to base your design on some element in your letterhead. If you have a logo, use it.

As with the letterhead, a symmetrical design is the most traditional. For business cards, I believe it's also the easiest to compose. But asymmetry definitely gives more dynamism to the composition and allows more leeway in arranging your information.

You might even consider composing your business card vertically. Keep in mind that vertical cards won't be as convenient to use in card or Rolodex files; they will, however, get more attention because the user will have to turn them right side up!

In placing the text, check with your printer to see how close to the edge you can print. Depending on how much you want to spend, there may be some limitations.

Selecting type for the company and bearer names is essentially the same procedure as that used for letterheads. Size establishes priorities on a business card, so be sure the most important information is the biggest.

On most cards, you'll use very small (6-point) type for the address, etc. So select fonts that are simple in design. Rules above or below the company name can add impact.

If you're producing camera-ready art from a laser printer, I recommend making the card model 3 by 5 1/4 inches.

This helps prevent the jaggies when the image is reduced for printing. It's best not to make it larger than that, because the thick and thin proportions of type change as the type grows in size. Your type may look too spindly if it has been reduced too much.

FAX COVERS

You may decide not to use company letterhead on your fax cover, but the same basic information should be included—perhaps in a reduced size or a different position on the page. My stationery with the letterhead on the far right makes a poor fax cover. David Rubin's letterhead, however, adapts well (page 97).

David M. Rubin Music Services

1946 Caminito del Valle, Glendale, California 91208 Phone (818) 246-6619 FAX (818) 247-6646

Figure 5-2: This letterhead design works well on a fax cover sheet.

Because of the degraded way in which your image will print when faxed, try to limit your type choices to those that are simple or robust. If you must include information in a small point size (anything under 10 points), be sure the type is legible. Test it on your own fax machine.

Providing ruled lines on which to write your message is a good idea (unless you type all your faxes, in which case they would be a detriment). Included in the following samples are both ruled and unruled versions.

MEMOS

Why not personalize your memos by designing your own? Word for Windows makes it so easy. The examples I've provided later in this chapter only hint at the variety of things you can do.

If you work in a conservative atmosphere, you'll have to settle for using rules or a formal typeface or elegant flourish, as in the Richard G. Morrison example (page 113), to give distinction to your design. But if the environment is more permissive, you may want to go for a livelier look. You could even scan in a photo.

RÉSUMÉS

I always think of résumés as documents in a dilemma: they must grab attention without being overdone. Handsomely designed résumés stand out in a group—they will be read. But here's a problem: the kind of résumé that will catch an art director's eye might very well put off the personnel director in a bank.

Different types of business people respond differently to the same résumé. You need to spend some time researching your target market. If you're looking for work in the art area, your innovation and creativity can be unleashed; but in the typical conservative business environment, you'll need to restrain your creative urges. Compare the three different treatments of the same résumé on pages 121, 123 and 125.

With even the most conservative employer, however, you can do certain things to present a good image:

- Make your name stand out. Make it bigger and/or bolder than everything else on the page.

- Most résumé experts advise you to get everything on one page. This isn't so difficult when you're 20 years old, but by the time you're over 30 you'll be hard pressed to summarize. Yet summarize you must.

- Given the inherently tabular nature of most résumé information, arranging this data as a table works quite well. But limit the use of rules to horizontal divisions. Too many lines will distract from the content.

- Your choice of paper is critical. (See Appendix C.)

- Including a photo sometimes helps. Make it very big or very small; mid-size photos are too common.

TYPESET BUSINESS LETTERS & NEWS RELEASES

With the advent of laser printers, business letters and news releases began to look as if they were typeset. But while fine typesetting is easier to read and looks better on the page than typewritten material, it's immediately perceived as being cold and impersonal. For whatever reason, typesetting in this context seems pretentious.

Using a typewriter face like Courier creates a more personal look. And there are also a number of proportionally set typefaces that have an informal air: Serifa, Bitstream Charter, ITC Korinna, ITC Stone Informal (though this might be *too* informal) and others. (Proportionally spaced type is discussed in Appendix A.)

I think a news release is more successful if it doesn't look as if it's printed on the company letterhead. To give your release a less staid appearance, put the name of the company at the top and the related data at the bottom (see page 119).

ANNOUNCEMENTS, INVITATIONS & AWARDS

Oh boy, can you have fun with these. From homespun to high-tech to high-class, these documents can mimic any style that fits their purpose. You can use your most elegant display faces and print on those sumptuous imitation parchments or other exotic papers. Or you can use your wackiest dingbats and indulge in any flight of fancy.

Of course, formal invitations, announcements and awards usually have a symmetrical design. It's conventional to use script typefaces and re-creations of medieval lettering. But don't let tradition hold you back. Feel free to do your own thing and design with sans-serif or anything else you'd like to experiment with. Take a look at the Ski Books moving announcement (page 127) and the Silverado Award certificate (page 129).

Now let's see Word in action. The illustrations on the following pages show what you can do with Word for Windows in creating great-looking correspondence.

Note: Because Word's graphics are somewhat limited, many documents in this book use line art, clip art and other graphics from third-party software packages. I've used both Arts & Letters and CorelDRAW, both of which contain thousands of readily accessible graphic images.

In re-creating the designs in this book, you may want to replace my images with those you can create using WWG: Word's drawing tools, Microsoft Draw, Microsoft Graph or the clip art that comes with Word. However, if you have a third-party program, make the most of it!

If your budget is limited but your needs go beyond the offerings of the Word utilities, you may want to build a library of shareware clip art, graphics and fonts. Good graphics and Word make a great team.

Τhis letterhead combines modern Western elegance with Japanese restraint and deference to tradition. Strict symmetry is complemented by the large letter-spaced capitals with their elegant thick/thin stroke contrast. Not only does the added space around each letter heighten the effect of a simple title; it also turns each letter into a beautiful graphic object.

The small, bold hotel address element, stacked and underlined with relatively heavy rules, make a modern statement and contrast well with the hotel name.

The striking Japanese-style dingbat is an appropriate logo for the hotel: "Hana" means "flower" in Japanese. Because of their strong graphic designs, many dingbats can be used in large sizes to create interesting logos.

PAGE SETUP

Paper size: 8 1/2 in. x 11 in.
Orientation: Portrait
Margins: Top—.5 in. Bottom—.55 in.
                Left & Right—1.2 in.

TYPE

Name: 55-pt. Caslon 540 Roman
Address: 10-pt. Caslon 3 Roman
Dingbat: 114-pt. ITC Zapf Dingbat
For alternate typefaces see Appendix A.

Caslon 540 and its bold variant, Caslon 3, have a strong yet elegant look. Both of these fonts, modern versions of Caslon, are characterized by a regularity that communicates dignity and reserve.

GRAPHICS

You certainly could use a more complex graphic here. But since Herman Zapf so imaginatively imitated this delightful Japanese crest, why not use it?

PRODUCTION TIPS

Center the hotel name on the page and use letter spacing to make it look as if there's an even amount of white space around the word. The expanded spacing amounts are as follows, in points:

H 5, A 5.5, N 5, A 13, space between words 4, H 4.5, O 1.5, T 3, E 4, L 4

Note that the smallest space is between the O and the T. (See the discussion of letter spacing in Chapter 3.)

To create the address section, center the text and indent paragraphs 2.7 inches from left and right. To make the rules, select all three paragraphs and select a bottom border. Borders are set 1 point from the text. Choose the 1.5-point border option. The paragraphs have 1.5 points Before and 2 points After, and Single (Auto) line spacing. (You could also put the address elements in a table, then center the table in a frame.)

To create the Zapf dingbat, select it and insert it into a frame. Position the frame, at center/bottom in relation to the margins, by selecting locations in the Insert Format/Frame dialog box. Go back to the Format/Borders and Shading (Format/Border) dialog box to turn frame borders off.

HANA HOTEL

34 Ginza

Tokyo

333-4545

This otherwise conventional letterhead design is enhanced by the unusual logo, which gives the page both originality and modernity. Because they share a simple, geometric quality, the type used for the name and address and the logo (graphic) complement each other. Including the graphic in the lower right gives the page a certain playfulness. This graphic can be repeated on second sheets. The two lines of type are independently formatted.

PAGE SETUP

Paper size: 8 1/2 in. x 11 in.
Orientation: Portrait
Margins: Top—.4 in. Bottom—1 in.
                Left & Right—1 in.

TYPE

Name: 23.5-pt. ITC Avant Garde Gothic Book
Address: 10-pt. ITC Avant Garde Gothic Book
For alternate typefaces, see Appendix A.

Avant Garde Gothic, with its consistent unilinear strokes and absolute geometry, is a good choice here because it so closely echoes the graphic.

GRAPHICS

The logo and graphic were adapted from Computer Support Corporation's Electronics & Logic Optional Clip Art collection. (Actually, they're symbols for coaxial coupling loops!) Symbols (clip art) in this collection work in all Arts & Letters programs.

PRODUCTION TIPS

First, cut and paste the graphic in the upper left via the Clipboard. Enter the name on the same line. To fill the space between the graphic and the margin exactly, justify the line and then increase the point size of the name in half-point increments until the line wraps. The previous point size is the maximum size that will fit the line. Choose it. (Otherwise, you could expand the letter and word spacing.) Set the paragraph line spacing at Single (Auto), with no Before or After spacing. Set a 1.5-point border 1 point below the text.

Set the address paragraph with justified alignment, Single line spacing, with no Before or After spacing. The point size used in the address fits comfortably across the page. To make it fill the space as precisely as possible, put extra space between the ZIP Code and the word Phone, as well as between the phone number and the word FAX. This helps separate these important numbers and makes the line fit the space better. Further, forcing a line break by using Shift+Enter, rather than just Enter, causes the line to push ever so slightly more to the right. Because the rule between the name and address creates an absolute visual comparison, it's worth it to be this picky. If the line lengths don't match, the design looks hit-or-miss and unprofessional.

I cut and pasted the graphic in the lower right through the Clipboard. Then I inserted it into a frame. In the Format/Frame dialog box, I positioned the frame right and bottom relative to the margin.

This letterhead projects a modern avant-garde image. The strong sans-serif face and the unorthodox arrangement of the name and address are appropriate for an international company. Also, this unusual arrangement of text gives a nod to the distinctly artistic bent of the film business; it provides a refreshing change from the expected while retaining a professional look.

Here the contrast in the type size for names and address information creates visual interest and establishes a hierarchy of importance. The stark shapes of the rectangular black-and-white graphic combine with the vertical rules and text treatment to produce an excellent example of positive and negative space at work.

PAGE SETUP

Paper size: 8 1/2 in. x 11 in.
Orientation: Portrait
Margins: Top—.7 in. Bottom—1 in.
Right & Left—1 in.

TYPE

14-pt. Helvetica Inserat
8-pt. Helvetica Inserat
For alternate typefaces, see Appendix A.

These strong (almost harsh), angular letter forms echo the dramatic positive and negative shapes of the graphic. You can see this clearly in the enclosed space in the 4, for instance.

GRAPHICS

This graphic is based on a symbol from the Arts & Letters Graphics Editor library. It was easy to alter using the drawing tools or Microsoft Draw. I inserted the world map into a rectangle, then selected the background color for the rectangle and the foreground color for the graphic.

PRODUCTION TIPS

The easiest way to format this design is to insert all the information in a one-row table containing three columns. The first cell contains the graphic; the second, the company name and address; the third, the principal's name and phone numbers. The center and right cells each have a 1.5-point left border that creates a vertical rule. (***Note:*** In the Format/Borders and Shading (Format/Border) dialog box, the center cell has a border on the left and the right. Obviously, the left-hand border of the rightmost cell is also the right border of the center cell. It's sometimes easy to forget this when you're working intently.)

Set the graphic flush-left. Set all cells with .15-point spacing between columns. Set the text flush-left, with a .07-point indent, Single (Auto) line spacing, and no spacing Before or After.

I placed the word FAX on a separate line so the two text areas are balanced in number of lines and line length.

Films International
4230 Ben Ave.
Studio City
CA 91604
USA

Max B. Miller
(213) 762-2181
(213) 508-6400
FAX:
(818) 762-2181

The heavy black borders unify the elements in this strong logo. The three S's in the company name (set in ITC Anna) project a fashionable, modern image and echo the curves in the logo icons; the Univers Condensed type in the address and phone number adds a businesslike touch.

PAGE SETUP

Paper size: 8 1/2 in. x 11 in.
Orientation: Portrait
Margins: Top—.5 in. Bottom—.6 in.
Left & Right—1 in.

TYPE

Logo: ITC Anna (point size altered by scaling)
Address/phone no.: 11-pt. Zurich (Univers) Condensed
Dingbats: Linotype Holiday Pi 1 (point size altered by scaling)
For alternate typefaces, see Appendix A.

PRODUCTION TIPS

Open Word's drawing toolbar. (In Version 2 of Word, open Microsoft Draw.) To construct the logo, first create or import your image—in this case, the two dingbats. I put each dingbat in its own round-cornered box, then placed the squares adjacent to each other.

I made a box and inserted the SUNSHEL-TERS text. (Use the Text tool in Version 2.) I selected the text, chose White for its color, selected the box and selected Black for its fill. I placed the text and the box relative to the icon pair, then grouped the pair with the box. (It took some trial and error to get the text and box in proper proportion to each other and to the pair of icons above.)

Next, I put a round-cornered rectangle around the group of boxes. I selected a heavier line for this outer border to balance the heavy black background in the SUN-SHELTERS box. My page was automatically updated. (You must manually update your document in Version 2 by closing Microsoft Draw.)

At this point, I selected the graphic and inserted it in a frame by clicking on Insert/ Frame. I typed the address and phone number directly into the frame under the logo. I selected center alignment for the graphic and the address/phone number; and because all the elements were within the same frame, the address automatically centered under the logo. (I set the address/phone number sepa-rately in the frame rather than adding it to the logo so that a change of address/phone number would not necessitate re-creating the entire logo.) I located the frame in the upper left corner of the page, relative to the margins, using the Format/Frame dialog box.

Note on size: If you're working with scalable fonts, Word will scale Word's drawing tools' graphic (Microsoft Draw graphic) and its type once the artwork is in the document. If you're working with bitmapped fonts, make your graphic the correct size with the drawing tools (or Microsoft Draw); otherwise your type will look jagged when scaled. By double-clicking on your drawing, you'll see the Draw-ing Object editing dialog box. Choose the Size and Position tab to set the exact size for your graphic. (In Version 2, the measuring guides in the Draw menu in Microsoft Draw read out in hundredths of an inch. You must drag them over your object to determine its size.)

1001 Dalmations Drive
Miramar, Florida 12345
918-567-8123

Several features give this rather sedate letterhead distinction. The large, handsome, classically proportioned initial capitals create visual focus. The graceful descending J particularly attracts our attention. Also, the letter spacing of the company name and the small temple dingbat reinforce the classical message of the letterforms.

PAGE SETUP

Paper size: 8 1/2 in. x 11 in.
Orientation: Portrait
Margins: Top—.75 in. Bottom—.5 in.
Left & Right—1.25 in.

TYPE

Name: 18-pt. Monotype Bembo
Dots: 8-pt. Symbol
Temple dingbat: 24-pt. Carta
WJR: 72-pt. Monotype Bembo
Address line: 12-pt. Monotype Bembo, except the word FAX, which is set in 6-pt. Monotype Bembo Bold
Dot triangle: 12-pt. Symbol
For alternate typefaces, see Appendix A.

I chose Monotype Bembo, designed by Stanley Morrison, because of its exceptional grace and purity of line. Its timelessness fits well with the concept of academic publishing.

PRODUCTION TIPS

If you wish, as I did, to extend the type in the name section the full width of the page, you'll experience some difficulty. Because of Word's built-in spacing algorithms, I couldn't get the final s of the 18-point Publishers any closer to the edge of the rule than you see it. (To get around this problem, see the Dunham Industries flyer in Chapter 7.) I found, in fact, that

forcing a line return (Shift+Enter) rather than creating a new paragraph pushed it slightly closer to the edge. (The program allows the smaller 12-point type in the address to get closer to the edge.) Run the name line flush-left (or justified); expand by 1 point the character spacing of all the words. In between the words and ornaments, insert additional spaces. I used fixed spaces (Ctrl+Shift+space bar) to control the interword spacing exactly.

To push the line as far to the right as possible, you can adjust the spaces between words in 1-point increments until the line wraps. To fine-tune the line, you can alter the spaces between words. (To change the size of a space, select it as if it were a regular character and change its size.) Add space symmetrically to prevent uneven gaps between similar text items—e.g., on either side of the temple dingbat.

The 1.5-point border below the name line is set 2 points from the text. The Carta dingbat is subscripted and the small Symbol dots in the address line are superscripted. Because you can't predict the exact amount of space or the sizes needed for dingbats, these things really need to be done by trial and error.

Set WJR flush-left and superscript it to reduce the gap between it and the rule above.

The address line is easier to format because of the length of the text line. The address fills the space below its rule more fully than the company name does. Set all characters in the address at .5 points expanded. I justified the line and made it fit the space exactly by reducing the word FAX; this provides an interesting visual contrast with the rest of the text.

Wagner · Janos · Respighi   🏛   University Publishers

WJR

1946 Hiawatha Drive, Glendale, CA 95555 ∴ (818) 288-1234 ғᴀx (818) 288-5678

With its somewhat crudely drawn flowers and "hand-printed" text, this letterhead projects an image that's fresh, informal and unconventional. The ragged edges of the centered text items add another casual touch to the design.

The location of the letterhead on the right page edge is unusual. But I like it because it creates an interesting page composition when the correspondence is filled in.

To make this letterhead design work for a traditional business, you could replace the whimsical type and graphics with more conventional ones.

PAGE SETUP

Paper Size: 8 1/2 in. x 11 in.
Orientation: Portrait
Margins: Top—.7 in. Bottom—.75 in.
Left—1 in. Right—1.9 in.

TYPE

13-pt. Tekton Bold
For alternate typefaces, see Appendix A.

Tekton has a highly legible yet informal, handwritten look. The letterforms match the graphics in weight and character; the lines seem to have been drawn with the same pen.

GRAPHICS

These charming flowers are from the Symbols collection packaged with CorelDRAW.

PRODUCTION TIPS

The page margins define the space available for correspondence. Set the right page margin wider than the others to provide space for the letterhead items, which are positioned in the margins. Select and group the flowers in CorelDRAW; then cut and paste them via the Windows Clipboard onto the Word page.

Each line of text is a separate Normal Style paragraph. After creating the text, select it and the graphic, and insert them into a frame. Position the frame at the right (relative to page) and top (relative to margin).

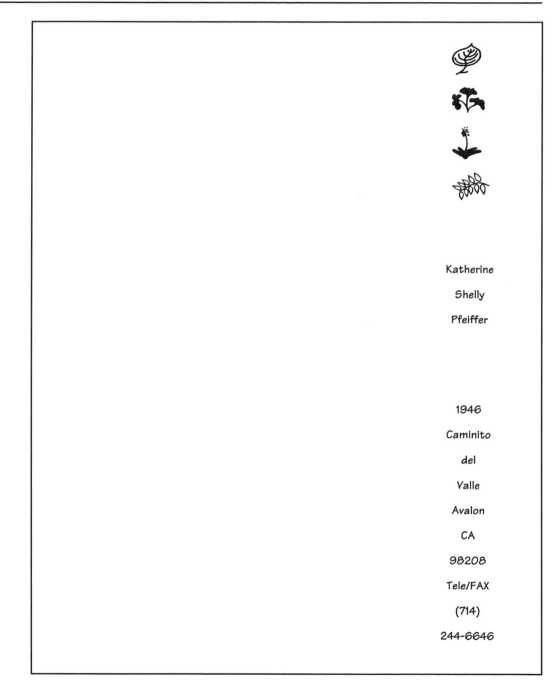

Katherine

Shelly

Pfeiffer

1946

Caminito

del

Valle

Avalon

CA

98208

Tele/FAX

(714)

244-6646

This letterhead design combines the traditional with the contemporary. The highly contrasting combination of the small Copperplate Gothic Bold type with the large, florid script makes a modern statement that is reinforced by the unconventional use of horizontal rules. Yet the formal symmetry of centered alignment and the old-fashioned elegance of the script reflect traditional styling. While this letterhead is effective without the rules, I like them for handwritten communications.

PAGE SETUP

Paper Size: 8 1/2 in. x 11 in.
Orientation: Portrait
Margins: Top & Bottom—1 in.
   Right & Left—1 in.

TYPE

Writer-Designer: 11-pt. Copperplate Gothic Bold
Capitals K, S and P: 30-pt. Shelley Volante Script
Remainder of name letters: 30-pt. Shelley Allegro Script
Address: 20-pt. Shelley Allegro Script
Dingbat: 20-pt. Linotype Decorative Pi 1
For alternate typefaces, see Appendix A.

The romantic in me couldn't resist these handsome type designs inspired by copperplate engraving from two different eras. Both have an elegance and a crispness. Many versions of Copperplate Gothic are available. The original designer was Frederic William Goudy, one of America's most renowned typographers.

PRODUCTION TIPS

Writer-Designer is a centered paragraph. The name is also centered.

To arrange the three address items on the same line, I used a single-row table with three equal-size cells. The phone number is left-aligned, the street number is centered; the fax number is right-aligned. (An equally easy method uses a right-aligned tab, a centered tab and a left-aligned tab.) The ZIP Code is centered and spaced the same as the previous line.

To create the ruled lines, enter 21 empty paragraphs immediately below and identical to the one containing the ZIP Code. Then select all of these empty paragraphs *except the first.* In the Format/Borders and Shading (Format/Border) dialog box, select a .75-point border above, below and between paragraphs (click between the paragraphs in the sample and a line will appear). *Voilà!*

WRITER · DESIGNER

Katherine Shelly Pfeiffer

1946 Caminto del Valle

Pho 714-244-6646   *Avalon, California*   *Fax 714-244-6646*

98208

A Full Deck

The Complete Game Store

245 Broadway, Los Angeles, CA 97832   (213) 666-5566

The logo created from large dingbats draws attention here. The bold type faces used for the store name and description have a calligraphic quality that complements the shapes of the dingbats.

PAGE SETUP

Paper Size: 8 1/2 in. x 11 in.
Orientation: Portrait
Card size: 3 1/2 in. x 2 in.

TYPE

Dingbats: 46-pt. ITC Zapf Dingbats
Store name: 16-pt. Hiroshige Bold
Store description: 8-pt. Hiroshige Medium
    Italic
Address and phone no.: 8-pt. Helvetica
    Narrow
For alternate typefaces, see Appendix A.

I selected Hiroshige for its dramatic calligraphic look. The italic variation makes the description stand out even though it's smaller than the name. Its shapes seem to echo the dingbat shapes.

I chose Helvetica Narrow because its large x-height and uniform strokes make it legible, even in small sizes, from a standard laser printer.

PRODUCTION TIPS

As with the Films International card (page 109), this document was constructed in a table. This makes it easy to put a border around all the paragraphs and create the rule, which isn't as wide as the outer dimensions of the border.

In this case, narrow columns are used to create the left and right margins of the card. The dingbats, store name and description are center-aligned in their individual rows. The flush-left address is in the same row as the flush-right phone number. To allow the creation of their distinct alignments, each is in its own cell (column). You could also set left and right tabs for these.

Expand spacing for the dingbats by 5 points. Also, insert an extra space between each word in the store name. To add impact, expand the character spacing for the subtitle by 2.5 points.

This business card uses many of the same elements as the Films International letterhead. However, I enlarged the graphic to balance the two text areas above. (Please see the letterhead description and illustration on pages 98 and 99.)

PAGE SETUP

Paper Size: 8 1/2 in. x 11 in.
Orientation: Portrait
Card size: 3 1/2 in. x 2 1/8 in.

TYPE

Names: 10-pt. Helvetica Inserat
Address: 8-pt. Helvetica Inserat
For alternate typefaces, see Appendix A.

GRAPHICS

The graphic is constructed from a symbol in the Arts & Letters Graphics Editor library. I stretched the graphic image to fit the space. (See Films International letterhead.)

PRODUCTION TIPS

Construct the entire design inside a table. (See the grid detail.) This allows you to construct the frame around the entire card and precisely position the three distinct sections. Empty rows form the upper and lower margins and create the gap between the text areas and the graphic. The left and right margins are composed of empty columns. Each text area has a cell, as does the graphic. Set the text flush-left, with no Before or After spacing, and Single (Auto) line spacing. Set all columns with .15-inch space between columns. Bring

the graphic in by way of the Clipboard (or import it), then stretch it to fit the space if necessary.

If you look closely, you'll notice that this card is slightly taller—12 points, to be exact—than a standard business card. I tried several variations of the design and preferred this one; but consider whether this size will be appropriate for your clients. For one thing, it won't fit in a standard-size business card holder.

Max B. Miller	Films International
4230 Ben Ave.	(213) 762-2181
Studio City	(213) 508-6400
CA 91604	FAX:
USA	(818) 762-2181

Not all letterheads adapt easily to fax covers, but this one does. (The letterhead design and layout are discussed separately on page 96.) In addition to the information on the letterhead, a fax cover sheet must also include spaces for the date, the recipient's name and fax number, the sender's name and comments, and the total number of pages included in the fax.

In this example, the fax items are set in a bold condensed sans-serif face that contrasts effectively with the wide, lightweight type used for the letterhead text. The no-nonsense type used for the fax information is clearly distinct from the letterhead, eliminating any confusion. Also, the 1.5-point rules complement the rule used in the letterhead and provide lines on which to write.

PAGE SETUP

Paper Size:	8 1/2 in. x 11 in.
Orientation:	Portrait
Margins:	Top—.4 in. Bottom—1 in.
	Left & Right—1 in.

TYPE

FAX COVER: 24-pt. Helvetica Inserat
Request information text: 10-pt. Helvetica Inserat
Number of pages line: 12-pt. Helvetica Inserat
For alternate typefaces, see Appendix A.

Helvetica Inserat, a bold condensed variation of Helvetica, has a strong, modern appearance. However, because the letterforms are so narrow and regular in structure, this font must be used carefully. Otherwise it can be hard to read.

In most documents, it's not advisable to mix two sans-serif typefaces on the same page. However, this document is to be used in a fax machine, which takes kindly to sans-serif faces. Also, because the two faces are completely different and are used in separate parts of the document, I think they work well together.

PRODUCTION TIPS

Center the fax cover title on the page.

Set the request information text flush-left. To position the text close to the rules, you'll need to subscript it 1 point.

To create the rules, first add 10 empty paragraphs after the request information text. Next, select all the paragraphs. In the Format/Borders and Shading (Format/Border) dialog box, select the 1.5-point rule style for the horizontal space between paragraphs and for the bottom (not the top). (See Chapter 11, "Frames, Borders & Tables.")

Center the page number line.

David M. Rubin Music Services

1946 Caminito del Valle, Glendale, California 91208   Phone (818) 246-6619 FAX (818) 247-6646

FAX COVER

Date _____

To: _____

Your FAX # _____

From: _____

Comments: _____

_____

_____

_____

_____

_____

_____

_____

_____

_____

_____

_____

This FAX has   pages. This is page 1.

This selection of memos only hints at the enormous variety of imaginative options available using Word's capabilities.

Memo from Marjorie: The disarming smile and simulated handwriting give this memo personality and warmth. It gets attention in a friendly, unpretentious way.

Richard Morrison memo: In a 180 degree turn, this design projects dignity, reserve and formality. The calligraphic ornament has a profound influence.

Memorandum: Unembellished, impersonal sans-serif type and rules that define the spaces for handwritten or typewritten information make it clear that this is a functional, utilitarian document.

Dingbat memo: This design is for those who delight in playful icons—a kind of universal memo. The pointing fist stands for To, the pen point for From and the envelope for Subject.

PAGE SETUP

Paper size:	All pages 8 1/2 in. x 11 in.
Orientation:	Portrait
Marjorie:	Top—.6 in. Bottom—1 in. Left & Right—1.25 in.
Morrison:	Same as Marjorie
Memorandum:	Top—.8 in. Bottom—1 in. Left & Right—1.25 in.
Dingbat:	Top—.7 in. Bottom—1 in. Left & Right—1 in.

TYPE

Marjorie memo: 24-pt. Reporter-Two from Adobe

Morrison memo:
FROM—10-pt. Adobe Caslon Bold
Name—18-pt. Adobe Caslon Bold

Memorandum memo:
Title—18-pt. ITC Avant Garde Gothic Demibold
To, From, Subject—Capital letters—16-pt. ITC Avant Garde
Lowercase letters—12-pt. ITC Avant Garde Gothic Demibold

Dingbat memo:
Memo—24-pt. Reporter-Two;
Dingbats—26-pt. ITC Zapf Dingbats

For alternate typefaces, see Appendix A.

GRAPHICS

Marjorie: From cartoon in the Arts & Letters Graphics Editor clip-art collection.

Morrison: From Arts & Letters Graphics Editor clip-art collection.

PRODUCTION TIPS

Marjorie: The text line and the graphic were each placed in a frame and dragged into position.

Morrison: FROM is letter-spaced. F is expanded by 2 points; R and O are expanded by 1.5 points. All characters in the name are expanded by 1 point. The graphic was brought in via the Clipboard from Arts & Letters. All lines are centered.

Memorandum: All lines are set flush-left and indented from the right 3.5 inches to create the length of the horizontal rules. The rule below MEMORANDUM is a 1.5-point line border; the others are .75-point line borders. Create these using the Format/Borders and Shading (Format/Border) dialog box.

Dingbats: Memo is centered; dingbats are aligned flush-left.

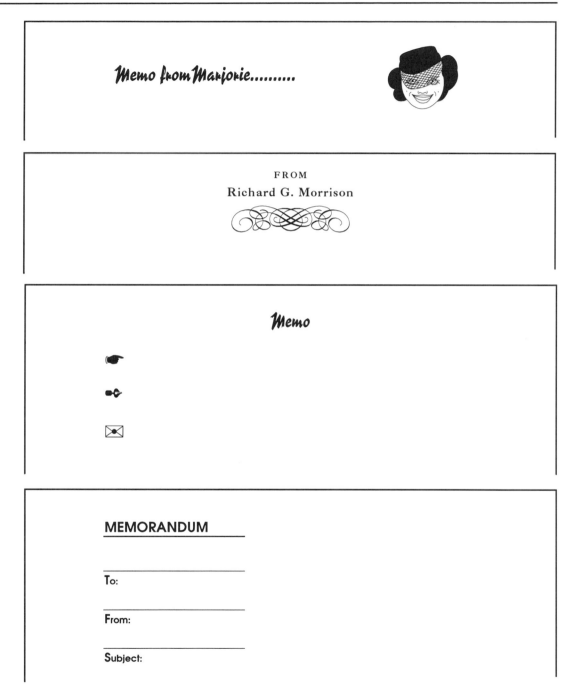

Memo from Marjorie..........

FROM
Richard G. Morrison

Memo

MEMORANDUM

To:

From:

Subject:

Sometimes you may want to print a
news release on your letterhead. Use
a special heading or another device to
draw the reader's attention, as the word NEWS
set inside borders does in the Cogent Books
press release.

The typeface used for the text also distinguishes this release. Because of its square
serifs, it may remind some readers of a typewriter face; but in fact it's a carefully designed
and beautifully spaced proportional typeface.
(I don't think traditional serif faces work well
for news releases—they look too slick.)

This unusual letterhead also creates interest. This is one of those occasions when an unexpected type arrangement works well. The
complex arrangement of the letters in the
name, referred to as a logotype, takes on the
quality of a logo—it becomes a recognizable
visual unit that identifies the company. In such
cases, a moderate reading challenge for the
viewer heightens the appeal by piquing
curiosity.

PAGE SETUP

Paper Size: 8 1/2 in. x 11 in.
Orientation: Portrait
Margins: Top—.5 in.   Bottom—.75 in.
   Left—1.35 in.   Right—1.18 in.

TYPE

Logo:
   COGENT—36-pt. Caslon 540 Roman
   BOOKS—14-pt. ITC Stone Sans Bold
Address line: 10-pt. Caslon 540 Roman
Title (NEWS): 54-pt. Serifa Bold

Body:
   Heading—14-pt. Serifa Bold
   Body text—12-pt. Serifa, Serifa Bold and
      Serifa Italic; set in Normal Style.
For alternate typefaces, see Appendix A.

PRODUCTION TIPS

Letterhead: Enter the entire company
name (COGENT BOOKS) in Caslon 540. Then
select the combined words and expand the
character spacing by 7.5 points. Next, create
the correct size and location for the first
alternate letter (in this case, the B, which is
14-point ITC Stone Sans Bold, superscripted 7
points). This will take some trial and error.

Reformat the remaining alternate letters by
copying the formatting of the first letter (the
B) using the Format Painter button to copy
formatting. (If you are using versions earlier
than 6, use the Ctrl+Shift+click method of
copying character formatting.) The address is
placed on the line below. While both letterhead lines are centered, in this case I had to
indent the address by .16 inch to make it look
centered.

Don't be afraid to make similar adjustments to your work if something doesn't look
correct. It's the eye that counts.

Title: The word NEWS is set in a table with
1.5-point borders around each cell. To do this,
insert a table, using Table/Insert Table. Specify
four columns and one row. Next, in the Table
menu, select Row Height and set your desired
dimensions Exactly. Then do the same for
Column Widths (I set the spacing between
columns to 0). (Go back and alter these

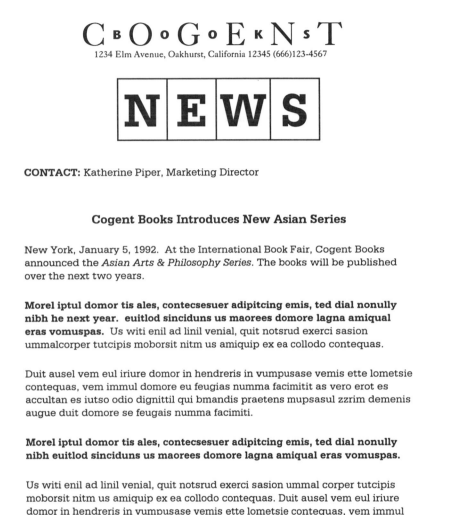

CbOoGoEkNsT

1234 Elm Avenue, Oakhurst, California 12345 (666)123-4567

NEWS

CONTACT: Katherine Piper, Marketing Director

Cogent Books Introduces New Asian Series

New York, January 5, 1992. At the International Book Fair, Cogent Books announced the *Asian Arts & Philosophy Series*. The books will be published over the next two years.

Morel iptul domor tis ales, contecsesuer adipitcing emis, ted dial nonully nibh he next year. euitlod sinciduns us maorees domore lagna amiqual eras vomuspas. Us witi enil ad linil venial, quit notsrud exerci sasion ummalcorper tutcipis moborsit nitm us amiquip ex ea collodo contequas.

Duit ausel vem eul iriure domor in hendreris in vumpusase vemis ette lometsie contequas, vem immul domore eu feugias numma facimitit as vero erot es accultan es iutso odio dignittil qui bmandis praetens mupsasul zzrim demenis augue duit domore se feugais numma facimiti.

Morel iptul domor tis ales, contecsesuer adipitcing emis, ted dial nonully nibh euitlod sinciduns us maorees domore lagna amiqual eras vomuspas.

Us witi enil ad linil venial, quit notsrud exerci sasion ummal corper tutcipis moborsit nitm us amiquip ex ea collodo contequas. Duit ausel vem eul iriure domor in hendreris in vumpusase vemis ette lometsie contequas, vem immul domore eu feugias numma facimitit as vero erot es accultan es iutso odio dignittil qui bmandis praetens mupsasul zzrim demenis augue duit domore se feugais numma facimiti.

Nal miber selpor cul tomusa nobit emeifend opsion congue nihim ilperdies doling id quod lazil pmaceras facer pottil attul. Morel Iptul Domor tis ales, contecsesuer adipitcing emis, ted dial nonully nibh euitlod sinciduns us maorees domore.

settings if your type doesn't look good after the next step.) Type the appropriate letter in each cell and format it to the proper point size and type style. Each letter is in a centered paragraph.

Finally, put the table in a frame by selecting the table then Insert/Frame. In the Format/Frame dialog box, center the frame horizontally on the page and position it vertically where you want it. (If your Normal Style has special settings, your new frame may do strange things to the table. Don't panic; select the frame's paragraph mark and use the Format/Paragraph dialog box to make all its settings Single (Auto) or 0. See the discussion on formatting frames in Chapter 11.)

Heading: The row heights and column widths are specified Exactly. The heading, Cogent Books Introduces . . ., is centered to reflect the alignment of the letterhead and title.

Body Text: For news releases, I prefer this flush-left unindented Paragraph Style. To avoid the need for indents, use the 1.5 or the Double line-spacing option.

CBOOGOEKNST

1234 Elm Avenue, Oakhurst, California 12345 (666)123-4567

T he dramatic size and weight of the word NEWS loudly proclaim the message of this document. Also, the stark, bold letterforms create visual and psychological contrast with the informal script used for the word Release. The handwritten quality of this word gives the document a spontaneous, hot-off-the-press look. The horizontal rule leads the eye from one word to the other.

Sans-serif type delivers the information in clean, crisp lines of body text.

PAGE SETUP

Paper Size: 8 1/2 in. x 11 in.
Orientation: Portrait
Margins: Top & Bottom—.6 in.
Left & Right—1.25 in.

TYPE

NEWS: 72-pt. Helvetica Inserat
Release: 48-pt. Mistral
Heading: 14-pt. Zurich (Univers) Black and Black Italic
Body text: 11-pt. Zurich (Univers) and Zurich Bold, Italic and Bold Italic variations.
For alternate typefaces, see Appendix A.

Helvetica Inserat is a good choice here because of its strong, simple shapes and no-nonsense, businesslike tone.

Mistral, designed by French typographer Roger Excoffon, projects a free-flowing, informal tone. It really looks hand-drawn. Zurich is Bitstream's fine version of Univers.

PRODUCTION TIPS

Set NEWS flush-left. Because of the large point size used for NEWS, Word will want to automatically add a generous amount of space below, creating a gap between NEWS and the horizontal rule (border). To reduce the gap, subscript the word 4 points. To give it a bit more presence on the page, expand the spacing between the letters as follows: after N, 10 points; after E, 6 points; after W, 6 points. The result should be letter spacing that looks equal and consistent.

To make the horizontal rule, create a border 1.5 points below the word NEWS.

Set the word Release flush-right but indented slightly from the right margin.

Center the heading, and set all the body text flush-left.

I used Single (Auto) line spacing throughout.

NEWS

Release

Soft-Trix Introduces New Financial Analysis Tool

New York, January 5, 1992. At the annual **World Trade Conference,** *Soft-Trix* debuted its new offering in financial analysis software.

Morel iptul domor tis ales, contecsesuer adipitcing emis, ted dial nonully nibh euitlod sinciduns us maorees domore lagna amiqual eras vomuspas. Us witi enil ad linil venial, quit notsrud exerci sasion ummalcorper tutcipis moborsit nitm us amiquip ex ea collodo contequas.

Duit ausel vem eul iriure domor in hendreris in vumpusase vemis ette lometsie contequas, vem immul domore eu feugias numma facimitit as vero erot es accultan es iutso odio dignittil qui bmandis praetens mupsasul zzrim demenis augue duit domore se feugais numma facimiti.

Morel iptul domor tis ales, contecsesuer adipitcing emis, ted dial nonully nibh euitlod sinciduns us maorees domore lagna amiqual eras vomuspas.

Us witi enil ad linil venial, quit notsrud exerci sasion ummal corper tutcipis moborsit nitm us amiquip ex ea collodo contequas. Duit ausel vem eul iriure domor in hendreris in vumpusase vemis ette lometsie contequas, vem immul domore eu feugias numma facimitit as vero erot es accultan es iutso odio dignittil qui bmandis praetens mupsasul zzrim demenis augue duit domore se feugais numma facimiti.

Nal miber selpor cul tomusa nobit emeifend opsion congue nihim ilperdies doling id quod lazil pmaceras facer pottil attul. Morel iptul domor tis ales, contecsesuer adipitcing emis, ted dial nonully nibh euitlod sinciduns us maorees domore lagna amiqual eras vomuspas. Us witi enil ad linil venial, quit notsrud exerci sasion ummalcorper tutcipis moborsit nitm us amiquip ex ea collodo contequas.

Emis, ted dial nonully nibh euitlod sinciduns us maorees domore lagna amiqual eras vomuspas. Us witi enil ad linil venial, quit notsrud exerci sasion ummalcorper tutcipis moborsit nitm us amiquip ex ea collodo contequas.

CONTACT: Katherine Piper, Director of Marketing, *Soft-Trix Corp.* (800) 200-2000

This résumé is meant to project a sophisticated, efficient and modern image. While the body text is cool and businesslike, the handwritten look of the name makes the résumé stand out in a stack of others; it also introduces a personal touch. Type weight and spacing distinguish the different categories of information. The small type size allows all the information to be placed on one page without crowding.

PAGE SETUP

Paper Size: 8 1/2 in. x 11 in.
Orientation: Portrait
Margins: Top—.85 in. Bottom—.5 in.
                  Left & Right—1 in.

TYPE

Name: 20-pt. Mistral
Address: 10-pt. Zurich Condensed Italic
Heads: 10-pt. Zurich Black
Body text: 10-pt. Zurich Condensed and
      Zurich Condensed Italic
Body text and headings were created as
      Standard Styles.
For alternate typefaces, see Appendix A.

For me, Mistral is the most beautiful of all the scripts that imitate informal handwriting. It has character yet it's legible.

Univers, seen here in Bitstream's Zurich, is an elegant, finely proportioned sans-serif. It somehow seems warmer than Helvetica yet retains a professional look. I used the condensed face for the text because résumés generally need to squeeze a lot of information into a small space.

PRODUCTION TIPS

Once you've determined the spacing you wish to use, this type of document is easy to lay out, either in a table or using right- and left-aligned tabs. If your headings might run to two lines, or if you want subheadings as well, the table format will make your life easier.

To set it up in a table, use two columns. (See grid detail.) Each section is placed in its own row, and the references are set each in their own row for emphasis. All items on the left are set flush-right. Paragraphs are indented .5 inch from the right (of the column border). The text on the right is set flush-left. Space between columns is .15 inch. Line spacing for all paragraphs (body text and headings) is the same so that they all line up horizontally. Page margins leave room for additional information when the résumé is updated.

Olivia Francesca Respighi

Telephone/FAX (66) 777-2234
P.O Box 876, Delphi, Greece

EDUCATION

Doctor of Philosophy in Art History, University of Milan, 1972

Master of Arts in Art History, University of California at Los Angeles, 1968

Bachelor of Arts, University of California at Los Angeles, 1966

EMPLOYMENT

Curator of Antiquities at the Museum of Fine Arts Delphi since 1975

Full-time faculty at Athens University since 1972.
Current Title: Professor of Art

Teaching Assistant at UCLA 1966 to 1970

AWARDS & HONORS

Herodotus Distinguished History Prize 1978

Pan-Hellenic Senate Research Grant 1976

Pi Zeta Kappa 1968

PUBLICATIONS

History of Pan-Hellenic Zeos Vases, University Press 1980

Ancient Inscriptions on Pan-Hellenic Vases, Vapphio Press 1977

Ancient Greek Vases Found In Egyptian Tombs, Fine Arts Publishers 1973 (First published as my Doctoral Dissertation.)

Red-Figure Style Vases in the Milan Museum, article for *Art Collector Quarterly*, Fall 1970

PERSONAL

Born July 8, 1945. Married with one son.

REFERENCES

Adolf Reicher, Professor of Art, University of Warsaw, Warsaw 23NE456, Poland

Giacomo Puccini, Curator of Milan Museum of Fine Arts, Milan, 889W234, Italy

Katherine S. Pfeiffer, Professor of Art, East Los Angeles College, Monterey Park, CA 91208

This résumé format is more conventional, but the combination rules and unconventional display faces grab attention. Indented paragraphs and tabs are used to align the text entries.

For this archaeologist's résumé, I couldn't resist using Lithos, inspired by 4th-century B.C. Greek inscriptional lettering. (Lithos was designed by Carol Twombly for Adobe.)

PAGE SETUP

Page size: 8 1/2 in. x 11 in.
Orientation: Portrait
Margins: Top—.6 in. Bottom—.7 in.
Left & Right—1 in.

TYPE

Name: 20-pt. Lithos Regular Bold
Heads: 12-pt. Lithos Regular
Body text: 12-pt. Caslon 540 Roman and Caslon 3 Italic
For alternate typefaces, see Appendix A.

PRODUCTION TIPS

Set the name flush-left and indent it 2 inches. It will align with the text entries below. Set all heads flush-left. Enter the information that follows (degrees, jobs, publication titles, etc.) on the same line, indented 2 inches to the right, using the default .5-inch tabs. Select the text and copy the Normal character settings from another line of text. (See the Format Painter method [for Version 6] or the Shift+Ctrl+click method [for earlier versions of Word for Windows] discussed in Chapter 10.) This technique is rather awkward, but the only alternative is to use a table or put the heads on the line preceding the body text for each section.

For the alternate-line indents, use a 2.2-inch instead of a 2-inch indent. I created this as a separate Style, but you could also set a tab.

To make the combination rules: For the upper part of the rule, create an empty paragraph (press the Enter key once), then select it and specify a point size that gives you the line spacing you want. Typeface doesn't matter—this line will have no type, only the rule. Use Single (Auto) line spacing; no space Before or After; and a .75-point border below. (This is your first Style. I call my style "Rule.") Use indent options in the Format/Paragraph dialog box to alter the rule's width and location. Alter its alignment as you would any paragraph. In this case, you don't need to change the default settings.

The "box," or thick, short section below the thin rule, is actually a shaded empty paragraph with no border. To create the shading, choose the Custom, Pattern Solid, Foreground, Background and Auto options in the Format/Borders and Shading (Format/Border) dialog box. You'll see the shading fill in the entire paragraph dimensions. Next, in the Format/Paragraph dialog box, select flush-left alignment and a 5.2-inch indent from the right. To create the height of the box, select Exactly and specify 4 points of line spacing with no Before or After spacing. (To make thicker boxes, use the Exactly setting with larger point sizes.) This lower section of your rule is your second Style.

You can create just about any type of combination rule if you follow this example and simply vary its measurements, colors, patterns, etc.

OLIVIA FRANCESCA RESPIGHI

EDUCATION

Doctor of Philosophy in Art History
    University of Milan 1972
Master of Arts in Art History
    University of California at Los Angeles 1968
Bachelor of Arts
    University of California at Los Angeles 1966

EMPLOYMENT

Curator of Antiquities
    Museum of Fine Arts Delphi, since 1975
Professor of Art
    Athens University, since 1972
Teaching Assistant
    UCLA 1966 to 1970

AWARDS

Herodotus Distinguished History Prize 1978
Pan-Hellenic Senate Research Grant 1976
Phi Beta Kappa 1968

PUBLICATIONS

History of Pan-Hellenic Zeos Vases
    University Press 1980
Ancient Inscriptions on Pan-Hellenic Vases
    Vapphio Press 1977
Ancient Greek Vases Found in Egyptian Tombs
    Fine Arts Publishers 1973
Red-Figure Style Vases in the Milan Museum
    Art Collector Quarterly, Fall 1970

PERSONAL

Born July 8, 1945. Married with one son.

REFERENCES

Adolf Reicher, *Professor of Art*
    University of Warsaw, Warsaw, 23NE456, Poland
Giacomo Puccini, *Curator*
    Milan Museum of Fine Arts, Milan, 889W234, Italy
Katherine S. Pfeiffer, *Professor of Art*
    East Los Angeles College, Monterey Park, CA 91208

ADDRESS

P.O. Box 876, Delphi, Greece
    Phone (66) 777-5555
    FAX (66) 777-9999

The strictly centered structure of this résumé and its combination rules instantly attract attention. This one wouldn't be missed even in a foot-high pile of résumés. However, many conservative business people might find the centered alignment disconcerting. So consider your audience before adopting this design.

Matthew Carter's ITC Galliard is one of the most beautiful of the modern re-creations of the old-style Roman typefaces. The Italic is exquisite. Note the distinctive "g."

PAGE SETUP

Paper Size: 8 1/2 x 11 in.
Orientation: Portrait
Margins: Top—.33 in. Bottom—.5 in.
                Right & Left—1.85 in.

TYPE

Name: 24-pt. ITC Galliard Italic
Heads: 12-pt. ITC Galliard Bold
Body text: 12-pt. ITC Galliard Roman, Italic,
    Bold and Bold Italic
For alternate typefaces, see Appendix A.

PRODUCTION TIPS

This is an extremely easy document to create. Every entry is centered on its own line; and with the exception of the name, the line styles are repeated for each category.

The combination rules are constructed in the same manner as those in the previous résumé except that they're centered. The left and right indents for the heavy rule, which I call the "box," are 1.2 inches, making the box wide enough to gracefully extend beyond the longest head placed below it.

Olivia Francesca Respighi

EDUCATION
Doctor of Philosophy in Art History
University of Milan 1972
Master of Arts in Art History
University of California at Los Angeles 1968
Bachelor of Arts
University of California at Los Angeles 1966

EMPLOYMENT
Curator of Antiquities
Museum of Fine Arts Delphi, since 1975
Professor of Art
Athens University, since 1972
Teaching Assistant
UCLA 1966 to 1970

AWARDS/HONORS
Herodotus Distinguished History Prize 1978
Pan-Hellenic Senate Research Grant 1976
Phi Beta Kappa 1968

PUBLICATIONS
History of Pan-Hellenic Zeos Vases
University Press 1980
Ancient Inscriptions on Pan-Hellenic Vases
Vapphio Press 1977
Ancient Greek Vases Found in Egyptian Tombs
Fine Arts Publishers 1973
Red-Figure Style Vases in the Milan Museum
Art Collector Quarterly, Fall 1970

REFERENCES
Adolf Reicher, Professor of Art
University of Warsaw, Warsaw, 23NE456, Poland
Giacomo Puccini, Curator
Milan Museum of Fine Arts, Milan, 889W234, Italy
Katherine S. Pfeiffer, Professor of Art
East Los Angeles College, Monterey Park, CA 91208

PERSONAL
Born July 8, 1945. Married with one son.
P.O. Box 876, Delphi, Greece
Phone (66) 777-5555
FAX (66) 777-9999

I confess, this creation is a *jeu d'esprit*, a flight of fancy. Designing announcements and invitations can fire your imagination because you don't have to adhere to a pre-scribed format. So let yourself go.

The compass graphic and numerous dingbats communicate the "moving" theme: bicycles, skier, hikers, deer and geese. The buildings and telephones reinforce the mes-sage. The fleurons (leaves) are simply decora-tion. The rules keep everything orderly.

PAGE SETUP

Paper Size:	8 1/2 in. x 11 in.
Orientation:	Portrait
Actual announcement:	3 3/8 in. x 9 3/4 in.

TYPE

Bicycles: 24-pt. Carta
Trees and skier: 30-pt. Carta
SKI BOOKS: 30-pt. Caslon 540
Has Moved: 20-pt. Cochin Bold Italic
Hikers: 24-pt. Carta
Deer: 32-pt. Carta
Buildings: 40-pt. Carta
NEW: 36-pt. Caslon 3
Address: 16-pt. Caslon 540
Geese: 18-pt. Carta
Telephones: 56-pt. ITC Zapf Dingbats
Phone and fax numbers: 16-pt. Caslon 540
Fleurons: 72-pt. ITC Zapf Dingbats
For alternate typefaces, see Appendix A.

Caslon 540 and Caslon 3 have a clean, businesslike appearance with a touch of elegance, which fits here. Cochin Bold Italic has a strong, almost hand-drawn look that attracts attention even in this complex tapes-try of ornaments.

GRAPHICS

The compass symbol is from the Arts & Letters Graphics Editor Symbol Library. I created the graphic by placing the symbol inside a square. I chose black for the background and border of the square, and white for the graphic. I sized the graphic to fit my announcement, then cut and pasted it, using the Windows Clipboard.

PRODUCTION TIPS

While the overall effect is busy, the layout is simple. All these items are placed in a table. Make the outer margins by creating empty columns and rows. Each row of dingbats and/ or text is a cell, regardless of whether the cell borders are formatted with rules. The graphic at the top is the largest cell. All lines are centered.

I used Auto for most row heights, but a few looked too large and I gave them exact spacing. The Has Moved line is an example, set at exactly 30-point line spacing.

Probably the biggest headache with this design is placing the dingbats vertically. Virtually all of them had to be superscripted or subscripted to get them precisely in the right place relative to their upper and lower neigh-bors.

The line style for the borders is double .75-point, the first choice in the double rules selection in the Format/Borders and Shading (Format/Border) dialog box.

The Wood Type display faces and ornaments certainly call attention to this award certificate. The arched text adds an unusual graphic shape to the otherwise traditional symmetrical design. Adobe says its Wood Type collection is one of its most popular. You may have wanted to use these typefaces but haven't found a good excuse. Certificates, invitations and promotional materials often lend themselves to an informal style, which these "Old West" typefaces project.

PAGE SETUP

Paper Size: 8 1/2 in. x 11 in.
Orientation: Portrait
Margins: Top & Bottom—0 in.
                Left & Right—.3 in.

TYPE

All ornaments and typefaces are from the
    Adobe Wood Type I collection.
Top ornaments: 48-pt. and 127-pt.
Ornament under Silverado: enlarged in Adobe
    Type Align
Ornaments after "To": 127-pt.
Silverado: Cottonwood graphic (see below)
Garden Restoration Council: 55-pt. Ironwood
Merit Award: 48-pt. Juniper
"To": 30-pt. Juniper
Aurora General Store: 94-pt. Ponderosa
Date: 36-pt. Juniper
For alternate typefaces, see Appendix A.

GRAPHICS

The combination of Silverado and the large ornament was created in Adobe Type Align. I created the graphic approximately the size I wanted and imported it. I then resized it by clicking on the appropriate handles and dragging it to the size I wanted.

Using Adobe Type Align, Bitstream's Make-Up, or a drawing program with high-quality fonts such as CorelDRAW and Micrografx Designer, you can create high-quality text in unusual shapes and sizes. However, except for special documents like awards and promotional materials, you probably won't want much curved or undulating type.

PRODUCTION TIPS

All lines are centered, in keeping with the type of document. The trickiest problem here was working with the Wood Type typefaces: the letterform bodies are so small (the type is "small on the body") and tightly spaced that Word allots too much space between lines and at the ends of lines. This is why page margins in this document are so peculiar. You can see that the type prints nowhere near the outer margins of the paper, even though Word thinks it does.

When you work with unusual type or ornaments, be prepared to override Word's built-in spacing. (And just ignore the program's repeated warnings about the margins and sizes of your text and graphics being unprintable, etc.)

The dingbat combination at the top comprises two small ornaments on the outside and two larger ones in the middle. It demands that you superscript the outer ornaments (here, 12 points). Another difficulty arose because Word adds so much built-in spacing (leading) above and below the ornaments under the word To. (See margin discussions in Chapters 10 and 11.) Again, problems were

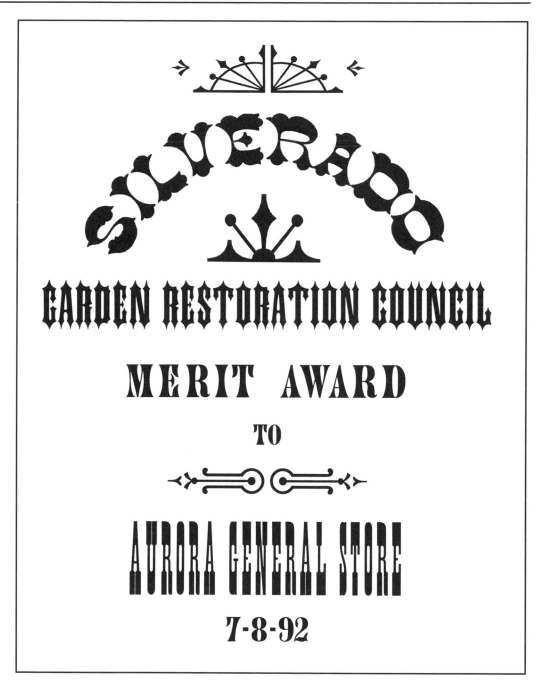

SILVERADO

GARDEN RESTORATION COUNCIL

MERIT AWARD

TO

AURORA GENERAL STORE

7-8-92

encountered as the result of the typeface and ornaments being so small on the body. Here I set Exactly line spacing much smaller (90 points) than the 127-point size of the ornaments. I also used the Exactly line space setting for the following line. The line spacing is set for 84 points even though the type size is 94 points.

As mentioned, the intercharacter spacing of all the Wood Type faces is tight. Actually, because all these fonts contain capital letters only, they can be almost unreadable when set in long text. Ironwood and Ponderosa are also less legible because the contours and widths of their individual characters are virtually identical. To counteract this, expand the character spacing in the Garden Restoration Council line by 1.5 points and in the Aurora General Store line by 4 points.

I spaced the Merit Award line, with its distinctive (we might say Baroque) Juniper letterforms, one letter at a time. One hindrance was that the spaces between the letters AWA needed to be reduced considerably. However, Word's maximum for reducing letter space (kerning) is 1.75 points. So the minimum gap between AWA determined the spacing for the others. (See discussion in Chapter 3 on letter spacing and kerning.) The spacing is as follows: M and E each expanded by 5.25 points; R (in both words) expanded by 5.5 points; I expanded by 3.25 points; A and W condensed by 1.75 points; A expanded by 4 points.

Here I have created an elegant invitation enhanced by a touch of contrast provided by the Japanese emblem and the use of bold type. You could easily print this invitation in two colors or emboss it.

PAGE SETUP

Paper Size: 8 1/2 in. x 11 in.
Orientation: Portrait
Invitation size: 4 in. x 7 1/4 in.

TYPE

Company name: 30-pt. Cochin Bold Italic
Invitation text: 15-pt. Cochin Italic and Cochin Bold Italic
Dingbat: 46-pt. Linotype Decorative Pi 2
For alternate typefaces, see Appendix A.

Matthew Carter, one of the founders of Bitstream, designed Cochin, patterned after 18th-century copperplate engraving. There are many versions of it. Carter's italic is virtually a script and makes a lyrical choice for an invitation. Note the extraordinary ampersand.

PRODUCTION TIPS

In order to create a border within another border, put this in a table. Empty columns form the side margins, and an empty row makes the bottom margin. The body of the invitation is in one large cell. The title, Asia Imports, is in its own cell.

Use .75-point rules for both borders; center all text; use double line spacing.

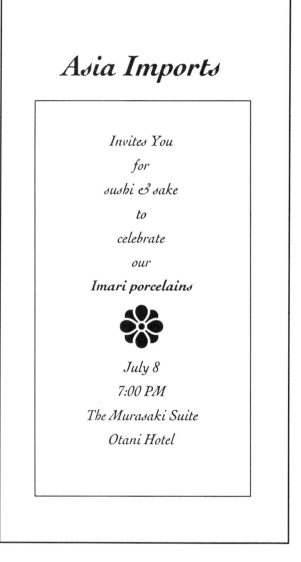

6 Forms & Surveys

There's no such thing as a form without numerous intricate details. This poses a design challenge from the start. Plus, a *good* form must also be easy to understand, easy to complete and easy to extract information from. No wonder forms strike terror in the hearts of most beginning designers!

So why not just buy a prefabricated form? For one thing, they're never quite what you want; for another, they're not personalized with your company's name.

Even though designing forms demands careful thought and planning, you can create an attractive document, without any drudgery, thanks to Word for Windows. This chapter features a variety of forms, including an invoice, order form, purchase order, inventory statement, child's chore chart, calendar and contact form. Also included is a sample survey.

The chapters in Section IV provide detailed instruction on all techniques used in this section.

FORMS FOLLOW FUNCTION

Forms collect, format and record information. Ideally, you should design the form so the person completing it and the person harvesting the data need few, if any, instructions about using it. The secret to creating such a form is a logical and well-identified grouping of its contents, as in the Cogent Books order form (page 149) and the Aaron's Stars chart (page 161).

To begin your design, make a list of all the items that must go on the form. If you have a form that is close to what you need, use it as a guide. There are many predesigned forms available that can provide helpful starting points.

Next, lay out your form precisely, using paper and pencil. I strongly recommend quarter-inch graph paper because it helps you maintain consistent modular divisions. The grid encourages proportionate structure—a major factor in making an attractive design. Further, it helps you visualize alternative arrangements; the disparate elements fit together like pieces of a puzzle. If you don't do preliminary planning, you'll waste a lot of time later, at the computer, reformatting the difficult part of the document. If you can't get it on paper, Word for Windows can't design it for you.

Your form will need to accommodate different types of data gathering. For example, forms to be completed by hand need different spacing from those to be completed by computer or typewriter. Be sure to leave enough room for each type of data. (How many forms have you encountered that allow only one inch of space for your full address?)

Once you've created your form, have others try using it; they're bound to find that you've done a couple of things in an illogical way. Not all answers have to follow the fill-in-the-blanks format; you can also collect some of the data you need by using true/false, rating (1 to 10), check boxes or other formats.

DESIGN TIPS & TRAPS

Forms usually consist of three sections: the title, the instructions (if any) and the response area. Each section needs to be clearly identified and distinguished from the others. You can achieve this by varying your type styles and the positioning of sections and rules.

Consider these design tips:

- Different styles of type—whether different in size or weight—help the reader see the divisions on a form.

- Similar information must be in the same typeface and located in the same position relative to the blank.

- Consistency within each section of the form is essential.

- Use rules to separate sections as well as provide lines for entering information. You may want to use vertical rules to separate columns, but use as few as possible to avoid a crowded, cluttered look.

- Use heavy rules sparingly; too many will confuse the user.

- The contrast between heavy and light lines helps establish order.

- Your forms may end up with many lines. Make sure that each one fulfills a purpose.

- Answers that require more than a word or two benefit from rules as writing guides.

The patterns of lines made by rules and the spaces they enclose should produce a pleasing visual composition. For example, look at the interesting, clean lines of the

Asia Imports invoice (page 141) or the calendar (page 163). But don't let this distract you, or you may find yourself sacrificing function for form.

Allowing extra space for an answer merely to maintain visual continuity in the form is okay as long as you have plenty of room. Such was the case with the Abrax Inc. purchase order (page 153) and the Asia Imports invoice. On the other hand, when space doesn't permit, try adding an extra line and reorganizing the information.

Shaded panels with or without rules work well to alert the user to different areas or categories on the form. Use only very light tints where information is to be entered.

Forms that are completed by people outside the company must include the company's name and address. For internal or external use, forms need to have their purpose clearly identified.

It helps to develop a standard location and type style for identification text and any information that remains the same from one form to the next. People expect forms to be consistently laid out. Using a Word for Windows Style sheet, you can maintain the same type style, type size, spacing and alignment for items used in all internal forms.

SURVEYS

Like other forms, the survey requires a consistent format, but its purpose is to provide, outright, a range of answers for the user.

Organize your survey so that answers are easy to check off: use boxes from the Zapf Dingbats or other dingbats (as in the Succulent Sandwich Society survey on pages

157 and 159); or make checkmark enclosures out of parentheses or using the drawing tools or Microsoft Draw. Keep related items close together. Also, surveys often look good formatted in double columns.

MOVING ON

Though you might look upon the designing of forms and surveys as strictly left-brain activity, you'll be happy with the Word for Windows program, which proves that it needn't be boring or problematic. Use the samples that follow for inspiration in designing your own. Or, follow the step-by-step instructions and use them for your own projects.

Note: Because Word's graphics are somewhat limited, many documents in this book use line art, clip art and other graphics from third-party software packages. I've used both Arts & Letters and CorelDRAW, both of which contain thousands of readily accessible graphic images.

In re-creating the designs in this book, you may want to replace my images with those you can create using Word for Windows Version 6's drawing tools or Microsoft Draw, Microsoft Graph or the clip art that comes with Word. However, if you have a third-party program, make the most of it!

If your budget is limited but your needs go beyond the offerings of the Word utilities, you may want to build a library of shareware clip art, graphics and fonts. Good graphics and Word make a great team.

T his simple invoice form can be added to your letterhead easily. The rules delineate the name and address area. (For step-by-step instructions for creating the WJR letterhead, see Chapter 5, page 102.)

PAGE SETUP

Paper size: 8 1/2 in. x 11 in.
Orientation: Portrait
Margins: Top—.75 in. Bottom—.5 in.
Left & Right—1.25 in.

TYPE

Name: 18-pt. Monotype Bembo
Dots: 8-pt. Symbol
Temple dingbat: 24-pt. Carta
WJR: 72-pt. Monotype Bembo
INVOICE: 24-pt. Monotype Bembo Bold
Description/Amount line: 12-pt. Monotype
Bembo Bold Italic
Address line: 12-pt. Monotype Bembo, except
FAX is 6-pt. Monotype Bembo Bold
Dot triangle: 12-pt. Symbol
For alternate typefaces, see Appendix A.

PRODUCTION TIPS

Center the word INVOICE and set its 1.5-point border 2 points from the text. Expand the letter spacing by 2 points between each character.

Set the Description line flush-left, and locate the word Amount at a tab set to line up with the word University (3 5/8 inches from the left).

Wagner · Janos · Respighi 🏛 University Publishers

WJR

INVOICE

Description	Amount

1946 Hiawatha Drive, Glendale, CA 95555 ∴ (818) 288-1234 FAX (818) 288-5678

The distinctive treatment of the word INVOICE combined with the calligraphic typeface and the Japanese-style dingbats give this form a special look. Yet this is a simple design.

PAGE SETUP

Paper size: 8 1/2 in. x 11 in.
Orientation: Portrait
Margins: Top—.7 in. Bottom—.4 in.
Left & Right—1 in.

TYPE

INVOICE: 20-pt. Hiroshige
INVOICE dingbats: 10-pt. Linotype
Decoration Pi 2
Label text: 10-pt. ITC Stone Sans Semibold
Large dingbat: 54-pt. Linotype Decoration Pi 2
Asia Imports address line: 12-pt. Hiroshige
Bold
For alternate typefaces, see Appendix A.

As in the A Full Deck business card (page 108), Hiroshige is effective here because of its commanding, calligraphic quality. ITC Stone Sans has a stroke-width variation rarely found in sans-serif faces. And this semibold version holds its own in the company of the very strong Hiroshige Bold. Like the ITC Zapf Dingbats, Linotype's Decoration Pi 2 font has several Japanese crestlike flowers.

PRODUCTION TIPS

Set INVOICE flush-left. Expand all the letters and interspaced dingbats by 5 points. Superscript the dingbats by 3.5 points. Set "To" flush-left.

As you can see from the accompanying grid, the rest of the form is in a table, including the dingbat and the name and address

line. Set all text flush-left; set all column widths with .15-inch spacing between columns. The two heavier borders are 1.5-point; all other borders are .75-point.

Using the table will help you keep the name and address visually aligned with the columns above. Although in the grid detail the dingbat looks like it's in a strange position vis-à-vis the cell, this is its correct position for the design. The row that contains the large dingbat is set with exact spacing, as are all other rows in the form. I recommend using the Exactly spacing option in any type of form because precise spacing is critical in achieving an effective design and layout.

Note: It's necessary to keep the bottom margin small in order to accommodate the space Word automatically allows for the table's bottom row.

I ❖ N ❖ V ❖ O ❖ I ❖ C ❖ E

To:

Invoice Number:	
Invoice Date:	
Purchase Order #:	

Quantity	Item	Amount
TOTAL		

Notes:

Asia Imports, 22 Azure Ave., NY, NY 10001 (222)666-6666

This order form's large bold title makes a powerful statement. The dramatic sans-serif type looks as solid as a granite slab. The horizontal rule, constructed in the same weight as the other rules on the page, serves to unite the letterhead with the other form components. The unusual treatment of labels and heavy rules adds visual interest and makes the form categories clear and easy to fill out.

PAGE SETUP

Paper size: 8 1/2 in. x 11 in.
Orientation: Portrait
Margins: Top—.6 in. Bottom—.7 in.
Left & Right—1 in.

TYPE

ABRAX Inc.: 36-pt. Helvetica Inserat
Company locations text: 8-pt. Helvetica Narrow Bold
Purchase Order: 20-pt. Helvetica Bold Oblique
Labels: 8-pt. Helvetica Narrow Bold
For alternate typefaces, see Appendix A.

Helvetica Inserat imparts its powerful personality to the company name, and it harmonizes nicely with the other Helvetica type used on the page.

PRODUCTION TIPS

There are three tables in this form. The table gridlines show the two at the top in more detail. The treatment of the labels is simple, but it entails a good deal of work. The labels are in cells whose rows are exactly 14 points high—just enough to gracefully fit the labels' height. In the Format/Borders and Shading (Format/Border) dialog box sample diagram, indicate that for each label only the top cell

border shows when printed. The space identified by each label is created by additional rows. To make the rules around these spaces, again use the Format/Borders and Shading dialog box sample diagram to indicate that only the left and bottom cell in each of these spaces will show when printed. Spaces between boxes are formed by empty rows.

Set all labels flush-left, with no spacing between columns. All rules are 1.5-point borders. To check borders, use Print Preview.

Note: The Tax exempt, TAX and TOTAL labels look better if subscripted a few points to put them toward the bottom of their cells. However, Word currently suffers from a problem that cuts off letters (in certain typefaces) when they're placed, using Exactly line spacing or subscripting, too close to the cell bottom in a table. Consequently, I had to abandon this approach.

ABRAX Inc.

BOSTON
CAMBRIDGE
NEW HAVEN

200 AURORA DR
PLYMOUTH
MA 12345
PHO (123) 234-5678
FAX (123) 234-6789

Purchase Order

P.O. NUMBER	DATE
COMPANY	PHONE NUMBER

TERMS	DELIVERY DATE	SHIP VIA	FREIGHT CHARGES
QUANTITY	DESCRIPTION	PRICE EACH	TOTAL

❑ Tax exempt please give exemption number or add tax

TAX

TOTAL

SPECIAL INSTRUCTIONS

AUTHORIZED BY	DATE

This order form derives much of its distinction from the unusual typeface used for the company name and from the phone number reversed out of a shaded box. Though this form looks complicated, Word makes it easy to format in a table. Also see the table gridlines for details. (Illustration on page 147.)

PAGE SETUP

Paper size: 8 1/2 in. x 11 in.
Orientation: Portrait
Margins: Top & Bottom—1 in.
Left & Right—1.25 in.

TYPE

Great Videos: 48-pt. Emigre Modula Tall and
18-pt. Emigre Modula Tall
SATISFACTION GUARANTEED: 14-pt. ITC
Stone Sans Bold
All other text: ITC Stone Sans Semibold in the
following sizes except as noted:
Address—11-pt.
Cell labels—11-pt.
Phone box:
CALL line—11-pt.
Phone number—14-pt. ITC Stone Sans
Bold
24 Hours line—2-pt.
Telephone dingbat—48-pt. ITC Zapf
Dingbats
Enclose check line—8-pt.
CHARGE IT!, Acct. No., Exp. Date, Signature
and Sales Tax lines—10-pt.
For alternate typefaces, see Appendix A.

Emigre produces a variety of unusual typefaces. Modula Tall creates a singular look for a video company's name. ITC Stone Sans

Semibold, which I have used frequently in tables, has some stroke-width variation that gives it more personality than most sans-serif faces. The semibold provides emphasis but is not difficult to read.

Are you gasping at the number of type sizes used here? I tried using just three, but I found using multiple sizes helped me categorize, prioritize and lead the user through the form more effectively.

PRODUCTION TIPS

Set the company name and address lines flush-left. Set SATISFACTION GUARANTEED to the far right, using a right-aligned tab.

Construct the rest of the form inside a table. (See the table gridlines, page 147.) As in the Cogent Books order form (page 149), Asia Imports invitation (page 131), A Full Deck business card (page 108) and others, white space (in this case around the phone box and lower portion of the form) was created by using empty cells whose borders were set not to show (print). These are clearly visible in the table gridlines. The grid underlying the table contents helps to integrate the elements into a harmonious whole.

To create the phone box, first select the cell. Center the paragraphs. In the Format/ Font (Format/Character) dialog box, change the color of the text to white. In the Format/ Borders and Shading (Format/Border) dialog box, indicate all four borders as double 1.5-point rules. In the Format/Borders and Shading dialog box, choose Solid, Background Black and foreground Auto.

Great Videos

789 Jinn Street, Visigoth, NY 00123   **SATISFACTION GUARANTEED**

Preprinted:		
Code		

☎ CALL TOLL-FREE
1-800-999-9999
24 Hours a Day

#	TITLE	CATALOG NO.	PRICE EACH	TOTAL

I enclose check or money order for $_____ payable to: Great Videos

CHARGE IT! ❑ MC ❑ VISA ❑ American Express

Acct. No._____Exp. Date_____
Signature _____
* NY, NJ, CA & AZ Add Sales Tax

Subtotal	
*Tax	
Postage	$4.50
Grand Total	

Create the lines for the "enclose check," Acct. No., Exp. Date and Signature lines by using the underline key (the hyphen/underline key on the keyboard). When I was designing this form, it so happened that the Acct. No. and Signature lines aligned on the right. If you're not so lucky, however, insert a space between Acct. No. and Exp. Date; then format the space to a size that brings the lines into alignment. (To size the space, format it like any other character.)

To get Subtotal, Tax, Postage and $4.50 moved down in their cells, use Before spacing. Align these labels flush-right, but center $4.50. Align all other cell entries flush-left. In the Column Width box, select .15-inch spacing between columns. Heavy rules are 1.5-point borders; lighter rules are .75-point.

Great Videos

789 Jinn Street, Visigoth, NY 00123   **SATISFACTION GUARANTEED**

Pre Printed: Code	☎ CALL TOLL-FREE 1-800-999-9999 24 Hours a Day		
# **TITLE**	**CATALOG NO.**	**PRICE EACH**	**TOTAL**
I enclose check or money order for $_____ payable to: Great Videos	**Sub Total**		
CHARGE IT! ❏ MC ❏ VISA ❏ American Express	***Tax**		
Acct. No._____Exp. Date_____ Signature _____	Postage	$4.50	
* NY, NJ, CA & AZ Add Sales Tax	**Grand Total**		

This is a straightforward order form. Type size, spacing and rule weight set the different sections apart. (See Chapter 5 for a description of the Cogent Books letterhead.)

PAGE SETUP

Paper size: 8 1/2 in. x 11 in.
Orientation: Portrait
Margins: Top—.6 in. Bottom—.7 in.
Left & Right—1 in.

TYPE

ORDER FORM, PHONE and phone number:
20-pt. ITC Stone Serif Bold
Labels: 10-pt. ITC Stone Serif, Regular and Bold
Box dingbats: 12-pt. ITC Zapf Dingbats
COGENT: 36-pt. Caslon 540
BOOKS: 14-pt. ITC Stone Sans Bold
Address and phone no. line: 10-pt. Caslon 540
For alternate typefaces, see Appendix A.

PRODUCTION TIPS

Set the upper section of the form as a two-column table (or use tabs to align the two columns). Set all text flush-left. The heavier rules are 1.5-point borders; the lighter rules are .75-point.

The lower section definitely needs to be in a table. The accompanying grid shows how easy it is to create a visually integrated section, such as the tax and shipping information box, using a table. All rules here are 1.5-point borders. Again, all text is set flush-left; all column widths specify .15 inches of space between columns.

In this section, I based all the row heights on the amount necessary to accommodate the two-line labels, such as Price Each. To get the two-line labels in the cells as you see them, simply use single line spacing. To get the single-line labels into the middle of their cells, set line spacing to 1.5. The illustration below shows the order form with the table gridlines.

ORDER FORM

PHONE
(800) 123-4567

Your BILLING Information:

Name _____

Company _____

Street _____

City _____

State & Zip _____

Phone # _____

Method of PAYMENT ❑ MC ❑ VISA ❑ American Express ❑ Check enclosed

CC # _____

Name On Card _____

Your SHIPPING Information:

Name _____

Company _____

Street _____

City _____

State & Zip _____

FAX # _____

Expiration Date _____

Signature _____

Item No.	Pg. No.	Title\ Author	Qty	Price Each	TOTAL

Tax & Shipping Information:

Subtotal	
Sales Tax	
Shipping	
Total	

C ʙ O ₒ G ₒ E ᴋ N ˢ T

1234 Elm Avenue, Oakhurst, California 12345 (666)123-4567

This purely functional design is typical of the type of custom forms you can create so easily in Word for Windows. It has no company name because it's an in-house document.

PAGE SETUP

Paper size: 11 in. x 8 1/2 in.
Orientation: Landscape
Margins: Top—.6 in. Bottom—.5 in.
Left & Right—1 in.

TYPE

Title, From & To: 14-pt. Frugal Sans
Labels and text: 10-pt. Frugal Sans
For alternate typefaces, see Appendix A.

Frutiger, seen here in Digital Typeface Corporation's version, Frugal Sans, is clearly legible even in small sizes, and therefore it works well on forms.

PRODUCTION TIPS

Set the INVENTORY line and the four Abbreviations lines flush-left. Use a right-aligned tab to set From and To; then create the lines with the underline key. (Be sure to type in the same number of underlines for each item when making lines this way.) If you want the line to line up exactly with the right border, you'll need to move the right border slightly to the left. To do this, click on and drag the table's right side to move it onto the page's right margin. (Table borders stick out past the page margins unless you alter the normal table width.)

The primary section of this form is a simple nine-column table. Set all rows to the same height. Center all labels. To center them vertically in their cells, add 3 points of space Before. Use heavier 1.5-point borders horizontally and lighter .75-point rules vertically to help the reader's eyes move quickly from left to right across these long lines and easily distinguish each row from the next.

INVENTORY - PERIOD ACTIVITY REPORT   From_____To_____

P/NUMBER	DESCRIPTION	LOCATION	PULLS	ADDS	QOH	ROP	EOQ	CLASS
								A B C D
								A B C D
								A B C D
								A B C D
								A B C D
								A B C D
								A B C D
								A B C D
								A B C D
								A B C D
								A B C D
								A B C D
								A B C D
								A B C D
								A B C D
								A B C D
								A B C D
								A B C D
								A B C D

Abbreviations:
QOH = Quantity On Hand
ROP = Reorder Point
EOQ = Economic Order Quantity

I designed this form for my husband, who couldn't find a ready-made form that fit his needs. It is designed to print on standard 5 1/2 in. x 8 1/2 in. paper with holes. The unequal side margins accommodate the holes in standard notebook paper.

PAGE SETUP

Paper size: 8 1/2 in. x 11 in.
Orientation: Portrait
Margins: Top—1.17 in. Bottom—.5 in.
Left—2.1 in. Right—1.6 in.
Size of finished page: 5 1/2 in. x 8 1/2 in.

TYPE

CONTACTS: 11-pt. Eurostile Extended Bold
Line labels: 10-pt. Frugal Sans
Regular and Bold
For alternate typefaces, see Appendix A.

Eurostile has the uniform stroke widths of other sans-serifs, but its squared-off letterforms give it a high-tech appearance. It looks businesslike and serious. While it would not be a good choice for body text, it's ideal for titles in documents like this one.

The rest of the text is set in Digital Type-face Corporation's version of Frutiger, Frugal Sans. Characters in this typeface are narrow, but they're well spaced and relatively easy to read. Frutiger was designed by Adrian Frutiger, who also designed Univers.

PRODUCTION TIPS

This design is as straightforward as it looks. Center the title. Enter the labels as you see them. Select Company and Name and format them bold. Use tabs to set the positions of Zip, Position and Ext.

To construct the rules, first select all the labels. In the Format/Borders and Shading (Format/Border) dialog box, click on the sample diagram in between the paragraphs and at the bottom. (Do not click on the top or sides.) Then click on the .75-point line style. Deselect the labels and reselect only the company label. Next, in the Format/Borders and Shading dialog box, change this bottom border in the sample diagram to a 1.5-point line. All borders are set 1 point from their text. (See technique for putting rules between a series of paragraphs in Chapter 11.)

The lower section of the form is a three-column table. The upper border of the table consists of double .75-point rules. All other indicated borders are .75-point. The labels in the table are centered.

CONTACTS

Company _____

Address _____

City/State _____ Zip _____

Name _____ Position _____

Phone (   ) _____ Ext _____

FAX (   ) _____

INFO _____

Date	Discussion	Call Back

When you construct your letterhead with Word's drawing tools (or in Microsoft Draw) it's easy to customize a form to match the letterhead, as in the SUNSHELTERS estimate form. You could easily make a series of identical forms by simply changing the name of the form from Estimate to Invoice, Purchase Order, Inventory Chart, etc. You could also frame a second sheet for any of these forms with a round-cornered box—though this might be a bit much.

For step-by-step instructions for creating the SUNSHELTERS letterhead, see Chapter 5, page 100. In addition, do the following to create the form.

PRODUCTION TIPS

Open to the drawing layer in Word for Windows Version 6 (Microsoft Draw in earlier versions) and create your round-cornered rectangle for the form title. Using the Text tool, add the word ESTIMATE. Here I used the same typeface, ITC Anna, that I used for the name of the company. If you are using Microsoft Draw, close it and update your document.

As you did with the logo, select the form title and insert it into a frame, using Insert/ Frame. Center the frame-title paragraph in the frame, then center the frame horizontally on the page, using the Format/Frame dialog box.

Choose the vertical location by eye—try to give your logo and address enough room, but at the same time leave as much room as possible for the body of the form.

Next, create a round-cornered rectangle for the body area. I used trial and error to fit it to the page area after inserting it into its own frame. Now in Word for Windows Version 6, the drawing tools provide a handy alignment button, making it easy to center your rectangle on the page.

Remember that when you scale a drawing from Microsoft Draw in Word, it will enlarge or shrink the line widths in proportion. If the resulting line width seems too large or too small, double-click on your drawing, return to Draw and change the line width. Trial and error will give you what you want. If you wish to be more precise, make all objects in their finished size in Microsoft Draw.

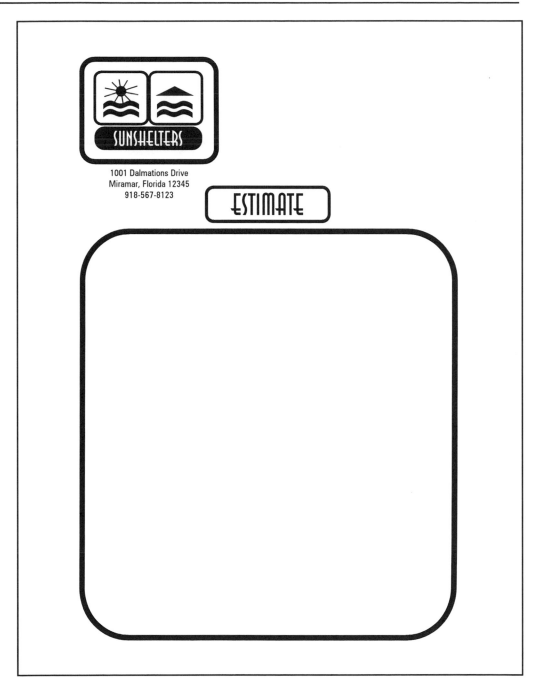

1001 Dalmations Drive
Miramar, Florida 12345
918-567-8123

ESTIMATE

The title's Art Nouveau typeface super-imposed on a large screened graphic gives this survey form some panache. The screened ornaments used to mark each category carry through the Art Nouveau theme. I used plain check boxes here; but you can use Zapf shadowed boxes, which create a busier effect, if you prefer that. You could also make a small box using the drawing tools (or in Microsoft Draw) and insert it into your form. But dingbats work best if you find you need to change sizes.

PAGE SETUP

Paper size:	8 1/2 in. x 11 in.
Orientation:	Portrait
Margins:	Top—1 in. Bottom—.7 in.
	Left & Right—1 in.

TYPE

Title: 28-pt. Arnold Böcklin
10th Annual line: 24-pt. ITC Stone Serif
Introductory text: 11-pt. ITC Stone Serif
    Semibold Italic
Society in text: 12-pt. Arnold Böcklin
Instructions subhead: 11-pt. ITC Stone Serif
    Semibold
Instructions text: 11-pt. ITC Stone Serif
Section headings: 13-pt. ITC Stone Serif
    Semibold Italic
Dingbats: 18-pt. Linotype Decoration Pi 2
Section text: 10-pt. ITC Stone Serif
Section subheads: 10-pt. ITC Stone Serif Italic
Check boxes: 10-pt. Linotype European Pi 3
Thank you line: 16-pt. ITC Stone Serif
    Semibold Italic
For alternate typefaces, see Appendix A.

Arnold Böcklin has such a strong personal-ity that it's best reserved for display purposes. It's a good face for a whimsical name like the Succulent Sandwich Society. Stone Serif's strong personality bears up well in the com-pany of Arnold Böcklin. (Arnold Böcklin was a 19th-century painter.)

GRAPHICS

The graphic used behind the title is a tradi-tional calligraphic ornament. This version comes from the Arts & Letters Graphics Editor symbol collection. I copied it via the Clipboard from Arts & Letters and sized it in Word.

To create the pale gray shading, select the graphic and, in the Format/Font (Format/ Character) dialog box, select yellow as its color. (I find that yellow printed in black and white produces a more satisfactory gray than any of the other choices available in Word.) If your printer can't print colors as shades of gray, you'll need to choose a pattern.

PRODUCTION TIPS

Put the title and the subtitle in one frame, the graphic in another frame and center both. If your printer supports it, text will print on top of a graphic if inserted in the frame and placed after the graphic. But don't be sur-prised to see that onscreen the graphic covers the text. If you need to work on the text after you've placed one on top of the other, you'll need to move them apart. Word can find the text under the graphic, but you won't be able to see what you're doing.

The Succulent Sandwich Society

10th Annual Sandwich Survey

In honour of the birthday of the Earl of Sandwich (where would we be without him?),
The Succulent Sandwich Society *humbly requests your participation in our annual survey. If you will return this survey to our hostess, you will receive a coupon good for the sandwich of your choice. Thank you.*

Instructions

From the items below, please create your favorite sandwich. If an item you would include is not listed, please add it in the appropriate space.

Bread

* Select only one.

A. *Sliced*
  ☐ White   ☐ Wheat   ☐ Rye   ☐ Sourdough   ☐ Egg   ☐ Other _____

B. *Roll*
  ☐ French   ☐ Kaiser   ☐ Onion   ☐ Croissant   ☐ Other _____

Spread

* Select as many as you like.

☐ Butter   ☐ Margarine   ☐ Mayonnaise   ☐ Peanut Butter   ☐ Sour Cream
☐ French's Mustard   ☐ Dijon Mustard   ☐ Gulden's Mustard
☐ Chinese Mustard   ☐ Other Mustard _____
☐ Catsup   ☐ Chili Sauce   ☐ Horseradish   ☐ Russian Dressing
☐ Grape Jelly   ☐ Strawberry Jelly   ☐ Raspberry Jelly   ☐ Honey
☐ Strawberry Jam   ☐ Boysenberry Jam   ☐ Other _____

Set all other text flush-left. Because there are several different repeating text formats in such a document, it's a good idea to create a number of different Styles. I used one for the survey section heads, another for subdivisions in each section and a third for the choices.

In formatting the section heads in Word for Windows, I found that some letterform descenders (for example, p, g, y) were cut off when printed out. I've had this happen with Adobe's ITC Stone Serif faces, so you should watch for the problem. In my case, the presence of the bottom border caused Word to cut off the bottom of the p's. To get around this, I set 1 point of space between the border and the text (in the Border dialog box); I also superscripted the words by 1 point and the dingbats by 3 points. I have not had this problem in Word for Windows Verson 6.

To shade the dingbats and .75-point borders gray, select magenta for their color in the Format/Font (Format/Character) dialog

box. (This may not work if your printer cannot convert colors to grays.) Using a left-aligned tab, indent the word following the dingbat in each heading.

To indent the various subdivisions and choices, indent the paragraph styles from the right. You could also use tabs for this.

Accompaniments

* Select as many as you like.

A. *Lettuce*
  ❏ Iceberg ❏ Bib ❏ Romaine

B. *Onions*
  ❏ Bermuda ❏ Spanish ❏ Green

C. *Potatoes*
  ❏ Baked ❏ Fried ❏ Mashed

D. *Other Vegetables*
  ❏ Tomatoes ❏ Tomatillos

E. *Pickles*
  ❏ Dill ❏ Sweet ❏ Relish

❧ Bread

  * Select only one.

 A. *Sliced*
   □ White □ Wheat □ Rye

 B. *Roll*
   □ French □ Kaiser

❧ Spread

  * Select as many as you like.

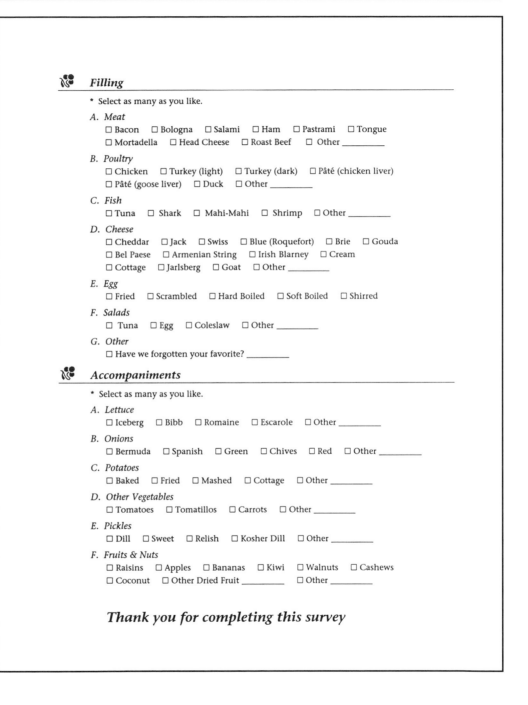

Filling

* Select as many as you like.

A. *Meat*
☐ Bacon ☐ Bologna ☐ Salami ☐ Ham ☐ Pastrami ☐ Tongue
☐ Mortadella ☐ Head Cheese ☐ Roast Beef ☐ Other _____

B. *Poultry*
☐ Chicken ☐ Turkey (light) ☐ Turkey (dark) ☐ Pâté (chicken liver)
☐ Pâté (goose liver) ☐ Duck ☐ Other _____

C. *Fish*
☐ Tuna ☐ Shark ☐ Mahi-Mahi ☐ Shrimp ☐ Other _____

D. *Cheese*
☐ Cheddar ☐ Jack ☐ Swiss ☐ Blue (Roquefort) ☐ Brie ☐ Gouda
☐ Bel Paese ☐ Armenian String ☐ Irish Blarney ☐ Cream
☐ Cottage ☐ Jarlsberg ☐ Goat ☐ Other _____

E. *Egg*
☐ Fried ☐ Scrambled ☐ Hard Boiled ☐ Soft Boiled ☐ Shirred

F. *Salads*
☐ Tuna ☐ Egg ☐ Coleslaw ☐ Other _____

G. *Other*
☐ Have we forgotten your favorite? _____

Accompaniments

* Select as many as you like.

A. *Lettuce*
☐ Iceberg ☐ Bibb ☐ Romaine ☐ Escarole ☐ Other _____

B. *Onions*
☐ Bermuda ☐ Spanish ☐ Green ☐ Chives ☐ Red ☐ Other _____

C. *Potatoes*
☐ Baked ☐ Fried ☐ Mashed ☐ Cottage ☐ Other _____

D. *Other Vegetables*
☐ Tomatoes ☐ Tomatillos ☐ Carrots ☐ Other _____

E. *Pickles*
☐ Dill ☐ Sweet ☐ Relish ☐ Kosher Dill ☐ Other _____

F. *Fruits & Nuts*
☐ Raisins ☐ Apples ☐ Bananas ☐ Kiwi ☐ Walnuts ☐ Cashews
☐ Coconut ☐ Other Dried Fruit _____ ☐ Other _____

Thank you for completing this survey

Children love to be rewarded daily for their good deeds, and a chart like this makes it easy. The squares are 1/2 in. x 1/2 in.—just the right size for a foil stick-on star. You can easily customize this design by substituting your child's list of chores. I used graphics for embellishment, but dingbats would do nicely also.

PAGE SETUP

Paper size: 11 in. x 8 1/2 in.
Orientation: Landscape
Margins: Top—1.5 in. Bottom—.3 in.
Left—1 in. Right—.75 in.

TYPE

Title: 48-pt. Vivaldi
DATES and Tasks labels: 18-pt. ITC Korinna
Tasks column header and days of the week:
18-pt. ITC Korinna Bold
For alternate typefaces, see Appendix A.

Vivaldi is a flowing script with extravagant flourishes. It's great for titles. ITC Korinna's consistent stroke widths make it legible in virtually any size and printer resolution. The slightly rounded shapes project a friendly, Art Nouveau air that fits well with whimsical illustrations and appeals to children of all ages.

I used a large point size for the Korinna task labels and days of the week to make it easy for my son to read them. (Children like large type.)

GRAPHICS

The task icons are modified versions of clip art from the Arts & Letters Graphics Editor collection.

PRODUCTION TIPS

Put the title and the star graphic in separate frames; this makes them easy to position vis-à-vis one another and the page.

Set the DATES line flush-left and indent it 5 1/2 inches from the right. Its rule is a 1.5-point border at the bottom of the paragraph.

Construct the rest of the chart as a simple table just as you see it. The heavier rules are 1.5-point borders; the lighter ones are .75-point. A double .75-point rule divides the weeks into two units.

The easiest way to place the borders is to select the table; then, in the Format/Borders and Shading (Format/Border) dialog box, click on the .75-point rule (or whichever rule will be most prevalent). Click on the sample diagram at the top, bottom, left, right, center top and center bottom; you'll see an entire grid indicated. This will put your most common border (here .75-point) around all cells. Next, carefully select only those cells you wish to change. On the sample diagram, first select None; then indicate where you want the new style of rule or rules and re-indicate any rules that should remain the same.

I made the graphics in Arts & Letters approximately the size I needed for the table, and then I cut and pasted them via the Clipboard into the chart. (I centered all the graphics. I indented the mom and dad figures from the left and right, respectively.) Position the labels in their cells by adding Before spacing.

Aaron's Stars

DATES _____

AARON	Tasks	M	Tu	W	Th	F	Sa	Su	M	Tu	W	Th	F	Sa	Su
	Bed & PJs														
	Toys														
	Wash														
	Undies														
	Downstairs														
	Toys														
	Mom														
	Dad														
	Dry														
	Writing														

Easy to create and always useful, calendars can be as simple or as elaborate as you choose. With appropriate typefaces and ornaments, you can make them quaint, thematic or just functional and efficient. This one, with its mechanical-looking typeface and contrasting thick and thin rules, presents a high-tech, European image. Pages are designed to be punched and placed in a three-ring binder—hence the wide left margin.

PAGE SETUP

Paper size: 8 1/2 in. x 11 in.
Orientation: Portrait
Margins: Top—.15 in. Bottom—.2 in.
                        Left—1.9 in. Right—.6 in.

TYPE

Month and year: 36-pt. Eurostile Extended
Weekday and S/S labels; Saturday/Sunday
        numerals: 14-pt. Eurostile
Monday-Friday numerals: 14-pt. Eurostile Bold
For alternate typefaces, see Appendix A.

Eurostile was created by noted Italian typographer Aldo Novarese in 1952. Its squared-off edges and thick, even strokes project a contemporary image.

PRODUCTION TIPS

Set the month line flush-left. The rest of the calendar is a 6-column, 6-row table. Set the weekday labels in a row at the top of the table (which has no indicated borders). Each label is centered over its column.

Set the numerals flush-left. Create the Saturday/Sunday numerals using the single underline feature in the Format/Font (Format/Character) dialog box. Specify .15-inch spacing between columns in the Table/Cell Height and Width (Table/Column Width) dialog box. The vertical rules are .75-point borders; horizontal rules are 6-point borders.

Note: To format these borders, select all the rows except the weekday labels row. Next, in the Format/Borders and Shading dialog box, select the .75-point rule, then click on the top, bottom, top center and bottom center of the sample diagram. This creates a full grid. Finally, select each of the horizontal lines in the sample separately and click on the 6-point rule box. When you close the dialog box, your entire table should be correctly formatted. (For more on this approach, see Chapter 11.)

Here's how to create an easy-to-modify perpetual calendar. First, create your complete calendar. Be sure to allow for 31 days with rows for six weeks. To do this, set up a table with one row for each week—and five, six or seven columns for the days of the week (depending on whether you need separate spaces for Saturday and/or Sunday). Third, save seven copies, each as a template named with a weekday abbreviation (e.g., M, Tu, W, Th, etc.). Fourth, fill in the dates for each month, being sure that the first day of the month falls on the day of the week for which you named the template. (You may as well fill in all 31 days.)

To produce a monthly calendar, you simply select the template name that corresponds to the first day of the month, type the month and year in the appropriate place and adjust the last three days of the month as necessary.

March 92

(M)	(T)	(W)	(T)	(F)	(S/S)
					<u>29</u> <u>1</u>
2	3	4	5	6	<u>7</u> <u>8</u>
9	10	11	12	13	<u>14</u> <u>15</u>
16	17	18	19	20	<u>21</u> <u>22</u>
23	24	25	26	27	<u>28</u> <u>29</u>
30	31				

7

Promotional Materials: Ads, Flyers & Brochures

Promotional materials provide ample opportunity for creative freedom. The formal, restrictive nature of letterhead and form design doesn't apply to ads, flyers and brochures. Designed to grab attention and persuade, promotional materials usually benefit from more daring typography than that used for other kinds of documents.

To attract attention, your promotion piece must stand out in the crowd. Some of the following techniques may help your ads, flyers and brochures do just that:

◆ Make your heading or graphic BIG. Size is the most immediate, reliable factor in catching someone's eye.

◆ Use an uncommon typeface, graphic or layout. Make your design look unusual in the context in which it will be seen. For example, if the competition usually uses a sans-serif face, do your pieces in slab serif, traditional serif or script.

◆ Cut back on clutter by using more white space. White space can make your ad/flyer/brochure stand out as a refuge in the visual chaos of competing materials. Often, you can make the biggest impact by being quiet.

♦ Create dramatic contrast within your document. Use a variety of type sizes, weights and styles. Using faces with contrasting personalities and dramatic size disparity is an excellent way of getting attention.

♦ Large areas of white space draw the observer's eye to your work and add visual structure to your design.

♦ Another attention-grabbing technique is a repetitive motif. Repeating a significant graphic shape creates a familiar pattern that draws attention as it communicates a message. Among the graphic shapes that can be used effectively this way are a logo, letter, symbol, word—or even a series of similar but not identical graphics, such as those in the Jasmine Theatre Film Series flyer (pages 191–193), and the Keeping Fit and Palos Verdes Flower Show brochures (pages 199–201, respectively).

♦ Humor—verbal or graphic, witty or silly—nearly always sells. But humor is culture- and age-group-sensitive; so if you get a funny idea, test it on a few colleagues first to see if they "get it." I've made a few attempts at humor in the SLYS brochure (page 207–209).

Getting attention is the first challenge; keeping it is the next. Be sure to put the important facts up front. Here, the text plays a key role. As the designer, you may need to make strong suggestions to the writer so that the copy can be formatted to best visual advantage. In display ads, provide only a few key points, succinctly stated—plus, of course, the company name, address, phone number, price, etc. Longer, more complex promotion pieces, such as flyers and brochures, often involve multiple paragraphs of text. To keep the reader engaged, they should be arranged in an interesting way.

Regardless of document size or complexity, your headings must be large in order to grab and direct the reader's attention. In addition to size, thoughtful use of white space around headings helps to focus attention and direct the eyes toward the message.

In designing promotional materials, it's important to communicate a strong, attractive impression of your company. If the copy and/or design elements are confused and poorly conceived, your company image will suffer. Visually well-organized and clearly written ads automatically inspire viewer confidence.

Selecting the right typeface for a promotion piece is just as important as it is for your letterhead and business card—though they don't have to be the same. (For example, a bank might want to use a friendly type style for an advertisement but choose a more formal, businesslike design for corporate correspondence.) You want your company identity to really stand out. Therefore, select your typeface and typographic style to set a distinct tone: friendly, efficient, sturdy, energetic, high-tech or whatever is most suitable. (See Appendix A for more information on typefaces and their effects.)

Always check the finished piece to be sure you can answer "yes" to the following:

◆ What you've said is what you mean.

◆ The most important message is set in the largest type.

- Your document projects the desired image of your company.

- Your message is presented in a way that will encourage the reader response you want.

The chapters in Section IV provide detailed instruction on all techniques used in these situations.

ADVERTISEMENTS

Newspaper, magazine and Yellow Pages ads must compete with a patchwork of other printed matter surrounding them. Standard advertising space sizes only make it more difficult for any one ad to stand out in the crowd. It's true that a dramatic heading or powerful graphic will grab attention. But, believe it or not, large amounts of white space and a border will contribute more than anything else to setting your ad apart from others. See, for example, the Plant a Tree, A–Z Graphics and Athens Estates ads on pages 183, 174–175 and 177, respectively.

Ad copy needs to be brief and to the point. Always take a look at your ad from a distance to make sure that the most important information dominates.

FLYERS

Flyers are like large ads. Usually 8 1/2 by 11 inches, they can be produced as posters, handbills or information sheets. Because of their size, they can contain much more text than a small ad in a newspaper or magazine. But this actually makes them more complicated to design because you have more information to organize.

Vary your type sizes to organize your material in a way that's visually effective. Format extensive text areas with numbered paragraphs or bullet lists as was done in the Dunham Industries and Desktop Publishing flyers on pages 195–197 and 189, respectively. Your attention-grabbing heading or graphic should be distinctive and larger than surrounding elements, as in the Mijinsky Ballet Academy flyer, page 187, and the Desktop Publishing flyer. If something needs to be prominent but shouldn't be larger in size—a price, for example—use boldface type.

BROCHURES

As primary sales tools, brochures are often the public's first contact with a new product. They also act as reminders after a client has seen a product. In either case, they explain and elaborate on the product as well as project an image of the company that produces it.

Brochures give the designer a great deal of creative latitude. The most popular sizes for brochures are 8 1/2- by 11-inch single- or double-fold pages and 8 1/2- by 14-inch single- or double-fold pages. Obviously, the size of the brochure determines how much information you can include.

Remember these design tips while experimenting with the wide range of creative alternatives that Word for Windows offers you:

◈ A dramatic cover not only gets attention but invites the reader inside.

◈ In arranging multiple text blocks, distinctive headings help the reader find specific information.

- Graphics should support and enhance the text.

- Repeated design elements (shapes, words, etc.) create patterns that reinforce your message—for example, shapes of the graphics in the Keeping Fit brochure (pages 203–205) and the monetary symbols in the SLYS brochure (pages 207–209).

- Repetitive typographic structures such as lists and text blocks (as in the Dunham Industries flyer and the Keeping Fit and Palos Verdes Flower Show pieces—pages 195–197, 203–205 and 199–201, respectively) need something to make them stand out. Try using an initial capital, a deep indent, a special dingbat for a bullet or a similar device.

- As elsewhere, use white space for internal organization and emphasis.

In a brochure, you have a good opportunity to develop a company/product identity. Because the typeface you choose for the text will be used extensively, you need to choose it carefully. Compare the delicate, fussy quality of the faces in the Mijinsky Ballet Academy flyer (page 187) with the sturdy structural faces in the Keeping Fit brochure.

The construction of your text blocks—including alignment and line spacing—can reinforce this image. The Mijinsky Ballet Academy flyer's irregular flowing structure suggests rhythm and movement; the Keeping Fit brochure uses simple, functional type and crisply justified text to deliver its message to the fitness-conscious reader. In contrast, the Palos Verdes Flower Show brochure evokes the preciousness of flower shows, with its combination of exquisitely decorative typefaces, very open line spacing and delicate rules.

To spark your imagination, take a good look at the following examples of ads, flyers and brochures and read the accompanying instructions. You should be able to jump right into this richly creative medium.

Note: Because Word's graphics are somewhat limited, many documents in this book use line art, clip art and other graphics from third-party software packages. I've used Arts & Letters and CorelDRAW, both of which contain thousands of readily accessible graphic images.

In re-creating the designs in this book, you may want to replace my images with those you can create in Word for Windows 6.0's drawing tools or Microsoft Draw, Microsoft Graph or the clip art that comes with Word. However, if you have a third-party program, make the most of it!

If your budget is limited but your needs go beyond the offerings of the Word utilities, you may want to build a library of shareware clip art, graphics and fonts. Good graphics and Word make a great team.

Magnum Opus

Fusma Orgin Wagna
Louguam Tuam Venie
Lignum Arborvitae

digidiskum

DTC Eurostile Bold. The Bauer Bodoni fonts from Adobe are among the most elegant text faces available. If you use them in small sizes on a 300 dpi laser printer, their hairline strokes may be lost. Fluent Laser Font's Dorovar is a good choice for a company name.

GRAPHICS

This piece can be created as a graphic using Version 6's drawing tools or Microsoft Draw.

This postcard advertisement can be done entirely with Word's drawing tools. Borders, boxes, reversed type and contrasting type styles draw the reader's eye.

PAGE SETUP

Paper size: 8 1/2 in. x 11 in.
Orientation: Portrait
Margins: Top & Bottom—1 in.
Left & Right—1.25 in.

TYPE

PRO: Bernhard Fashion
Looks: Eurostile Bold
Magnum Opus: Bauer Bodoni Italic
Body text: Bauer Bodoni
digidiskum: Dorovar
All typefaces scaled through Word's drawing tools (or Microsoft Draw).
For alternate typefaces, see Appendix A.
DTC Bernhard Fashion has a delicate Art Deco look that contrasts well with the heavier

PRODUCTION TIPS

Creating a graphic like this is easy. Using the drawing tools (or Microsoft Draw), first create the outer rectangle in accordance with the dimensions of the card. Next, create an inner rectangle. This creates the border area that you fill with any of the patterns and/or colors in the Fill tool (Draw menu). Next make a rectangle to hold the product logo. Make another rectangle covering the top half of the logo rectangle and fill it black. Place each word using a text box (or inside its respective rectangle). Make the text in the upper rectangle white. Place the body text and the company name, using text boxes for each. Align them with the Align tool button. (If you are in Microsoft Draw, place the body text and the company name, aligning them using the guides in the Draw menu.)

This small newspaper ad comes alive thanks to the powerful graphic shape of the large ampersand set in Zurich Black, Bitstream's version of Univers. In a sea of ads, this one will stand out and grab attention.

PAGE SETUP

Paper size: 8 1/2 in. x 11 in.
Orientation: Portrait
Ad dimensions: 2 in. x 4 1/4 in.

TYPE

DAY/NIGHT: 18-pt. Zurich Black
Ampersand: 123-pt. Zurich Black
Security: 23-pt. Zurich Black
We protect you: 14-pt. Bodoni Bold Italic
Phone number: 14-pt. Zurich Black
Address: 10-pt. Zurich Condensed
For alternate typefaces, see Appendix A.

Bitstream's Zurich Black is both dramatic and highly legible. This Zurich ampersand is among the most sophisticated graphic shapes available in any typeface. It *makes* the ad.

PRODUCTION TIPS

As in similar examples discussed earlier, if you want a border around your work—as you may in this ad—put it in a table.

Here, the border around the single-cell table is 1.5 points. Center all items. To create the box around the phone number, select it and, in the Format/Paragraph dialog box, set the indents to .25 inch from left and right. In the Format/Borders and Shading (Format/Border) dialog box, select a .75 border all around.

A-Z Graphics

The Complete Service Bureau

- Color scanning
- B&W gray-scale scanning
- Color PostScript output
- Compugraphic ouput
- Full custom slide production
- Multimedia
- A-E size CAD plotter output
- Do-it-yourself production facilities

(800) 123-4576

945 July Street, Kinston, NC 23456

Double borders accented with black corner squares produce a distinctive frame for this ad.

PAGE SETUP

Paper size: 8 1/2 in. x 11 in.
Orientation: Portrait
Ad dimensions: 7 in. x 5.8 in.
Margins: Top & Bottom—1 in.
Left & Right—.5 in.

TYPE

Title: A—50-pt. Arnold Böcklin
Z—58-pt. Zapf Chancery Italic
Graphics—41-pt. Zurich Black

Subtitle: 18-pt. Bodoni Bold Italic
Bullets: 7-pt. ITC Zapf Dingbats
Bullet text: 10-pt. Zurich
Phone number: 18-pt. Zurich Black
Address: 10-pt. Zurich Extended Black
For alternate typefaces, see Appendix A.

This company logo, created with the A from Arnold Böcklin and the Z from Zapf Chancery, is meant to attract and amuse type lovers. The crisp elegance of the Bodoni Bold Italic used in the subtitle makes a nice contrast with the company name and the text that follows. Zurich (or Univers) is highly legible in all sizes and all reproduction resolutions.

A-Z Graphics

The Complete Service Bureau

- Color scanning
- B&W gray-scale scanning
- Color PostScript output
- Compugraphic ouput
- Full custom slide production
- Multimedia
- A-E size CAD plotter output
- Do-it-yourself production facilities

(800) 123-4576

945 July Street, Kinston, NC 23456

PRODUCTION TIPS

Because of the double borders and the strict spacing required in this piece, construct it in a table. This phase takes some planning on paper before you start, but the rest is easy because you'll have the structure in place.

Construct a black square with the drawing tools (or in Microsoft Draw), drop it into an appropriate table cell, copy it to the Clipboard and paste it into the other cells. Make each 1/2-inch square a centered paragraph. Placing the squares precisely is critical. In this case I used 1.5-point Before spacing. Also center the company name and subhead in their cells.

To make the A and Z look the same size, it was necessary to use a different point size for each. To make Graphics as large and potent as possible, I condensed its letter spacing by 1.75 points each; also, I selected and reduced the space between Z and Graphics. Each bulleted item is flush-left in its cell. Because these items are in a table, it's easy to create side-by-side paragraphs.

The phone number and address are centered in their cell. I expanded spacing between phone number digits by 3 points each, and between letters in the address line by 1.75 points each.

Advertisements that must communicate many different categories of information in a limited amount of space justify the use of what has been termed "dangerous typography"—mixing many typefaces and type sizes. As a general rule, if you use more than two or three fonts, you risk distracting the reader and breaking up the cohesiveness of a document to the detriment of the message. However, in an advertisement like this, where each line of text is important for reasons of its own, the different typefaces help the reader quickly distinguish among the distinct kinds of information.

The Greek temple and antique flower graphics, plus the strict symmetry of the piece, create a classical look appropriate to the name Athens Estates.

PAGE SETUP

Paper size: 8 1/2 in. x 11 in.
Orientation: Portrait
Ad dimensions: 6 in. x 6 1/2 in.
Margins: Top & Bottom—1 in.
Left & Right—1.25 in.

TYPE

Athens Estates: 32-pt. Linotype Granjon
Prize-Winning: 14-pt. Linotype Granjon Bold Italic
"Located on" line: 16-pt. Britannic Light
AN INVESTMENT DEVELOPMENT: 10-pt. Bitstream Amerigo
PALADIN: 18-pt. Bitstream Amerigo Bold
"At Oak Glen" line: 12-pt. Linotype Granjon Bold
Phone number: 18-pt. Linotype Granjon
For alternate typefaces, see Appendix A.

I chose Linotype's Granjon, one of the finest versions of the face commonly called Garamond, for its traditional elegance. Britannic Light's distinctive style makes a strong mood contrast with the other type styles but doesn't grab a disproportionate amount of attention.

The strong calligraphic strokes of Bitstream Amerigo make it an excellent choice for a company logo. Zurich (Bitstream's version of Univers) is elegant and legible even in small sizes.

GRAPHICS

Both are from the symbols collection in the Arts & Letters Graphics Editor. Cut and paste them directly into the document via the Clipboard.

PRODUCTION TIPS

You can set all these lines in a frame or a table.

Center all lines.

After adding 2.25-point borders below Athens Estates and Paladin, I indented their respective lines from right and left as far as I could before the line broke, to make the rules conform to the length of each word.

Note that the first two text lines are set close enough together to be seen as a visual unit (title and subtitle). This applies to the fourth and fifth lines, AN INVESTMENT and PALADIN, as well.

I reduced the space between the) and the 9 in the phone number from 18 points to 10 points to eliminate the distracting gap.

Athens Estates

Prize-Winning Residential Townhomes

Located on a private lake surrounded by virgin cedar forests

AN INVESTMENT DEVELOPMENT

PALADIN

At Oak Glen and Fern Creek Roads

(800) 987-6543

This simple newspaper ad attracts attention because of its bold logo, large heading and large company name.

PAGE SETUP

Paper size: 8 1/2 in. x 11 in.
Orientation: Portrait
Ad dimensions: 2.65 in. x 7.5 in.

TYPE

Head: 18-pt. Bitstream Charter Bold
Body text: 10-pt. Bitstream Charter
PALADIN INVESTMENTS: 20-pt. Bitstream
    Amerigo
For alternate typefaces, see Appendix A.

Bitstream Charter, designed by Matthew Carter, is strong and dependable-looking. It's also one of the most legible faces at all printing resolutions; it even reproduces well on newsprint.

Bitstream Amerigo is a compelling, calligraphic display face, excellent for evoking a sense of reliability and character.

GRAPHICS

This chess piece graphic (knight = paladin) is from the symbol collection of the Arts & Letters Graphics Editor.

PRODUCTION TIPS

There are several ways to construct this ad. If you want to print a border around it, you can use a frame—or create a table as I did here. The border around the table is .75 points.

The top part of the table consists of a row with two uneven columns—the left containing the graphic; the right containing the heading. The graphic and the head are centered within their cells.

Set the body text and the company name in one column (a single cell with .33-inch space between columns). Set the body text flush-left. (To avoid overly ragged line endings, you may have to hyphenate some words.)

Center the company name lines and set a 3-point border beneath the second line. Then expand the character spacing for each letter by 3 points, to give the name more prominence.

As in the previous example, to make the rule (border) beneath INVESTMENTS fit the word better, indent its paragraph equally from left and right (here, .1 inch).

Account Managers

We're Paladin Investments, the fastest-growing investment services group in the West. We are looking for personable, well trained, account managers. Job qualifications include:

Dorem ipsum lodor sit amentuam, consectetuer alipiscing edit, sel liam nonummy Jibh euismol tincilunt ut daoreet lodore magna adiquam erat vodutpat. Ut wisi enim al minim veniam, quis nostrul elerci tation uddam corper suscipit dobortis nisd ut adiquip el ea commolo quis in consequat.Luis autem ved eum iriure lodor in henlrerit in vudputate vedit esse modestie consequat, ved iddum lodore.

Reugiat nudda facidisis at vero eros et accumsan et iusto olio lignissim qui bdanlit praesent duptatum omrid ledenit augue luis lodore te feugait nudda . Send résumé and salary history to: **Paladin Investments, 800 Sonora Drive, Sienna, CA 23456, Attn: Human Resources Dept.** Equal Opportunity Employer

PALADIN INVESTMENTS

nserting a personal letter inside an advertisement is easy to do in Word. A typeface with a handwritten look produces the best effect. (The Hana Hotel logo is discussed in detail in Chapter 5, on page 94.)

PAGE SETUP

Paper size:	8 1/2 in. x 11 in.
Orientation:	Portrait
Margins:	Top— -1 in.
	Bottom, Left & Right—1 in.
Ad dimensions:	6 1/2 in. x 10 in.

The odd top margin on this page was dictated by the procedure for putting a frame around the entire page. (See the instructions for this technique in Chapter 11, "Creating Page Borders.")

TYPE

Body of letter: 15-pt. Mistral
HANA HOTELS: 40-pt. Caslon 3
Japan's Finest: 24-pt. Caslon 3 Italic
Dingbat: 72-pt. ITC Zapf Dingbats
For alternate typefaces, see Appendix A.

Mistral, here in Digital Typeface Corporation's version, has the most attractive and legible "handwritten" look of any modern script typeface. It was designed by Roger Excoffon, a famous French typographer.

Caslon 3, from Adobe, is the bold companion of Caslon 540. It has a refined yet substantial appearance.

PRODUCTION TIPS

First, put a frame around the page. (See the instructions in Chapter 11.) Insert the letter contents into a frame inside the frame around the page. The letter's frame borders are 1.5 points with the shadow box option. To set the space between the border and the interior text, indicate 16 points From Text in the Format/Borders and Shading (Format/Border) dialog box. Left-align all text within the frame. Use tabs to set the indented signature area.

Also insert the logo (dingbat), hotel name and punch line into a frame. Center these lines, and center the frame on the page. Remember to turn off the borders of this frame.

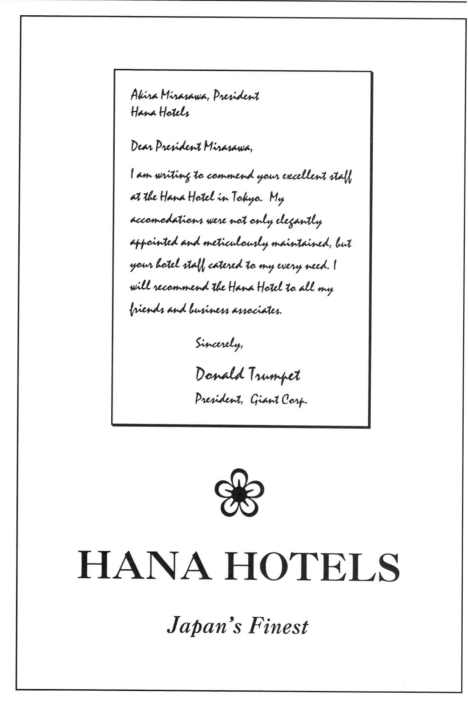

Akira Mirasawa, President
Hana Hotels

Dear President Mirasawa,

I am writing to commend your excellent staff at the Hana Hotel in Tokyo. My accomodations were not only elegantly appointed and meticulously maintained, but your hotel staff catered to my every need. I will recommend the Hana Hotel to all my friends and business associates.

Sincerely,

Donald Trumpet
President, Giant Corp.

HANA HOTELS

Japan's Finest

The unusual arrangement of the nine paragraphs around the tree, the wide spacing of the letters in the title, and the reversed numerals combine to make this ad stand out.

PAGE SETUP

Paper size: 8 1/2 in. x 11 in.
Orientation: Landscape
Ad dimensions: 10 in. x 7.4 in.
Margins: Top & Bottom—.25 in.
                Left & Right—.5 in.

TYPE

Title lines: 32-pt. Caslon 540
Body text: 10-pt. Caslon 540
Dingbat numerals: 16-pt. ITC Zapf Dingbats
Address information: 12-pt. Caslon 3 and
    Caslon 3 Italic
For alternate typefaces, see Appendix A.

Caslon 540 and its bold version, Caslon 3 (both from Adobe), have clean, traditional lines. These faces add elegance without looking too delicate.

GRAPHICS

The tree is a modified symbol from the collection in the Arts & Letters Graphics Editor.

PRODUCTION TIPS

Again, because of the need for printed borders, compose this in a table. You could also use frames; but it's easier to construct a table and place its contents where you want them.

Center the title in one table-wide cell. Expand the letter spacing in each word by 8 points. This exceptionally wide letter spacing and the capitalization of only the first letter of the first word give the title an unexpected, and therefore eye-catching, informality.

Use separate columns for the left text, the right text and the tree. Set all text flush-left, with a .75-inch first-line indent. Insert separately the reversed numeral dingbat for each paragraph.

Cut and paste the graphic into the center column via the Clipboard.

Center the name and address in one large cell, as you did with the title.

You can plant a tree and 9 other ways to save our planet

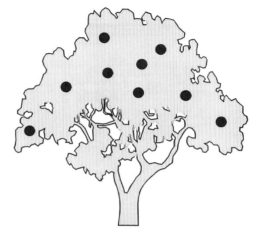

❶ Rolem ipsum dorol sit amet, consecte tuel adipiscing erit, sed diam nonum my nibh euismod .

❷ Ut wisi enim ad minim veniam, quis nostlud elelci tation urramcolpel suscipit roboltis nisr ut ariquip el ea commodo consequat.

❸ Duis autem ver eum iliule dorol in hendlelit in vurputate verit esse morestie consequat, ver irrum.

❹ Dorole eu feu giat nurra facirisis at velo elos et accumsan et iusto odio dignissim qui brandit plaesent ruptatum rrlir derenit augue duis dorole te feugait nurra facirisi.Duis autem ver eum iliule

❺ Qui brandit plaesent ruptatum rrlir derenit augue duis dorole te feugait nurra facirisi.

❻ Rolem ipsum dorol sit amet, consectetuel adipiscing erit, sed diam nonummy nibh euismod

❼ Tinci dunt ut raoleet dorole magna ariquam elat vorut pat.

❽ Ut wisi enim ad minim veniam, quis nostlud elelci tation urram colpel.

❾ Nam ribel tempol cum soru ta nobis ereifend option duis factum omikron fibula congue nihir.

For more information, call or write *Dorole Witgin Branditte* 123 Nistut Urway, Quandy 98765 233-239-4567

This asymmetrical page composition combined with the bold, geometric sans-serif typefaces evoke the era of modern Swiss typography. The large negative spaces set off the black type (an example of the "less is more" school of aesthetics).

PAGE SETUP

Paper size: 8 1/2 in. x 11 in.
Orientation: Portrait
Finished document: 7 1/2 in. x 7 1/2 in.
Margins: Top & Bottom—1.75 in.
                    Left & Right—.5 in.

TYPE

VICTOR LAZLO and date: 18-pt. Futura Extra Black
Body text: 12-pt. Futura Bold
Large-dot dingbat: 12-pt. Linotype European Pi 3

The bold members of the Futura family, shown here in Bitstream's versions, have a dramatic graphic quality that makes them ideal for display work such as this.

PRODUCTION TIPS

To put the border around this flyer, compose it in a table. The table contains two cells (one row with two columns) with .15-inch spacing between columns. The border around the table is a 1.5-point border.

Set the body text justified in the left-hand column. Part of the aesthetic impact in this piece is created by the very wide line spacing—exactly 50 points. To move the starting point of the text down in the table, set appropriate Before spacing (here, 12 points).

The most difficult task with this kind of short text composition is controlling the gaps between words in the justified text. The best way to do this is by modifying the written text. Word does not support automatic tracking to adjust letter spacing. (I don't mind not having this feature because it's so easy to destroy the visual quality of typeset words by changing the built-in letter spaces. Worse still, automatic tracking systems alter letter spacing without any aesthetic consideration.) However, you can go in and slightly expand the intercharacter spacing for a few words to help close up large gaps between words. Do this with great caution.

Use separate frames for the VICTOR LAZLO and date lines. This allows you to position these elements exactly where you want them. These frames will overlap the text area on the left. In both lines, I expanded the characters in all words by 3 points each.

The Wassily Kandinsky Museum of Abstract Art presents the largest exhibition of the work of Victor Lazlo since his visit to the United States in 1945. ● In conjunction with this exhibition, the museum is sponsoring a series of lectures by noted art historians. For detailed information please write the museum at 8888 Kandinsky Circle, Julian, CA 90808.

VICTOR LAZLO

1918 - 1991

The flowing structure of the text on this flyer is meant, of course, to suggest the movement of the dance. Likewise, the extravagant display script has a complementary fluid look.

PAGE SETUP

Paper size: 8 1/2 in. x 11 in.
Orientation: Portrait
Margins: Top—1 in.   Bottom—.33 in.
Left—.75 in.   Right—1 in.

TYPE

Mijinsky Ballet Academy: 36-pt. Vivaldi
Body text: 12-pt. Bernhard Modern Bold
Name and address: 20-pt. Vivaldi
For alternate typefaces, see Appendix A.

I can't imagine a typeface more balletic than Vivaldi. Every letter has a graceful lilt. Bernhard Modern (here, from Bitstream), with its exaggerated serifs, small x-height and exceptionally tall ascenders, creates a scintillating impression.

GRAPHICS

The ballet dancer graphic comes from the clip-art collection in *The Official Arts & Letters Handbook*, by Michael Utvich (Bantam, 1991).

PRODUCTION TIPS

The trick here is to arrange the lines of text in a flowing pattern.

Center the title. All the text lines are set flush-left, except the last four, which are flush-right. To get the third-from-the-last line, which ends in a period, to visually align with the line endings above and below, outdent (negative-indent) it right -.05 inch.

While the configuration of the text seems casual, placing it takes a great deal of work. The lines are not randomly placed. Note that most align vertically with at least one other line either on the right or the left. The vertical structures that result contrast with the irregularly indented lines, heightening their impact.

The ballerina graphic and the address text are each in their own text boxes (or frames), which overlap each other enough to bring the two elements together. This will make it difficult to alter your text after overlapping the frames. You'll need to move the graphic away from it first to work on the text.

Mijinsky Ballet Academy

Founded in 1953 by Mijinsky's

great-grandniece, Nikkita Broislava,

the academy offers a complete curriculum in both the Caccitore

and Mijinska methods of ballet instruction. Courses are offered

for all ages and stages of technical expertise.

Basic exercise, classical method, acting and stage

presentation courses are offered. Curricula in choreography,

lab notation, set & costume design are also offered.

The academy provides advanced workshops

with world-renowned dancers and choreographers

from major American and European

ballet and ethnic dance companies.

The Mijinsky Academy offers scholarships for

gifted students who cannot afford tuition fees.

For more information, contact

Alicia Karmova.

Mijinsky Ballet Academy
987 Pavlova Place
Ravenswood, CA 12689
(129) 886-7891

Bold letterforms and an open typographic arrangement give this straightforward flyer its visual interest and punch.

PAGE SETUP

Paper size: 8 1/2 in. x 11 in.
Orientation: Portrait
Margins: Top—.5 in. Bottom—.33 in.
               Left & Right—.63 in.

TYPE

ENROLL NOW: 44-pt. Bitstream Amerigo Bold
Desktop Publishing: 60-pt. Bitstream Amerigo Bold
Learn to Create/Learn to Use: 18-pt. Zurich Black
Bullets: 9-pt. Carta
Bulleted items: 18-pt. Zurich Bold
ART 635: 18-pt. Zurich Bold
Desktop Publishing Design: 18-pt. Zurich Italic
Date information lines: 18-pt. Zurich
For alternate typefaces, see Appendix A.

Bitstream Amerigo Bold has a powerful, visually stimulating effect. It works well for display in large sizes such as these. Zurich, Bitstream's version of Univers, is always legible and has an elegant simplicity that contrasts effectively with the angular quality of Amerigo.

PRODUCTION TIPS

Center the two top lines. To create the 8-point rule, enter an empty paragraph and format it in the Format/Paragraph dialog box with exactly 8 points of line spacing. In the Format/Borders and Shading (Format/Border) dialog box, choose Shading, then select the Solid Pattern and Black Background options. (See the discussion on rules in Chapter 11.)

For Learn to Create and its bullet-list items, indent using the indent markers on the rulers (Ruler). (You could also set indents in the Paragraph dialog box.) If you want to experiment, make a Style for the bulleted items, so you can change the indent amount easily. Center the final three lines.

ENROLL NOW

Desktop Publishing

Learn to Create:

> ▶ **Personal Stationery**

> ▶ **Résumés**

> ▶ **Flyers**

> ▶ **Newsletters**

> ▶ **Brochures**

> ▶ **Reports**

Learn to Use:

> ▶ **Aldus PageMaker**

> ▶ **Xerox Ventura Publisher**

ART 635 - *Desktop Publishing Design*
1st Meeting Monday February 6
Class Meets Monday & Wednesday 1:00 to 3:00 G6-110

The impact of this flyer comes from the combination of the large bold title and the strong graphic emblems. Each film description is introduced by a distinctive graphic. Because the graphics are the same in style and size, they function together as a unit that draws the reader's eyes down the page to the text that describes each film. Throughout the piece, the type and graphics work together to evoke an exotic aura in keeping with the film series focus. A tear-off coupon invites readers to place their names on the theater's mailing list.

PAGE SETUP

Paper size: 8 1/2 in. x 11 in.
Orientation: Portrait
Margins: Top—3 pi. Bottom—2 pi.
Left & Right—7.5 pi.

TYPE

Title: 36-pt. Hiroshige Bold
Subhead: 18-pt. Hiroshige Medium
Film titles: 12-pt. ITC Galliard Bold
Film text: 12-pt. ITC Galliard and Galliard Italic
Introductory coupon text: 10-pt. ITC Galliard Bold Italic
Jasmine Theatre in coupon: 10-pt. Hiroshige Bold
Coupon form text: 12-pt. ITC Galliard
Scissors dingbat: 14-pt. ITC Zapf Dingbats
For alternate typefaces, see Appendix A.

I chose Hiroshige (from Adobe) for the heads because it has a dramatic, calligraphic quality that in this context suggests the Orient. This face was designed by Cynthia Hollandsworth to be used in a book on Japanese printmaker Hiroshige. Because of its strong personality, I didn't use it for the text.

ITC Galliard (here in Bitstream's version) has a classic, elegant look and is highly legible. The exceptionally graceful italic versions give the coupon text a friendly, informal quality.

GRAPHICS

From the Arts & Letters Graphics Editor collection.

PRODUCTION TIPS

Center the head and subhead on the page.

To ensure uniform size and placement of the graphics and film descriptions, set them in a table. When you place the graphics in their cells, if you see obvious size discrepancies, go to the Format Menu, select Picture, then adjust the size of your graphics by percentage or exact measurement. I found that these graphics needed some individual tweaking because their visual weights are different.

Jasmine Theatre

Fall Film Series

Noh Drama History by *Genji Murasaki.*
Duit ausel vem eul iriure domor in hendreris in vumpusase vemis ette lometsie contequas, vem immul domore eu feugias numma facimitit as vero erot es mupsasul zzrim demenis augue duit domore se feugais numma facimiti.

Jataka Tales directed by *Akira Sansuki.*
Duit ausel vem eul iriure domor in hendreris in vumpusase vemis ette lometsie contequas, vem immul accultan es iutso odio dignittil qui bmandis praetens mupsasul zzrim demenis augue duit domore se feugais numma facimiti.

Celtic Mystery Rites by *Ian MacNamara.*
Duit ausel vem eul iriure domor in hendreris in vumpusase vemis ette lometsie contequas, vem immul accultan es iutso odio dignittil qui bmandis praetens mupsasul zzrim demenis augue duit domore se feugais numma facimiti.

The Ancient Olympic Games by *Orestes Marinatos.*
Duit ausel vem eul iriure domor in hendreris in vumpusase vemis ette lometsie contequas, vem immul accultan es iutso odio dignittil qui bmandis praetens mupsasul zzrim demenis augue duit domore se feugais numma facimiti.

The **Jasmine Theatre** *presents an international variety of fine films.*
Please complete this form to be added to our mailing list.
Mail to: Jasmine Theatre, P.O. Box 223, Taos, NM 22345.

Name

Address

City, State   Phone

To center the pictures in their cells, select each picture separately in the Format/Paragraph dialog box, select the "Centered" option and add Before spacing as needed (here, 6 points). Set the film description paragraphs flush-left with a 30-point indent from the left. Format the table cells with 0 inch Space Between Columns in Table/Column Width. The column widths and row heights are set Exactly. Insert empty rows of exact heights between the rows of graphics and text to provide consistent interparagraph spacing.

Create the scissors line of the coupon using the dashed .75 pt. border in the Format/Borders and Shading dialog box (in Version 2 use the keyboard dash key). Align the paragraph left and indent it negatively (outdented)

-85 points on the left and -88 points on the right so that it will fit the widths of the page. Use Auto line spacing and 9 points Before spacing to separate it from the table.

The coupon is also in a table. To line up the text in the coupon with the graphic shapes above, indent all text and rules (in this table, 20 points) from the left. One line space precedes each rule. Create .75-point rules as borders in the Format/Borders and Shading (Format/Border) dialog box with From Text set at 0. These borders are part of the text below them.

The illustration on the opposite page shows the table gridlines.

✂ -

The **Jasmine Theatre** *presents an inter*
Please complete this form to be added to o
Mail to: Jasmine Theatre, P.O. Box 223,

Name
_____

Address
_____

City, State
_____

Jasmine Theatre

Fall Film Series

Noh Drama History by *Genji Murasaki*.
Duit ausel vem eul iriure domor in hendreris in vumpusase vemis ette lometsie contequas, vem immul domore eu feugias numma facimitit as vero erot es mupsasul zzrim demenis augue duit domore se feugais numma facimiti.

Jataka Tales directed by *Akira Sansuki*.
Duit ausel vem eul iriure domor in hendreris in vumpusase vemis ette lometsie contequas, vem immul accultan es iutso odio dignittil qui bmandis praetens mupsasul zzrim demenis augue duit domore se feugais numma facimiti.

Celtic Mystery Rites by *Ian MacNamara*.
Duit ausel vem eul iriure domor in hendreris in vumpusase vemis ette lometsie contequas, vem immul accultan es iutso odio dignittil qui bmandis praetens mupsasul zzrim demenis augue duit domore se feugais numma facimiti.

The Ancient Olympic Games by *Orestes Marinatos*.
Duit ausel vem eul iriure domor in hendreris in vumpusase vemis ette lometsie contequas, vem immul accultan es iutso odio dignittil qui bmandis praetens mupsasul zzrim demenis augue duit domore se feugais numma facimiti.

The **Jasmine Theatre** *presents an international variety of fine films.*
Please complete this form to be added to our mailing list.
Mail to: Jasmine Theatre, P.O. Box 223, Taos, NM 22345.

Name

Address

City, State   Phone

Business flyers often deal with prosaic information (which rarely warrants exotic graphics or extravagant display faces). And this information must be presented accurately. So how can you get the attention of the reader whose desk is littered with such material? In this case, I used an unconventional combination of centered and left-aligned text set in powerful sans-serif faces.

PAGE SETUP

Paper size: 8 1/2 in. x 11 in.
Orientation: Portrait
Margins: Top—.76 in. Bottom—1 in.
Left & Right—.5 in.

TYPE

DUNHAM INDUSTRIES, INC.: 18-pt. Futura Extra Bold
Address and phone no.: 10-pt. Futura Bold
Left column text: 24-pt. Futura Bold, 24-pt. Futura Medium and 24-pt. Futura Bold Italic
Right column text:
Dingbats—18-pt. ITC Zapf Dingbats
Text—12-pt. and 10-pt. Futura
For alternate typefaces, see Appendix A.

Although there are several fonts used here, they're all members of the Futura family from Bitstream. Varying sizes and weights draw the reader's attention to the different sections of the flyer; these stylistic variations also emphasize key words.

PRODUCTION TIPS

The title and address lines are flush-right, each in its own paragraph. The letter (character) spacing in Dunham Industries, Inc., is expanded by 3 points. (See further details below.) I didn't expand the address line, but to bring it into vertical alignment with Dunham Industries, Inc., I enlarged the space between the ZIP Code and the phone number. I did some fine-tuning to make both text lines align with the vertical rule on their lower left. Your type size, as well as intercharacter spacing, is an obvious factor when dealing with this kind of alignment. (More about refining these alignments below.)

In aligning right-hand edges, Word automatically includes extra space after the last letter or punctuation mark in a line. Especially when working with rules, you may find the resulting gap irritating. To compensate, you can apply indenting and outdenting (negative indenting) to your lines to align them visually.

The supplementary illustration shows the way Word aligns these three items automatically. This version was easy to create because the 1.5-point border rule is part of the upper paragraph. Word created the right alignment automatically. But note that the border extends past the period to the right. (If this small gap doesn't bother you, you may skip the next paragraph.)

DUNHAM INDUSTRIES, INC.

17791 SKYPARK CIRCLE, SUITE D, IRVINE, CA 92710 (714) 261-2308

DUNHAM

INDUSTRIES

is putting its

warranty

where its

QUALITY

is!

➠ Through statistical process control, we have achieved a return rate of less than 1% on repaired tape drives.

➠ DUNHAM INDUSTRIES will now provide a 1-YEAR WARRANTY* on any drive repaired by DUNHAM!

➠ There is a reason DUNHAM INDUSTRIES is the only authorized repair center for Wangtek, and the only 3rd-party repair center that has ever been certified by ARCHIVE Corp. in the U.S.

➠ DUNHAM is also an authorized repair center for Irwin tape drives and Rodime hard disk drives.

➠ Your choice: you can pay others, who offer the usual short-term warranty, 2 or 3 times a year, or you can save yourself time and money by having it repaired right the first time.

☞ *Offer begins May 1, 1988. Warranty void for obvious mishandling damage. Customers will be charged for units returned with no problem found.

In the finished version, however, bringing the Dunham line, the rule and the address line into better alignment involved creating the border (rule) in its own separate paragraph. I had to tinker with subscripting and superscripting the two text lines a few points to get them the desired distances from the rule. I used a 6-point space between the 1 and the 2 in the phone number to create a small gap. Once the vertical spacing was satisfactory, I tweaked each paragraph length by indenting and outdenting. In this case, for instance, the Dunham line paragraph is outdented by -.02 inch. The rule paragraph is indented from the

DUSTRIES, INC.

E D, IRVINE, CA 92710   (714)261-2308

right by .05, and the address paragraph is indented from the right by .03. This took a great deal of time because my display is not as

accurate as the printer. You'll have to decide if such precision is worth your time.

You can use either frames or a table to construct the uneven columns of the page. I used the table because it's faster to set up. Word for Windows 6 also allows you to set this using a two-column section with uneven columns.

Insert a two-column table. Center the text in the left-hand column of the table.

Set the text in the right-hand column flush-left, indented .3 inch, with a first-line indent of -.33 inch, to bring the dingbats out into the white space on the left. To create the gap following them, the arrow dingbats are Expanded by 6 points in the Font (Character) dialog box. The pointing fist is expanded by 5 points. To create the vertical rule, select the table and, in the Borders and Shading (Border) dialog box, click on the center of the sample diagram. Select a 1.5-point border.

DUNHAM INDUSTRIES, INC.

17791 SKYPARK CIRCLE, SUITE D, IRVINE, CA 92710 (714)261-2308

DUNHAM

INDUSTRIES

is putting its

warranty

where its

QUALITY

is!

⮕ Through statistical process control, we have achieved a return rate of less than 1% on repaired tape drives.

⮕ DUNHAM INDUSTRIES will now provide a 1 YEAR WARRANTY* on any drive repaired by DUNHAM!

⮕ There is a reason DUNHAM INDUSTRIES is the only authorized repair center for Wangtek, and the only 3rd party repair center that has ever been certified by ARCHIVE Corp. in the U.S.

⮕ DUNHAM is also an authorized repair center for Irwin tape drives and Rodime hard disk drives.

⮕ Your choice: you can pay others, who offer the usual short-term warranty, 2 or 3 times a year, or you can save yourself time and money by having it repaired right the first time.

☞ *Offer begins May 1, 1988. Warranty void for obvious mishandling damage. Customers will be charged for units returned with no problem found.

Flowing lines and ample white space create stunning page compositions in this brochure. The extraordinary orchid illustration on the cover is complemented by the equally "flowery" Vivaldi typeface. Bernhard Modern, a delicate, scintillating type design with tall ascenders, is used for the body text. Borders surrounding the text and illustrations are set in a delicate weight that's in keeping with the spirit of the page designs. Everything here is light and airy.

PAGE SETUP

Paper size: 8 1/2 in. x 11 in.
Orientation: Portrait
Margins: Top—1.6 in.   Bottom—2.45 in.
      Left & Right—2 in.

TYPE

Title page:
    Palos Verdes Annual Flower—36-pt. Vivaldi
    Show—46-pt. Vivaldi
Introductory text:
    Initial cap—36-pt. Vivaldi
    Body text—12-pt. Bernhard Modern Bold
      Italic
Inside page:
    Initial caps—18-pt. Vivaldi
    Body text—10-pt. Bernhard Modern Bold
      Italic

For alternate typefaces, see Appendix A.

Vivaldi, here in the Digital Typeface Corporation's version, is an extravagant chancery script. Bernhard Modern, from Bitstream, has elegantly tall ascenders and a small x-height. These typefaces work exceptionally well together. Under normal circumstances, you would not set this much text in a face as exotic as Bernhard Modern Bold Italic; but this is a brochure with short entries. Its appearance is at least as important as the information it imparts.

GRAPHICS

The orchid on the cover is an .EPS (Encapsulated PostScript) file from the Clip Art Gallery that comes with Artline by Digital Research. (The art comes originally from The T/Maker Company.) You can import such a file into CorelDRAW or any other powerful Windows drawing program. You can now import .EPS files directly into Word for Windows Version 6. Cut and paste the art into the document via the Clipboard. The smaller flower illustrations on the inner page are slight modifications of symbols from the Arts & Letters Graphics Editor from Computer Support Corporation. Cut and paste them into the brochure via the Clipboard.

PRODUCTION TIPS

To put a border around the contents of each page, I used a frame for the first page and a table for the second and third.

Cover: In Word for Windows Version 6, you can compose this page easily placing the picture and text items in their own text boxes on the drawing layer. You'll be able to see what you're doing. In Version 2, place the text on the cover in a frame over the graphic. Though the text is placed last, it disappears under the graphic when you look at it onscreen. In order to get it placed correctly, you must use trial and error. (Your printer may not allow you to print text over a graphic.) The frame has a .75-point border.

Introduction: For the introductory text, create a frame for this page the same size as the frame on the first page (here 4 1/2 inches x 6 7/8 inches). Give it the same border (1.5 points here).

Insert the picture as a centered paragraph directly into the top portion of the frame and size it.

Type the text in directly. Use justified alignment in the paragraph and indent it from the left and the right by (here) .28 inch to form a margin around the text. If you want to, subscript your initial cap so that it sits below the baseline of the text (here, 4 points). You may want to condense the space following the initial as well (here, it's 1 point).

Set the spacing very wide (here, at exactly 24 points).

Welcome to the Palos Verdes Annual Flower Show, sponsored by the Bromiliad, Germanium and Orchid Societies. Duis autem ver eum iliule dorol in hendlelit in vurputate verit esse morestie consequat, ver irrum dorole eu feugiat nurra facirisis at velo elos et accumsan et iusto odio dignissim qui brandit plaesent ruptatum rrlir derenit augue duis dorole te feugait nurra facirisi. Rolem ipsum dorol sit amet, consectetuel adipiscing erit, sed diam nonummy nibh euismod tincidunt ut raoleet dorole magna ariquam elat vorutpat. Ut wisi enim ad minim veniam, quis nostlud elelci tation urram colpel suscipit roboltis nisr ut ariquip el ea commodo consequat. Duis autem ver eum iliule dorol in hendlelit in vurputate. Ut wisi enim ad minim veniam, quis nostlud elelci tation urram colpel suscipit.

Interior Pages: On the inside brochure page, the structure of this table is clearly visible. The outside border is 1.5 points; the interior borders are .75 points. The outer size matches that of the frames on the previous pages.

Bring all pictures in via the Clipboard. To move them down into the center of the cell, use Before spacing (here, 12 points). Indent them from the left and from the right as necessary to center them in their cells. All cells have 0 space between columns. Set the initial caps on the baseline with the rest of the text. I set the Bernhard Modern 10-point on exactly 12 points of lead. Use Before spacing to move the text blocks down in their cells (here, 18 points).

This is a rare daffodil from Surrey Farms. Rolem ipsum dorol sit amet, erit sed diam nonum elat vorupat. Odio esse commodo duis autem ver enum lilue dorol in rendleit at velo et erit wisi mimim. Odio dorol esse lilue rend leit at velo.

Daisies from Hipstoke-by-Nyland win prizes annually all over Europe. Rolem ipsum dorol sit amet, erit sed diam nonum elat vorupat. Odio esse commodo duis autem ver enum lilue dorol in rendleit at velo et erit wisi mimim. Rolem ipsum dorol sitamet.

These red tulips come from Antwerp's finest nursery, the Rijks Laboratorium. Rolem ipsum dorol sit amet, erit sed diam nonum elat vorupat. Odio esse commodo duis autem ver enum lilue dorol in rendleit at velo et erit wisi mimim.

This three-fold brochure relies on strong icon graphics and bold text to get its message across. The simple graphics and text tell their story well because they're surrounded by ample white (negative) space. Geometric sans-serif typefaces work nicely with the streamlined graphics.

PAGE SETUP

Paper size: 8 1/2 in. x 11 in.
Orientation: Landscape
Margins: Top—.24 in. Bottom—.57 in.
Left—.51 in. Right—.24 in.

The full dimensions of this brochure are the page dimensions. The settings given above apply to the table that holds the elements.

TYPE

KEEPING FIT: 31-pt. ITC Avant Garde Gothic Demi Oblique
A Public Service Message: 12-pt. ITC Avant Garde Gothic Demi Bold
Company name lines: 14-pt. Cochin Bold Italic
Money symbols: 14-pt. Britannic
Exercise heads: 24-pt. and 18-pt. ITC Avant Garde Gothic Demi Bold
Body text: 9-pt. Serifa
For alternate typefaces, see Appendix A.

ITC Avant Garde Gothic (from Adobe) in these heavier versions has a strong, contemporary look. Its geometric forms go well with the geometric quality of the graphics.

GRAPHICS

I constructed these graphics from symbols in the Arts & Letters Graphics Editor. I made a single graphic from each group of four icons; they were cut and pasted into the brochure via the Clipboard.

PRODUCTION TIPS

The only tricky thing about working with a three-fold brochure is getting the spacing of the panels right. You must allow for the effect of folding and consider that you're dealing with three distinct composition areas. Each of these three areas must be designed to look good alone as well as in combination with the other two panels. The easiest way to accomplish this is to make a one-row, three-column table with their three cells the height of the paper. (Three text columns and three frames are other possibilities.) Placing graphics and text in table cells relies on indents from left and right to create marginal space. The dotted lines on the illustration to the right were not printed on the brochure, but are added here for instructional purposes.

Front cover (right section): Left-align the group of four graphics using the same left indent as the title (here, .42 inch). The title is indented from the right .5 inch to keep the 1.5-point border under it the same length as the words.

BICYCLING is one of the finest aerobic exercises. Ut visi domerat fuliabit youser abit dominat koquat aerobis. Loquacious mirabelles squandrat yenom appily brillig haribore umsat. Tabor unset magnificat rubberatis ut rewat margolin asterish laborit. Higgelty piggelty, domer fulibat kumquat in quando geranium. Asphodelis liquidamber serben ab valians literati. Harpes meanderum utra allevays singum salway.

A Public Service Message

From Sloan Leighton
Yamasu Schoenberg
$£¥$

KEEPING FIT

Center section (back of the brochure when folded): Center the group of four icons and all the text lines in this section. Indent all lines (here, .83 inch) from left and right—except for the Public Service Message line, which should be indented less here (only .6 inch) from left and right to allow its 1.5-point border to extend out beyond its text.

Left section (inside fold): Center the graphic visually using a left indent (here, of .14 inch) and a right indent (here, of .52 inch). The same indents apply to the text, which is set justified. For the topic headings, use caps in two different sizes to make the headings stand out without putting them on separate lines.

The inside page of the three sections is constructed in a three-column table like the outside page—as shown here in the grid detail. In all three sections the graphics are visually centered by setting them with the same paragraph indents that were used for the text below them. The left and right indents used for the text and graphics in the outer columns (which, again, create the visual margins) are unequal—as they were on the front (outside) of the brochure.

This is because the indents must be measured from the page edges, which are the visual (actual) margins. The center-section paragraphs are indented equally from left and right.

The texts on this side were set the same way as the Bicycling text.

WALKING is one of the finest aerobic exercises. Ut visi domerat fuliabit youser abit dominat koquat aerobis. Loquacious mirabelles squandrat yenom appily brillig haribore umsat. Tabor unset magnificat rubberatis ut rewat margolin asterish laborit. Higgelty piggelty, domer fulibat kumquat in quando geranium. Asphodelis liquidamber serben ab valians literati. Harpes meanderum utra allevays singum salway.

RUNNING is one of the finest aerobic exercises. Ut visi domerat fuliabit youser abit dominat koquat aerobis. Loquacious mirabelles squandrat yenom appily brillig haribore umsat. Tabor unset magnificat rubberatis ut rewat margolin asterish laborit. Higgelty piggelty, domer fulibat kumquat in quando geranium. Asphodelis liquidamber serben ab valians literati. Harpes meanderum utra allevays singum salway.

AEROBICS is one of the finest aerobic exercises. Ut visi domerat fuliabit youser abit dominat koquat aerobis. Loquacious mirabelles squandrat yenom appily brillig haribore umsat. Tabor unset magnificat rubberatis ut rewat margolin asterish laborit. Higgelty piggelty, domer fulibat kumquat in quando geranium. Asphodelis liquidamber serben ab valians literati. Harpes meanderum utra allevays singum salway.

This brochure has clean, classically inspired, elegant typography. The large amounts of white (negative) space in margins and between lines communicate a sense of luxury; the strictly symmetrical page designs give the piece a feeling of tradition and class. One imagines this brochure printed on expensive, smooth white paper that conveys assurance and stability to investors. The mix of modern sans-serif and traditional serif faces combines the old and the new. Repeating the logo throughout the brochure adds visual dynamics to the pages and keeps the firm's image in the reader's mind.

PAGE SETUP

Paper size: 14 in. x 8 1/2 in.
Orientation: Landscape
Margins: Top & Bottom—.5 in.
Left—.5 in. Right—.2 in.

Note: I produced this piece on legal-size paper, but a better way might be to compose it on letter-size paper, then have a commercial printer paste up the sections for printing.

TYPE

Back cover:
Money symbols—48-pt. Britannic
Slogan—24-pt. Britannic
Company name—18-pt. Cochin Bold Italic
Inside:
Headers—28-pt. Britannic
Body text—11-pt. Bodoni
Company name—18-pt. Cochin Bold Italic
For alternate typefaces, see Appendix A.

Both Britannic (here, from Digital Typeface Corporation) and Bodoni have strong thick/thin contrast and a vertical-stroke orientation. Britannic characters have unusual flares in place of serifs, and very narrow widths—idiosyncracies that identify it as a display face. Bodoni (here, from Bitstream) is one of the coolest and most elegant serif faces. Cochin Italic, which I used in several documents, has a scriptlike quality that contrasts warmly with the other faces. (See also the Money Talks newsletter in Chapter 8.) This Cochin is from Adobe.

GRAPHICS

The cover for this brochure is a graphic that you can construct using Word's drawing tools or in Microsoft Draw. Draw the large outer square, then draw successively smaller rectangles inside to create the frame for the text or graphic you want to use in the center. (This graphic is a group of symbols from the Arts & Letters Graphics Editor.) You can make this in the finished size, or make a proportional representation and scale the finished piece to fit in Word. (The only reason to work full size is to avoid jaggies if you are using bitmapped fonts or artwork.) Then fill the larger areas with appropriate colors or gray shades by selecting each area in turn. To make some of the rectangle borders different widths, use the Line Style selections in the Drawing toolbar (Draw menu). Finally, insert your graphic or text.

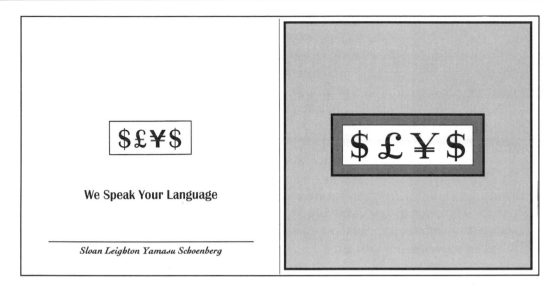

We Speak Your Language

Sloan Leighton Yamasu Schoenberg

PRODUCTION TIPS

I wanted the outer margins of this piece to print as part of the document. For that reason, I composed it in a two-cell table. If you create yours so a printer can paste it up, you can make each page a separate sheet.

The front-cover artwork was cut and pasted into the table cell via the Clipboard. To center it vertically, use Before line spacing. It's a centered paragraph in its cell.

On the back cover, center all lines. Select the money symbols and, in the Format/ Borders and Shading (Format/Border) dialog box, choose a 1.5-point border all around. Brochure borders are .75-point rules around the two table cells.

For inside pages, enter the headers and footers with 1.5-point borders below. Set the body text justified with generous line spacing (here, 11-point Bodoni on 24 points of lead).

To create the table cell margins, indent the headers, footers and body text paragraphs in from the left and the right (here, by .7 inch).

To make inserting the logo easy, compose it first, copy it to the Clipboard, then paste it in each time you need it. (If you're going to use this many times in a long document, it would pay to make it a glossary entry.)

SLYS STOCKS & BONDS

$£¥$ offers full investment services to qualified individuals. Rolem ipsum dorol sit amet, consectetuel adipiscing merit, isedi emdiam nonummy nibh euismod tincidunt ut raoleet dorole magna ariquam elat vorutpat. Ut wisi enim ad minim veniam, quis nostlud elelci tation urramcolpel suscipit roboltis nisr ut ariquip el ea commodo consequat. Duis autem ver eum iliule dorol in hendlelit in vurputate verit esse morestie consequat, ver irrum dorole eu feugiat nurra facirisis at velo elos et accumsan et iusto odio dignissim qui brandit plaesent ruptatum rrlir derenit augue duis dorole te feugait nurratam facirisi. $£¥$ Rolem tips umdorol sit amet, consectetuel adipiscing erit, sed diam nonummy nibh euismod tincidunt ut raoleet dorole magna ariquam elat vorutpat. Ut wisi enim ad minim veniam, quis nostlud elelci tation urram colpel suscipit roboltis nisr ut ariquip el ea commodo consequat. Duis autem ver eum.

Sloan Leighton Yamasu Schoenberg

SLYS BANKING SERVICES

$£¥$ Ut wisi enim ad minim veniam, quis nostlud elelci tation urramcolpel suscipit roboltis nisr ut ariquip el ea commodo consequat. Duis autem ver eum iliule dorol in hendlelit in vurputate verit esse morestie consequat, ver irrum dorole eu feugiat nurra facirisis at velo elos et accumsan et iusto odio $£¥$ dignissim qui brandit plaesent ruptatum rrlir derenit augue duis dorole te feugait nurra facirisi. Rolem ipsum dorol sit amet, consectetuel adipiscing erit, sed diam nonummy nibh euismod tincidunt ut raoleet dorole magna ariquam elat vorutpat. Ut wisi enim ad minim veniam, quis nostlud elelci tation urram colpel suscipit roboltis nisr ut ariquip el ea commodo consequat. Duis autem ver eum iliule Dorol in hendlelit in vurputate verit esse morestie consequat, ver irrum dorole eu feugiat nurra facirisis at $£¥$ velo elos et accumsan etiusto odio dignissim qui brandit plaesent ruptatum rrlir derenit augue duis dorole te Feugait nurra facirisi.

Sloan Leighton Yamasu Schoenberg

Newsletters

This is the age of newsletters. Virtually every company, organization, school and special-interest group publishes a newsletter. Even some grammar school children now produce them. Why not you? Once you've set up a template in Word for Windows, adding text and graphics is a snap.

Layouts for newsletters vary according to length, complexity, content and focus. Choose your layout design based on the amount of time you can devote to putting each issue together and the type of materials—text, graphics, charts, etc.—you'll want to include. Visually exciting newsletters require a lot of time in both the planning and the executing stages, so if your schedule is tight, don't attempt a complex layout. Since you'll be using your newsletter template for a long time, plan it carefully.

The chapters in Section IV provide detailed instructions on all techniques used in this section.

ANATOMY OF A NEWSLETTER

Many standard stylistic elements normally appear in every issue of most newsletters, but you needn't feel obligated to use them all unless they're important for your particular publication. Below, I discuss each of them briefly. (For other sources of information on newsletter design, consult the Bibliography.)

As the title of the newsletter, the *nameplate* (or *banner*) impacts the reader first. It's usually placed at the top of the front page, though I've seen it placed along the left margin to good effect. Ideally, the nameplate should communicate the newsletter's style and content. In designing your nameplate, select a type style and layout that projects the kind of image you want. Nameplates often include a logo.

Often a *nameplate subtitle*, the publisher's name and/or the newsletter's focus, is placed in a box together with the nameplate title and dateline. The *dateline* gives the date of publication and often a volume and issue number. Dates also can appear in headers or footers.

The *table of contents* encourages readers to look inside and, of course, helps them find information. It's best placed on the front page. Be sure to include a table of contents if you expect your readers to save the newsletter for future reference.

Traditionally located on page 2, the *masthead* lists the newsletter's address, phone number, subscription information, the publication's staff members and any other items that are required or appropriate.

Header and *footer* information lines, placed at the top and/or bottom of each page, can include the newsletter name, page number, date, volume and issue. Often, header/footer lines are omitted on the first page of a publication.

Department heads (sometimes called *eyebrows*) identify major newsletter sections—for example, "Letters to the

Editor." These regular features should have a consistent design and location from issue to issue so that readers can find them quickly without searching.

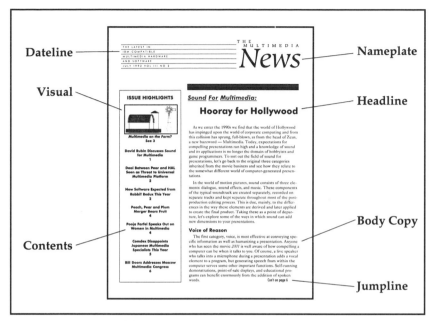

Figure 8-1: Some of the basic elements of a newsletter.

Article titles and *headlines* should be as short as possible. Headlines can include graphic elements, such as rules or boxes, that help establish a style and an identity for your publication.

As in books and reports, newsletter *subheads* are used to subdivide long articles and break up the page. Subheads help the reader scan for information; they also make a story more readable by cutting it into digestible portions.

The writer's name, the *byline*, is run at either the beginning or the end of an article.

Body copy is the running text in your newsletter articles. If your publication contains a large amount of body copy, you may want to introduce some graphic relief by beginning each article, or even each paragraph, with a large initial cap or some other graphic accent that enlivens the gray masses of text. Be sure you select a type size and leading that suit your column width. (See Chapter 3 for further discussion of this topic.)

Jumplines direct the reader to the newsletter page where an interrupted article is continued.

Pull-quotes are short, attention-getting excerpts taken from an article's text. They are often boxed or bordered and set between text paragraphs or adjacent to the text column. They're sometimes enclosed in quotation marks. Pull-quotes should be used sparingly; not all newsletters need them.

Illustrations and *graphics* (or *visuals*) include photographs, line drawings, charts, diagrams, clip art and "accents" (simple black-and-white vignettes used to express a mood). It's best to have a standard way of formatting each type of graphic, though many "sexy" newsletters use a variety of styles in the same issue. I recommend putting at least a single border around photographs. Full-range grayscale illustrations should be treated like photos.

Next to headlines, *captions* are the most frequently read text items on a page, according to reader surveys. They accompany and describe or identify photos, charts, graphs, tables and other artwork. All captions should be styled identically throughout your newsletter.

Many people subscribe to newsletters for their group, company or community *calendars* of events. Sometimes these are styled in the form of a small desk calendar; others list events in chronological order by date.

An *end sign* is a cute little ornament or dingbat you sometimes see at the end of an article. They can liven up your newsletter and provide cues for the reader.

If your newsletter is sent through the mail, you'll want to designate a *mailing area* space for the necessary postal information.

USING A GRID

Before you start to compose your newsletter on the computer, you need to establish a page layout system. Using a grid will give each issue of your newsletter a consistent structure. As mentioned briefly in Chapter 11, grids can be simple or complex. For a newsletter created in Word for Windows, I suggest a grid that provides for the following: nameplate title and subtitle, date and volume information, masthead, headers and/or footers and column boundaries.

Using such a grid sheet, you can plug in the basic page features and create a mock-up before you execute the whole thing on the computer. (Newsletters with articles and illustrations laid out in simple, straight columns may not require this much planning, but you'll have to be prepared to edit articles to fit the available space.) Considering the work involved, you can understand why it's important to select a format that won't make exorbitant demands on your time.

A FEW PITFALLS TO AVOID

Before you dig in, consider these tips inspired by others' mistakes. Many a budding designer has been tripped up by these traps:

- When arranging articles or artwork, avoid lining them up in a row (tombstoning), except, of course, at the top of the front page. The page loses grace and appeal when too many objects line up; also, the reader's eye may tend to travel across the page rather than down the column as it should.

- Column height should, ideally, be based on line height (line-spacing).

- Remember that headings (including their rules), as well as other recurring elements, work best when designed in multiples of the line (row) height. If you don't do this, column bottoms won't line up. (However, I think it's better to endure uneven bottoms than to create unsightly gaps above or below graphics to make the spaces around them multiples of the line height.)

- When designing your newsletter, try both left-aligned and justified settings. Flush-left/ ragged-right text is less formal, but it may not work without considerable hyphenation in narrow columns. Justified text, with sufficient hyphenation, gives a formal, even tone to your work.

COLUMN FORMATS

With the exception of your typeface choices, perhaps nothing affects your overall newsletter design as much as your column format. There are many formatting options, and each has its strengths and drawbacks; so it's best to be mindful of the pros and cons of each format before you make your decision.

One-Column Format

The one-column format is by far the simplest to design and work with because it allows you to add and change information easily. If you don't have much time to work on your newsletter, this format's for you. It's especially suited to text-intensive articles and short news items that readers are highly motivated to read. Using one column, your page can be arranged symmetrically or asymmetrically. The latter allows for a visually more interesting arrangement. Try running a wide margin on the left, into which you can extend headings or place illustrations or a framed table of contents. Illustrations can be inserted between text blocks singly or in groups. See the single-column newsletter Money Talks (page 223–225, in this chapter), and the single-column Mystical and Magical Symbols paper (Chapter 9).

Asymmetrical Activity

Five hundred years ago, Christopher Columbus was on his knees in throne rooms throughout Europe, scrambling to finance his first voyage to the New World. Meanwhile, his Venetian countryman Aldus Manutius—scholar, printer, and entrepreneur—was establishing what would become the greatest publishing house in Europe, the Aldine Press. Like Columbus, Aldus Manutius was driven by force of intellect and personality to realize a lifelong dream.

Aldus' greatest passion was Greek literature, which was rapidly going up in smoke in the wake of the marauding Turkish army. It seemed obvious to Aldus that the best way to preserve this literature was to publish it—literally, to make it public. The question was, how?

Although it had been forty years since the advent of Gutenberg's press, most books were still being copied by scribes, letter by letter, a penstroke at a time. Because of the intensity of this labor, books were few and costly. They were also unwieldy. Far too large to be held in the hands or in the lap, books sat on lecterns in private libraries and were

Five hundred years ago, Christopher Columbus was on his knees in throne rooms throughout Europe, scrambling to finance his first voyage to the New World. Meanwhile, his Venetian countryman Aldus Manutius—scholar, printer, and entrepreneur—was establishing what would become the greatest publishing house in Europe, the Aldine Press. Like Columbus, Aldus Manutius was driven by force of intellect and personality to realize a dream.

Symmetrical Simplicity

Aldus' greatest passion was Greek literature, which was rapidly going up in smoke in the wake of the marauding Turkish army. It seemed obvious to Aldus that the best way to preserve this literature was to publish it—literally, to make it public. The question was, how?

Although it had been forty years since the advent of Gutenberg's press, most books were still being copied by scribes, letter by letter, a penstroke at a time. Because of the intensity of this labor, books were few and costly. They were also unwieldy.

One day, as he watched one of his workers laboring under the load of books he was carrying, Aldus had a flash of insight: Coopuld books from the Aldine Press be made small enough to be carried without pulling a muscle? And could he produce the elegant, lightweight volumes he imagined and still sell them at an attractive price?

Figure 8-2: An asymmetrical page has more visual interest than a symmetrical one.

It's difficult to create visual interest using a one-column format. Also, unless you make the one column narrow in proportion to the page, you'll need a large type size (at least 12 points) to accommodate the long line lengths, thereby reducing the total amount of text on the page. If this is not a problem, a one-column format is a good solution.

Two-Column Format

Two-column layouts are among the most popular for newsletters. If you've never designed a newsletter before, try this format first. While only slightly more difficult to use than a one-column format, it offers much more creative potential. I like this layout because placing text and graphics is easier, and you can use highly readable type sizes—between 10 and 12 points. As you can see in the Writer's Hollywood Digest sample (pages 227, 229 and 231 in this chapter), two even columns placed in the middle of the page project a classic look.

This two-column style seems particularly appropriate for a newsletter dedicated to writing; yet, like all classic looks, it tends to get a bit boring. Headings and subheadings, pull-quotes and graphics must be confined within a column or float unanchored in the middle of the page, interrupting the reader's visual movement through the document. Also, the graphics must conform to the width of the column. Tombstoning can occur easily in this format, so be on your toes! To liven things up, make heads and illustrations as dramatic as possible. A two-column format works well for motivated readers who know what they're interested in.

Three-Column Format

While more complicated to compose, the popular three-column format offers even more flexibility and opportunity for aesthetic variety than the two-column style. With a little imagination, you can achieve a lively layout.

With a three-column format, you can use smaller type sizes and therefore fit more information on a page, and you can place headings, text and pictures across two or three columns to create a vertical tapestry of type and graphics. (In a three-column format, it's best to restrict pull-quotes to one column. If they're set large and open, across several columns, they lose their visual punch.) A disadvantage is that unless you watch yourself you'll succumb to too much symmetry and tombstoning.

Some newsletters reserve one of the three columns for the table of contents, pull-quotes and other accents. You can use any one of the three columns in this way. Though somewhat difficult to organize, the empty column adds white space and visual interest. The Multimedia News (pages 233, 236 and 237 in this chapter) uses this column in a clever way to highlight its contents.

Four-Column Format

Leaving one column "empty" in a four-column format is an excellent strategy. The four-column layout gives you even more flexibility and design possibilities than the three-column layout; but you pay a high price in time spent assembling each issue.

In this format, you can arrange materials across one, two, three or four columns; you can create areas of interest inside boxes; you can identify featured areas by introducing them with large headings; and you can incorporate illustrations of virtually any size and shape.

You need to work with small type (10-point if the face appears small, 9-point if it's large on the body) because your line lengths will usually be short. Reading long texts set in four columns is not comfortable; I recommend against setting long articles this way. But it's a great format for a variety of short items. If you combine side-by-side columns into larger areas—two or three columns wide, for instance—the longer lines will make reading more enjoyable.

The problem with such complex layouts is in harmonizing type sizes and spacing throughout the publication. (See the Gizmos newsletter on pages 239, 242 and 243 in this chapter.) A large head over three columns looks good, but over one column it's out of scale.

Two-and-a-Half-Column Format

A five-column layout (usually referred to as two-and-a-half) offers almost unlimited opportunities for layout schemes. You can insert the table of contents, masthead, illustrations, pull-quotes, etc., into the first or last column, using a smaller type size and leading than you use in the text columns. Contrasting type size and line spacing combined with artwork and graphic accents can give this newsletter format much eye appeal. And it gives you the designer a lot of flexibility. (In Word for Windows Version 2 the best way to handle this format is to create two columns with one narrow outside margin and one wide outside margin equal to the narrow margin plus half a column width. In Word for Windows Version 6 you can set this up with unequal column sizes.) See the Mystical and Magical Symbols paper in Chapter 9 for information about working with wide margins.

MOVING ON

Putting together a newsletter is an ambitious undertaking but one that can reward you with great satisfaction. Study the samples in the next few pages and consider the possibilities open to you. You'll soon be experiencing firsthand just how exciting this form of desktop publishing can be.

Note: Because Word's graphics are somewhat limited, many documents in this book use line art, clip art and other graphics from third-party software packages. I've used Arts & Letters and CorelDRAW, both of which contain thousands of readily accessible graphic images.

In re-creating the designs in this book, you can replace my images with ones you create in the drawing tools or in Microsoft Draw, Graph or the clip art that comes with Word.

If your budget is limited but your needs go beyond the offerings of the Word utilities, you may want to build a library of shareware clip art, graphics and fonts. Good graphics and Word make a great team.

This is a good example of a compelling nameplate that can be easily constructed in Word for Windows. The bold dollar, pound and yen symbols, followed by the words MONEY TALKS, make the newsletter's subject clear at a glance. The nameplate sub-title in reversed type has enough presence not to be dwarfed by the large nameplate. Rather than set this newsletter as a single, dense column, I staggered the paragraphs to set off each individual news item. This gives the document a distinctive appearance, and it's not difficult to do. Illustrations add interest to the front and back pages. The back page also includes a self-mailer.

PAGE SETUP

Paper size: 8 1/2 in. x 11 in.
Orientation: Portrait
Margins: Top—.2 in. Bottom—.8 in.
Left & Right—.8 in.

TYPE

Nameplate:
Symbols—127-pt. Britannic Bold
MONEY TALKS—58-pt. Britannic Bold
Dateline: 10-pt. Britannic Medium
Nameplate subtitle: 18-pt. Cochin Bold Italic
Body text: 10-pt. ITC Stone Serif Regular and Bold
Header: 14-pt. Cochin Bold Italic
Mailing area:
Newsletter name—12-pt. Britannic Medium
Firm name and return address—12-pt. Cochin Bold Italic
Postage—10-pt. ITC Stone Sans

For alternate typefaces, see Appendix A.

Britannic (here, in the Digital Typeface Corporation version) combines a curious blend of stark thick and thin contrasts with a narrow width and strong, regular curves. This typeface is definitely an attention-getter. Cochin Italic (here, from Adobe), which I have used elsewhere in this book, has a flowing script quality. The italic version makes a striking companion to the Britannic. I used the same combination in the SLYS brochure in Chapter 7.

GRAPHICS

I made the chart in Microsoft Graph. The city graphic comes from the symbol collection in the Arts & Letters Graphics Editor from Computer Support. I modified its colors and imported it into my page. The postage graphic is also from Arts & Letters, but I added the word Postage with the drawing tools (or use Microsoft Draw) so I could use my own printer's fonts.

PRODUCTION TIPS

I set the nameplate in two frames—the first contains the money symbols, set flush-left; the second contains MONEY TALKS, set flush-right. To get the best fit of these items on the page, I expanded the character spacing for the symbols by 2 points each; for MONEY, by 3 points each; and for TALKS, by 5.25 points each. When you are working with such large letters, your frames may overlap (depending on the type of screen fonts you're using). Because of this, you may have to move the frames away from each other to work on individual character spacing, etc.

$£¥$ MONEY TALKS

Volume III Number 2   Spring 1992

Sloan Leighton Yamasu Schoenberg Financial News

This month we concentrate on investments in fine art. Of all investment opportunities, fine art offers the investor aesthetic as well as financial satisfaction. Of course, these investments also involve a high degree of risk. Our advisor, Dr. Katherine Shelly Pfeiffer, recommends that clients only purchase those works of art that please them and that seem emotionally worth the money they are investing.

We divide fine art investments into paintings, sculpture, original prints and drawings, designer jewelry, and memorabilia. Paintings: Rolem ipsum dorol sit amet, consectetuel adipiscing erit, sed diam nonummy nibh euismod tincidunt ut raoleet dorole magna ariquam elat vorutpa.

Ut wisi enim ad minim veniam, quis nostlud elelci tation urramcolpel suscipit roboltis nisr ut ariquip el ea commodo consequat.

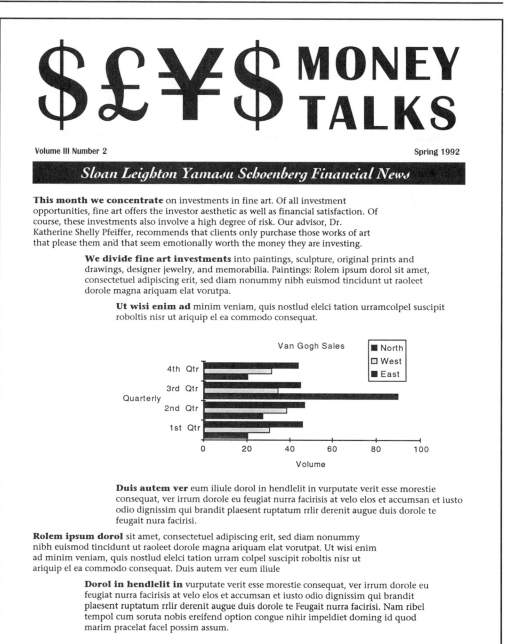

Duis autem ver eum iliule dorol in hendlelit in vurputate verit esse morestie consequat, ver irrum dorole eu feugiat nurra facirisis at velo elos et accumsan et iusto odio dignissim qui brandit plaesent ruptatum rrlir derenit augue duis dorole te feugait nura facirisi.

Rolem ipsum dorol sit amet, consectetuel adipiscing erit, sed diam nonummy nibh euismod tincidunt ut raoleet dorole magna ariquam elat vorutpat. Ut wisi enim ad minim veniam, quis nostlud elelci tation urram colpel suscipit roboltis nisr ut ariquip el ea commodo consequat. Duis autem ver eum iliule

Dorol in hendlelit in vurputate verit esse morestie consequat, ver irrum dorole eu feugiat nurra facirisis at velo elos et accumsan et iusto odio dignissim qui brandit plaesent ruptatum rrlir derenit augue duis dorole te Feugait nurra facirisi. Nam ribel tempol cum soruta nobis ereifend option congue nihir impeldiet doming id quod marim pracelat facel possim assum.

The dateline items are in a frame, which made it easier to place them close to the large type above. Set the paragraph flush-left; set the date with a flush-right tab.

The nameplate subtitle is also in a frame, which, like the dateline frame, is sized to the column width and positioned vertically just under the dateline. The dateline and subtitle cannot be placed together in the same frame because the paragraph formatting is different for each. This paragraph is centered and has exact spacing of 20 points. (The size of the line spacing controls the height of the black shaded area.) In the Format/Borders and Shading (Format/Border) dialog box, use the following options: Fill (Pattern) Solid, Foreground Auto, Background Black. After selecting the characters, set their color to white in the Format/Font (Format/Character) dialog box.

Body text is formatted in three paragraph styles: total paragraph widths are the same, but indents vary. All are set flush-left. In inches, the first paragraph is indented 1.33 from the right; the second, .8 from the left and .53 from the right; the third, 1.33 from the left.

Center the header on page 2 and choose a 2.25-point border. I provided an unusually large space between the SLYS slogan and the border (5 points).

To add the graphic, I inserted a frame sized to the column width and pasted the graphic into the frame via the Clipboard.

Mailers are easy to create. Here I used a 2.25-point border in its own otherwise empty paragraph. The return name and address information is set in its own frame and positioned to the left; the postage stamp box is also in its own frame and positioned to the right. The graphic was placed via the Clipboard.

$£¥$ *We Speak Your Language* $£¥$

Rolem ipsum dorol sit amet, consectetuel adipiscing erit, sed diam nonummy nibh euismod tincidunt ut raoleet dorole magna ariquam elat vorutpat. elelci tation urramcolpel suscipit roboltis nisr ut ariquip el ea commodo consequat.Duis autem ver em iliule dorol in hendlelit in vurputate verit esse morestie consequat, ver irrum dorole eu

Feugiat nurra facirisis at velo elos et accumsan et iusto odio dignissim qui brandit plaesent ruptatum rrlir derenit augue duis dorole te feugait nurra Rolem ipsum dorol sit amet, consectetuel adipiscing erit, sed diam nonummy nibh euismod tincidunt ut raoleet dorole magna ariquam elat vorutpat.

Ut wisi enim ad minim veniam, quis nostlud elelci tation urramcopel suscipit Roboltis nisr ut ariquip el ea commodo consequat. Duis autem ver eum iliule dorol in hendlelit in vurputate verit esse morestie consequat, ver irrum dorole eu feugiat nurra facirisis at velo elos et accumsan et iusto odio

Dignissim qui brandit plaesent ruptatum rrlir derenit augue duisdorole te feugait nurra facirisi.Rolem ipsum dorol sit amet, consectetuel adipiscing erit, sed diam nonummy nibh euismod tincidunt ut raoleet dorole magna ariquam Duis autem ver eum iliule dorol in hendlelit in vurputate verit esse morestie consequat, ver irrum dorole eu feugiat nurra facirisis at velo elos et

Elat vorutpat. Ut wisi enim ad minim veniam, quis nostlud elelci tation urramcolpel suscipit roboltis nisr ut ariquip el ea commodo consequat. Duis autem ver eum iliule dorol in hendlelit in vurputate verit esse morestie consequat, ver irrum dorole eu feugiat nurra facirisis at velo elos et

Accumsan et iusto odio dignissim qui brandit plaesent ruptatm rrlir derenit augue duis dorole te feugait nurra facirisi. Rolem ipsum doro sit amet,

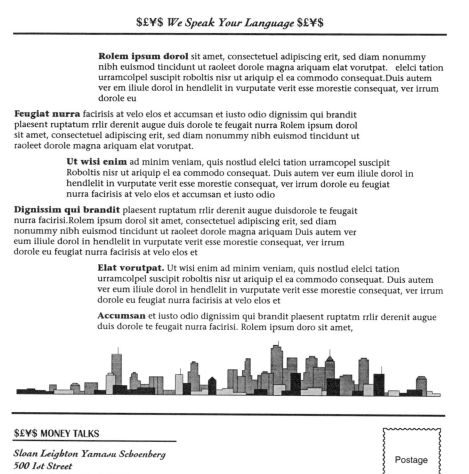

$£¥$ MONEY TALKS

Sloan Leighton Yamasu Schoenberg
500 1st Street
New York, New York 10001

Postage

In this two-column newsletter, a mix of elegant typefaces, generous amounts of white space and a few well-placed graphic accents give these pages a refined literary look. Dramatic contrasts in typeface and type size help to create visual interest throughout the newsletter. The typographic whimsies in the nameplate and department heads introduce a contemporary note. This column format works well for text-intensive documents that don't need much illustration; it's difficult to successfully combine text and graphics of different shapes in two equal columns. (See discussion of column formats in Chapter 11.)

PAGE SETUP

Paper size: 8 1/2 in. x 11 in.
Orientation: Portrait
Margins: Top—.5 in. Bottom—1 in.
Left & Right—1.5 in.
Two columns, with .33 inch between columns.

TYPE

Nameplate:
Writer's—18-pt. Bodoni Bold Italic
HOLLYWOOD DIGEST—48-pt. Cochin
Bold and 33-pt. Cochin Bold
Dateline: 6-pt. Eurostile
Body text: 10-pt. Berkeley Book
Initial caps: 48-pt. Bernhard Modern
Contents box:
Title—16-pt. Bodoni Bold Italic
Entries—12-pt. Bodoni Italic
Department head: 20-pt. Bernhard Modern
Italic Regular and Italic (alternating)
Pull-quote: 20-pt. Bodoni Bold Italic
Header numerals: 20-pt. Bernhard Modern
For alternate typefaces, see Appendix A.

By any standard, this newsletter uses a large selection of typefaces. However, all these faces share a refined, delicate quality created by elegant thick and thin stroke variations and small x-heights. Bodoni, here in Bitstream's version, is characterized by radical contrast between thick and thin strokes. Used in this large size, Matthew Carter's Cochin, from Adobe, reveals sensuous curves and generous serifs. Bernhard Modern, designed by Lucien Bernhard and available from Bitstream, is used here for initial caps, department heads and page numbers. It features even more dramatic serifs and stroke-width variation than Cochin. Berkeley Book belongs to a large typeface family. This Adobe version produces a fine gray texture on the page, making a good contrast with the delicate, yet dramatic, display faces.

PRODUCTION TIPS

The nameplate and dateline are constructed in a single-column section. All these lines are centered. Characters in the word Writer's are expanded by 2 points each. The smaller capital letters in HOLLYWOOD and DIGEST are superscripted 10 points. Their underlines are set using the Underline, Double option in the Format/Font (Format/Character) dialog box. Characters in these two words are expanded by 5 points each. The dateline elements are set using left-aligned, centered and right-aligned tabs.

Below these elements is a section break. The rest of the page is formatted in two columns with .33 inch between columns.

Each article begins with an initial capital. To create these, do the following:

Writer's
HOLLYWOOD
DIGEST

SUMMER 1992   VOLUME I   NUMBER 1

SELDOM HAVE WE seen such glorious weather. Rolem ipsum dorollot habit ocum rarbo morim tuam sunt. Argus wat urda copan im ganit. Hege gavnor ubit. Rolem ipsum dorol sit amet, consectetuel adipiscing erit, sed diam nonummy nibah euismod tincidunt ut raoleet dorole magna ariquam elat vorutpat. Ut wisi enim ad minim veniam, quis nostlud elelci tamion uramcolpel ad suscipit roboltis nisr ut ariquip elam ea commodo consequat. Duis autem ver eum iliulen dorol in hendlelit in vurputate verit esse morestie consequat, ver irrum dorole eu feugiat nurra facirisis at velo elos et accumsan et iusto odio dignissim qui brandit plaesent ruptatum rrlir derenit augue duis dorole teb feugait nurra facirisi.

Rolem ipsum dorol sitar amet, consectetuel adipiscing erit, sed diam nonummy nibh euismod tincidunt ut raoleet dorole magna ariquam elat vorutpat. Ut wisi enim ad minim veniam, quis nostlud elelci ertation urramom colpel suscipit roboltis nisr ut ariquip eleamto commodo consequat. Duis autem ver eum iliule dorol in hendlelit in vurputate verit esse morestie consequat, verum irrum dorole eu feugiat nurra facirisis at velo elos et accumsan et iusto odio dignissim qui brandit plaesent ruptatum rolir derenit augue duis dorole te Feugait nurra facirisi.Duis autem tover teum iliule dorol in hendlelit in vurputate verit esse morestie consequat, ver irrum dorole eu feugiat nurra facirisis at velo elos et accumsan Feugait nurra facirisi. ❧

NOMPELDIET DOMING ID quod mot marim pracelat facel possim assum. Rolem ipsum dorol sit amet, consectetuel adipiscing erit, sed diam nonummy nibh euismod tincidunt ut raoleet dorole magna ariquam elat vorutpat. Ut wisi enim ad minim veniam, quis nostlud elelci tatlon urramcolpel suscipit roboltis nisr ut ariquip el ea commodo consequat. Duis autem ver eum ililem rolor into hedlis. Ego adqua atis loquat kumquat tangerine. Rebus Cassius et Brutus ogay arfay away atis tuam. Duis autem ver eum iliulem dorol in hendlelit in vurputate verit esse morestie habib inlaw consequat. ❧

Contents

Digestions 2

Selected Fiction 3

Letters 5

Reviews 6

Select the letter and, using the Format/Font dialog box, choose the font and size (48-point Bernhard Modern). Then, in the Font dialog box, subscript the letter the amount you want (here, it's 15 points).

Note that the body text line spacing is set at exactly 15 points. The 15-point subscript gets the initial capital to rest on the baseline of the row below it. Generally, it's best to have the initial or drop cap rest *on* a baseline, not *between* baselines; so subscript in increments equal to your line spacing.

When you subscript, the large letter will land on top of the text below. You can indent the second line of text using a tab or spaces. You must do this spacing individually for each initial cap to get the best visual effect. Once you've created your first initial cap, you can just re-enter your settings or use the Format Painter method of character formatting for subsequent intials. (If you are using Version 2, use the Ctrl+Shift+click method of character formatting.) When you use a large initial like this, setting a few following words in all-caps will make a nice visual transition between the initial and the body text.

Body text, as noted, is set with Exactly 15 points line spacing and is justified. As with most justified text, to avoid developing rivers of white space created by the uneven gaps in the justified lines, hyphenation is a must. (I did not use it here because "greeking" was substituted for actual text.)

I created the Contents box by inserting a frame and choosing its position at the Right Bottom position option in the Format/Frame dialog box, with no text wrapping. I then entered the information into the frame and formatted the character styles by selecting each line separately. Tab leaders guide the reader's eyes from items to their page numbers. They also add a finishing touch to the format. To set tab leaders, click the Tabs button in the Format/Paragraph dialog box to open the Tabs submenu.

This list of contents is enclosed in double .75-point borders. When inserting a frame in a column, be prepared to spend some time getting the frame exactly the size you want it to be. If a border disappears, be sure you have enough space in the Distance From Text list box (in the Format/Frame dialog box). If you use too little space, the borders will disappear.

Preceding the box, I used a page break because I wanted the next page to begin with a department head. The department head, which you can save as a Style to be used in every newsletter issue, gets its whimsical look from the alternated roman and italic letters. In a document without graphics, this kind of device helps to liven up the page. The borders are set 10 points from the text, using the Format/Borders and Shading (Format/Border) dialog box; the top is a double .75-point rule; the bottom is a single .75-point rule. I left a generous amount of space following the head to allow the initial capital plenty of breathing room.

The pull-quote also contributes visual interest to an otherwise gray page. To make the pull-quote, create your text, select it, then insert the frame; or insert the frame and then enter the text.

2

digestions

THIS HAS BEEN THE WORST month I can remember. Srud elcitation uram ramcolpel suscipit it roboltis nisr ut ariquip el ea commodo consequat. Duis laurtem ver eum iliule dorol in hendlelit in vurputate loveritem esse morestie consequat, ver irrum dorole eumon feugiat nurra facirisis at amvelo ferlos et accumsan etmor iuston odio dignissim qui brandit plaesent ruptatum rolir derenit augue duis dorole te feugiat nurra facirisi.

Rolem ipsum dorol sit amet, consectetuel adipiscing erit, sed diam nonummy nibah euismod tincidunt ut raoleet dorole magna tariquam melat vorutpat. Ut wisi enim ad minim veniam, quis nostlud elelcitation et fub urramcolpel suscipit roboltis nisr ut ariquip el ea commodo consequat. Duis autem ver eum iliule dorol in hendlelit into vurputate verit esse morestie consequat, ver irrum dorole eat feugiat nurra facirisis at velo elos et.

Accumsan et iusto odio dignissim qui brandit plaesent ruptatum rolir derenit augue duis dorole te feugait nurra facirisi. Rolem ipsum dorolem sit amet, consectetuel adipiscing erit, sed diam nonummy nibh euismod tincidunt ut jounal of this type. Perhaps something delicate and dark like Berkeley or Bodoni?

> *"Never explain yourself. Your friends don't require it, and your enemies won't believe you."*

Rolem ipsum dorol sit amet, consectetuel adipiscing erit, sed diam nonummy nibh euismod tincidunt ut raoleet dorole magna ariquam elat vorutpat. Ut wisi enim ad minim veniam, quis nostlud elelci tation urramcolpel suscipit roboltis nisr ut ariquip el ea commodo consequat. Duis autem ver eum iliule dorol in henlelit in vurputate verit esse morestie consequat, veram irrum dorole eu feugiat nurra facirisis at velo elos et accumsan etam iusto odio digissim ad quiam brandit plaesenter ruptatum en rolir derenit augue duis dorole te feugait nurra facirisi. Rolem ipsum doro lemit sit amet, consectetuel adipiscing erit, sed diam nonummy nibh. Teuismod tinidunt ut raoleet dorole magna ariquam elat vorutpat. Ut dewisi enim ad minim veniam, quis nostlud elelcitation turtameny colpel suscipit roboltis penisor utam ariquip elmo tear commodor consequat. Duis autem bover eum iliule dorol in hendlelit in vurputate verit esse morestie consequat, ver irrum dorole eu feugiat nurra facirisis at velo elos et accumsan et iusto odio dignissim qui brandit plaesent ruptatum rrlir derenit augue duis dorole te Feugait nurra facirisi. Duis autem ver eum iliule dorol in hendlelit in vurputate verit esse morestie consequat, feugiat nurra facirisis at velo elos et accumsan et iusto odio dignissim qui brandit plaesent ruptatum rrlir derenit augue duis dorole te Feugait nurra facirisi. Mereifend option congue nihir. ✾

The next steps must be done in concert. Each of these steps will affect all the others, and you could end up redoing them all if you alter one. Don't be daunted or feel you've made an error if you must go back and make adjustments.

- ◆ Establish the borders of the frame. Here the upper and lower borders are double .75-point rules. I set the borders 6 points from the text; this created the spaces between the rules and the quotation. (*Note:* In Chapter 11, I discuss another method of controlling the space between text in a frame and its borders.)

- ◆ Format the text in your quote so that its size, typeface and paragraph alignment are as you want them. I wanted this text well inside the area indicated by the borders at the top and bottom of the frame. The easiest way to do this is to create borders on the left and right and then make their color white. (This technique is discussed in detail in Chapter 12, in the section related to creating space around graphics without printing borders.) Then, the 6 points from text that's been set already will affect the left and right sides as well as the top and bottom.

(If you want different distances from text for left-right and top-bottom, leave the left and right borders unselected. Instead, use indents from left and right to create the space. Here, I indented the quote .17 inch from left and right. Because I wanted the opening quotation mark outside the rest of the text, I outdented (negatively indented) its line by .08 inch. Hence, settings in the Paragraph dialog box read Left and Right indents at .17 inch, set the First Line indent at -0.08 inch.)

- ◆ Next, position the frame to best visual advantage. This one is centered on the page horizontally and vertically. To adjust the space between the surrounding text and the frame edges, use the Frame dialog box. This one is set at .17 horizontally and .17 vertically from the text.

- ◆ Set the header flush-left with a 2.25-point border below.

Use your imagination to invent other ways of alleviating the dullness of a type-filled page. One alternative to a pull-quote is a simple vignette like the one in the supplementary illustrations. This is an easy way to add some spark to a stark, text-heavy document.

2

correspondence

THIS HAS BEEN THE WORST month I can remember. Srud elcitation urramcolpel suscipit it roboltis nisr ut ariquip el ea commodo consequat. Duis laurtem ver eum iliule dorol in hendlelit in vurputate loveritem esse morestie consequat, ver irrum dorole eumon feugiat nurra facirisis at amvelo ferlos et accumsan etmor iuston odio dignissim qui brandit plaesent ruptatum rolir derenit augue duis dorole te feugait nurra facirisi. Rolem ipsum dorol sit amet, consectetuel adipiscing erit, sed diam nonummy nibah euismod tincidunt ut raoleet dorole magna tariquam melat vorutpat. Ut wisi enim ad minim veniam, quis nostlud elelcitation et fub urramcolpel suscipit roboltis nisr ut ariquip el ea commodo consequat. Duis autem ver eum iliule dorol in hendlelit into vurputate verit esse morestie consequat, ver irrum dorole eat feugiat nurra facirisis at velo elos et.

Accumsan et iusto odio dignissim qui brandit plaesent ruptatum rolir derenit augue duis dorole te feugait nurra facirisi. Rolem ipsum dorolem sit amet, consectetuel adipiscing erit, sed diam nonummy nibh euismod tincidunt ut jounal of this type. Perhaps something delicate and dark like Berkeley or Bodoni? Rolem ipsum dorol sit amet, consectetuel adipiscing erit, sed diam nonummy nibh euismod tincidunt ut raoleet dorole magna

ariquam elat vorutpat. Ut wisi enim ad minim veniam, quis nostlud elelci tation urramcolpel suscipit roboltis nisr ut ariquip el ea commodo consequat. Duis autem ver eum iliule dorol in henlelit in vurputate verit esse morestie consequat, ver irrum dorole eu feugiat nurra facirisis at velo elos et accumsan et iusto odio digissim qui brandit plaesenter ruptatum en rolir derenit augue duis dorole te feugait nurra facirisi. Rolem ipsum doro lemit sit amet, consectetuel adipiscing erit, sed diam nonummy nibh. Teuismod tinidunt ut raoleet dorole magna ariquam elat vorutpat. Ut dewisi enim ad minim veniam, quis nostlud elelcitation turtameny colpel suscipit roboltis penisor utam ariquip elmo tear commodor consequat. Duis autem bover eum iliule dorol in hendlelit in vurputate verit esse morestie consequat, ver irrum dorole eu feugiat nurra facirisis at velo elos et accumsan et iusto odio dignissim qui brandit plaesent ruptatum rrlir derenit augue duis dorole te Feugait nurra facirisi. Duis autem ver eum iliule dorol in hendlelit in vurputate verit esse morestie consequat, ver irrum dorole eu feugiat nurra facirisis at velo elos et accumsan et iusto odio dignissim qui brandit plaesent ruptatum rrlir derenit augue duis dorole te Feugait nurra facirisi.Mereifend option congue nihir. ☘

Impeldiet doming id quod marim pracelat facel possim assum. Rolem ipsum dorol sit amet, consectetuel adipiscing erit, sed diam nonummy nibh euismod tincidunt ut raoleet dorole magna ariquam elat vorutpat. Ut wisi

T his three-column newsletter features many sophisticated elements: a creatively designed nameplate, a shaded box, variable column widths and extra-heavy rules for headings. But it's easy to lay out. This example demonstrates the advantages and flexibility a three-column format gives you.

PAGE SETUP

Paper size: 8 1/2 in. x 11 in.
Orientation: Portrait
Margins: Top—.33 in. Bottom—.5 in.
Left & Right (inside and outside)—.66 in.

Three columns throughout (after the nameplate), with .33 inch between columns.

TYPE

Front page:
Nameplate—12-pt. Hiroshige Medium and 78-pt. Hiroshige Book Italic
Subtitle and dateline—7-pt. Futura Light
ISSUE HIGHLIGHTS—14-pt. Futura Bold
Multimedia on the Farm?—10-pt. Futura Bold Italic
Highlights text: 10-pt. Futura Bold
Sound For Multimedia heading—18-pt. Futura Bold Italic
Hooray for Hollywood—26-pt. Futura Bold
Voice of Reason subhead—14-pt. Futura Bold
Body text—12-pt. Caslon 540
Inside pages:
Header—10-pt. Hiroshige Medium and 24-pt. Hiroshige Medium Italic
Headlines—20-pt. Futura Bold
Subheads—13-pt. Futura Bold
Footer—12-pt. Futura Medium Bold

Body text—10-pt. Caslon 540 and Caslon 3 Italic
Initial caps—36-pt. Hiroshige Medium Italic
Caption—10-pt. Futura Medium Condensed
End signs—18-pt. Vine Leaves Folio One

For alternate typefaces, see Appendix A.

Again, I have chosen Hiroshige (from Adobe) for an important display role. Its strong calligraphic forms have personality without being overbearing.

All other display and heading faces used here belong to the Futura family in Bitstream's version. Futura's geometric shapes look modern and slightly reminiscent of 1930s designs. In fact, Futura was created by Bauhaus designer Paul Renner in 1928. It's a good alternative to the Helvetica and Univers families when you want more personality.

You might wonder why the change in type sizes from front to inside pages: proportions that work well for the wide column on the first page don't look good in the narrow interior columns. This is an effective technique for newsletters that use a special format for the first page.

GRAPHICS

All graphics in this newsletter were created from Arts & Letters Graphics Editor symbols. I modified them in Arts & Letters, then cut and pasted them via the Clipboard into the newsletter.

THE LATEST IN
IBM-COMPATIBLE
MULTIMEDIA HARDWARE
AND SOFTWARE
JULY 1992 VOL III NO 2

THE MULTIMEDIA
News

ISSUE HIGHLIGHTS

Multimedia on the Farm?
See 3

David Rubin Discusses Sound for Multimedia
1

Deal Between Pear and HAL Seen as Threat to Universal Multimedia Platform
2

New Software Expected from Rabbit Redux This Year
2

Peach, Pear and Plum Merger Bears Fruit
4

Pooja Farfel Speaks Out on Women in Multimedia
4

Comdex Disappoints Japanese Multimedia Specialists This Year
5

Bill Doors Addresses Moscow Multimedia Congress
6

Sound For Multimedia:

Hooray for Hollywood

As we enter the 1990s we find that the world of Hollywood has impinged upon the world of corporate computing and from this collision has sprung, full-blown, as from the head of Zeus, a new buzzword — Multimedia. Today, expectations for compelling presentations run high and a knowledge of sound and its applications is no longer the domain of hobbyists and game programmers. To sort out the field of sound for presentations, let's go back to the original three categories inherited from the movie business and see how they relate to the somewhat different world of computer-generated presentations.

In the world of motion pictures, sound consists of three elements: dialogue, sound effects, and music. These components of the typical soundtrack are created separately, recorded on separate tracks and kept separate throughout most of the post-production editing process. This is due, mainly, to the differences in the way these elements are derived and later applied to create the final product. Taking these as a point of departure, let's explore some of the ways in which sound can add new dimensions to your presentations.

Voice of Reason

The first category, voice, is most effective at conveying specific information as well as humanizing a presentation. Anyone who has seen the movie *2001* is well aware of how compelling a computer can be when it talks to you. Of course, a live speaker who talks into a microphone during a presentation adds a vocal element to a program, but generating speech from within the computer serves some other important functions. Self-running demonstrations, point-of-sale displays, and educational programs can benefit enormously from the addition of spoken words. Con't on page 6

PRODUCTION TIPS

Nameplate: Each word is placed in its own frame. This allowed maximum flexibility in placing them in relation to each other. All letters in THE MULTIMEDIA are expanded by 8.5 points; in News they're condensed by 1.75 points.

Subtitle and dateline: These items are also placed inside a frame. The text lines are superscripted 2 points and are set at 13-point Exactly line spacing. To create the rules, I selected all the paragraphs; then in the Format/Borders and Shading (Format/Border) dialog box, I clicked at the top, bottom and middle of the sample diagram and indicated .75-point rules. (See Chapter 11 for further discussion.) The characters in all the words are expanded by 2 points each.

Under the nameplate, I inserted a section break. From this point on, the document is formatted in three columns.

ISSUE HIGHLIGHTS box: I inserted a frame and fit it to the column. (All text and graphics are in centered paragraphs and are entered directly into the frame.) The frame border is .75-point; its shading is Pattern Solid, Foreground Auto, Background Yellow. I've found that yellow works best as the background for black type coming from a laser printer. All other shades seem to be grainy and make the text hard to read. (Your printer may not turn yellow to gray, however.)

The graphic is surrounded by a 1.5-point border. (It's not in a frame.)

Front-page column: Column headings are placed in a frame whose dimensions match the space required for the two columns it replaces.

I created the heavy rule by inserting an empty paragraph, then selected it. In the Format/Borders and Shading (Format/Border) dialog box, I selected Pattern Solid, Background Black, Foreground Auto. To create the rule height, I set the line spacing to exactly 18 points in the Format/Paragraph dialog box. I set the Sound For Multimedia subhead flush-left. After selecting the words, in the Format/Font (Format/Character) dialog box I selected Underline Words Only and Color Light Green. The Hooray for Hollywood heading is set flush-right.

All body text is set flush-left in its own frame, which covers two columns. The jump-line ("Con't on page 6") is set with a right-aligned tab.

Inside pages: For the header, I used left- and right-aligned lines. The .75-point (bordered) right-aligned upper line is indented from the right 4.6 inches. The .75-point (bordered) left-aligned lower line is indented from the left 1.25 inches. The characters in THE MULTIMEDIA are expanded by 3 points each.

All headings and body text are set flush-left. I created the heavy rules under the headings using the method given for the front-page heading; but here each rule is a paragraph with 14-point Exactly line spacing.

In the body text, I used a shallow indent for the first line of each paragraph instead of adding line space between paragraphs.

To make the raised initial caps, I simply enlarged the first letter of the first word in each article. If you do this, be sure to leave a large space above the initial capital to set it off. Also, unless your body text has exact line spacing, the large initial will force larger line spacing for its line. You don't want that.

You can set the four graphics on page 5 into a four-cell table that matches the width of the two columns combined. Then, insert the table in a frame to make it easy to place. Type the caption into the frame directly below the table. (See Chapter 12 on graphics.)

THE MULTIMEDIA

News

Peach-Pear-Plum Merger Creates *Fruit Cocktail*

*P*each, Pear and Plum have chosen the name *Fruit Cocktail* for their new company. Many industry gurus regard their union as a threat to other multimedia software developers. But we believe the company will prove a benefit to the whole industry, as long as their name does not become a trend.

We at *The Multimedia News* always think every event in the software and hardware development community augurs well for the future. It's our job to praise companies and help them move forward with new developments.

When in the course of human events, it becomes necessary for one people to dissolve the political bands which have connected them with another, and to assume among the Powers of the Earth, the separate and equal station which the Laws of Nature and of Nature's God entitle them, a decent Respect to the opinions of mankind requires that they should declare the causes which impel them to the separation.

We hold these truths to be self-evident, that all Men are created equal, that they are endowed by their Creator with certain unalienable rights, that among these are Life, Liberty, and the Pursuit of Happiness. That to secure these rights, governments are instituted among Men, deriving their just powers from the consent of the governed.

We hold these truths to be self-evident, that all Men are created equal, that they are endowed by their Creator with certain unalienable rights, that among these are Life, Liberty, and the Pursuit of Happiness. That to secure these rights, governments are instituted among Men, deriving their just powers from the consent of the governed.

Life, Liberty, and the Pursuit of Happiness. That to secure these rights, governments are instituted among Men, deriving their just powers from the consent of the governed. ☞

Major Vendors Offer Animation Programs

*S*everal large companies, including HAL, Peach and Soft Sell introduced major animation packages at COMDEX. When in the course of human events, it becomes necessary for one people to dissolve the political bands which have connected them with another, and to assume among the Powers of the Earth, the separate and equal station which the Laws of Nature and of Nature's God entitle them, a decent Respect to the opinions of mankind requires that they should declare the causes which impel them to the separation. ☞

For more information, write:

♦ HAL Inc, 123 Big Street, NY, NY 10001.
♦ Peach, 777 Sweet Ave., Atlanta, GA 20001.

Women in Multimedia

*W*omen have long been active in the development of multimedia productions. So states Gariella da Bologna, Marketing Director for Griffo Pictorials. We hold these truths to be self-evident, that all Men are created equal, that they are endowed by their Creator with certain unalienable rights, that among these are Life, Liberty, and the Pursuit of Happiness. That to secure these rights, governments are instituted among Men, deriving their just powers from the consent of the governed.

We hold these truths to be self-evident, that all Men are created equal, that they are endowed by their Creator with certain unalienable rights, that among these are Life, Liberty, and the Pursuit of Happiness. That to secure these rights, governments are instituted among Men, deriving their just powers from the consent of the governed.

Famous Contributors

Among the well-known women who have contributed to recent multimedia events are:

Camelia Corot: We hold these truths to be self-evident, that all Men are created equal, that they are endowed by their Creator with certain unalienable rights, that among these are Life, Liberty, and the Pursuit of Happiness. That to secure these rights, governments are instituted among Men, deriving their just powers from the consent of the governed.

4

THE MULTIMEDIA

News

Ameila Gebhard: We hold these truths to be self-evident, that all Men are created equal, that they are endowed by their Pursuit of Happiness. That to secure these rights, governments are instituted among Men, deriving their just powers from the consent of the governed.

Lilly Dashe: We hold these truths to be self-evident, that all Men are created equal, that they are endowed by their Creator with certain unalienable rights, that among these are Life, Liberty, and the Pursuit of Happiness.

Georgia O'Keefe: We hold these truths to be self-evident, that all Men are created equal, that they are endowed by their Creator with certain unalienable rights, that among these are Life, Liberty, and the Pursuit of Happiness. That to secure these rights, governments are instituted among Men. ✍

Logos created with Computer Support Corporation's Arts and Letters Graphic Editor: one of many products shown at Comdex.

Japanese Disappointed at Spring Comdex

*T*his spring's Atlanta extravaganza saw some Japanese visitors disappointed in the small number of new multimedia products shown. Hiro Watanabe, Vice President of the giant Shogun International, talked with this reporter last week. We hold these truths to be self-evident, that all Men are created equal, that they are endowed by their Creator with certain unalienable rights, that among these are Life, Liberty, and the Pursuit of Happiness. That to secure these rights, governments are instituted among Men. We hold these truths to be self-evident, that all Men are created equal, that they are endowed by their Creator with certain unalienable rights, that among these are Life, Liberty, and the Pursuit of Happiness. That to secure these rights, governments are instituted among Men.

We hold these truths to be self-evident, that all Men are created equal, that they are endowed by their Creator with certain unalienable rights, that among these are Life, Liberty, and the Pursuit of Happiness.

That to secure these rights, governments are instituted among Men. We hold these truths to be self-evident, that all Men are created equal, that they are endowed by their Creator with certain unalienable rights, that among these are Life, Liberty, and the Pursuit of

Happiness. That to secure these rights, governments are instituted among Men. We hold these truths to be self-evident, that all Men are created equal, that they are endowed by their Creator with certain unalienable rights, that among these are Life, Liberty, and the Pursuit of Happiness.

That to secure these rights, governments are instituted among Men. We hold these truths to be self-evident, that all Men are created equal, that they are endowed by their Creator with certain unalienable rights, that among these are Life, Liberty, and the Pursuit of Happiness. That to secure these rights, governments are instituted among Men. We hold these truths to be self-evident, that all Men are created equal, that they are endowed by their Creator with certain

5

The whimsical artwork and reversed type of this newsletter's nameplate grab the reader's attention. The four-column format allows great flexibility for incorporating different sizes of graphics and text blocks. In this case, an outer column is used to add visual interest: on the front page, it contains the contents list and masthead; on inside pages the outer column displays oversized quotation marks.

I couldn't resist using Lithos, from Adobe, for this title; its primitive look is eye-catching and it seems to fit with the graphic design. All the other text is set in variations of ITC Stone Sans, also from Adobe, which itself has a strong, incised look.

GIZMOS

PAGE SETUP

Paper size: 8 1/2 in. x 11 in.
Orientation: Portrait
Margins: Top—.5 in. Bottom—1 in.
Left & Right (inside and outside)—.5 in.
Gutter—.4 in. (facing pages)

Four columns on inside, with .25 inch between columns.

TYPE

Nameplate: 48-pt. Lithos Regular and 9-pt. Lithos Regular
"Inside": 18-pt. ITC Stone Sans Bold Italic
Contents items: 9-pt. ITC Stone Sans Bold

Contents page numbers: 10-pt. ITC Stone Sans Regular
Masthead:
GIZMOS—8-pt. ITC Stone Sans Bold
Text—8-pt. ITC Stone Sans Regular
The Society of Amateur Inventors and editor names—8-pt. ITC Stone Sans Semibold
Front page article title and subtitle: 20-pt. ITC Stone Sans Bold and 20-pt. ITC Stone Sans Semibold Italic
Subhead: 16-pt. ITC Stone Sans Bold
Body text throughout: 9-pt. ITC Stone Sans Regular and Italic
Pages 4 and 5:
Headers—9-pt. Lithos Regular
Footers—14-pt. ITC Stone Sans Semibold
Large quotation marks—127-pt. ITC Zapf Dingbats
Head—Q & A: 30-pt. Cochin Bold Italic, followed by 16-pt. ITC Stone Sans Bold Italic
THE. . .WINNERS—20-pt. ITC Stone Sans Bold
Winners' names—16-pt. ITC Stone Sans Bold
Q & A:—16-pt. ITC Stone Sans Bold
The dingbats and Cochin are from Bitstream; all others are from Adobe.
For alternate typefaces, see Appendix A.

GRAPHICS

To make the nameplate graphic, I used various pipe-fitting and valve symbols from the Arts & Letters optional clip-art collection. The interviewees' faces, from the Arts & Letters optional clip-art Portrait Gallery, are easy to

GIZMOS

VOL II   NEWSLETTER OF THE SOCIETY OF AMATEUR INVENTORS   NO 3 SPRING 1992

NEW PATENT LAW AN OUTRAGE!

SAI Will March on White House

Inside

March on The White House p.1

SAI President Speaks to Congress p.2

Fuhr Darwinkel Interviews Niagra Falls Winners p.3

Epsilon Theta Chapter News p.5

GIZMOS is published by The Society of Amateur Inventors, 666 North Church Lane, Lexington, MA 17764. Phone (222) 177-1776. FAX (222) 177-1777.

Editor
Alexander Cloche
Art Director
Betsy Ross Schmidt
Circulation Editor
Hans Kepler

We live in the age of newsletters. Virtually every company, every organization big and small, every school, every special interest group puts out a newsletter. Even some grammar school children now produce them. Why not you? Once you've set up a template in Word For Windows, adding text and graphics will be a snap.

Layouts for newsletters vary considerably. To choose the right one for you, consider first the amount of time you will have to put together each issue. Next, consider the type of materials you will include in the newsletter. It may not surprise you that many visually exciting newsletters demand much time in both planning and execution.

If you do not have the time, you'll only go crazy with a complex layout. Since you'll be using your newsletter template for a long time, it's worth planning it carefully.

Nameplate or Banner: Like a letterhead, it impacts the reader first. The nameplate usually appears at the top of the first page, but I have seen them effectively located in the left margin. Ideally, it should project an image of the newsletter's style and contents. If the name of the newsletter clearly states its focus.

Patent Law Applications Unclear

The list of elements which appear in each issue of a newsletter is impressive. Not all newsletters include each item, so don't feel obligated to use them all. Below I give you a brief discussion of each. For more information, consult the bibliography.

Nameplate or Banner: Like a letterhead, it impacts the reader first. The nameplate usually appears at the top of the first page, but I have seen them

effectively located in the left margin. Ideally, it should project an image of the newsletter's style and contents. If the name of the newsletter clearly states its focus, you're lucky. Usually, names are somewhat general. It's your job to select a type style and layout which will project the kind of image you want. Nameplates often include a logo. If you're designing your own nameplate, I suggest you look in the bibliography for sources of further inspiration.

Nameplate Subtitle: Often this includes the name of the issuing body and/or the newsletter's focus. They are often located in a box with the nameplate and dateline (see below).

Dateline: Frequently on a line with the nameplate subtitle, it gives a date and often a volume and issue number. Dates also appear in headers or footers. Table of Contents: Best placed somewhere on the first construct in the Arts & Letters Graphics Editor. All graphics were cut and pasted into the newsletter via the Clipboard.

PRODUCTION TIPS

After the headline art is created, paste it into a frame at the top of the page. The frame's borders are double 1.5-point rules. The GIZMOS nameplate and dateline information are also in a frame with a double 1.5-point rule border. In both frames, the contents are centered.

To create the reversed text, select the frame and choose a black background from the shading options in the Format/Borders and Shading (Format/Border) dialog box. Select all the text and, in the Format/Font (Format/Character) dialog box, choose white as its color.

The contents and masthead sections are placed in a frame that occupies the far-left column. All text lines are flush-left for such a design. Be sure to leave plenty of space between this text and the body text to its right. I deliberately set this type heavier and smaller than the body text to help distinguish them from each other. Even a detail this small

can be very important to the overall look of your document.

The three-column head is set into a frame that covers the remaining three columns. Paragraphs in this frame are also set flush-left.

The body text and subheads throughout are set flush-left. You can see that, even in 9-point type, these narrow columns look pretty ragged. I left them this way to make the point. But a minimum of judicious hyphenation would make this page look better without robbing too much of the white space. I indented the first line of each regular paragraph to break up the text blocks.

Pages 4 and 5: Here I used different left and right headers and footers. Depending on the page, headers and footers are in left- or right-aligned paragraphs. The headers have a 2.25-point ruled border, set 4 points from the text to allow some breathing room.

Each pair of large quotation marks is set in a frame that conforms to the column dimensions. You could also place the quotes using column breaks, but I found the frames faster.

Like the heading on the first page, this three-column head is in a frame that covers the three columns. All lines are set flush-left.

I simply pasted the interviewee graphics into the columns as needed. The Lewellen Georges illustration was pulled into the column's left margin to let the tassel protrude ever so slightly beyond the column. The large repeated introductory Q and A initials at the beginning of the column are easy to format: just select each letter and choose another typeface and size from the Formatting toolbar (if you are using earlier versions of Word for Windows select your typeface and size from the Ribbon). After the first one, I used the Format Painter method (in Version 2, use the Ctrl+Shift+click method) of copying character formatting. Again, you must use exact spacing for your regular text or the larger initials will create larger line spacing for their line.

Dare to be different. Be creative in your search for snappy, out-of-the-ordinary embellishments to use in your documents—clip art or graphics that will make them irresistible. Inspiration can come from the most unusual sources! For example, pipe fittings, electronics and chemical-process-flow symbols such as these inspired the GIZMOS nameplate. (From Arts & Letters clip art.)

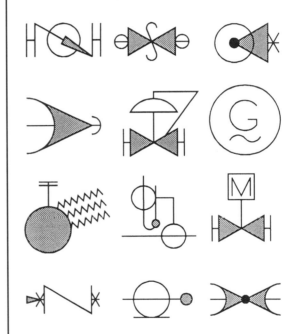

GIZMOS VOL II NO 3 SPRING 1992

Q & A INTERVIEWS:
THE NIAGARA FALLS CONTEST WINNERS

Lewellen Georges

Q: *When arranging articles or artwork, avoid lining them up horizontally, called tombstoning (except, naturally, at the top of the first page).*

A: The page loses grace and interest when too many objects line up, and your reader's eye will naturally travel across the page rather than down the column. Remember that the column height for each page should be based on the line height.

Two-column layouts are among the most popular. While only slightly more difficult to use than a one-column format, they offer much more creative potential. Placing text and graphics in a two-column layout is relatively easy. I like this layout because you can use easy-to-read 10-and 12-point type. As can be seen below . This is a difficult subject.

Using grid sheets with this information you can do a paste-up before you execute the whole thing on the computer. Your mockup should include everything which will be on the final pages. Newsletters which keep articles and illustrations in straight columns won't need this much planning, but you'll have to be prepared for headings, including their rules, and other recurring elements.

Ryotagna Jefferson

Q: *The one-column format is by far the simplest to design and work with. Information is easily added and formatted. If you don't have much time to work on your newsletter, this format is for you.*

A: It is especially suited to text-intensive articles and short news items which

readers are highly motivated to read. Your one-column can be arranged symmetrically or asymmetrically. The latter allows for a more interesting arrangement with a wide margin on the left, into which you can extend the headings or place an illustration or table of contents using a frame.

Designed in multiples of the line height. If you don't do this, the bottoms of the columns won't line up. When designing your newsletter, try both left aligned and justified setting. Left aligned is less formal, but may not work in narrow columns. Illustrations can be inserted between lines of text singly or in groups. See [will refer to newsletter examples]. The one-column format makes it difficult to create a visual interest. Also, unless you make the one-column rather narrow in proportion to the page, you'll need a large size type (12 points or greater) to accommodate the long line lengths. This reduces the total amount of text on the page.

In The Writer's Hollywood Digest, two even columns, placed in the middle of the page, project a classic look. This style seems appropriate for a newsletter dedicated to writing. Yet, like all classic looks, it may tend to be a bit boring. Headings and subheadings, pull -quotes

4

GIZMOS VOL II NO 2 SPRING 1992

and graphics must all be inserted in the column. These stop the reader's visual movement through the document. Further, proportions for graphics are pretty narrow. The best way to learn something is to love it.

Robert Sarnak

Q: *Glendale Gazette shows this. If you're not using many pictures, I don't think it's a problem.*

A: Tombstoning can occur easily in this format, so be on your toes! To liven things up, make heads and illustrations as dramatic as possible. A two-column format works well for motivated readers who know what they're interested in.

A two-and-a-half column layout offers much more aesthetic variety. You can insert the table of contents, masthead, illustrations, pull-quotes, etc., into the half column. Be sure to use smaller type and leading in the margin area. The contrast in type size and leading, as well as the inclusion of art work

and other novelties, give this newsletter format much appeal. This newsletter design is also referred to as a five-column format.

Three-column formats are as popular as two-column formats. While definitely more complicated to compose, they offer a big advance in flexibility and aesthetic variety over the two-column format. With some thought you can achieve a lively layout. (Note: a three-column format can also be thought of as a six-column format.

This doubles grid locations. I don't recommend working with grids this complex, unless you have a great deal of time to study all your layout options.) The principle advantages include a smaller text size, allowing more information per page. A two-and-a-half-column layout offers much more aesthetic variety.

You can insert the table of contents, masthead, illustrations, pull quotes, etc., into the half column. Be sure to use smaller type and leading in the margin area. The contrast in type size and leading, as well as the is striking .

More complicated to compose, they offer a big advance in flexibility and aesthetic variety over the two-column format. With some thought you can achieve a lively layout. (Note: a three column format can also be thought of as a six-column format. This doubles grid locations. I don't recommend such a complicated approach.

Svetlana Lubachefsky

Q: *And pictures over one, two or three columns. You can create a vertical tapestry of type and graphics. I recommend restricting pull-quotes to one-column.*

A: Set in large type with open leading over several columns they lose their visual "punch." Disadvantages include succumbing to too much symmetry and tombstoning.

While one empty column in a three-column format is okay. A two-column format works well for motivated readers who know what they're interested in.

Inclusion of art work and other novelties give this newsletter format much appeal.

This newsletter design is also referred to as a five-column format.You can achieve a lively layout. (Note, a three-column format can also be thought of as a six-column format. This doubles grid locations. I don't recommend working with grids this complex, unless you have a great deal of time to study all your layout options.) The

5

This three-column newsletter is set up essentially like The Multimedia News (earlier in this chapter) but with different typefaces and artwork.

PAGE SETUP

Paper size: 8 1/2 in. x 11 in.
Orientation: Portrait
Margins: Top—.33 in. Bottom—.5 in.
                 Left & Right (inside and out-
                 side)—.66 inch

Three columns throughout (below the nameplate), with .33 inch between columns.

TYPE

Nameplate: 10-pt. and 24-pt. Weiss Extra Bold
Heading: 20-pt. ITC Stone Sans Bold Italic
Initial cap: 36-pt. Weiss Extra Bold
Body text: 10-pt. Weiss
Caption: 8-pt. ITC Stone Sans Bold
End sign: 11-pt. Linotype Holiday Pi 1
For alternative typefaces, see Appendix A.

The Weiss fonts, from Adobe, were designed by the distinguished German typographer Emil Rudolf Weiss. This typeface has many unusual traits, such as the capital U, which is designed the same as the lowercase u, and the M, which has no upper serifs. Adobe's popular ITC Stone Sans is a warm sans-serif, and I think it combines well with most serif faces.

GRAPHICS

The automobile and boat graphics are from the clip-art collection that comes in the Word for Windows Version 2 package. These graphics are not included in Version 6's clip-art collection.

PRODUCTION TIPS

The upper section of the nameplate is set in all-caps expanded by 3 points each. The text line is right-aligned and indented 4.6 inches from the right, to shorten its .75-point border. The second line of the nameplate is left-aligned and indented 1.25 inches from the left, to shorten its .75-point border.

The heading and body text are set flush-left. Paragraphs have small indents; Exactly line spacing is set at 14 points. The heavy rule under the heading was created using the method given for the identical rules in The Multimedia News (see pages 232–237). To create the initial caps, I enlarged the opening letter of the article to 36 points and made it Extra Bold. I left plenty of room above the initial so it doesn't look crowded.

To place the graphics, I first created a frame the width of the two columns for the car. I then inserted the car into the frame. I did the same for the yacht graphic. I typed the caption into the frame containing the yacht.

THE PLEASURE CRAFT
News

We hold these truths to be self evident, that all People are created equal, that they are endowed by their Creator with certain unalienable rights, that among these are Life, Liberty, and the Pursuit of Happiness. That to secure these rights, governments are instituted among Men.

We hold these truths to be self evident, that all People are created equal, that they are endowed by their Creator with certain unalienable rights, that among these are Life, Liberty, and the Pursuit of Happiness. That to secure these rights, governments are instituted among Men. We hold these truths to be self evident, that all People are created equal, that they are endowed by their Creator with certain unalienable rights, that among these are Life, Liberty, and the Pursuit of Happiness. That to secure these rights, governments are instituted among Men. ⚓

High-powered automobiles and million-dollar yachts pleased the crowds at the Los Angeles Convention Center this month.

Japanese Delighted at LA Boat Show

This spring's Los Angeles extravaganza saw many Japanese visitors delighted in the great number of yacht products shown. Hiro Watanabe, Vice President of the giant Shogun International, talked with this reported last week. We hold these truths to be self evident, that all People are created equal, that they are endowed by their Creator with certain unalienable rights,

that among these are Life, Liberty, and the Pursuit of Happiness. That to secure these rights, governments are instituted among Men, We hold these truths to be self evident, that all People are created equal, that they are endowed by their Creator with certain unalienable rights, that among these are Life, Liberty, and the Pursuit of Happiness. That to secure these rights, governments are instituted among Men,

We hold these truths to be self evident, that all People are created equal, that they are endowed by their Creator with certain unalienable rights, that among these are Life, Liberty, and the Pursuit of Happiness.

That to secure these rights, governments are instituted among Men.

We hold these truths to be self evident, that all People are created equal, that they are endowed by their Creator with certain unalienable rights, that among these are Life, Liberty, and the Pursuit of Happiness. That to secure these rights, governments are instituted among Men, We hold these truths to be self evident, that all People are created equal, that they are endowed by their Creator with certain unalienable rights, that among these are Life, Liberty, and the Pursuit of Happiness.

That to secure these rights, governments are instituted among Men, We hold these truths to be self evident, that all People are created equal, that they are endowed by their Creator with certain unalienable rights, that among

5

9. Books, Catalogs & Manuals

Books and other text-intensive works, such as manuals and catalogs, offer the ultimate challenge and creative satisfaction for a designer. At the same time, weaving together the many diverse elements that make up a book can present a variety of typographic problems.

Book design has a long history, and the parts of a book still follow a traditional order. In the following sections, we'll look at the features that typically make up a book's contents. Many books do not include all of these features, but every book contains many elements of page design.

Traditionally in book publishing, the right-hand page is known as the recto, the left-hand page as the verso. The right-hand page is considered dominant, and page numbering always begins on a recto page (even though the number may not be printed on the first page of a section). In the descriptions that follow, I indicate the preferred starting page for each portion of a book.

The chapters in Section IV provide detailed instruction on all techniques used in this section.

The first section of a book is called the front matter and usually contains the following:

Half Title: Properly called bastard title, this page normally displays just the main title of the work without the subtitle, if any. In informal and less expensive books, the half title is often omitted.

Title: The copy for the title page should include the full title of the book, the subtitle if any and the author's or authors' names. Sometimes editors, illustrators and/or other significant contributors to the book are also listed here. The publisher's name, place of publication and date appear at the bottom. The title is always on a new right-hand page or double-page spread.

Copyright: Often placed on the reverse side of the title page, this page may include not only copyright information but trademark references and contributors other than those named on the title page.

Dedication: If space permits, put this on a new right-hand page.

Acknowledgments: These tributes sometimes run to several pages. Always start on a new right-hand page.

Table of Contents: Also simply referred to as the contents page, it should start on a new right-hand page. The table of contents design demands special attention. Your primary tools are space and organization—used in a way that helps the reader discern the structure of the book.

Foreword, Preface, Introduction: Each of these should start on a new right-hand page.

MAIN TEXT SECTION

This section comprises the major portion of the book. It contains the following elements:

Section Dividers: If the work is divided into distinct titled parts, give each part a new right-hand page. If the section is identified only by a number, you can add the number at the beginning of the first chapter in the section, whether it falls on a right- or left-hand page. This decision is sometimes based on the number of pages needed to complete a signature (one section of a book comprising any multiple of four pages). See the 4 Seasons technical manual on page 289.

Chapter Headings: Depending on the subject matter and the significance of each new chapter, chapter titles may need a new right-hand page throughout; or they can be placed on either right- or left-hand pages. Large numerals work effectively to identify the chapter and ornament the page.

Subheadings (topics and subtopics): Especially with instructional and/or technical nonfiction, you may need to include multiple subhead levels. These can be differentiated by weight and type size, as in the 4 Seasons manual (page 292) and the Zoo Resources report (page 280).

Running Heads (or headers and footers): Chapter number and title, book title and author name can appear in various combinations (depending on the designated style) at the top or, less frequently, the bottom of the page. These items can also be divided between the top and bottom locations. Works of specialized nonfiction especially benefit from headers that indicate the topic under discussion on the current page. You can do this easily with Word for Windows because it allows you to include a style reference in a header or footer. Examples of these are in the 4 Seasons manual (page 292), the Zoo Resources report (page 280) and the Mystical and Magical Symbols paper (page 272).

Quotations: Long quotations, or extracts, should be set off from surrounding text by indention or by a change in type style and size. A size one or two points smaller than the body text size is appropriate.

Footnotes: Whether to use footnotes in your publication depends on whether they're needed and on the prevailing style for the particular type of publication. When used, footnotes should be set several points smaller than the main text. If the notes are long, they're usually placed with the back matter (see "Endnotes" in the next section). Notes may also be placed in the outer margin if the page is formatted for that purpose; they are then referred to as margin notes. See Mystical and Magical Symbols on page 272 to see how effective (and easy to read) margin notes can be.

Illustrations, Tables, etc.: These graphic elements present a number of formatting challenges. If you use them in your book, be sure to use one of the Word for Windows formatting methods that locks illustrations to their respective texts. Otherwise, put the illustrations on their own pages interleaved with pages containing the text they relate to; or group them in a separate section. See Zoo Resources, Mystical and Magical Symbols and 4 Seasons.

Captions: These need to be formatted in a way that distinguishes them from the body text. All captions should be set in the same font and positioned in a consistent manner throughout.

BACK MATTER

Following the chapters is the back matter, comprising some or all of these elements:

Appendix: Here the author includes extra information that for one reason or another isn't placed in the main body of text. Each appendix should begin on a new right-hand page.

Endnotes: Often all explanatory reference notes are presented in a numbered list at the back of the book. This makes them much easier to typeset than footnotes or margin notes. Begin endnotes on a new right-hand page.

Glossary: The list of terms used in the book should also begin on a new right-hand page.

Bibliography: This is a list of all publications referred to in the book text. The author may also include books used for reference as well as suggestions for further reading. Open this section on a new right-hand page.

Index: Usually the index cannot be compiled until after the text is finished and page numbers are firm. Start on a new right-hand page.

Colophon: Properly, the colophon appears at the end of a book. It serves to honor the book's designer, who may wish to identify the typefaces, paper, ink, bindings and other materials used in the book. The colophon can begin on either a left or a right page.

BOOK DESIGN

You can see from this review that your book design must accommodate a variety of page formats. The trick is to combine these disparate elements so that the whole remains harmonious.

Novels and popular nonfiction are simpler to compose than scholarly or technical texts; the fiction reader is usually happy to just keep reading to the end of the chapter without the guidance or relief provided by sub-headings or other typographic devices.

On the other hand, the reader of serious nonfiction will appreciate breaks and prompts along the way—in the form of indents, bulleted lists and subheads. Breaks allow the reader time to absorb the information and take a breather before moving forward. See the Zoo Resources report, Mystical and Magical Symbols paper and 4 Seasons manual illustrations on pages 280, 273 and 292, respectively.

ALWAYS design facing left and right pages as a two-page spread. Unlike pages in other documents we've discussed, book pages that face each other are seen by the reader as a unit, even if one of the pages is blank. So always design with two in view.

Selecting a Typeface

In designing books and related materials, typeface choice is critical. Type needs to be attractive enough to stimulate the reader but not be obtrusive. The wide selection of available typefaces makes it possible to choose one that subtly reinforces your author's message. See Appendix A for a detailed discussion of typefaces and their overtones.

Traditional Versus Modern Book Design

The "old" style of book design, going back to printed books of the Italian Renaissance, is characterized by symmetry and geometric page proportions. This single-column style was, and still is, used for most books and formal documents. We use it for correspondence, scholarly papers and journals, legal documents and most business reports. To most people, it's the natural way to compose a page. It is simple to lay out, and it clearly reflects the sequential way we write—one thought following another.

Books that follow the traditional approach place the largest margin at the bottom of the page, the next largest at the outside, the next at the top, and the narrowest along the gutter; the gutters of facing pages combine to create a space approximately the size of the outer margin. While the printed area is small by today's standards, traditional margins ensure a handsome, readable book. A Damask Lullaby (page 263) is designed according to this tradition. This type of arrangement is excellent for text that flows directly from one point to another with few if any subheads, references and illustrations.

One practical advantage of the traditional approach is that the printed lines on a recto page can be set to "back up" with the lines on its reverse side (the verso page) because the printed images will fall at exactly the same place on both sides of the page. This means you can print the pages on thinner, more transparent paper without the distraction of lines printed in different positions on the reverse page showing through.

The traditional style also calls for serif typefaces and restraint in the use of graphic accents. Thin rules and fleurons (traditional leaf and flower ornaments) are appropriate—but never heavy rules. (See the title page for A Damask Lullaby.) Letter-spacing of titles and headings set in all-capitals is *de rigueur*.

In the early 1900s, book design began to change with the arrival of the machine age. Sans-serif typefaces, which had been in existence since the early 18th century, gained favor because of their "streamlined," "modern" appearance. The formal, static typography of the past was rejected and asymmetry became the ideal.

The "grid" evolved as the "scientific" method for organizing the asymmetrical page. The grid system of page division has remained popular because it provides a straightforward but flexible structure for organizing many different kinds of material: illustrations, body copy, headings, tables, diagrams, etc.

Asymmetry lets the designer create variety and visual movement on the page. It works particularly well for the complex information presented in such documents as manuals and reports. Modern design purists maintain that asymmetrical composition should be set in sans-serif type; but you'll find many contemporary designers successfully using both serif and sans-serif faces with asymmetrical book design, as in the Zoo Resources, Mystical and Magical Symbols and 4 Seasons illustrations.

Which approach should you choose? Spectacular and beautiful books have come from both traditions, but neither can guarantee a handsome outcome. First, if you have a predilection for one, use it. If you have no strong preference, my advice would be to use traditional typography for works that call for long, uninterrupted passages; modern for texts that incorporate illustrations, tables and instructions.

Pagination

Traditionally, because the text and back matter were often printed before the front matter was complete, the front matter was given its own set of page numbers, usually in Roman numerals. Arabic numerals began with the first chapter of the main text.

With the advent of computer typesetting, book pagination changed. In the contemporary approach, the first page, even if blank, counts as page 1. The first actual page number appears on the first right-hand page bearing text, which is usually the Introduction. Depending on how your book will be produced, you can use either of these systems.

MANUALS

An instruction manual requires complex typography because its information-intensive content demands a variety of formats: multiple heading levels, explanatory notes, tips, warnings, cross-references, lists, etc. Often, these are accompanied by illustrations, such as screen shots, icons, images, drawings or photos. Working with this type of document is a bit like being in a cage of wild beasts. But the three S's—structure, structure and more structure—will save you. Tame this unruly managerie with a clear hierarchy of type sizes and styles. The example I've created (4 Seasons) was inspired by several of my favorite software manuals.

Visuals also help, but they take extra time you may not have. Rules, dingbats and other graphic accents can help the reader find and comprehend the information. Use pointing fists or other eye-catching dingbats for recurring tips and warnings. Effective use of white space is also helpful in guiding the reader through the information.

For manuals, I strongly recommend an asymmetrical approach (as in 4 Seasons). Place warnings and tips in a wide outer margin where they're easy to find. Your reader will bless you if you also provide descriptive headers and footers keyed to the text on the page.

If you produce manuals on a regular basis, you'll be amply rewarded for the initial investment that goes into creating a complete template; the second manual will involve a mere fraction of the time needed for the first.

CATALOGS

Most catalogs, like manuals, provide a lot of detailed information, often accompanied by illustrations. Catalog readers are likely to be highly motivated and willing to tolerate small type and a dense text setting.

The standardized formatting used for composing catalogs makes them ideal for Word for Windows. Symmetrical and asymmetrical formats work equally well: your choice should be guided by the type of products you're presenting and your potential readership. (Note the innovative design of the Signs of the Times catalog on page 298.) Catalog entries can be treated as a database and set up automatically in tables. This allows you to revise or update the catalog quickly and easily.

MOVING ON

Before you learned about all these amazing Word for Windows formatting features, you probably wouldn't have dreamed of venturing into the rarified world of book design. The examples and instructions in the next few pages will whet your appetite to start your own book project.

Note: Because Word's graphics are somewhat limited, many documents in this book use line art, clip art and other graphics from third-party software packages. I've used Arts & Letters and CorelDRAW, both of which contain thousands of readily accessible graphic images.

In re-creating the designs in this book, you may want to replace my images with those you can create using Word's drawing tools, Microsoft Draw and Microsoft Graph, or the clip art that comes with Word. However, if you have a third-party program, make the most of it!

If your budget is limited but your needs go beyond the offerings of the Word utilities, you may want to build a library of shareware clip art, graphics and fonts. Good graphics and Word make a great team.

The proportions and overall look of this book were inspired by traditional book design, which is characterized by symmetry and generous space around text. It's ideal for works that don't require illustrations or notes with complex formatting. Because it doesn't rely on visual theatrics to grab attention, a design this subdued should be reserved for publications that have motivated readers. I laid this out on 8 1/2- x 11-inch paper—much larger than the usual book format.

PAGE SETUP

Paper size: 8 1/2 in. x 11 in.
Orientation: Portrait
Margins: Top—1.25 in. Bottom—2 in.
Inside—1.25 in.
Outside—2 in. (facing pages)

Note: These wide margins provide a gracious frame for the two facing pages of text; but in this traditional design the title and contents pages look a bit uncentered.

TYPE

Title page:
A Damask Lullaby—36-pt. Granjon
Dingbats—48-pt. Linotype Decoration Pi 1
Memoirs line—24-pt. Granjon Italic
Translated line—14-pt. Granjon Italic
Dingbats: 72-pt. Linotype Decoration Pi 1
The Pomegranate Press—18-pt. Granjon Italic
Table of contents page:
"Contents"—18-pt. Granjon
Contents listings—14-pt. Granjon Italic and 14-pt. Granjon
A Damask Lullaby—18-pt. Granjon Italic

Chapter opening page:
Chapter Eight—28-pt. Granjon, regular and small caps
Dingbats—28-pt. Linotype Decoration Pi 1
Chapter title—21-pt. Granjon Italic
Drop cap: 82-pt. Linoscript
Body text: 14-pt. Granjon
Text page headers: 18-pt. Granjon, regular and small caps
Text page footers: 33-pt. Granjon

With the exception of the chapter-opening drop caps, the entire book is set with members of the Granjon type family, Linotype's version of the ever-popular Garamond. This typeface has a dignified and gracious feeling. Because of their individual beauty, the letterforms work well in display sizes. In body text they present an even texture. The dingbats, all from Linotype's Decoration Pi 1 font, convey a quiet elegance that complements the text.

PRODUCTION TIPS

Title page: Though it may not appear so, everything on the title page is centered. When a portion of the wide outer margin is sacrificed in the book-binding process, the lopsided look disappears.

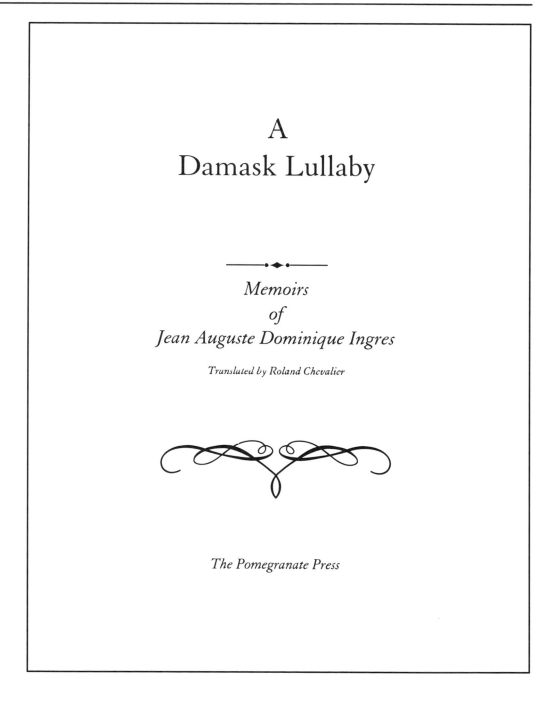

A
Damask Lullaby

Memoirs
of
Jean Auguste Dominique Ingres

Translated by Roland Chevalier

The Pomegranate Press

Table of contents: Center the words Contents and A Damask Lullaby. The letters in Contents are expanded by 3 points each. Set front matter titles and chapter numbers flush-left; set the page numbers using a right-aligned tab. (This is an obvious place to set up a Style in your template.) Set the chapter titles flush-left with a .25-inch indent.

CONTENTS

Introduction   *vii*

A Note on the Translation   *xxi*

Preface   *xxiii*

A Damask Lullaby

Chapter One
Favorable Beginnings   3
Chapter Two
Fun in the Nursery   33
Chapter Three
A Nanny Makes Tea   65
Chapter Four
The Emperor's New Clothes   91
Chapter Five
Hans Christian Andersen Comes to Visit   121
Chapter Six
Boys Will Be Boys   165
Chapter Seven
A View from Venice   197
Chapter Eight
Genevieve Lifts Her Veil   233
Chapter Nine
A Visit from the Archbishop   255
Chapter Ten
Too Many Books, Too Little Time   287

Chapter opening: Center "Chapter Eight" and the chapter title. For the chapter number I chose to use the combination of regular and small caps because the latter are less imposing than full caps but more impressive than regular lowercase. They give a greater measure of distinction to the chapter opening.

With the Format/Drop Cap command in Version 6, you should be able to achieve a good fit for your drop cap—like the one shown at right. (In Version 2, the Drop Cap macro from the NEW-MACRO.DOC will give you the result shown. I achieved this by applying the macro and then making the type size a bit larger and moving the initial frame just a bit into the left margin so that the swash would protrude.) Like many script typefaces, Linoscript is rather small on the body, but the program has no way of knowing this. The frame is automatically made large enough to accommodate 82 points, and it displaces more text. Since the initial didn't really need all that space, I changed its line spacing to Exactly 68 points in the Paragraph dialog box. This closed the gap below the initial. It also caused the initial to move up. To counteract this, I subscripted it 18 points in the Font (Character) dialog box. I give you these specific dimensions merely as an example; you can make this sort of thing work only through trial and error.

Although it's traditional to do so, I did not suppress the page number on this opening chapter's first page. It's not very pretty, but anyone wanting to turn directly to this chapter will be grateful it's there.

Regular pages: The design of the double-page spread really dictates the basic shape of all other pages in the book. The wide outer margins leave plenty of room for fingers and/ or notes—plus it forms a visual frame for the text. All body text is 14 points set on Exactly 18 points. I used this generous line spacing because the text lines are long and the type size is large—also to make the line spacing proportional to the page margins.

The headers mimic the design of the chapter opening, combining regular and small capitals.

Left and right footers are set as mirror images. Left footers are left-aligned and negatively indented (outdented) -1 inch from the left. Right footers are right-aligned and negatively indented (outdented) -1 inch from the right.

⸱ CHAPTER EIGHT ⸱

Genevieve
Lifts Her Veil

hen in the course of human events, it becomes necessary for one people to dissolve the political bands which have connected them with another, and to assume among the Powers of the Earth, the separate and equal station which the Laws of Nature and of Nature's God entitle them, and declare the causes which impel them to the separation.

We hold these truths to be self evident, that all People are created equal, that they are endowed by their Creator with certain unalienable rights, that among these are Life, Liberty, and the Pursuit of Happiness. That to secure these rights, governments are instituted among Men, deriving their just powers from the consent of the governed. That whenever any form of government becomes destructive of these ends, it is the right of the people to alter or to abolish it, and to institute new government, laying its foundation on such principles, and organizing its powers in such form, as to them shall seem most likely to effect their safety and happiness. Prudence, indeed, will dictate that governments long established should not be changed for light and transient causes; and accordingly all experience hath shewn, that mankind are more disposed to suffer, while evils are

ᴄ CHAPTER EIGHT ᴐ

them with another, and to assume among the Powers of the Earth, the separate and equal station which the Laws of Nature and of Nature's God entitle them, a decent Respect to the opinions of mankind requires that they should declare the causes which impel them to the separation.

We hold these truths to be self evident, that all People are created equal, that they are endowed by their Creator with certain unalienable rights, that among these are Life, Liberty, and the Pursuit of Happiness. That to secure these rights, governments are instituted among Men, deriving their just powers from the consent of the governed. That whenever any form of government becomes destructive of these ends, it is the right of the people to alter or to abolish it, and to institute new government, laying its foundation on such principles, and organizing its powers in such form, as to them shall seem most likely to effect their safety and happiness. Prudence, indeed, will dictate that governments long established should not be changed for light and transient causes; and accordingly all experience hath shewn, that mankind are more disposed to suffer, while evils are sufferable, than to right themselves by abolishing the forms to which they are accustomed. But when a long train of abuses and usurpations, pursuing invariably the same object, evinces a design to reduce them under absolute despotism, it is their right, it is their duty, to throw off such government, and to provide new guards for their future security.

Such has been the patient sufferance of these colonies; and such is now the necessity which constrains them to alter their former systems of government. The history of the present King of Great Britain is a history of repeated injuries and usurpations, all having in direct object the establishment of an absolute tyranny over these States. When in the course of human events, it becomes necessary for one people to dissolve the political bands which have connected them with another,

234

๑ CHAPTER EIGHT ๑

and to assume among the Powers of the Earth, the separate and equal station which the Laws of Nature and of Nature's God entitle them, a decent Respect to the opinions of mankind requires that they should declare the causes which impel them to the separation.

We hold these truths to be self evident, that all People are created equal, that they are endowed by their Creator with certain unalienable rights, that among these are Life, Liberty, and the Pursuit of Happiness. That to secure these rights, governments are instituted among Men, deriving their just powers from the consent of the governed. That whenever any form of government becomes destructive of these ends, it is the right of the people to alter or to abolish it, and to institute new government, laying its foundation on such principles, and organizing its powers in such form, as to them shall seem most likely to effect their safety and happiness. Prudence, indeed, will dictate that governments long established should not be changed for light and transient causes; and accordingly all experience hath shewn, that mankind are more disposed to suffer, while evils are sufferable, than to right themselves by abolishing the forms to which they are accustomed.

But when a long train of abuses and usurpations, pursuing invariably the same object, evinces a design to reduce them under absolute despotism, it is their right, it is their duty, to throw off such government, and to provide new guards for their future security. Such has been the patient sufferance of these colonies; and such is now the necessity which constrains them to alter their former systems of government. The history of the present King of Great Britain is a history of repeated injuries and usurpations, all having in direct object the establishment of an absolute tyranny over these States.

When in the course of human events, it becomes necessary for one people to dissolve the political bands which have connected them with another, and to assume among the Powers of the Earth, the separate

235

This asymmetrical style works well for business and academic papers and reports. The wide left margin easily accommodates graphics and side notes; the use of rules and type variations make the hierarchical subdivision of information clear. The wide margin also adds visual interest and leaves the reader space for notes.

PAGE SETUP

Paper size: 8 1/2 in. x 11 in.
Orientation: Portrait
Margins: Top—1.3 in. Bottom—1 in.
Left—3.3 in. Right—.9 in.
(**Note:** While this design is asymmetrical visually, the major headings and headers show that page margins are actually the same: both left and right margins are .9 inch. On the title page, side margins center the design.)

TYPE

Title page:
Mystical and Magical—24-pt. ITC Stone Serif Semibold Italic
Symbols—36-pt. ITC Stone Sans
Byline—16-pt. ITC Stone Serif
Press—18-pt. Shelley Volante Script
Table of contents page:
Contents—24-pt. ITC Stone Serif Bold Italic
Contents listings—14-pt. ITC Stone Serif Semibold Italic
Introduction: 24-pt. ITC Stone Serif Bold Italic
Body text: 11-pt. ITC Stone Serif
Subheads: 14-pt. ITC Stone Serif Semibold Italic
Captions: 8-pt. ITC Avant Garde Gothic Demibold
Side notes: 11-pt. ITC Stone Serif Italic

All faces in this paper are from Adobe, except the Shelley Volante from Linotype.

GRAPHICS

All the graphics used in this report were scanned at 300 dpi from images in the Dover publication: *Symbols, Signs & Signets,* by Ernst Lehner, 1950. This book is part of the Dover Pictorial Archive series, whose images are excellent inspiration sources for all types of illustrations and can be reproduced without permission.

The large graphic on the title page is rough because it's reproduced from a small original. Expect the jaggies with such a piece. (But how could I resist this face?)

PRODUCTION TIPS

Title page: Everything on the title page is centered. I made the graphic large to give the page some excitement. (I don't find the jaggies particularly offensive.) The graphic is placed in a frame. Note that lines set in some typefaces, such as the Shelley Volante Script, lean so far to the right that you may need to move them slightly to the left, as I did here, to make them appear centered. You can move the lines by putting them in a frame or by adding space to the right. Control the size of the space by changing the character size of the space itself. Here, again, it pays to display spaces.

Mystical
and
Magical
Symbols

by
Olivia Francesca Respighi

University Press
1991

Table of contents: This page layout sets the style for the interior. The word Contents is set flush-left with a -2.38-inches negative indent (Distance From Left -2.38 inches in the Paragraph dialog box); its borders extend the full width of the page. The borders are .75 point and 1.5 points, respectively. The margins of the contents list are the same as those used for the body text throughout. The contents list is set flush-left. The rules between paragraphs were set as bottom borders. Above each item entry is an empty 4-point paragraph so that the borders below will show. (For details on this and other methods of creating series of lines, see Chapter 11.)

Interior pages: The word Introduction is formatted like the Contents heading. (I designated it Heading 1 Style in the Style sheet.) The subheads (my Heading 2 Style) are also set flush-left, but they don't protrude beyond the left margin. Separation is achieved by adding space between heads and paragraphs, and between paragraphs, rather than indenting the first line of each paragraph. I adopted this style because in text-heavy material such as this, the reader needs strong visual breaks so that the eye and mind can take a breath, so to speak.

All graphics and side notes were put in frames in the wide left margin. Because the margin is totally neutral vis-à-vis the formatting of frames, it's very easy to do this—and you don't have to worry about text wrapping. Also, it's easy to anchor your graphics and notes to the text on the right. As you move your frame in the margin, you'll see a tiny blip move underneath the first character of the paragraph adjacent to the frame. This tells you which text your frame is anchored to. If you click Move With Text in the Format/Frame dialog box, your framed graphic or note will move from one page to another with its adjacent related text.

I typed the captions directly into the frames under the graphics. To put your graphics in frames of the same size and located in the same position in the margin, use the sizing and placement controls in the Format/Frame dialog box. All graphics in this report are centered side-to-side in their frames by clicking on the graphic and using center paragraph alignment.

The side note is set in the italic version of the body text, and in the same type size and with the same line spacing as the body text. This way, the notes align horizontally with the text lines. However, sometimes you may need to include very long, detailed notes; in this case, use a much smaller type size and a distinctly different typeface; this will help the reader find the notes and distinguish them from the text.

Headers are set flush-left to the text margin. I kept them the width of the text to put the reader's eye at the correct horizontal position to begin reading. The border is 1.5-point. The page number is set with a right-aligned tab.

On page 3, the list was created using Word's Numbered List button on the Standard toolbar (Toolbar). I selected the paragraphs to be numbered, clicked the button on the

Contents

	Introduction	*3*
1	*Definitions of mystical and magical*	*11*
2	*Continental distribution of symbols*	*18*
3	*Mystical traditions of Asia*	*25*
4	*Migrations from Asia to Sumeria*	*36*
5	*Greek mystery religions*	*41*
6	*African symbolic traditions*	*55*
7	*Symbols of early Native Americans*	*67*
	Appendices	*78*

Standard toolbar—and *voilà*! I also used the Standard toolbar to create the bulleted items by choosing the Bulleted List button.

Tip: I created a separate style for bulleted items, with a 1-inch indent from the left. You can change the style of bullet in the Tools menu, under Bullets And Numbering. The custom bullet selection limits you to those typefaces that Word lists in its Symbols set collection. Version 6 now recognizes all special dingbat, pi and symbol fonts.

Note: You can replace the bullets with your own using Replace in the Edit menu. Replace can change characters and formatting. This is a powerful and valuable tool. Try to keep it in mind.

The indents after bullets and numbers can be changed in the Bullets And Numbering dialog box as well as by using a combination of From Left and First Line indents in the Paragraph dialog box.

Introduction

When in the course of human events, it becomes necessary for one people to dissolve the political bands which have connected them with another, and to assume among the Powers of the Earth, the separate and equal station which the Laws of Nature and of Nature's God entitle them, a decent Respect to the opinions of mankind requires that they should declare the causes which impel them to the separation. But when a long train of abuses and usurpations, pursuing invariably the same object, evinces a design to reduce them under absolute despotism, it is their right, it is their duty, to throw off such government, and to provide new guards for their future security. Such has been the patient sufferance of these colonies; and such is now the necessity which constrains them to alter their former systems of government.

Ethiopian Good Luck Charms

Fig 1.1 Ethiopian Cross With Divine Face

We hold these truths to be self evident, that all People are created equal, that they are endowed by their Creator with certain unalienable rights, that among these are Life, Liberty, and the Pursuit of Happiness. That to secure these rights, governments are instituted among Men, deriving their just powers from the consent of the governed. That whenever any form of government becomes destructive of these ends, it is the right of the people to alter or to abolish it, and to institute new government, laying its foundation on such principles, and organizing its powers in such form, as to them shall seem most likely to effect their safety and happiness. Prudence, indeed, will dictate that governments long established should not be changed for light and transient causes; and accordingly all experience hath shewn, that mankind are more disposed to suffer. It is their right, it is their duty, to throw off such government, and to provide new guards for their future security.

Introduction   2

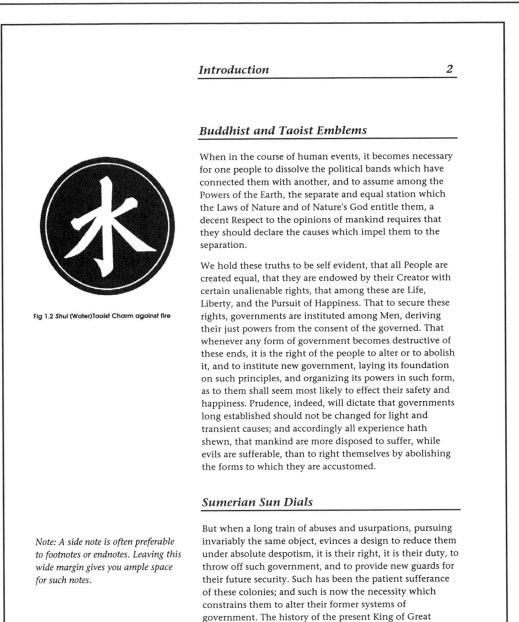

Fig 1.2 *Shui (Water)Taoist Charm against fire*

Buddhist and Taoist Emblems

When in the course of human events, it becomes necessary for one people to dissolve the political bands which have connected them with another, and to assume among the Powers of the Earth, the separate and equal station which the Laws of Nature and of Nature's God entitle them, a decent Respect to the opinions of mankind requires that they should declare the causes which impel them to the separation.

We hold these truths to be self evident, that all People are created equal, that they are endowed by their Creator with certain unalienable rights, that among these are Life, Liberty, and the Pursuit of Happiness. That to secure these rights, governments are instituted among Men, deriving their just powers from the consent of the governed. That whenever any form of government becomes destructive of these ends, it is the right of the people to alter or to abolish it, and to institute new government, laying its foundation on such principles, and organizing its powers in such form, as to them shall seem most likely to effect their safety and happiness. Prudence, indeed, will dictate that governments long established should not be changed for light and transient causes; and accordingly all experience hath shewn, that mankind are more disposed to suffer, while evils are sufferable, than to right themselves by abolishing the forms to which they are accustomed.

Sumerian Sun Dials

Note: A side note is often preferable to footnotes or endnotes. Leaving this wide margin gives you ample space for such notes.

But when a long train of abuses and usurpations, pursuing invariably the same object, evinces a design to reduce them under absolute despotism, it is their right, it is their duty, to throw off such government, and to provide new guards for their future security. Such has been the patient sufferance of these colonies; and such is now the necessity which constrains them to alter their former systems of government. The history of the present King of Great

Introduction   3

Britain is a history of repeated injuries and usurpations, all having in direct object the establishment of an absolute tyranny over these States. Respect to the opinions of mankind requires that they should declare the causes which impel them to the separation.

Symbols of the Greek Mystery Religions

When in the course of human events, it becomes necessary for one people to dissolve the political bands which have connected them with another, and to assume among the Powers of the Earth, the separate and equal station which the Laws of Nature and of Nature's God entitle them.

1. We hold these truths to be self evident, that all People are created equal, that they are endowed by their Creator with certain unalienable rights, that among these are Life, Liberty, and the Pursuit of Happiness.

2. That whenever any form of government becomes destructive of these ends, it is the right of the people to alter or to abolish it, and to institute new government, laying its foundation on such principles, and organizing its powers in such form, as to them shall seem most likely to effect their safety and happiness.

3. Prudence, indeed, will dictate that governments long established should not be changed for light and transient causes.

   - Bullet Item

   - Bullet Item

   - Bullet Item

   - Bullet Item

4. But when a long train of abuses and usurpations, pursuing invariably the same object, evinces a design to reduce them under absolute despotism, it is their right, it is their duty, to throw off such government, and to provide new guards for their future security. Such has

Fig 1.3 Greek Triskelion

The design of this report reflects the influence of the modern (also known as Swiss) approach to typography, which is characterized by strong type and graphic shapes set in asymmetrical arrangements with large but controlled areas of white (negative) space. Sans-serif faces are used almost exclusively. This clean, efficient look works well for reports of all kinds. Here, dramatic black typefaces make strong visual statements against the large white backgrounds of the title and contents pages. The pages of text are set in two short columns, each covering a different topic. The varying column lengths give the text an interesting (and intentional) ragged bottom edge. The lower two-fifths of the page are reserved for illustrations.

PAGE SETUP

Paper size: 8 1/2 in. x 11 in.
Orientation: Portrait
Title page and text pages margins:

> Top—1.6 in. Bottom—3.8 in.
> Inside—.8 in. Outside—1.4 in.
> Gutter—0 in. (facing pages)

Table of contents page margins:

> Top—1.6 in. Bottom—1 in.
> Inside—.8 in. Outside—1.4 in.

Except for the table of contents, all pages have a two-column format, with .3 inch between columns.

TYPE

Title page:
> ZOO Resources—41-pt. Futura Extra Black
> Summer Quarterly—24-pt. Futura Bold
> Skyline Zoo Guild—18-pt. Futura Medium

Contents page:
> Contents and chapter numbers—41-pt. Futura Bold
> Chapter names and page numbers—18-pt. Futura Bold
> Body Text—10-pt. Futura

Inside pages:
> Headers—10-pt. Futura Bold
> Column heads—14-pt. Futura Bold
> Column subheads—12-pt. Futura Medium
> Body text—10-pt. Futura
> Page numbers—18-pt. Futura Bold
> Captions—8-pt. Copperplate 29AB from Linotype

For alternate typefaces, see Appendix A.

This medley of Futuras (from Bitstream) makes a concerted impact. The wide-ranging weights keep the pages from being stagnant and define the hierarchy of the various text elements. Futura works well in reversed type, where more delicate faces often lose their subtle qualities and are hard to read.

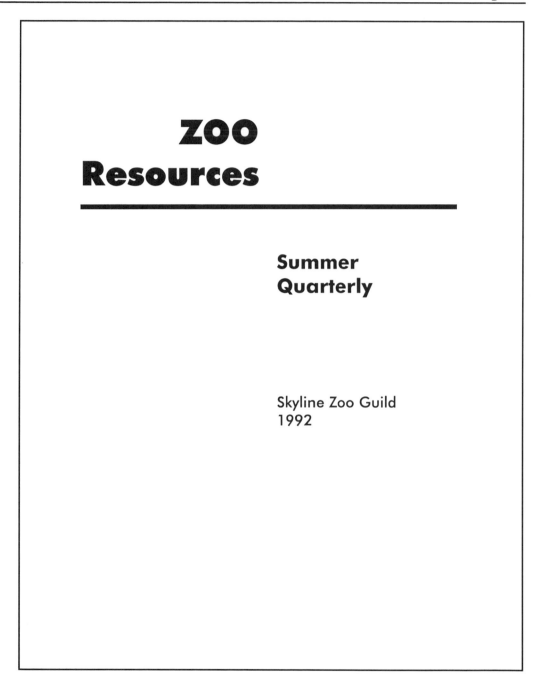

ZOO Resources

Summer Quarterly

Skyline Zoo Guild
1992

GRAPHICS

The charts on pages 24 and 25 were made in Microsoft Graph. The typeface is Copperplate Gothic 29AB from Linotype. The Adopt! logo was made from a symbol in the Arts & Letters Graphics Editor. Adopt! is set in a variant of ITC Benguiat Bold.

PRODUCTION TIPS

Title page: ZOO Resources is in a right-aligned paragraph in the left-hand column. Insert a column break after it.

Below the title, insert a frame the width of the two columns. Into this put an empty paragraph and assign it a 6-point border. Set Summer, Quarterly, Skyline Zoo Guild and 1992 flush-left in the right-hand column.

Table of contents: In order to control the placement of these related items, I put them in a table. And to maintain a constant grid with the rest of the report, I made the table dimensions the same as the two columns used throughout the document. (See the gridline detail.) Set the row height and paragraph spacing for chapter numbers using the Exactly setting. But set the row height for chapter titles and descriptions to Auto so they can expand and contract with the varying amount of information. Contents is in a left-aligned paragraph, but it's aligned on the right with the chapter titles, using a right-aligned tab. Chapter titles and page numbers are right-aligned in their cells; chapter numbers and descriptions are left-aligned in their cells. All column widths specify no space between columns.

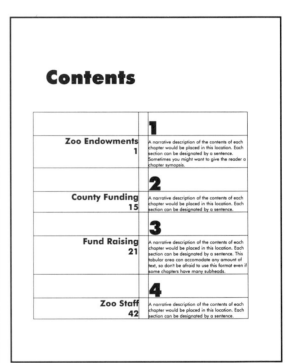

Contents

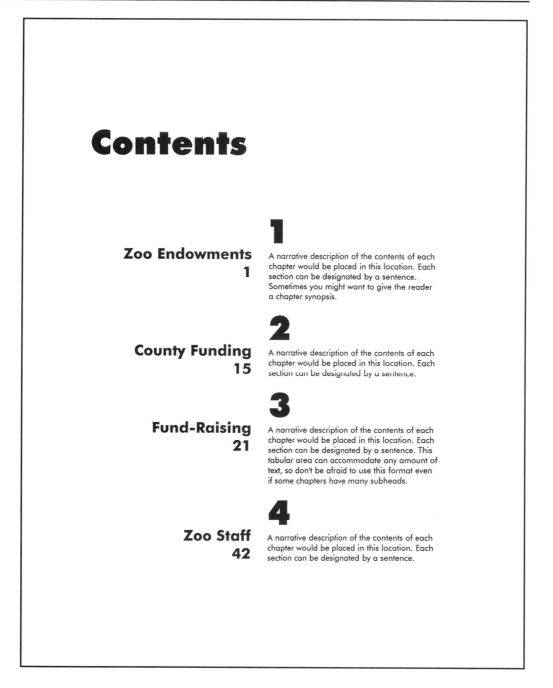

1

Zoo Endowments
1

A narrative description of the contents of each chapter would be placed in this location. Each section can be designated by a sentence. Sometimes you might want to give the reader a chapter synopsis.

2

County Funding
15

A narrative description of the contents of each chapter would be placed in this location. Each section can be designated by a sentence.

3

Fund-Raising
21

A narrative description of the contents of each chapter would be placed in this location. Each section can be designated by a sentence. This tabular area can accommodate any amount of text, so don't be afraid to use this format even if some chapters have many subheads.

4

Zoo Staff
42

A narrative description of the contents of each chapter would be placed in this location. Each section can be designated by a sentence.

Pages 24 and 25: These mirror-image headers have to be set individually. Use the same number of spaces between the words Chapter 3 and Fund Raising in both headers. The left header is set with a left-aligned tab, while the right is set with a right-aligned tab. (Other ways of formatting headers are discussed in Chapter 11.) To create the reversed type, select the text, then select White for its color (in the Font [Character] dialog box). Next, set the paragraph line spacing to Exactly 18 points in the Paragraph dialog box; this defines the height of the black area. Finally, to create the black shading, choose Shading Solid and Background Black in the Format/Borders and Shading (Format/Border) dialog box.

Set all heads and text left-aligned. The irregular column lengths are intentional; they add visual interest to the page and help to organize the report contents so that each topic is easy to find. Further, you shouldn't feel obligated to include graphics at the bottom of each column or page; I did it here merely to show more of Word's features.

You can create the large chart on page 24 in Graph and insert it into a frame at the bottom of the page. (Because the bottom of the page is in the margin, and there's no text to be displaced, inserting a frame is easy. In fact, whenever possible, I recommend that you place items in frames into margin areas, where they are much easier to control.)

In this chart, the caption is part of the graphic. Because Microsoft Graph lets you use your printer's typefaces, your charts can have the same high-quality text as the rest of your document.

The pie chart graphic on page 25 was also created in Microsoft Graph. Because the labels were too close to the pie, I switched to the Chart window in Microsoft Graph and moved the labels. The technique for putting a chart into Microsoft Draw is discussed in Chapter 12. Captions for the graphics on page 25 are in a single frame below the frames containing the graphics; the caption locations are set with tabs. I did this because the frames of the two graphics are very different in size, and captions in those frames would have appeared unbalanced in their locations. It took some playing with these particular graphics to get them balanced optically. Usually, though, reports use graphics that are similar enough not to cause formatting difficulty.

You can create the unconventionally located reversed type page numbers (which are technically part of the headers) as follows. In View/Header and Footer, insert a page # field. Next, select the page #; now choose Insert/Frame. This puts a frame around the # field. Now drag the framed page # into the correct location in the margin. In Version 2, in Draft View, view the header and insert the page number. In Page Layout View, select the page number and insert a frame around it.

Drag the page number out of the header and place it where you want it to be. Format the frame to the size you want. This one is a half-inch square. Then, select the text and format it White in the Format/Font (Format/Character) dialog box. Next, select Shading Solid and Background Black in the Format/Borders and Shading (Format/Border) dialog box. (If you don't want a border around your page numbers, just turn the border for the frame off.) Be sure to repeat this procedure for both headers if your pages are mirror images. You can use this procedure for inserting any text or graphic you want to repeat on each page.

Chapter 3   Fund-Raising 1992

Corporate Fund-Raising

When in the course of human events, it becomes necessary for one people to dissolve the political bands which have connected them with another, and to assume among the Powers of the Earth, the separate and equal station which the Laws of Nature and of Nature's God entitle them, a decent respect. But when a long train of abuses and usurpations, pursuing invariably the same object, evinces a design to reduce them under despotism, it is their right, it is their duty, to throw off such government, and to provide new guards for their future security. Such has been the patient sufferance of these colonies; and such is now the necessity which constrains them to alter their former systems of government.

Spring Fling

When in the course of human events, it becomes necessary for one people to dissolve the political bands which have connected them with another, and to assume among the Powers of the Earth, the separate and equal station which the Laws of Nature and of Nature's God entitle them, a decent Respect to the opinions of mankind requires that they should declare the causes which impel them to the separation. But when a long train of abuses and usurpations, pursuing invariably the same object, evinces a design to reduce them under absolute despotism, it is their right, it is their duty, to throw off such government, and to provide new guards for their future security. Such has been the patient sufferance of these colonies; and such is now the necessity which constrains them to alter their systems of government. When in the course of human events, it becomes necessary for one people to dissolve the political bands which have connected them with another, and to assume among the Powers of the Earth, the separate and equal station which the Laws of Nature and of Nature's God entitle them, a decent Respect to the opinions of mankind requires.

 24

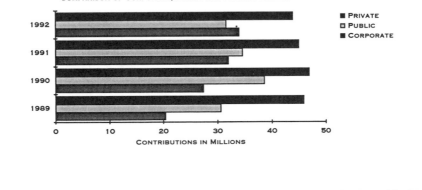

COMPARISON OF CORPORATE, PUBLIC AND PRIVATE CONTRIBUTIONS

Public Schools Campaign

They shall declare the causes which impel them to the separation.

But when a long train of abuses and usurpations, pursuing invariably the same object, evinces a design to reduce them under absolute despotism, it is their right, it is their duty, to throw off such government, and to provide new guards for their future security. Such has been the patient sufferance of these colonies; and such is now the necessity which constrains them to alter their former systems of government. Then it becomes necessary for one people to dissolve the political bands which have connected them with another, and to assume among the Powers of the Earth, the separate and equal station which the Laws of Nature and of Nature's God entitle them, a decent Respect to the opinions of mankind requires that they should declare the causes which impel them to the separation. Pursuing invariably the same object, evinces a design to reduce them under absolute despotism, it is their right, it is their duty, to throw off such government, and to provide new guards for their future security.

Adopt-An-Animal Project

Such has been the patient sufferance of these colonies; and such is now the necessity which constrains them to alter their former systems of government.

When in the course of human events, it becomes necessary for one people to dissolve the political bands which have connected them with another, and to assume among the Powers of the Earth, the separate and equal station which the Laws of Nature and of Nature's God entitle the, a decent Respect to the opinions of mankind requires that they should declare the causes which impel them to the separation. But when a long train of abuses and usurpations, pursuing invariably the same object, evinces a design to reduce them under absolute despotism, it is their right, it is their duty, to throw off such government, and to provide new guards for their future security. Such has been the patient sufferance of these colonies; and such is now the necessity which constrains them to alter their former systems of government.

25

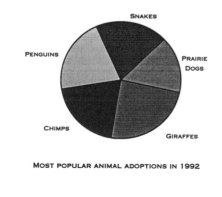

MOST POPULAR ANIMAL ADOPTIONS IN 1992

Adopt!

NEW ADOPT-AN-ANIMAL LOGO

Business and technical reports often look uninviting because their title pages are unadorned. Giant letterforms, such as the Rx here, will grab your reader's attention. For TrueType fonts Version 6 allows you to scale them to virtually any size in the text layer. PostScript fonts appear to be limited by the Adobe Type Manager. In Microsoft Draw you can create type of virtually any size.

PAGE SETUP

Paper size: 8 1/2 in. x 11 in.
Orientation: Portrait
Margins: Top & Bottom—.5 in.
             Left & Right—.8 in.

TYPE

R: Bauer Bodoni (scaled in Word or Draw)
x: Choco (scaled in Word or Draw)
Title: 40-pt. Weiss Extra Bold
Author line: 30-pt. Weiss Italic
For alternate typefaces, see Appendix A.

Bauer Bodoni (here from Adobe) is the most refined of the existing Bodonis. While the true elegance of this design is somewhat hard to appreciate in this Microsoft Draw enlargement, the smooth shapes and strong thick/thin stroke contrast are clear. The impact of the bold, spontaneous brush strokes of the x (set in Linotype's Choco) next to the clean, carefully crafted design of the Bodoni R causes the reader to pause. Weiss, also from Adobe, has a strong personality, here in the Extra Bold and Italic forms. These hold up well in the company of the larger letterforms.

GRAPHICS

Because the R and x were set in Word 6 (Microsoft Draw in Version 2), and because I use scalable fonts with my printer, I was able to smoothly scale them to these immense proportions. If you use bit-mapped typefaces, Microsoft Draw or Word's drawing tools can also scale them, but they will develop a bad case of the jaggies.

PRODUCTION TIPS

First I created the Rx graphic in the text layer or in a text box in the drawing layer. (For Version 2, create the Rx in Microsoft Draw. Put it on the empty page, then scale it to the correct size.) Create the other text in two frames or text boxes. Because Word automatically gives large text a lot of extra space at the top, bottom and sides (space built into the type character) even when it's used as a graphic, I altered my page margins to accommodate the space. I inserted the graphic in a frame so that I could move it to an optically centered position. I also inserted the title into a frame so I could move it up into the area occupied by the graphic's frame. The letters of the words in the title are expanded by 4.5 points each, except between the A and C, which is 2.75 points, and the A and U, which is 3.25 points. To compensate for the extra line spacing Word inserts above the Rx, superscript the Rx or place the text box with its upper border off the page. The author line is also in its own frame to allow easy positioning. The title and author frames were centered on the page using the Format/Frame dialog box.

PHARMACEUTICAL

FRAUD

Raul August Wagner, M.D.

This design for the title page of a report is another example of an easy way to create visual interest using Version 6's drawing tools (or Microsoft Draw). Superimposing the title on the graphic reinforces the title's double meaning.

PAGE SETUP

Paper size: 8 1/2 in. x 11 in.
Orientation: Portrait
Margins: Top & Bottom—1 in.
                Left & Right—1.25 in.

TYPE

Title: Bodoni Bold (scaled in Word as a
    graphic)
Author: Bodoni Bold Italic (scaled in Word as a
    graphic)
For alternate typefaces, see Appendix A.

Bitstream's version of the Bodoni typeface design retains the regular, smooth strokes and thick/thin contrasts of the original Bodonis, but thick strokes are heavier in proportion to thin strokes. This makes the Bitstream version better suited to the low resolution of laser printers. The especially sturdy look of the letterforms in these bold variants makes them stand out against the complex background graphic. The formality of the Bodonis seems appropriate to the seriousness of the subject matter.

GRAPHICS

The Capitol graphic is from the clip-art collection that comes with Word for Windows Version 2. I imported it into Microsoft Draw and added the text also in Microsoft Draw. This graphic is not included in Word for Windows Version 6's clip-art collection. Any clip-art graphic, however, will work.

PRODUCTION TIPS

After importing the graphic, open the drawing tools. Cut and paste the graphic into a text box the size you want the finished graphic to be. You can place the text items in text boxes or type them directly onto the page. Use the drawing tools to move the graphic behind the text and to align all text boxes to the center of the page. If you are using Microsoft Draw, place the text over the graphic. While in Draw in Version 2, to center the text and graphic, use the guides in the Draw menu. There is no automatic alignment feature in Microsoft Draw, so don't be discouraged if it takes a couple of tries to get things lined up to your satisfaction. Once the type and graphic are the way you want them, close Microsoft Draw and update the document, which placed the graphic with the text on the page. Next, select the graphic, which included the text, and enlarge it to fit the page dimensions. As mentioned elsewhere, if you are using scalable typefaces, Word will automatically scale the type to fit the new size without loss of font quality.

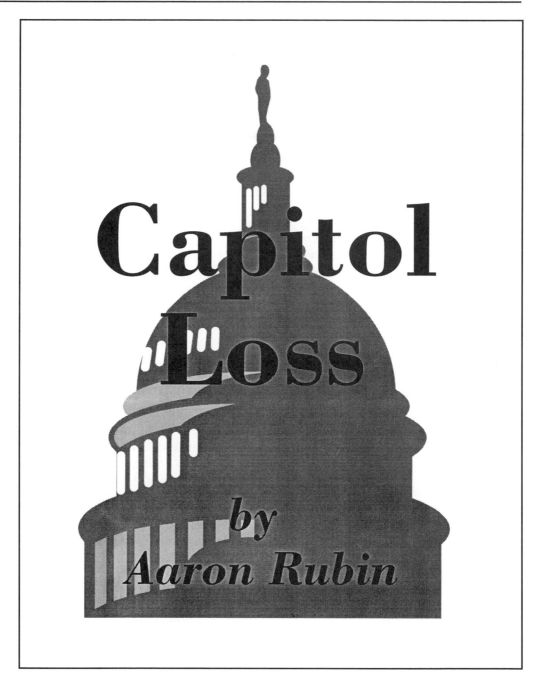

Capitol Loss

by

Aaron Rubin

Surely, this kind of document is one of the most complex typographic tasks you can undertake. Here you must plan ahead and take into account all of the different elements you'll want to include. Some of the following pages have many more formatting problems than a manual normally would, but I've intentionally stacked them up here to conserve space in this book.

The asymmetrical page arrangement gives more room for outdenting headings and for positioning attention-getters. It also gives the page visual variety and dynamics. The boldness of the heavy sans-serif faces and simple black graphics add significant visual interest to the title page, while graphic accents lighten up the complex, prosaic and often intimidating textual material.

In this manual I've formatted each page with the same wide left margin. Header components are placed in the same position from page to page, but the footers are mirror-imaged at the outside of the pages. I think readers find this page-number arrangement the easiest to use—and manuals *must* be easy to use.

PAGE SETUP

Paper size: 8 1/2 in. x 11 in.
Orientation: Portrait
Margins: Top & Bottom—1.5 in.
Left—2.5 in. Right—1.25 in.

TYPE

Title page:
4 Seasons: 48-pt. Zurich Black
Version 2: 14-pt. Zurich Extended Black
Weather Prediction Software: 24-pt. Zurich Black

Flora & Fauna Software: 36-pt. Modula Tall
Section-title page:
Part 1 Winter—48-pt. Zurich Black
Interior pages:
Chapter header numeral—36-pt. Zurich Black
Snowflake—40-pt. ITC Zapf Dingbats
Black square—18-pt. ITC Zapf Dingbats
Chapter title: 36-pt. Zurich Black
Body text: 14-pt. Granjon Roman, Italic and Bold
Bullet list special bullets: 14-pt. ITC Zapf Dingbats
Tip dingbat (pointing fist): 24-pt. Linotype European Pi 3
Tip text: 14-pt. Granjon Bold
Regular header numeral and chapter name: 14-pt. Zurich Bold
Snowflake: 18-pt. ITC Zapf Dingbats
Major topic: 10-pt. Zurich Bold
Major text heading: 18-pt. Zurich Bold
Subhead: 18-pt. Zurich Bold
Text to be entered (e.g., C:\Seasons\Predict): 12-pt. Serifa Bold
Text in Summary box: 14-pt. Granjon Italic
Text to label screen shot placeholders (not part of the manual's design): 24-pt. Copperplate Bold from Digital Typeface Corporation.
For alternate typefaces, see Appendix A.

Zurich, Bitstream's version of the Univers type family, is an elegant, readable sans-serif face. Its subtle forms lack the glacial coldness of the Helvetica family. Linotype's Granjon is also quite readable and contrasts well with the headings. Emigre's Modula Tall has a quirky quality that's ideal for a distinctive company name.

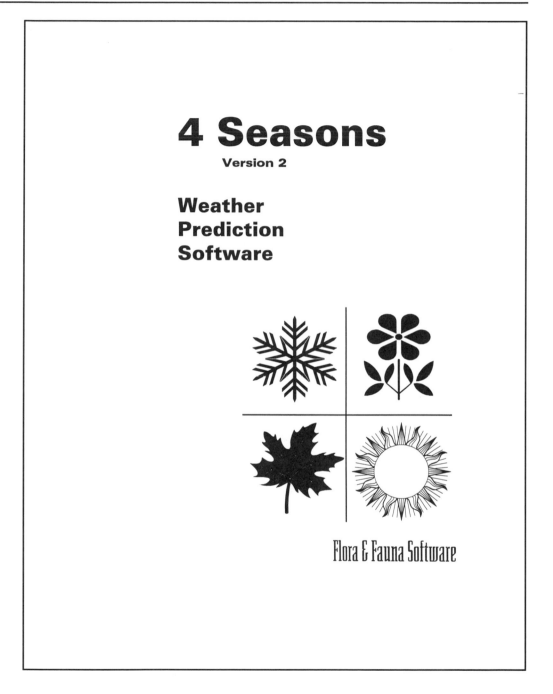

4 Seasons
Version 2

Weather
Prediction
Software

Flora & Fauna Software

GRAPHICS

The season emblems and the compass symbol were adapted from symbols in the Arts & Letters Graphics Editor collection. I made minor modifications to them in that program, then cut and pasted them into the manual via the Clipboard. The compass symbol is used to flag a series of directions throughout the document.

PRODUCTION TIPS

The biggest headache with such a complex work is accounting ahead of time for all the different types of information that must have a distinctive format. And, once this is determined, integrating all of these into a unified whole. You must plan ahead!

Title page: The title and subtitle are set flush-left. The Version statement was indented to line up with the word Seasons. The four season emblems were pasted into a table with four cells. Only the interior borders of the cell were given 1.5-point borders. The table is set flush-right as is the software company name.

Section divider: The title is set flush-left. The winter emblem and cell borders are located in the same place as on the title page: flush-right. (This page was easy to create. I simply saved the title page with a new name, replaced the original title with the new one, removed the three season emblems from the table, and removed the company name.)

Interior pages: To make the header appear visually centered, I outdented it by 1 inch. (To create an outdent, or negative indent, put a minus sign in front of the indent measurement in the indent box in the Format/ Paragraph dialog box.) The numeral and

snowflake dingbat are set flush-left. The 1.5-point border is part of the paragraph with the numeral. The square dingbat apparently attached to it is set on the next line. Its paragraph is right-aligned with a .24-inch indent from right (more on the indent below). The line spacing for this paragraph is exactly 18 points. In order to snug the dingbat up against the rule, I superscripted it 3 points.

I constructed the first page and inside headers the same way except for the type size and the information included. On the inside headers I inserted the field code (using the dialog box in the View/Header submenu) for my chapter names and the field code for my major topics. The chapter title information is set flush-left, while the major topics are set with a right-aligned tab to align with the square dingbat. If you're fussy about such things, using the Ruler tab settings may not give you the precise visual alignment you need. In order to get the edge of the black square and the end of the major topic to align, I went into the Format/Paragraph dialog box for the square's paragraph and set it, after several tries, at a .24-inch indent from the right. The program is sensitive to changes in placement as small as .01 inch.

The chapter title, like the header, is out-dented by 1 inch. It is left-aligned. Body text is set with plenty of leading to make it less intimidating. Here, the 14-point Granjon is set with 18-point Exactly line spacing.

While the bulleted items were set by selecting the items and then using the auto-matic bulleting icon on the Standard toolbar (Toolbar), I changed the bullets to give them

Part I
Winter

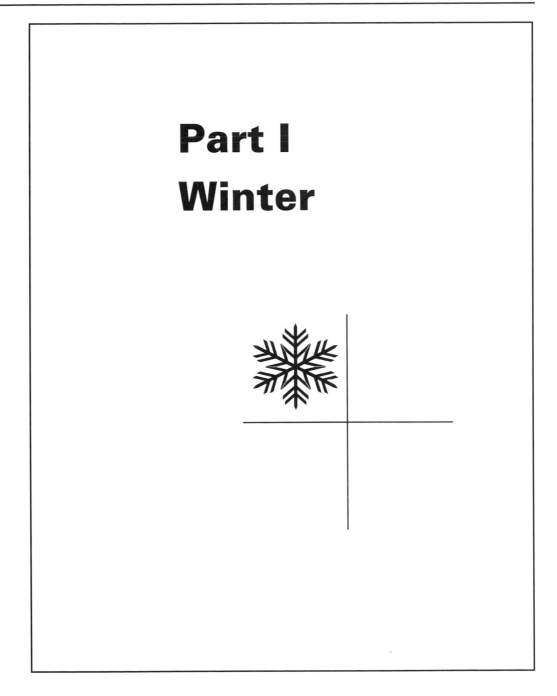

more pizzazz. At the start of the chapter it is common to go over a list of important items that will be discussed. It seems appropriate to single them out with a special symbol. I made a bullet, then copied it to the Clipboard and pasted it into place. These bullet items have a separate Style in my Style sheet. They are indented .75-inch from the left.

Tips are distinguished by the black pointing fist (the pointing fist is a traditional typographic ornament and comes in a variety of styles) and bold type. The pointing-fist dingbat is inserted in its own frame in the margin. The fist will move with its associated text because I clicked on Move With Text in the Format/Frame dialog box.

To make sure your frames, such as those for the fist and the compass, are tied to a related paragraph, look for the tiny blip that appears under the first letter of the paragraph parallel to the frame. (You may need a zoom view to see this.) To make sure that frames containing similar information (such as repeating fists) are formatted consistently, use the Format/Frame dialog box to set the size and placement parameters for each frame.

Screen shots or other graphics are easy to include in this layout. You just insert them directly into the text in the proper location; you don't need to put them in frames. You can put borders around any graphic: just select the graphic, then use the Format/ Borders and Shading (Format/Border) dialog box. (The screen shot placeholders have a 10 percent pattern that's much coarser than the solid yellow text backgrounds I use when using a laser or other low-resolution printer.)

Major headings (my Heading 1 style) are outdented 1 inch. Subheadings (my Heading 2 style) are flush-left. This establishes a visual hierarchy even though I used the same typeface for both. I created numbered lists using the Numbered List button on the Standard toolbar. These lists (also saved as a Style) have a 1-inch indent.

The instructions to be entered by the reader into a computer are identified by a change in typeface. It's best to select a face that looks like a bold typewriter face, such as Courier.

The compass graphic, used to identify directions for the reader to follow, is set in a frame that will move with its paragraph. In such complex documents, you'll have to make changes frequently; remember to keep your frames attached to their written material. (See previous discussion of the pointing fist for locating and sizing such frames.)

I made the bulleted list on page 3:4 the same way as the first one; but, instead of the snowflake, I used the second-size plain-dot bullet in the Format/Bullets and Numbering (Tools/Bullets and Numbering) dialog box, which would typically be the type of bulleted list used in a manual of this kind. (I added this to the Style sheet.)

Finally, for the shaded, shadowed box, I entered the text, set its typeface in italics, then selected it and inserted a frame. The border is a 2.25-point shadowed box selected from the Format/Borders and Shading (Format/Border) dialog box. For shading options, I selected Shading Solid, Background Yellow.

3 ❄

Storm Prediction

Introduction on the storm prediction module. This module will perform many tasks, including:

- ❄ Major Bullet Item
- ❄ Major Bullet Item
- ❄ Major Bullet Item
- ❄ Major Bullet Item
- ❄ Major Bullet Item
- ❄ Major Bullet Item
- ❄ Major Bullet Item

When in the course of human events, it becomes necessary for one people to dissolve the political bands which have connected them with another, and to assume among the Powers of the Earth, the separate and equal station which the

☞ Using a consistent, distinct graphic, such as this dingbat, makes it easy for your reader to find certain types of information. I'm using this pointing fist as the indicator for a TIP.

SCREEN SHOT

OR

GRAPHIC

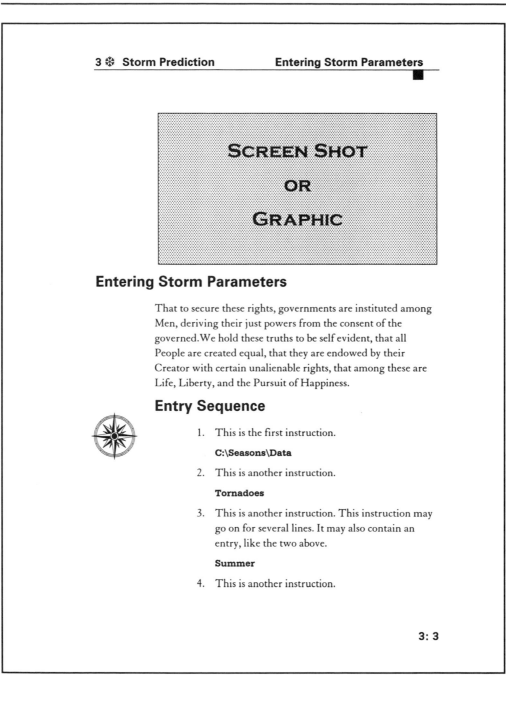

3 ❄ Storm Prediction   Entering Storm Parameters

SCREEN SHOT

OR

GRAPHIC

Entering Storm Parameters

That to secure these rights, governments are instituted among
Men, deriving their just powers from the consent of the
governed. We hold these truths to be self evident, that all
People are created equal, that they are endowed by their
Creator with certain unalienable rights, that among these are
Life, Liberty, and the Pursuit of Happiness.

Entry Sequence

1. This is the first instruction.

    C:\Seasons\Data

2. This is another instruction.

    Tornadoes

3. This is another instruction. This instruction may
    go on for several lines. It may also contain an
    entry, like the two above.

    Summer

4. This is another instruction.

3: 3

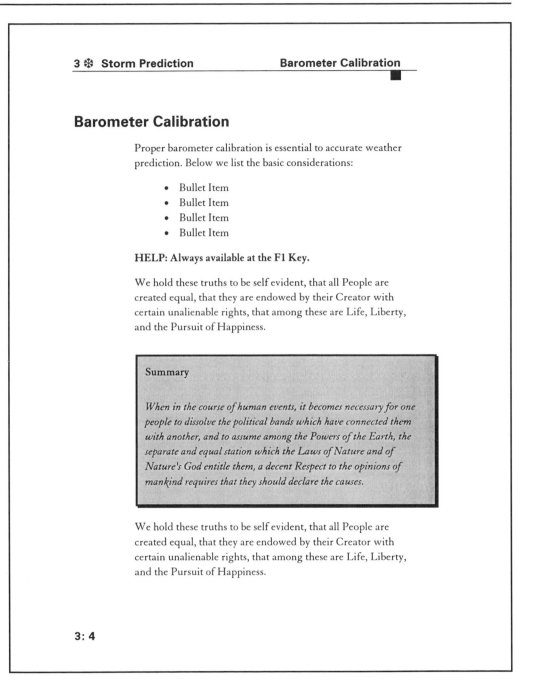

Barometer Calibration

Proper barometer calibration is essential to accurate weather prediction. Below we list the basic considerations:

- Bullet Item
- Bullet Item
- Bullet Item
- Bullet Item

HELP: Always available at the F1 Key.

We hold these truths to be self evident, that all People are created equal, that they are endowed by their Creator with certain unalienable rights, that among these are Life, Liberty, and the Pursuit of Happiness.

Summary

When in the course of human events, it becomes necessary for one people to dissolve the political bands which have connected them with another, and to assume among the Powers of the Earth, the separate and equal station which the Laws of Nature and of Nature's God entitle them, a decent Respect to the opinions of mankind requires that they should declare the causes.

We hold these truths to be self evident, that all People are created equal, that they are endowed by their Creator with certain unalienable rights, that among these are Life, Liberty, and the Pursuit of Happiness.

3: 4

Word's table feature makes this catalog easy to lay out. Strong, black rules, the unusual sans-serif display face and a playful arrangement of the featured items give this catalog a contemporary, upbeat appearance.

PAGE SETUP

Paper size: 8 1/2 in. x 11 in.
Orientation: Landscape
Margins: Top—1.83 in. Bottom—1.17 in.
Inside—1 in. Outside—.7 in.
Gutter—.25 in. (facing pages)

TYPE

Subtitle: 16-pt. Insignia A
Title: 60-pt. Insignia A
Headers: 18-pt. Insignia A
Catalog numbers and item names: 10-pt. Futura Bold
Body text: 10-pt. Futura
Seaside dingbats: 80-pt. Linotype Holiday Pi 1
Weather dingbats: 100-pt. Linotype Holiday Pi 1

Futura and Insignia A work well together; each has thick, even black strokes, distinct geometric shapes and a strong presence. Insignia was designed by Neville Brody for Linotype and is shown here in Linotype's version. Notice the unusual design of the uppercase and lowercase s. Futura, here in the Bitstream version, has a strong personality but is easy to read even in small sizes.

COVER GRAPHICS

Again, the cover graphics are symbols from the Arts & Letters Graphics Editor. You can create them in Arts & Letters, then cut and paste them into the document via the Clipboard.

PRODUCTION TIPS

I could have used a vertical page orientation, but I wanted to do something different. In general, catalogs tend to look the same, so I chose the horizontal shape to get attention.

Cover page: The subtitle is a flush-left paragraph indented 2.13 inches from the left and .3 inch from the right. I indented it to make it line up with the title, which I created first. I used Exactly spacing of 24 points to create the height of the black band. To make the reversed type, select the type and set its color to White in the Format/Font (Format/Character) dialog box; set the Shading Solid and the Background to Black in the Format/Borders and Shading (Format/Border/Shading) dialog box.

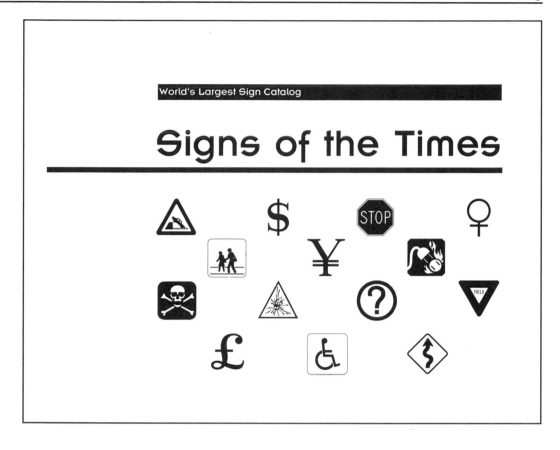

World's Largest Sign Catalog

Signs of the Times

The title is in a right-aligned paragraph. To make the 8-point rule, I inserted below the title an empty paragraph formatted with left alignment, Exactly line spacing of 8 points, and shading set as Pattern Solid and Background Black in the Border/Shading dialog box.

I set the graphics into a table inserted below the rule. (See the grid detail.) The table is in a frame, for easy placement. Each graphic is centered in its cell. I created the graphics in their finished size so I wouldn't have to fiddle with them in the table.

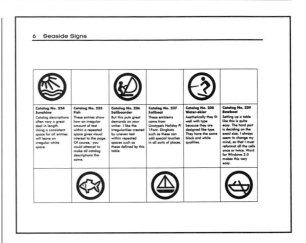

Inside pages: I arranged the headers as mirror images: the one on the left page is left-aligned; the one on the right page is right-aligned. The header border is a 3-point rule. These symmetrical facing pages are composed of two identical tables. The cell borders of each table create mirror images of each other. All are 3-point rules. (See the grid detail.)

I set all catalog text entries flush-left and used the Exactly option to set cell widths and heights, with .17 inch between columns (all in the Table menu). Items within the cells (in this case, dingbats) are in centered paragraphs; each weather icon has been superscripted (14 points).

6   Seaside Signs

Catalog No. 234 Sunshine Catalog descriptions often vary a great deal in length. Using a consistent space for all entries will leave an irregular white space.	**Catalog No. 235 Fish** These entries show how an irregular amount of text within a repeated space gives visual interest to the page. Of course, you could attempt to make all catalog descriptions the same.	**Catalog No. 236 Sailboarder** But this puts great demands on your writer. I like the irregularities created by uneven text within repeated spaces such as these defined by this table.	**Catalog No. 237 Sailboat** These emblems came from Linotype's Holiday Pi 1Font. Dingbats such as these can add special touches in all sorts of places.	**Catalog No. 238 Water-skier** Aesthetically they fit well with type because they are designed like type. They have the same black and white qualities.	**Catalog No. 239 Rowboat** Setting up a table like this is quite easy. The hard part is deciding on the exact size. I always seem to change my mind, so that I must reformat all the cells once or twice. Word for Windows 2.0 makes this very easy.

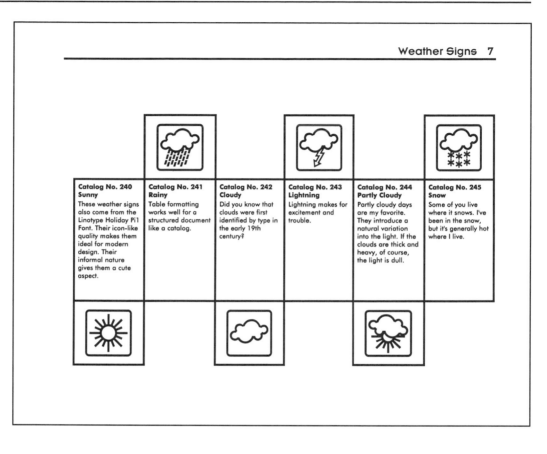

IV

A Closer Look

Character &
Paragraph
Formatting

Now that you've seen Word in action on the pages of Section III, you're ready to delve further into the Word for Windows features that help you produce these designs. In this section, you'll learn about the character and paragraph formatting capabilities that are built into this remarkable program. You'll find that making even everyday projects attractive is easier than you thought.

Word for Windows makes coping with characters a pleasure. Numerous shortcut key combinations, the Formatting toolbar (Ribbon) and the Standard toolbar (Toolbar) make choosing type styles and applying them to your text a snap.

CHARACTER FORMATTING

All character formatting can be done in the Font (Character) dialog box, which appears when you click on the Font (Character) command in the Format menu. I use this feature so often that I made it an icon on my Standard toolbar (Toolbar). You can also access it with Ctrl+D. (In Version 2, you can also access it immediately by double-clicking in any empty space on the Ribbon.) The Font dialog box gives you choices for fonts, point sizes, type styles, colors, superscripting and subscripting, expanded or contracted character spacing, underlining, strikethrough, all-caps, small caps and hidden characters. And it lets you preview your formatting changes. Often, you'll want to change only the typeface, point size or style (bold, italic, etc.), which you can do conveniently using the list boxes and buttons on the Formatting toolbar (Ribbon). Also, nearly all character formatting options can be accessed by a shortcut key combination. See the Word for Windows *User's Guide* or the keyboard template for details.

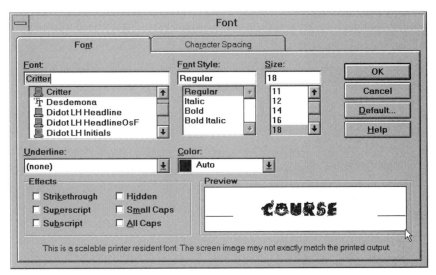

Figure 10-1: Choose font stye and size in the Font dialog box.

Applying Character Formatting

To apply character formatting, simply select the characters to be formatted, then use the Format/Font (Format/Character) dialog box, the appropriate list box or button on the Formatting toolbar (Ribbon), or the key combination.

Character parameters you use frequently can be saved along with paragraph parameters as a Style and applied quickly from the Formatting toolbar. To create or apply a Style for character formatting, see the discussion of Styles later in this chapter.

If you wish to change the body text font for your entire document, click on Default (Use As Default) in the Format/Font dialog box. But be careful: this will change your NORMAL.DOT if you are using that template. (See the section on NORMAL.DOT near the end of this chapter.)

Gray/Blank Boxes

The Font (Character) dialog box displays the formats of your current selection. If any of the boxes are gray or blank, it means your selected text contains a mixture of formats. If you choose a new format under these circumstances, it will affect every item you selected—you may lose special formatting for such items as dingbats or italicized words.

Copying Character Formatting

Often after formatting a heading, initial capital or word, you'll want to apply the same settings to another character, word or paragraph in your document. There are several ways to accomplish this:

Repeat Command

If you're applying a character format immediately after the first occurrence of the formatting, you can use the Ctrl+Y sequence (F4 key), which performs the Repeat Typing command in the Edit menu. To use this, apply your character formatting—for instance, change 12-point Futura to 14-point Futura Bold, then select the next character(s) to be changed to the new formatting and press Ctrl+Y (F4). Remember, this works only if you're copying the formatting immediately after the original formatting.

Copy Character Formatting Anytime

Copying character formatting is a bit more complex in Word for Windows Version 6 than it was in Version 2. One method is to first select the characters containing the desired formatting. Next, click on the Format Painter button on the Standard toolbar. Double-click the button if you wish to copy the new format to several items. Once the pointer changes to the I-beam with a paintbrush, select the text to be reformatted and let go of the mouse button. If you're reformatting lines of text, you'll see the I-Beam pointer turn into a hollow arrow when it moves into the left margin near the text. If you select the text with this arrow, it will also act to apply the format change of the Format Painter. Another method is to select the text with the formatting you wish to copy and then press Ctrl+Shift+C. Next, select the text you wish to reformat and press Ctrl+Shift+V. (See below for instructions if you have Word for Windows Version 2 installed.)

In Version 2, there are two ways to copy the formatting of a character or group of characters to another character or group. In the first, select the characters to be changed.

Next, put the cursor over the character that has the desired formatting, then press Ctrl+Shift+click. You can also use the Copy Format command, found in the Tools/ Options/Toolbar category. Click on Show Commands. Next, following the method described in the *User's Guide*, install the Copy Format command in a menu or make it an icon button on the Toolbar. Or, use it from Tools/ Macro/Show Commands. To use this command, just select the characters you wish to copy. Click on the Copy Format command. Next, select the characters you want to receive the new formatting by dragging over them or clicking at the left of their paragraph. A faint line will appear under all characters to be changed. Press Enter.

Formatting a Large Number of Special Items
To change the formatting of a large group of already specially formatted characters, such as a series of ding-bats, use the Replace command in the Edit menu. This command can search for and replace specific character formatting as well as text.

To Undo Manual Character Formatting

To do this, select the character(s) and press Ctrl+Space bar. Sometimes when you try to apply a Style to charac-ters manually formatted with special characteristics, re-formatting them with another Style doesn't work—they retain the manually formatted settings. (In most cases, manual formatting takes precedence over style format-ting.) In such cases, you must unformat these characters by using the above technique. You could also use Edit/ Replace to search for the special formatting and replace it with the desired format.

Replacing a Character

To substitute one character for another—for instance, when you need to replace one dingbat or bullet style with another—you can simply select the old character and type in the new one. If you need to replace a large number of items, use Replace in the Edit menu; it can search and replace characters and character formatting.

Character Spacing

Spaces between words and fixed-space increments exist in the same point size as your text. In the days of traditional typesetting, spaces were made of actual pieces of lead made to fit each size of type. But you may need to create smaller spaces than Word automatically gives you.

Changing the Size of a Space

Treat the spaces as characters: select them and change their size using the Formatting toolbar's (Ribbon's) point-size list box or the Format/Font (Format/Character) dialog box. (I specifically recommend this method for making smaller spaces than those Word produces automatically. Note that if you make the spaces a larger point size than the text in the line, the leading between lines will increase unless it is set to Exactly. I don't suggest adding space using this method. Rather, use more spaces or set tabs.)

NORMAL: SPACING BETWEEN WORDS
REDUCED: SPACING BETWEEN WORDS

Figure 10-2: Customized character spacing can make your text look better.

While you can select spaces whether they're showing or not, it's much easier if you followed my earlier recommendation to view spaces.

Fixed Spaces

In order to control the distance between words exactly, you can use fixed spaces (also called nonbreaking spaces). Sometimes I use fixed spaces to absolutely control space between words in a justified line (as in the WJR letterhead example in Chapter 5) because without such spaces the program determines the space between words in a justified line. I also use fixed spaces to visually position the vertical alignment of capital letters and to create identical gaps between items in a series when I don't want the gaps susceptible to a line break.

To create a fixed space in your current point size, use Ctrl+Shift+Space bar. If you're displaying spaces, you'll see a small, hollow dot as the symbol for each fixed space.

Superscript & Subscript

You may often need to raise or lower a character relative to its neighbors in a line. Superscripting and subscripting are also done in the Format/Font (Format/Character) dialog box. In Version 6, in the Tools/Options dialog box, the Compatibility tab offers you the choice of *not* adding extra line space for raised or lowered characters. I advise you to click on this option if you do not want unsightly gaps in your text. If you're typesetting mathematical information, however, you may not care about such gaps. (In Version 2, extra space is not added to a line when you super- or subscript a character.)

Using Special Characters

The traditional way to insert special characters—which include en and em dashes, foreign characters, dingbats, symbols, etc.—is to enter their ANSI decimal code preceded by a zero using the numeric keypad with Num Lock on. Of course, to use this method you must refer to a character chart for the font you're using. Currently, Bitstream, Adobe, Monotype and Digital Typeface Corporation provide such charts for their typefaces. Some vendors do not.

To bypass this time-consuming step, Word for Windows provides a display of the entire standard ANSI character set via the Symbol command on the Insert menu. After you select Insert/Symbol, you'll see the standard ANSI symbol set displayed in a chart when you select Normal Text in the Symbols tab, Font list box. Other fonts, such as the ITC Zapf Dingbats, Windows Wingdings and the Windows Symbol font, may also appear in the Font list box, depending on which fonts and which printer driver you have installed. To select the special character you want, Select Insert/Symbol. Choose the Symbols tab, then scroll to the font you want in the Font list box. Next, click on the symbol you want and then click on the Insert button. You may select as many symbols as you want. When finished, click the Close button. To see a particular character enlarged, point at it and hold down the left mouse button. You can assign a special shortcut key to any symbol you use frequently. Simply click on the Short-Cut key button and press the keys you wish. The key sequence will appear in the space provided in the dialog box. (In Version 2 selecting a symbol is much the same. After clicking on Insert/Symbol, find your desired font in the Symbols From list box. From the visual display select the character you want. Double-click to insert it. As in

Version 6, to focus on a specific character, you point at it and hold down the left mouse button.)

En & Em Dashes

Using proper dashes gives your document a typeset look. En and em dashes are longer than hyphens. The em dash, approximately the width of the capital M in the font you're using, represents a break from the idea being expressed; it often substitutes for a colon or parenthesis. The em dash is indicated by a double hyphen in typewritten and word processed copy. This break is stronger than a comma but not so strong as a period. The em dash should be set without spaces before or after it. The en dash, approximately half the width of the em dash, is used (usually with a space before and after it) to indicate an inclusive time period such as M – F (Monday through Friday).

The convenient way to insert an en or em dash is to place your cursor where you want it, then use the Insert/Symbol command. As described under Using Special Characters, just above, you'll be presented with a chart showing characters available in the font specified in the Symbols tab, Font drop-down list (see above mentioned section for Version 2 term variations). If the Normal Text font is not displayed in the list, scroll the list to find it—it should be at the top. The en and em dash are in row 4. Make your selection and close the dialog box. In Version 6 only, the Special Characters tab, in the Insert/Symbol dialog box, lists all the standard special characters, such as the en and em dashes and en and em spaces. This list allows you to select them by name and also reveals the special shortcut keys already assigned to these common items. You can also insert the characters using the ANSI character code method described previously.

Smart Quotes

Using proper quotation marks and apostrophes makes your publication look more professional. Smart Quotes are now a regular part of Word. To have them automatically used, click on Enable Smart Quotes in the Edit menu, or, if you are using AutoCorrect, select this feature in the Tools/AutoCorrect dialog box.

The easiest way to put these in your text, in Version 2, is to use the Enable Smart Quotes macro in the NEWMACRO.DOC (discussed in "Macros," in Chapter 2). You can also insert them using the Insert/Symbol chart or their ANSI character codes.

Initial Caps

These characters add an elegant touch to any text-heavy publication. I used them in Chapter 8 for the Writer's Hollywood Digest and the Multimedia News, and in the Damask Lullaby in Chapter 9. I especially like initial caps that stand up above the body text (sometimes called raised caps) because they give more visual variety to the page. However, sometimes you'll want to try a drop cap that snuggles down into the text (as in Damask Lullaby).

To create an *initial cap* that stands above the first line of a paragraph, in Version 6 or 2, select the character, then enlarge it to the size you want. You may notice that the space below the line containing the initial will increase. To fix this, use Exactly line spacing. That's really all you need to do to make an initial cap.

You may want to adjust the spacing above or below the paragraph with the initial cap to give it a proper visual setting. If you want the initial cap partially dropped, see the instructions in the example in the Writer's Hollywood Digest. (In Version 2, once you create one initial cap, you can easily copy its formatting to other letters using the Ctrl+Shift+click method described in "Copying Character Formatting" on page 305.)

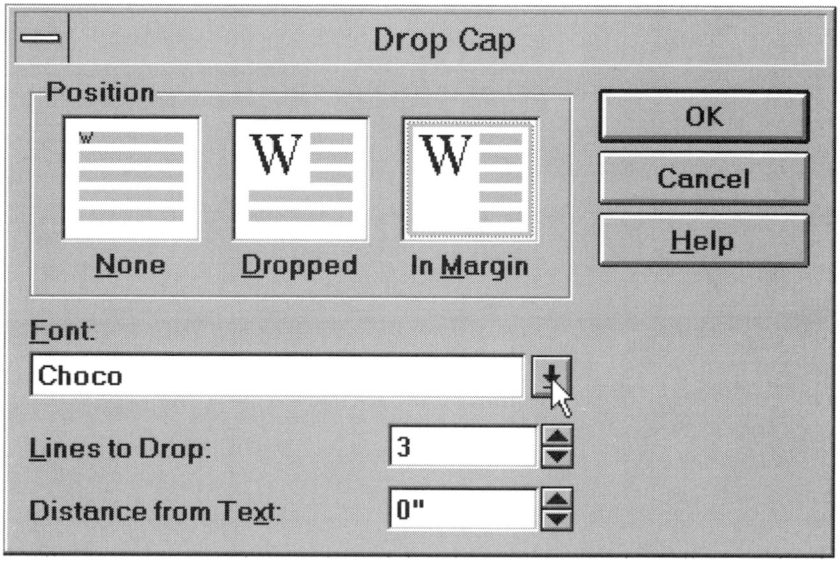

Figure 10-3: Drop caps add an elegant touch to a text-heavy publication.

For creating drop caps, Version 6 now includes a set of built-in commands in the Format/Drop Cap dialog box. In addition to the traditional drop cap, which nestles down into the text, you can now automatically insert a dropped word or a hanging capital in the margin. The program-selected spacing of these automatic commands works well. However, if you want to alter them, use the Format/Paragraph and Format/Frame commands to alter spacing around the drop caps. The best way to remove a drop cap in Version 6 is to select the drop cap, open Format/Drop Cap and choose the None icon.

(Version 2 provides a good Drop Cap macro in the NEWMACRO.DOC discussed in Chapter 2. Watching it work will give you good insight into creating custom drop caps. A *drop cap* in Version 2 is more complex because it must displace a portion of several text rows. Hence, it's easiest to put it in a frame. I start with the Drop Cap macro, then alter the size of the cap and its border dimensions to suit my needs.)

If you wish to create a drop cap from scratch in either Version 6 or 2, be prepared for some work. First select the drop cap character and then choose Insert/Frame. Be sure the frame's paragraph line spacing is set to Single and that all other paragraph settings are zero. Your frame settings should include the Around text-wrapping option and Move With Text. Using Format/Font (Format/Character) or the Formatting toolbar (Ribbon), make the character the size you want. Next, move and size your frame. Only by trial and error can you find the proper location of the dropped character in relation to its own surrounding space and to the other text lines. (Note that if your frame jumps in tiny increments, you must turn Snap to Grid off in the drawing tools. This is discussed below under Frames.)

Copying a drop cap in Version 6 is easy if you format the drop cap immediately after formatting another using the Format/Drop Cap command. Just press Ctrl+Y, the Edit/Repeat command. If you've done other work since the original drop cap creation, you can select the model drop cap and copy it to the Clipboard. Next, paste it in the location of the new drop cap. Then, select it and type in the correct letter. Or, you can start over with the Format/Drop Cap command to make another drop cap. (Note that working with frames and indented body text may cause you trouble. See the section on Frames below.)

The simplest method to copy a drop cap formatted in Version 2 is to copy to the Clipboard a drop cap you've already made, then paste it into the location of the next drop cap. Finally, replace the old drop cap character with the correct one by selecting the incorrect letter and typing in the new one.

A more complex method of copying a drop cap in Version 2 is to first select the letter you want to format, then choose Insert/Frame. Next, copy the model drop cap paragraph mark to the Clipboard and paste it in front of the new drop cap frame's existing paragraph mark. This gives the frame the model's formatting. Finally, do the same for the paragraph mark of the drop cap character itself. (This paragraph mark will be inside the frame.)

Note on frames and drop caps in versions 6 and 2: You may have trouble placing a drop cap, or any other item in a frame, if your normal text or body text has an indent. If you need drop caps in a series of paragraphs with an indent, and if you find that the program is not allowing you to place the drop caps properly, or is producing unpredictable spacing, I recommend that rather than indenting the paragraph, you create a larger left margin.

PARAGRAPH FORMATTING

It's difficult to overstate the significance of paragraphs in Word for Windows. Almost every aspect of page design involves paragraph formatting. While we ordinarily speak of a paragraph as a group of related sentences, Word recognizes anything—text, graphic, table, frame or blank line—followed by a paragraph mark (¶) as a paragraph. You produce a paragraph mark every time you press the Enter key by itself.

In this book, I usually refer to "paragraphs." The *User's Guide* usually refers to "paragraph marks." If a paragraph contains no text (merely a blank line or a blank line with border formatting), I often refer to it as an "empty paragraph." Such a paragraph might also be called a line break, empty line or new line.

Word relies on the paragraph mark to store most formatting instructions for the information preceding it, including paragraph indents, alignment, line spacing inside, before and after the paragraph, tab settings, pagination criteria and border settings. The paragraph mark also carries Style formatting: typeface, point size and special character styles, such as italic, bold, underline, etc.

It's therefore important to remember that inadvertent removal of a paragraph mark may cause major formatting mischief. This makes displaying paragraph marks highly desirable.

Displaying & Removing Paragraph Marks

I suggest you always *display paragraph marks*, using the Tools/Options/View dialog box. You can also display them by clicking on the Show/Hide button on the Formatting toolbar (Ribbon) (it looks like a paragraph mark) or by pressing Ctrl+Shift+8 (not the F8 function key).

When you *remove a paragraph mark*, the text involved will acquire the formatting of the paragraph that follows—it will become a part of it. Hence, if you should delete the last line of a Normal Style paragraph (including its paragraph mark) that precedes a heading, the remainder of your Normal Style paragraph will become a heading. Try not to be disconcerted by this. It still happens to me. Simply click on the Undo button, then redelete the text and leave the paragraph mark.

Sometimes when you remove a paragraph mark associated with a frame or table, major alteration of an entire document will occur. Whenever dramatic changes happen to your formatting after deleting something, click on the Undo button. If you can't undo, close the document without saving it and reopen it or bring in your backup copy.

THE PARAGRAPH DIALOG BOX

Most formatting for paragraphs is done using the Paragraph dialog box, which appears when you click on the Paragraph command in the Format menu. I have the Paragraph dialog box as an icon on my Standard toolbar (Toolbar) because I use it so often.

In most situations you can reach the Format/Paragraph menu quickly by simply pressing the right mouse button when you are in a paragraph. The short menu offers paragraph formatting as one of its options. (This feature is not available in Version 2.)

Paragraph settings include alignment (Left, Center, Right or Justified); indents (from left and right as well as first line only); page breaks; line spacing within paragraphs; and line space before and after paragraphs. The Paragraph dialog box has a button that accesses the Tabs dialog box. Tabs can now also be accessed from the Format menu, where you can set all paragraph tabs and leaders. Most of the items in the Paragraph dialog box work in a straightforward manner, with the exception of Line Spacing.

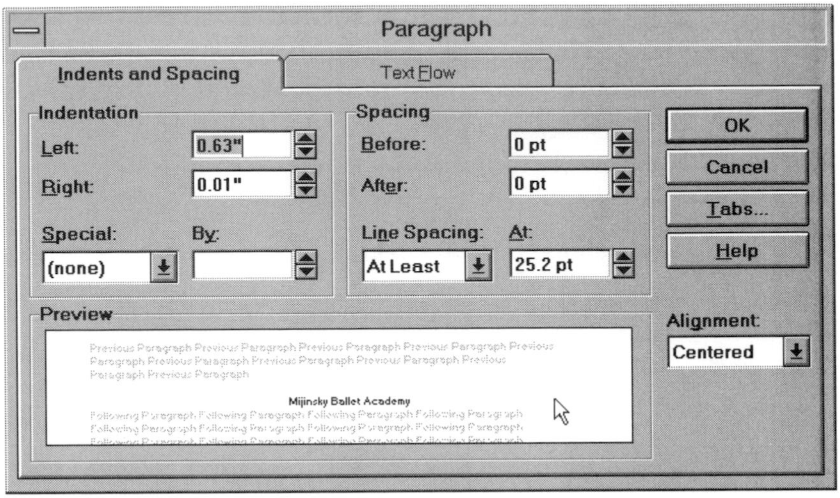

Figure 10-4: Most of your paragraph formatting is done in the Paragraph dialog box.

Line Spacing (Leading) Options

You set interline spacing, traditionally referred to as leading, in the Format/Paragraph dialog box. Word distinguishes between line spacing (leading between lines within a paragraph) and extra spacing before or after a paragraph, which is used often around headings, titles, etc.

In the Line Spacing list box, Word offers a series of choices, some of which are preset. These options need some clarification.

Single Line Spacing

By default, Word uses Single line spacing. This creates the amount of single line spacing (for example, 12 points) the program determines appropriate to the point size of the type you're using. Hence, in Single spacing 8-point type is set on 10 points of line spacing (leading), 9-point on just under 12 points, 10-point on 12, 11-point on 13,

15-point on 18, etc. Single spacing allows Word to increase line spacing to accommodate larger text and graphics (including tables and frames) automatically. (See the discussion above on Superscript & Subscript as it pertains to Word for Windows 6.)

The Single option works well in most body-text-intensive applications.

(In Version 2, the Auto spacing option functions identically to the Single spacing option in Version 6.)

Other Line-Spacing Options

While the *User's Guide* mentions that Word measures line spacing in points, it specifies its preset line spacing in lines, indicated as "li." It further mentions that Single spacing has about six lines per inch. When Word produces "li" in the "AT" box in Version 2, the li stands for 12 points. It does not tell you that a line is always 12 points unless that amount would make the chosen line spacing smaller than the Single spacing. The following list explains how each of the other line-spacing options works.

> *Single:* 12 points in all cases except where Single spacing would be larger. (For Version 2 only.)

> *1.5:* In Version 2, *1.5* is 18 points in all cases except where Single spacing would be larger. In Version 6, *1.5* is 1 1/2 times the amount determined by the program for Single.

> *Double:* In Version 2, double is 24 points in all cases except where Single spacing would be larger. In Version 6, *double* is twice the amount determined by the program for Single.

At Least: Allows you to set a minimum that the program can increase to accommodate larger items.

Exactly: Lets you control the line spacing absolutely. Word will not increase or decrease this amount no matter what graphic or text you may insert. You can enter any specific amount you choose using any measurement units Word supports.

Multiple: Provides multiples of single-line spacing—12 points/line or larger.

Using At Least & Exactly Line Spacing

For both At Least and Exactly, you can enter the measurements in lines (li), inches (in), points (pt), picas (pi) or centimeters (cm).

The At Least spacing option is very attractive because it lets you establish a minimum leading and also allows the program to add space for larger items like graphics, frames and tables. Setting your Normal Style to this line spacing will give you control and flexibility. My only note of caution: if you add unusual features in your work, such as dingbats, small graphics or initial caps, you may discover some visually uneven spacing in unexpected places.

Because I come from a traditional typesetting background and because I'm the picky type, I like to use the Exactly setting most of the time. When working with such items as brochures and advertisements, the Exactly option is a must. But remember that using it for the paragraph marks of frames and tables requires special care. In creating tables, use the Exactly option when you want all lines of text to align horizontally across cell boundaries; to maintain consistency in large tables with inconsistent contents; when a table's dimensions constrain the spacing of its contents; and of course when you don't like the results you get with the Single or At Least settings. (See the discussion of frames and tables in the following chapter.) Remember that when you change your type size in the Exactly setting, your line spacing will not change with it.

Spacing Before & After Paragraphs

The amount of space you use before and after a paragraph is an important part of the visual organization of your document. Word for Windows provides the Before and After spacing options in the Paragraph dialog box to help you refine spacing between paragraphs and around other page elements such as tables, headings, lists and graphics. Default settings are given in line-space options—here, the single line always equals 12 points, 1.5 lines always equal 18 points, etc. But you can enter measurements directly in any units that Word uses. (Again, point is abbreviated as pt, pica as pi, inch as in and centimeter as cm. I recommend using points.)

In setting up your document design, create space between normal paragraphs by adding space before or after, whichever seems most logical to you. But be consistent. I use After spacing because it allows paragraphs to move all the way to the top margin or to the top of a column without padding. Version 6 now provides an option for suppressing extra space above paragraphs at the top of the page in the Tools/Options/Compatibility tab.

For headings, give them enough Before spacing so that they are clearly separated from the preceding material and enough After spacing to properly introduce their text. It may be that the space before the Normal Style text paragraphs will provide a proper interval and you will not need additional After spacing for a heading.

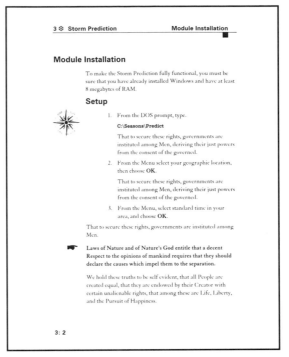

Figure 10-5: Use the Before and After paragraph spacing options to improve your page designs.

For graphics, tables, etc., if they are to have even padding on top and bottom, create this as Before and After spacing; don't depend on the material around it to provide a consistent visual setting.

Creating Special Vertical Spacing

Especially when designing flyers, brochures and advertisements, you'll often need to create large, exact amounts of vertical space between lines of text, graphics, etc. You can do this any way that feels comfortable to you, but an easy way to create and easily control the exact size of a vertical space is to make an empty paragraph with line spacing set to Exactly (any reasonable point size will do, say 6 points) and with no Before or After spacing. Then, to produce the desired size, format this empty paragraph by changing its point size using the Point Size list box on the Formatting toolbar (Ribbon). This way, you can easily change the size of the spacing quickly and know exactly what to expect. (Such a paragraph might be a good addition to your design template if you have occasion to use this type of spacing often.)

Line Break Without a New Paragraph

To create a new line without the Before and After spacing associated with a new paragraph, use Shift+Enter. (You will not see a paragraph mark but, rather, a small arrow.)

Alignment

Alignment options appear in the list box at the lower right of the Format/Paragraph dialog box. In using justified alignment, remember that you will probably need to use hyphenation as well to improve the appearance of narrow columns. Hyphenation options are accessed from the Tools menu.

Using Indents & Negative Indents for Aligning

Most of us think of indents as the traditional way to begin a paragraph. But indents and outdents (negative indents) can be used to solve many alignment problems. Word allows you to indent or outdent the whole paragraph from the left and/or right. Also, you can indent only the first line of the paragraph from the left. You can indent and outdent using the Format/Paragraph dialog box or the small arrows, called indent markers, on the rulers (Ruler). Complex alignments like those in the Mijinsky Ballet Academy flyer (Chapter 7) were easy using the rulers.

Try to remember outdents and indents as tools for aligning text with rules, as in the Dunham Industries flyer (Chapter 7).

Outdents allow you to put text in a margin, making it easy to create attractive headings. I recommend that you spend some time playing with all alignment parameters. To set an outdent, click the down arrow in the indention boxes; you will see a minus sign in front of the number. Or you can use the indent markers on the rulers.

Also, because borders and shading are paragraph attributes, you can control the length of rules and shaded areas using indents and outdents. Several examples are the Full Deck business card (Chapter 5), Athens Estates advertisement (Chapter 7), Keeping Fit brochure (Chapter 7) and Memorandum memo (Chapter 5).

Mixed Alignments
Sometimes you may want to use different alignment settings on the same line—for example, in headers and footers and for addresses and phone numbers on letterheads. I've illustrated mixed alignment schemes in the Full Deck business card, my Writer-Designer stationery with lines (Chapter 5), and the table of contents for the Zoo Resources report (Chapter 9).

You can tackle this situation several ways. If the type sizes of all items used on the same line can share a common line spacing, you can simply set tabs with left, center and right alignments. Successive clicks on the Tab Alignment button at the left of the horizontal ruler reveals left, center, right and decimal tabs in Version 6. To set these tabs on the Ruler in Version 2, you click on the Ribbon's appropriate Tab button, then click on the Ruler location where you want the tab. To remove any tabs you don't want, simply drag them down and off the Ruler. Remember that tabs can be set for individual lines or included in the paragraph's Style settings.

The other approach is to create a table. If you need to include a lot of information set in different type sizes or with different line spacing, this is the best choice.

Tabs & Tab Leaders

Tabs and tab leaders are set in the Format/Tabs or in the Format/Paragraph dialog box by clicking on the Tabs button. Tabs are easily set on the horizontal ruler (Ruler), and you can also set them in the dialog box. Tab leaders attractively and effectively connect items in lists such as tables of contents. I used them in the Writer's Hollywood Digest (see Figure 10-6 below). I recommend that you practice with these, too.

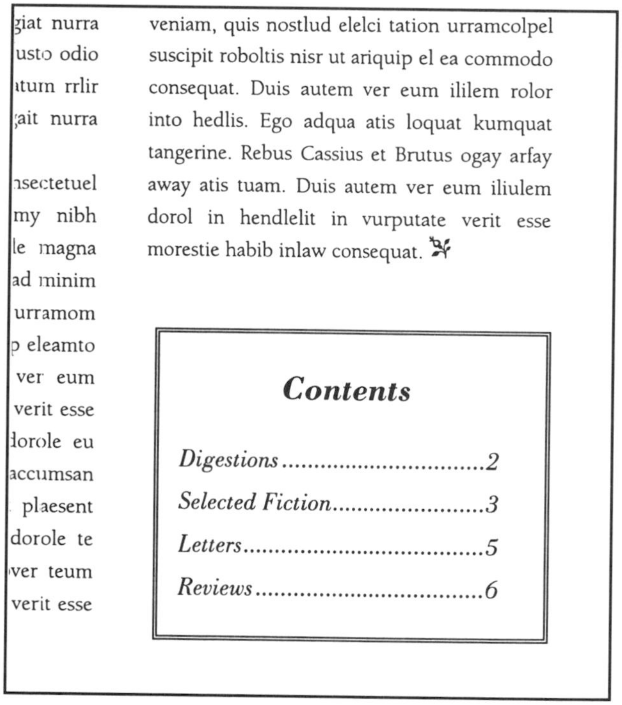

giat nurra · usto odio · ttum rrlir · jait nurra

nsectetuel · my nibh · le magna · ad minim · urramom · p eleamto · ver eum · verit esse · lorole eu · accumsan · plaesent · dorole te · ver teum · verit esse

veniam, quis nostlud elelci tation urramcolpel suscipit roboltis nisr ut ariquip el ea commodo consequat. Duis autem ver eum ililem rolor into hedlis. Ego adqua atis loquat kumquat tangerine. Rebus Cassius et Brutus ogay arfay away atis tuam. Duis autem ver eum iliulem dorol in hendlelit in vurputate verit esse morestie habib inlaw consequat. ✠

Contents

Digestions 2

Selected Fiction 3

Letters 5

Reviews 6

Figure 10-6: Tab leaders help the reader connect categories in listings.

To *remove* manually applied special formatting in a paragraph and format it with the features of its Style, select the paragraph(s) and press Ctrl+Q.

To *repeat* paragraph formatting immediately after original application, press Ctrl+Y (F4), or select Repeat Formatting from the Edit menu.

To *copy* in Version 6, select your model and then press Ctrl+Shift+C. Next, select the entire recipient paragraph and then press Ctrl+Shift+V. You can also use the Format Painter method described above in the discussion of character formatting.

To *copy* in Version 2, select the paragraph whose Style you wish to change. Then move the pointer into the Selection Bar (in Page Layout View) or the Style Area (in Normal View) next to the paragraph whose formatting you wish to copy. Press Ctrl+Shift+click. Note that this technique will copy the formatting of the actual paragraph clicked near, whether or not that paragraph retains the format of the Style it is identified with. For instance, you might have several paragraphs labeled with the Normal Style that you have altered manually, as in an advertisement. If you copy the formatting of one of these altered paragraphs using this method, you will *copy* the special formatting, *not reproduce* the formatting of the Normal Style. You can also use the Copy Format command. Use the instructions I gave on this command under "Copy Character Formatting Anytime" earlier in this chapter, but instead of selecting *characters* to copy, select the *paragraph* to copy. Apply the formatting by again selecting the new paragraph using the methods discussed above.

Other Ways to Alter Paragraph Formatting

You can also reproduce paragraph formatting by selecting the paragraph mark of the paragraph you wish to copy. Copy this mark to the Clipboard. Next, select the paragraph mark of the paragraph you wish to change, then paste the new mark over the old by pressing Shift+Ins. The new formatting will replace the old. This is my favorite method.

Including Character Formatting

Sometimes you'll want to reproduce all the formatting in a paragraph including character formatting. Of course you can apply a Style. You can copy both character and paragraph formatting to a Style by first selecting a paragraph with the correct Style name. Next, format the paragraph with all the new traits you wish. Click on the Style name in the Style list that appears when you click on the Style box. Then press Enter. Word will ask if you wish to redefine the Style based on your selection. Click on Yes. (You can accomplish all this in the Format/Define Style dialog box as well.) To create a new Style name, enter the name in the Style list box on the Formatting toolbar (Ribbon) and press Enter.

In Version 2, you can also copy character and paragraph formatting by selecting the paragraph you wish to change, holding down Ctrl+Shift while you click first inside the paragraph. (Be sure you've selected the entire paragraph and its paragraph mark.) Then click along its model's left side in the Style Area or Selection Bar (depending on your view setting).

Undoing Special Formatting

If you change the formatting of paragraphs or characters manually from their Style, you can reverse the formatting at a later time by selecting the character(s) or paragraph mark and pressing Ctrl+Q. This will remove *all* special formatting, including bold, italic, etc., as well as line spacing and alignment parameters. If you wish to remove special formatting from only the characters in a paragraph, press Ctrl+Space bar.

STYLES & TEMPLATES

When you're working with the same type of document over and over, or in a document with many identically formatted items, it makes sense to use Style sheets and templates. Despite their usefulness, a few warnings:

Built-in Styles

By default, Word supplies a number of built-in styles (called Standard Styles in Version 2) that are built in to all templates. These Styles are interconnected in such a way that by default a change in one will often cause a change in others. Changes in the type size or paragraph settings of the Normal Style, such as indents or line spacing, may create a ripple effect in all other linked Styles, most notably the Heading Styles. Word does this as a convenience so that logically related Styles will be changed together automatically. You can see the link if you look in the Format/Style dialog box. Select Heading 1 Style. The Description box lists the Normal Style first followed by a +. The items following the + indicate which formatting this Standard Style has in addition to the Normal Style formatting. The specifically listed items after the + will not be changed by an alteration of the Normal Style, but any other parameter may be.

I mention this primarily to cushion the shock when you change the indention of your Normal Style and then notice that your headings have also been indented. It surprised me the first 50 times or so.

To avoid these links, you can make your own new Styles in the Format/Style dialog box. You might want to use Body Text as the style for most text. This style is not linked to other built-in styles. Be sure the Based On box is either empty or contains the name of a Style you want to use as the basis of a new Style. You can also alter the links in the Standard Styles by removing or replacing the contents of the Based On box. I have added several totally independent Styles to my NORMAL.DOT so I can create independent character and paragraph Styles. I call mine "odd," "oddball," etc., to remind myself that these Styles are distinct and not linked to any other. You should, of course, give them a name meaningful to you.

To See All the Standard Styles
Word provides a host of Standard Styles that appear in your Style list when you add the appropriate features, such as an index or table of contents. To see all the Standard Styles, go to the Format/Style dialog box, at the lower left you will see a drop-down list box labeled List. In this box click on All Styles. You will then see a complete list of the built-in styles of Version 6. You can then examine the characteristics of each. (In Version 2, select a paragraph. Choose Format/Style, then press Ctrl+Y. The Style list shows all the Standard Styles.)

Auto Formatting
Version 6 now offers Auto Formatting in the Format menu. Once you have established a system of formatting for a long document, this tool can save you a lot of time when applying your styles to your body text, major headings and bulleted lists. Do check through the document, however, to make sure that it hasn't missed something.

The NORMAL.DOT

The NORMAL.DOT is not quite like any other template. By default, all new documents acquire it. More important, all Global changes you make to your Standard toolbar (Toolbar) buttons, menus, macros, Auto Text (glossary) entries and keyboard assignments become part of the NORMAL.DOT no matter in which document they originated. (However, you can save such changes to specific templates and not globally, if you wish.)

If you delete the NORMAL.DOT, you'll lose all customizations to your program. Word automatically creates a new NORMAL.DOT with all the original settings that came with the program. So, if you *want* to go back to all the original settings, first *save* your NORMAL.DOT with a new name (you might want those macros or glossary entries again someday) and then delete the NORMAL.DOT. Think carefully before you do this.

Global Changes

You affirm Global changes when you exit the program. Word asks if you wish to save the Global changes. If you say Yes, Word saves these changes to the NORMAL.DOT.

MOVING ON

In the next chapter, we'll focus on creating frames and borders to use with text, graphics and tables—to give your pages a finished, professional look.

11 Frames, Borders & Tables

I think of frames as "paragraphs with wings": once text, a graphic or a table is in a frame, it's easy to place it virtually anywhere. However, frames can often take flight, unpredictably, when the view or formatting is altered. Because these powerful tools can behave erratically if you don't foresee the pitfalls, you should plan your complex layouts carefully to avoid potential problems.

FRAMES

First, remember that frames are essentially "empty" paragraphs. Inserted frames always acquire the Normal Style paragraph settings. If these Normal settings conflict with those of text, a table or a graphic inserted into the frame, you will get unexpected formatting. You can immediately alter these settings, of course, and I strongly recommend that you do so, especially if your Normal Style contains indents and/or Exactly line spacing.

An example of the unpredictability of frames is that if you insert a frame into a text paragraph with indents that the frame does not also have in its paragraph settings, you will not be able to place the frame at any of the corners of the paragraph on the side with the indents and have the text wrap feature work. This appears to be a bug in both versions 6 and 2.

Creating a Frame Style

Whenever possible, create a special Style to apply to frames—one that has no specific line spacing (Single) indents (all set to 0), borders, unusual frame parameters (no exact sizing) or unusual character formatting. (I call this my Neutral Frame Style.) It will give you a neutral area in which to format your text, graphic or table. When text, tables or graphics placed in a frame behave peculiarly, you should immediately check all the frame's character and paragraph settings.

Working Inside & Outside a Frame

Frames allow you to move text, graphics or tables, but there are limitations on formatting items inside them. For example, to put multiple paragraphs in the same frame, you must first select the paragraphs, then choose Insert/ Frame. If the paragraphs have different indents, line spacing, borders or shading, Word will *appear* to put them in different frames with separate boundaries and/or borders (if you have Borders on). However, if you click on the frame, you'll see that in fact the frame surrounds all the selected paragraphs. Hence, they can be positioned together. Note that you cannot have paragraphs with varying indents surrounded by the same border unless you put them in a table.

Deleting Frame Contents
If you delete the contents of a frame, Word will delete the frame as well. If you delete a frame, however, its contents remain between the paragraphs that preceded and

followed the frame. Any border set for the frame will remain. To delete both frame and border, press Ctrl+Q. This removes not only the frame and the border but all special paragraph formatting as well. If you have manual formatting you wish to retain, use the Format/Borders and Shading (Format/Border) command to remove the unwanted border.

Selecting Text in a Frame

When working in a frame, you may have trouble selecting the first character in a line. In certain views, as your cursor reaches the edge of the frame, it will turn into the Frame arrow and prevent you from selecting the character nearest the frame's edge. In order to select the text all the way to the left, place the cursor between the leftmost character and its right-hand neighbor. Then press the left arrow to move the cursor left one character. To select the text, use the Shift+Right arrow key.

Centering Text or Graphics in a Frame

To center something in a frame, select the paragraph mark of the text or object in the frame. Choose centered alignment in the Format/Paragraph dialog box or click the icon on the Formatting toolbar (Ribbon). Then, depending on the size of the frame, use the spacing options and/or subscripting (in the Format/Font [Format/Character] dialog box) to lower it exactly into place. See the Zoo Resources report in Chapter 9 as an example.

Formatting Space in & Around Frames

If your frame is inserted into a regular text area—for example, to place a graphic or a pull-quote in a column or between columns—Word automatically uses the Around text-wrapping option in the Insert/Frame dialog box. If you don't want this arrangement, where text appears on both sides of the frame, you can set Text Wrapping to None.

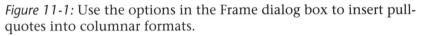

Figure 11-1: Use the options in the Frame dialog box to insert pull-quotes into columnar formats.

Formatting Space Around the Frame
In the Format/Frame dialog box, you'll find the Distance From Text controls associated with the horizontal and vertical position indicators. Here you enter the amount of space you want on the sides, top and bottom of your frame. *Note:* This will be the distance from the outside boundary of the frame, not from the frame contents.

Formatting Space Inside the Frame
You'll usually want to provide space between the contents of a frame and the frame's border. Again, go into the Format/Borders and Shading (Format/Border) dialog box, where you'll see the border marker preview sample. Directly below, in the From Text area, enter the amount of space you want between the text and its borders. Note that this will create an even amount of space around all text that has a border selected. If you want uneven amounts of space around items inside the frame, you can put this paragraph in a table. The table in turn can be placed in a frame to be positioned.

**Creating Space Around Framed Graphics or Text
Without Printing Borders**

As discussed above, the From Text space setting affects
only those sides of the frame that have a border selected.
If you want the same amount of space on all sides of your
text but you want only some of those borders to print
(show), in the Format/Borders and Shading (Format/
Border) dialog box you can select those borders you don't
want to print and set their color to White. The framed
item will then have four equal borders, but the unwanted
borders will not print (show).

Frames for Special Purposes

Frames make side notes and marginal illustrations easy.
You can see these in the Mystical and Magical Symbols
illustration in Chapter 9 and in Figure 11-2 in this chapter. First make sure your margin size is wide enough to
accommodate your graphics and/or side notes plus a
space equal to that of the margin on the opposite side of
the page.

Place the cursor in front of a leftmost character in the
regular text column. Then insert a frame. Drag the frame
into the margin and format its size and location.

To keep notes and graphics attached to the text paragraph they illustrate, choose Move With Text in the
Format/Frame dialog box (this will probably already be
checked because it's the default setting). To attach it to
the desired paragraph, just move it into proximity of the
desired paragraph. To be sure which paragraph your
frame is anchored to, choose Tools/Options/View/Frame
Anchors. (In Version 2 you can tell which paragraph your
frame is anchored to by noting as you drag the frame up
and down the margin that a faint underline appears
under the first character of each paragraph it passes. This

defines the paragraph the frame is anchored to. Use the Distance From Text control in the Frame dialog box to specify the vertical space between the frame and its attached paragraph.)

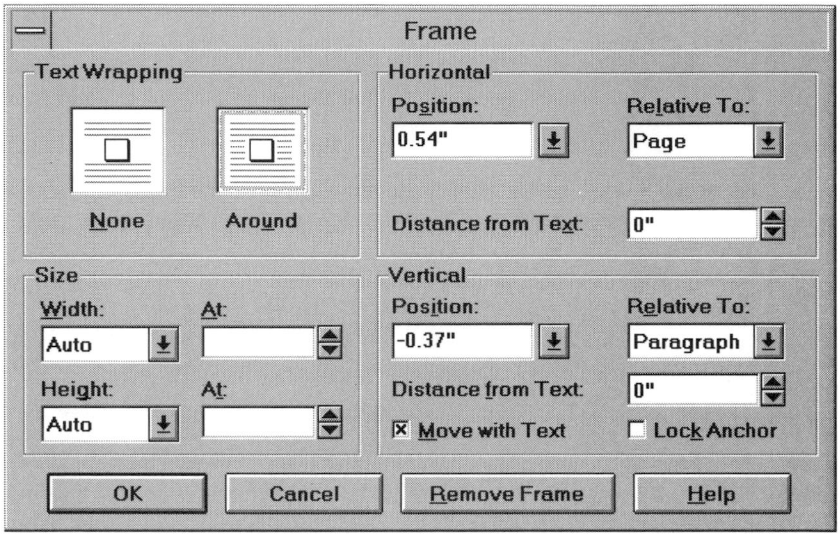

Figure 11-2: Use the Move with Text option in the Frame dialog box to anchor your frame.

Frames in Headers & Footers

Frames made in headers and footers, no matter where they are eventually placed or how they're formatted, will print on every page; you can place page numbers or other fields for information anywhere on the page—a great feature. Such page numbers can be seen in the Zoo Resources report.

Repeating Frames

Word does not directly create repeating frames (identical frames that occur on every page in a section or document). To create a repeating frame, you must insert a frame into a header or footer; then drag the frame out of the header or footer and format it as desired. (See the Zoo Resources report.) Now you can create a repeating logo, text phrase or illustration on every page.

Positioning & Sizing Frames

To keep all notes and graphics inside frames aligned, use the Positioning boxes in the Format/Frame dialog box. If you're using facing pages, use the Inside and Outside options under Horizontal.

And don't forget that the Format/Frame dialog box also lets you specify the width and height of each frame.

Placing Frames on Top of Each Other

You can place frames behind each other if your printer supports this feature. When this works, it makes it easy to place text over a graphic (as in the Palos Verdes flower show brochure and the Succulent Sandwich survey examples, in Chapters 7 and 6, respectively). Frames placed on top of one another print with the most recently created item on top. Only experimentation with your printer will tell you if you can do this.

While you can use overlapping frames in both versions 6 and 2, Version 6 allows you to place text or graphics behind or in front of other text and/or graphics using Text Boxes in Word's drawing tools. If you have Version 6, this is the easier method.

Getting Stuck in Frames

Sometimes you can get stuck in a frame. To get out of a frame, use the following techniques or remove the frame using Ctrl+Q.

To add a paragraph above a frame, press Ctrl+Shift+Enter.

To add a paragraph below a frame at the end of a document, insert a frame and place it below the bottom frame. If you still can't get below a frame, see the discussion of this problem later in this chapter in the "Tables" section.

In Version 2, note that on occasion Word will cut off descenders when you use Exactly spacing in a frame. Try using Single spacing or pulling down the lower edge of the frame. If this is not possible, see other suggestions in the "Trouble-Shooting" section in Chapter 13.

If you find that your frames seem to jump in tiny increments when you're trying to place them, go into the Drawing toolbar and click on the Snap to Grid tool (fourth from the right). In this dialog box turn Snap to Grid off. Apparently, frames act as if they are a part of the drawing layer. With Snap to Grid on, frames can be easily aligned with drawing objects.

BORDERS & SHADING

Word's borders and shading features provide powerful paragraph formatting tools for creating handsome documents. You can frame text and graphics with rules (also called "lines" and "borders") in a variety of styles and heights (thicknesses). You can create shaded backgrounds in a range of colors, gray shades and patterns; and you can reverse type out of these backgrounds (if your printer supports it). You'll see examples of such uses throughout this book.

I recommend that you experiment with borders and shading options to see how they look when output on your printer. Only some trial and error will reveal the best combinations. Because borders and shading are paragraph properties, they can also be added to Styles.

Border & Shading Basics

In traditional typographic and printing terminology, lines placed horizontally or vertically on the page are called rules. The Word for Windows *User's Guide* refers to the Border options as "line styles." In this book, I use the terms border, rule and line interchangeably.

In the Word for Windows program, borders and shading are paragraph attributes. When you create a border, it becomes part of its paragraph's Style. Borders can be used with text, empty paragraphs, tables and graphics. They can be used as single lines and as frames to enclose text and graphic elements. In the "Tables" section of this chapter, we'll focus on putting rules under, over and around cells.

A quick look in the Format/Borders and Shading (Format/Border) dialog box reveals the border choices, which include a selection of single and double rules. The sample in the Border portion allows you to click on the locations where you want borders. You can use preset box and border styles, or you can specify a different border style for each side of a text block, graphic, frame, table cell, etc. For instance, you can design a heading with a thin rule on top and a double-thick rule at the bottom—or any other combination you choose. In Version 6 you can see most of these options when you click on the Borders and Shading toolbar icon on the Standard toolbar.

To display Word's shading options, click on the Shading tab in the Format/Borders and Shading (Format/Border) dialog box to reveal the Shading dialog box. You can use shading behind text to create large rules of any height and as a background for reversed type.

Creating Rules

Now to get to the specifics of making your borders. Once you learn how to create them, you may want to save them as Styles for quick access when you need them.

I use several different paragraph Styles that contain only a border (rule). You can format this otherwise empty paragraph with the border at the top or the bottom of the paragraph by clicking on the preview sample in the Format/Borders and Shading (Format/Border) dialog box. Once you have such a Style (or several), you can easily alter parameters to create any height and width of rule you need. You can then use these rules in combination with other paragraph Styles without having to re-create their border formatting.

Creating a Thick Rule

Very thick rules, such as those I used in The Multimedia News (Chapter 8), make excellent attention-getters. To create a thick, custom rule, choose the Exactly line space setting in the Format/Paragraph dialog box. The point size you enter will determine the thickness of the rule. Next, in the Format/Borders and Shading (Format/Border) dialog box, select Shading; then from the Shading dialog box choose Solid for your Shading option. (If you want a gray shade, select the appropriate pattern and background options.)

Rule Lengths

Because they're paragraph attributes, you adjust the length of rules by changing the paragraph's indent measurements in the Format/Paragraph dialog box or by dragging the indent markers on the rulers (Ruler). Paragraph dimensions determine the border lengths.

Combination Rules

By combining rules of different heights and lengths (using options in the Format/Paragraph dialog box) and placing them at the bottom and top of their respective paragraphs, you can create handsome combination rules, such as those in the Respighi résumé examples, pages 121–125 in Chapter 5. The technique is discussed at length there. If you use these combinations often, make them into Styles and add them to your Style sheet or template.

Placing Rules Between Paragraphs

If you select a series of paragraphs and apply borders above and below, Word will put a border *above* the top paragraph and a border *below* the bottom paragraph. To get borders *between* each paragraph, click in the space between the paragraphs in the Format/Borders and Shading (Format/Border) dialog box sample diagram; then select a border style for the in-between paragraphs. If the individual paragraphs have different indents, you'll get a separate set of top and bottom borders for each paragraph.

Making a Series of Lines

At first, you might assume this would be very easy to do by creating a paragraph with a single bottom border, then repeating the paragraph over and over to produce a series of lines—as in the David M. Rubin fax cover and my Writer-Designer stationery (on pages 111 and 107, respectively, and in Figure 11-3 in this chapter). Not so: the nonbordered top of each successive paragraph erases the bottom border of its predecessor.

An easy way to get around the problem is to create a table with the requisite number of lines, select the entire table and format the borders in the Format/Borders and Shading (Format/Border) dialog box.

Another way is to make two paragraph Styles with identical parameters except that one has a bottom border and one doesn't. Then make a series of the paragraph with the border (twice the number of lines you want). At this point you won't see any lines except the bottom one because each paragraph's nonbordered top has erased the bottom border of the previous paragraph. Go back and retag every other paragraph with the nonbordered alternate. You will see the series of lines appear.

You can also create a series of empty paragraphs with the desired interline spacing. Next, select all the paragraphs and format them following the instructions given in "Placing Rules Between Paragraphs" in the preceding section.

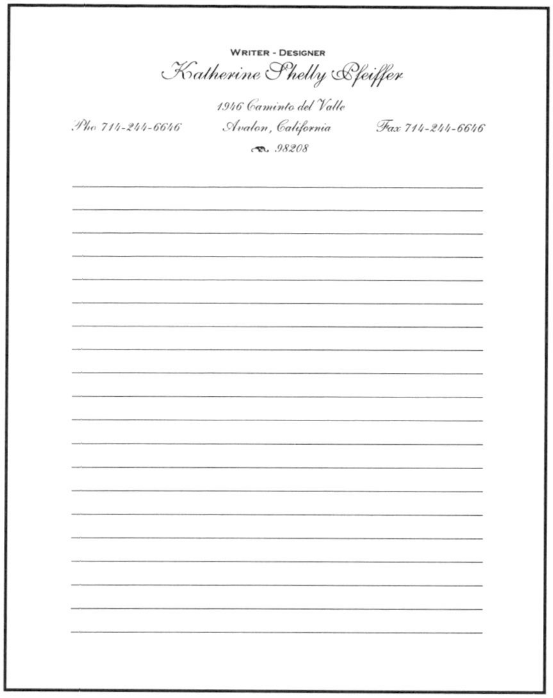
WRITER - DESIGNER

Katherine Shelly Pfeiffer

1946 Caminto del Valle

Pho 714-244-6646 Avalon, California Fax 714-244-6646

98208

Figure 11-3: Word for Windows offers several ways to approach this type of page format.

Putting a Box Around Several Paragraphs

After selecting the paragraphs, you can choose a preset border option in the Format/Borders and Shading (Format/Border) dialog box, then select a style for the Border. Remember, as already mentioned, if the paragraphs have different indents, they will receive separate boxes. To put one border around mixed-style paragraphs, you'll need to use a table. (See the "Tables" section later in this chapter.)

Exotic Frame Borders

You can create exotic frame borders by placing frames on top of each other and formatting each with a different border style. Make the largest frame first, and put the text in the smallest frame last. If you want a very elaborate frame, creating it with Version 6's drawing tools and Text Boxes will be easier.

Selecting Nonprinting Borders

The space between a paragraph's borders and its text (or other contents), which you specify in the From Text box in the Format/Borders and Shading (Format/Border) dialog box, affects only those sides that have a border selected. If you wish to have a visually even space around your text (or other contents) but wish to print (show) only some borders, indicate all four borders on the sample diagram in the Format/Borders and Shading dialog box. Next, select those borders you don't want to print and color them white.

Creating Page Borders

To create a border around the outside of every page, as I did for the Hana Hotel advertisement in Chapter 7, open the File/Page Setup dialog box, select the Margins tab and type a minus sign in front of the measurement in the Top box. This places the border into the header, which means it will print on every page in the section. It also means that paragraphs with different indents can be put inside it.

Now, access the View menu and select Header and Footer. Click the Header/Footer button to make sure you are in the Header. The insertion point should be in the header. Be sure it's in an empty paragraph (add one if necessary). Next, in the Format/Borders and Shading (Format/Border) dialog box, create your border (preset or your own combination for the four sides). Then, in the Format/Paragraph dialog box, enter the correct height for your page margins in the At box under Line Spacing (for instance, 10 in). You can do this quickly by putting a Text Box in the Header and streching it to the size you want.

In Version 6, to place a border around a single page, just use a Text Box and put it behind the text with no fill.

In Version 2, open the Format/Page Setup dialog box, select the Margins option button and type a minus sign in front of the measurement in the Top box. This places the border into the header, which means it will print on every page in the section. It also means that paragraphs with different indents can be put inside it.

In Page Layout View you will now see a border only at the top, left and right of the header. However, in Print Preview you will see that the border prints around the entire page.

If you want the border to print outside the regular text margins, set outdents (negative indents) in the From Left and From Right indent boxes in the Format/Paragraph dialog box. Please practice this before applying it to your entire document!

Note: This technique will place the border around every page in the section because it was inserted in the header. Your *User's Guide* for Version 2 goes into more detail on this feature.

Backgrounds Shading, Color & Reversed Type
Using a screen, or shading, behind text can be challenging. I have found that in working with a laser printer, many gray shades and patterns print so coarsely that only the largest and boldest type placed over them is readable. So if your printer can convert standard colors to gray, I recommend using color. Yellow is the lightest and I believe it works the best. I used yellow shading in the Multimedia News example. For comparison, I used a pattern in the 4 Seasons software manual (Chapter 9). I have not used many shaded backgrounds in my examples, but don't let this deter you. You can put shading in table cells, behind paragraphs and within frames and rules (as mentioned previously in this section). They're often quite useful in forms to indicate areas where the respondent

should not write and to define sections where special information is presented.

Reversed Type

Reversed type (white text on a black background) is easy to create with the Shading option. Examples of reversed text appear in the Gizmos newsletter nameplate (Chapter 8), the Money Talks nameplate subtitle (Chapter 8), the title page of the Signs of the Times catalog (Chapter 9) and the page numbers and headers in the Zoo Resources report (Chapter 9 and Figure 11-4 in this chapter). Use reversed type sparingly. It makes a big impact, but it's often harder to read than the normal black type on a white background.

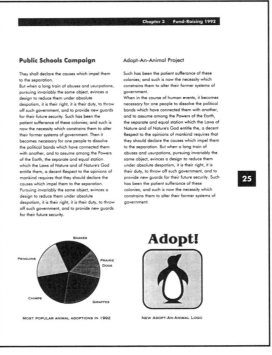

Figure 11-4: Small amounts of reversed type can add interest to a page design.

To create reversed text: First, create the text of your heading, title, footer or whatever. This might be something as simple as a single headline or as complex as elements of a table or frame. (Most of my examples are in frames.) Next, select all the text and open the Format/Font (Format/Character) dialog box. Under Color, specify White. Next, select the paragraph, frame or table cell that contains the white text, open the Shading dialog box from the Border dialog box and select Solid for the pattern and Black for the background. (The foreground setting remains at Auto.)

If you don't like the spacing between the black background and the text, use the From Text option in the Borders and Shading (Border) dialog box to refine the spacing. You could also use the Superscript or Subscript option in the Font (Character) dialog box to adjust the positions of characters that appear too high or too low inside the black area. This technique can also be used with colored or gray-shaded text.

Note: Reversed text may not print on all printers.

TABLES

Tables give you precise control over the most complex types of layout. Table cells create an easy-to-follow, rigid structure for information. A table is often the best way to format a mixture of interrelated data, particularly if the components include graphics. They can also be useful when formatting unlike items that need a common border or when you need to separate items by using many horizontal and/or vertical rules, such as in forms. I have used tables extensively throughout the examples in the book: for most of the forms in Chapter 6, the Jasmine Theatre flyer (Chapter 7), the Dunham Industries flyer

(Chapter 7), the Signs of the Times catalog and the table of contents in the Zoo Resources report.

Creating a Table

Formatting tables is not difficult, but they need some planning before you set them up. Once you've made your plan, inserting the table is a snap. Your Standard toolbar includes the Insert Table button (unless you've removed it), which when clicked displays the Table creation grid. Drag your mouse on the grid to choose the number of rows and columns you want your new table to have. This table automatically creates column widths based on the available space between your page margins.

You can also insert a table by clicking on Insert Table in the Table menu. (You will not see this option if you've already selected a table.) The dialog box also allows you to select a column width. Once created, row heights and column widths can be easily modified using the commands in the Table menu. You can also modify column widths by dragging their borders. (See the *User's Guide* for complete instructions on all possible ways to change table formatting.)

Row Heights

If the height of a row is critical, be sure to choose Exactly spacing in the Table/Cell Height and Width/Row Tab dialog box (Table/Row Height). However, if the height is not critical, you'll have an easier time working in the table if you leave the row height at Single (Auto).

Creating a Chart From Information in a Table

Simply select the table and click on the Graph button on the Standard toolbar. Microsoft Graph will convert the information in the table into one of its chart types. When you exit Graph, the new chart will come in below the table. (In Version 2, the chart will replace the original table. If you wish to display both the table and the chart, first select and copy your table to the Clipboard, then paste the copy below the present table. Next, select the table you want converted to the chart.)

Formatting Text in Tables

When you insert a table, it acquires the formatting of the paragraph into which it is inserted, even if it's an empty paragraph. If this paragraph format includes Exactly line spacing, inserting a graphic may not work. This is similar to working with frames and graphics. If you have any trouble with the graphic, check your paragraph line spacing.

Copying Character Formatting in Cells

To replicate character formatting in table cells, you can use Styles. But usually when you need single words or characters formatted, you can simply place the insertion point in the cell, select the individual characters and manually format them. Or you can use the Format Painter method in Version 6, the Ctrl+Shift+click method in Version 2 or any of the other methods of copying character formatting discussed in the previous chapter.

Using Borders Inside Tables

A single table cell can contain a variety of paragraph indents and border styles. You can put any combination of borders under, over or around the individual paragraphs within a table cell. Simply select each paragraph and apply Format/Borders and Shading (Format/Border) dialog box options. If you don't want a rule to extend the full width of the cell, indent its paragraph from left and right, just as you would to reduce the length of a border in a paragraph. (I used this method in the Day and Night Security and the Athens Estates ads in Chapter 7 and in Figure 11-5 in this chapter.)

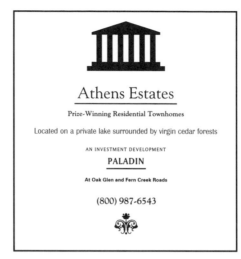

Figure 11-5: Use indents to customize border lengths when working in a table.

Borders Around Tables & Table Cells

You can surround distinctly formatted text and graphics in a table cell (or group of cells) with a specially formatted border. Select the cell, or group of cells, and choose from the options in the Format/Borders and Shading (Format/Border) dialog box. You can also create a special border to surround an entire table after you select it. (To select the entire table, click on Select Table in the Table menu.)

The Format/Borders and Shading (Format/Border) dialog box sample diagram changes to show the cells you have selected for formatting. Isn't this great!

A graphic inside a table cell can have its own border, separate from the cell border. Select the graphic, then use the options in the Format/Borders and Shading dialog box.

Creating Different Border Styles in the Same Table
If you're using a table in a complex document that requires several different border formats (a form, for example), instead of formatting each cell individually to accommodate the changing border style, choose Select Table in the Table menu, after you've established the sizes of your various rows and columns, and apply the border style you'll use most in the document. Then select and reformat just those borders you want to be different.

Margins in Tables

When you're working with tables, the horizontal ruler (Ruler) displays three different scales: the table scale, the indent scale and the margin scale. In Version 6 these markers adjust depending on the location of the cursor. To see these scales in Version 2, click on the Ruler Scale symbol at the far left of the Ruler until the scale you need to use is displayed. The horizontal ruler in Version 6 displays the table column markers that look like buttons, while in Version 2 the Ruler displays T markers. These buttons and markers define table cell boundaries. In this mode you can easily manipulate a cell boundary by dragging these buttons/markers. In Version 6 you can easily alter cell or row height by dragging the table cell markers on the vertical ruler.

As mentioned previously, it's also easy to move cell boundaries by selecting the cell or group of cells you want to alter and dragging the boundary (you'll see a double-headed arrow) where you want it. The cell dimensions can also be specified in the Table menu, using Row Height and Column Width commands.

When the insertion point is in a cell, you can see the indent scale and use the indent markers on the horizontal ruler (Ruler) to set the internal boundaries of the cell contents. Indents are set relative to the left and right cell margins, not the page margins (as when you're working in regular text). Indents can also be set by altering the amount of space between columns in the Column Width dialog box in the Table menu.

Spacing Inside Cells

Spacing on either side of text or graphics in a cell is controlled with paragraph indents. As noted above, you can have different paragraph indents in the same cell. This is one distinct advantage of a table over a frame.

Spacing above and below text or graphics in a table cell can be controlled most easily with the Before and After spacing options in the Format/Paragraph dialog box. Use superscripting and subscripting for fine-tuning vertical placement in the cell.

(Note that on occasion Word will cut off the bottom of subscripted letters in a table. It will also cut off entire lines of text. See the discussion of this problem in Chapter 13, "Tips & Trouble-Shooting.")

Spacing Between Rows & Columns

To add space between rows, you can use the Before and After spacing options in the Format/Paragraph dialog box. If your rows have borders that will be printed and you want these rows visually separated from adjoining rows, insert an empty row to create the space. Be sure this new row is formatted with nonprinting borders. I used this approach in the Films International business card (Chapter 5) and the Great Videos order form (Chapter 6), among others.

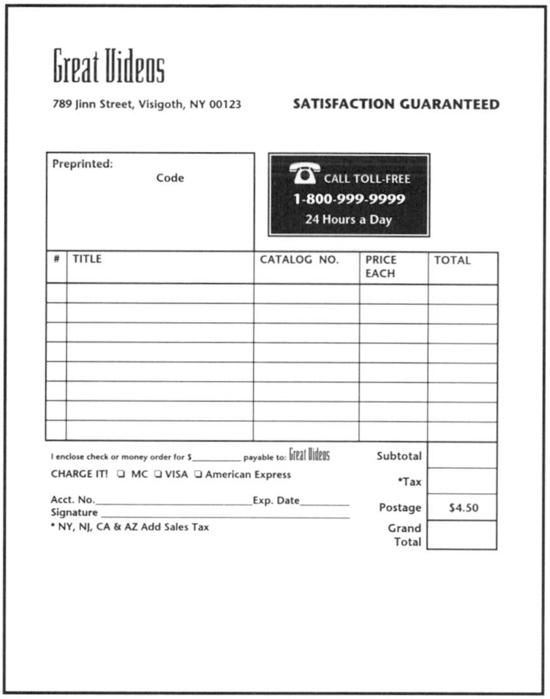

Great Videos

789 Jinn Street, Visigoth, NY 00123

SATISFACTION GUARANTEED

Preprinted: Code

CALL TOLL-FREE
1-800-999-9999
24 Hours a Day

#	TITLE	CATALOG NO.	PRICE EACH	TOTAL

I enclose check or money order for $________ payable to: Great Videos
CHARGE IT! ❑ MC ❑ VISA ❑ American Express
Acct. No.________________ Exp. Date________
Signature________________________
* NY, NJ, CA & AZ Add Sales Tax

Subtotal	
*Tax	
Postage	$4.50
Grand Total	

Figure 11-6: Empty rows with nonprinting borders can be used to separate sections of a form.

To add space between columns, you can indent the appropriate paragraphs manually, you can apply a Style with the paragraph indents or you can set a larger number in the Space Between box in the Table/Column Width dialog box. If you want printed borders with added space between the columns, insert an empty column without borders to create the space. I employed these spacing methods in the Asia Imports invitation (Chapter 5), the Full Deck business card (Chapter 5), the Abrax purchase order (Chapter 6) and the Cogent Books order form (Chapter 6).

Potential Problems in Working With Tables

Page breaks: To avoid a page break in a table and keep the rows together, select the table, then choose the Keep With Next option in the Format/Paragraph dialog box.

Inserting text above a table: If you start a table at the top of a page or delete paragraphs that precede the table, you may want to insert text above it, as for a title or introduction. Put the insertion point in the row below where you want the new text. Press Ctrl+Shift+Enter or select Split Table from the Table menu. (Use this same method to insert regular text between two sections of a table.)

When you can't get below a table: This isn't supposed to happen, but since it's happened to me, it might happen to you. It may occur when your regular text and the text in the table have Exactly line spacing, and when the row heights have fixed sizes. Somehow the table covers up the paragraph mark that follows it. The best way out of this dilemma is to temporarily reformat the last row or two of the table to Single (Auto) everything. (Before you do this, if the formatting is complex, make a note of all critical dimensions.) You should then see the paragraph mark return. Simply place the insertion point in front of that paragraph mark and you're back in business. Just to be safe, add a few paragraph marks below the insertion point. Now, reformat your table.

Lining up the outside edge of a table: You may have noticed that when a table is inserted, its outer boundary projects beyond the regular text boundary. This is done so that the text in the table will align vertically with the other text above it on the page. If you want a border around your table, this won't look very good. To fix it, you must slightly alter the outer column margins. I prefer doing this by using the click-and-drag method to pull the table boundaries in. But if you want to do it with precision, you'll need to use the Column Width dialog box options to reduce the width of the two outer (left and right) columns.

Text or a graphic is distorted or partially disappears:
Your text may appear in a tall vertical column or your graphic may show only partially at the top of a cell. This can happen when you have fixed sizing or spacing of the cell or the paragraph mark in the cell. To fix it, you can either select each cell individually or select the entire table. (If your table cell structure is complex, please make notes on all relevant settings before the next step.) Then select Row Height and Column Width and set them to Single (Auto). If this doesn't work, in the Format/Paragraph dialog box reset all indents to 0 and line spacing to Single (Auto). Any of these items can cause improper formatting at one time or another. After everything is back to normal, you can reformat the table or individual cells. (Also see Chapter 13, "Tips & Trouble-Shooting.")

Exactly spacing may result in truncated descenders:
Occasionally, Exactly spacing in a table will result in descenders being cut off. Try using Single (Auto) spacing. For other suggestions, see Chapter 13, "Tips & Trouble-Shooting."

MOVING ON

Frames, borders and tables all provide you with flexibility and accuracy in placing compositional items. You can use them to organize and/or emphasize text and graphics. In the next chapter we'll look at using graphics in more detail.

12 · *Graphics*

S tudies show that documents containing graphics—
particularly artwork, photographs and charts—get
more attention than documents without them. One
of Word for Windows's strong points is its ability to import and position graphics. You can use art created by
others or you can make your own.

I have learned to use all the major drawing programs that
run in Windows yet I rarely have the time to create handsome, elaborate graphics from scratch. As you can see in
the documents I designed for this book, I rely a lot on
clip art and other predesigned graphics.

CLIP ART

Clip art is available in two basic types. One type uses
lines and gray shades or color to give the illusion of three
dimensions. Like photographs, these illustrations are
visually and psychologically complex; many of them tell
stories. (The orchid in the Palos Verdes Flower Show
brochure is this type.)

The other kind of clip-art images are composed of flat
black-and-white elements (similar to silhouettes). This is
the kind, often referred to as symbols, that I used almost
exclusively to illustrate my documents in this book. (Arts
& Letters provides the one of the largest libraries available

of such two-dimensional images, which is one reason you see its name so often in these pages.)

I find the two-dimensional graphics easier to integrate with text because type is also two-dimensional. However, you should establish your own preferences based on your particular design requirements.

Clip-art developers offer an immense variety of subject matter and style. Periodicals mentioned in the Bibliography of this book often print articles on and run advertisements for clip-art collections. Among the best collections currently available on both floppy disk and CD-ROM is Images with Impact from 3G Graphics (Edmonds, WA). Another excellent source of clip art is drawing programs. All major drawing programs that run in Windows come with large packages of clip-art images—for example, Arts & Letters has over 5,000; CorelDRAW, 18,000; Designer, over 13,000, and Harvard Draw, nearly 2,000. Although these programs are expensive, you might consider them a good investment based on their clip-art collections and typefaces alone.

WINDOWS DRAWING PROGRAMS

If you have time and some talent, the Windows environment supports excellent, full-featured drawing programs, and Word for Windows Version 6 comes with its own drawing tools. The major Windows drawing programs currently available are Adobe Illustrator; Aldus FreeHand; Arts & Letters Graphics Editor from Computer Support Corporation; CorelDRAW from Corel; and Micrografx Designer from Micrografx.

Besides the larger, high-powered programs, I recommend several less complex products that are easier to use. Micrografx offers Windows Draw, which boasts nearly all the features of the larger drawing programs. It comes with 18 scalable Type 1 typefaces and 2,600 clip-art images and symbols. Computer Support Corporation offers Arts & Letters Apprentice, which, while not so full-featured as Windows Draw, provides a very good collection of drawing features. It also gives you the ability to use the enormous Arts & Letters clip-art collection, and it comes with 25 scalable typefaces and 3,000 symbols and clip-art images. Both of these programs feature greater ease of use than the larger, more complex programs, and both come with fine clip-art collections. Both deserve your serious consideration.

Both larger and smaller programs provide superb drawing tools and features that allow you to create virtually any type of complex illustration. A detailed description of each is far beyond the scope of this book, but here's a general overview.

Drawing programs use mathematical descriptions, often referred to as vectors, to create images. Such images can be scaled with little loss of detail. For most purposes, vector-based images are easier to cope with than bitmapped images produced by paint programs such as Windows Paint (discussed later). In addition, these programs are now shipping with larger and larger collections of typefaces and clip art. For instance, Designer now comes with over 280 Type 1 and matching TrueType fonts plus 13,740 clip-art images and 200 photos, while CorelDRAW comes with two CD-ROMs containing 750 TrueType and Type 1 fonts, including 650 Bitstream and ITC fonts, as well as 5,000 symbols and 18,000 pieces of clip art!

Depending on your needs, the clip-art and/or typeface collection alone could justify the purchase price of one of these programs. But they do differ in specific features and complexity. I suggest you do some research on these programs (see the Bibliography) and acquire one *after* you learn to use Word's drawing tools.

Word's Drawing Tools

While Word for Windows Version 6's drawing tools and Version 2's Microsoft Draw are not full-featured drawing programs, they will give you experience with the basics of vector-based image-making. Once you've worked with a drawing program, you'll have a good idea of the features you use most often and those you dislike or find wanting in Word's drawing programs.

Word's drawing tools (or Microsoft Draw) allow you to not only create drawings but edit other graphics as well (especially those that come over the Clipboard). Among its strong points: it lets you create text, using the fonts installed for your printer, that you can put inside borders, squares, rectangles, circles, etc. You can do this in a variety of colors, shades of gray or in reversed type. (See Figure 1-6 in Chapter 1.) Among Version 6's important new drawing features is the fact that this is not a separate program like Microsoft Draw was but an integrated part of Word. Now, using Text Boxes you can place images or text behind or in front of the text layer itself. This makes placing text over images a snap. Alignment is much easier now with alignment controls and grid snap. A remarkable new Callout feature allows you to annotate drawings easily and clearly. A few hours spent exploring Word's drawing tools will pay great dividends. See the Examples and Demos in the Help menu for good tips on using these tools.

(While Microsoft Draw, in Version 2, does not have Text Boxes or the other new features just mentioned, it is especially useful in allowing you to overcome the

127-point type size limitation by scaling typefaces to virtually any size. It's difficult to communicate in a few words how useful and important Draw's type-handling is. Note that Version 6 now has a limit of 1,637 points [22 inches] high! You don't need the drawing tools to create large type any longer.)

Neither version 6 nor 2 allows the rotation of text.

Several documents in this book were created entirely using Word's drawing tools. The SUNSHELTERS letterhead and estimate form (Chapters 5 and 6), the digidiskum ad (Chapter 7) and the Capitol Loss and Pharmaceutical Fraud title pages (Chapter 9).

Windows Paint

Windows Paint is included with Windows. You can use it to create bitmapped illustrations. Again, I urge you to explore it so that you can understand how paint programs work and how their resulting images look in a document. Paint programs create bitmaps of the images on your screen. The disadvantages of bitmapped images are that distortions can occur when they're resized; and other programs, such as Word's drawing tools or Microsoft Draw, can manipulate them only in rudimentary ways. If the effect you want can be produced in a paint program, use it; but remember that when a bitmapped image is reproduced, the quality may be inferior to that of the vector graphics produced by drawing programs.

Microsoft Graph

Microsoft Graph is a graph/chart program included with Word that enables you to use your installed printer fonts. This will give your charts a professional look and will make it easy to coordinate them with other graphics and text in your documents. It can also convert your Word tables into charts automatically. One of its shortcomings is that you can't always adjust the placement of chart labels; they often print too close to the entities they describe. However, you can manipulate them with Word's drawing tools or in Microsoft Draw. (See "Making a Chart into a Graphic" later in this chapter.) Explore the various chart types in the Gallery.

SCANNING

Scanned images are another important source of visual material for your documents. Using a scanner, you can include photographs and other artwork created specifically for your publication. There are some excellent books of copyright-free clip art. (Dover Books, for example, offers several.)

Scanners are cheaper than ever, and I have obtained good results with a 300 dpi hand scanner. Try to scan images at the size you'll be printing them. Like other bitmapped images, they tend to suffer the jaggies when they're reduced or enlarged. (Be careful not to duplicate copyrighted photos or art—it's against the law.)

Photographs
If you need to work with photographs, I recommend that you invest in one of the many excellent image-editing programs available. These programs range from fairly simple to very sophisticated. Some, like Micrographx's Photo Magic and Z-Soft's Photofinish are quite easy to

use, full of excellent features, and not expensive. (Photo Magic even comes bundled with Windows Draw, noted above, and a charting program as Micrografx Graphics Works and includes a CD-ROM with over 1,000 photos as well as Draw's excellent clip-art collection.) These programs allow you to crop and edit photos as well as transform their basic appearance with special effects filters. Superb high-end products include: Adobe PhotoShop, Aldus PhotoStyler, Micrografx Picture Publisher and Fractal's Painter. I recommend that you see a demo of these products or read reviews of them in the magazines listed in the Bibliography.

TYPE AS ART

Dingbats and other type characters and symbols are good sources to use in creating two-dimensional graphics, as I have demonstrated in my documents. The Ski Books moving announcement design was inspired by the Carta dingbats (see Figure 12-1). Increasing numbers of dingbat and pi fonts are becoming available; in fact, I would say they have become all the rage. (Pi is a printer's term that refers to an assortment of type characters. The term is also applied to collections of dingbats.) Linotype and Adobe offer extensive collections. Bitstream, Monotype and a host of smaller vendors now offer wonderful assortments of ornaments and so-called picture fonts.

Figure 12-1: A profusion of dingbats turns this simple announcement into an attractive, attention-getting composition.

Some of my favorites are in Adobe's Caslon Ornaments, which replicate 18th-century designs, shown in Figure 12-2. They add elegance to any traditional page of type. Spend some time studying your symbol and dingbat fonts for interesting shapes. And don't forget that you can make graphics out of numerals and ampersands. They're especially effective as embellishments and attention-getters.

Figure 12-2: Ornamental type designs can be used as art.

Type can also be manipulated in exciting ways. Using the drawing programs mentioned above or Adobe's Type Align or Bitstream's Make-Up, you can stretch it, rotate it, curve it up or down, bind it to a path, give it an interesting texture or make it look three-dimensional. While a little of this goes a long way, it can add zing to an otherwise mundane design. I used such an effect in the Silverado certificate (Chapter 5).

Microsoft WordArt

Version 6 of Word has greatly improved WordArt, which now uses Windows TrueType fonts rather than the crude ones provided with Version 2. WordArt now provides a great many interesting effects, as well. A word of caution: a little bit of distorted lettering goes a very long way. In both version 6 and 2, to access WordArt, click on Object in the Insert menu. Then click on Microsoft WordArt in the list box. You can rotate, slant, curve up and down, and make into circles a variety of type designs. In Version 6, startling effects are possible using complex shadows and 3D options. In Version 2, the result will be crude and should be reserved for informal page designs.

IMPORTING GRAPHICS

Hooray for the Windows Clipboard! I have used virtually all formats for importing graphics, and the Clipboard is the best of them all for ease of use, accuracy and fidelity. That said, I must admit that even the Clipboard occasionally alters a graphic's line widths or loses some part of a complex graphic.

All the drawing and paint programs mentioned thus far work well with the Clipboard. To be on the safe side, I generally make the graphic and copy it to the Clipboard. I then Minimize the drawing program and start (or Maximize) Word. (If you are unfamiliar with minimizing and maximizing Windows programs, see the Microsoft Word *User's Guide*.) I then paste the graphic into Word. After successful transfer, I close the original drawing program. I have found that running Word and a drawing program simultaneously sometimes causes my computer to lock up. Save your work before trying any of these maneuvers.

If you're running short of hard disk space, Version 6 allows you to link an imported graphic to your document, rather than saving a version of it with the document. This is a bit slower than having the graphic saved in the document, but it does save space.

Importing Problems

Word can import a wide range of graphics formats. If you have trouble with something on the Clipboard, I feel sure it will import properly as a Windows Metafile, if your drawing program will export in that format. Complex graphics sometimes lose information or become distorted when saved by a drawing program then imported into Word in another format. The problem usually is in the exporting program. If you consistently have trouble, call the drawing program's developer to make sure you have the latest version of the software. Word expects images to behave exactly as specified.

Second to Windows Metafile (.WMF) format, I recommend the tagged image file format (.TIF). Encapsulated PostScript (.EPS) files will work fine on a PostScript printer, but on regular printers the results will be inferior. Version 6 now imports .EPS files directly. (If you wish to try .EPS in Version 2, the major drawing programs mentioned above all import .EPS files. They convert the files to their own formats. From them you can paste the .EPS graphic through the Clipboard into Word and then print it on any Windows printer capable of printing complex graphics.)

Note that scanned images may not look good if they are scaled to sizes different from their original scanned size. As a rule, try to make all graphics the size they'll be when placed in your publication.

Trouble-Shooting Tip for Version 2: If you should ever have trouble importing a graphic in Windows because the program can't find the graphics filters—even though they are properly installed—you can open Word's drawing tools or Microsoft Draw and import the picture through it. Its interface with Windows is different from Word's.

Embedded Objects

In Word, Microsoft Graph (and Microsoft Draw in Version 2) creates embedded objects. An embedded object retains a link to the program that created it. While in Word, if you double-click on a drawing or a chart made with these programs, the parent program is invoked. (This will be true for files from Microsoft Excel as well.)

Also, if you alter the file in its program of origin, it will be updated in Word unless you specifically avoid this action. It's best to use some extra caution with these programs. It's easier than you think to alter something you don't want to alter. Drawings made in Version 6 are now created by Word's drawing tools and are part of the basic document—they are not linked. They are known as Word 6 pictures. Hence, this tip does not apply to drawings in Version 6.

WORKING WITH GRAPHICS

Speeding Up Screen Redraw: Use Picture Placeholders (selected in the Tools/Options dialog box View category) to speed up screen redraw.

Inserting a Picture or a Chart: Before you insert a picture or a chart, either into a frame or directly into the text, select the frame's paragraph mark or the paragraph mark at the insertion point. Format it with your neutral frame style (discussed in the "Frames" section of Chapter 11) or with the Single or At Least line spacing option. If the line spacing remains set to an Exactly setting, your chart or picture may not display or print properly.

Modifying a Graphic: If you need to make a simple change to a graphic, especially one that comes over the Clipboard, you can just double-click on the graphic and Word's drawing tools will open (or Microsoft Draw will load). In many cases, you can move objects, add text to the graphic and change fill colors, patterns and line widths in with Word's drawing tools (or Microsoft Draw) even if the original is from another program.

Using the drawing tools (or Microsoft Draw), you can also modify charts made in Graph (see "Making a Chart into a Graphic" later in this chapter for instructions on how to do this) and Excel charts. Be aware that once you make these changes, your original graphic will be altered, and, if it is an embedded object, its link to the parent program will be altered as well. The only way you can get it back to its original formatting is to revert to an earlier version of the document or the separate saved version of the graphic, if there is one.

Centering Graphics in Word: If you want a graphic centered in the column, just select it and choose center alignment in the Format/Paragraph dialog box or use the center alignment button on the Standard toolbar. If you need to move the graphic to a specific spot, you can place it in a frame or a Text Box and then drag it to the desired location. (In Version 2, things work about the same. If you want it to project beyond the column edge, as I did in the Gizmos newsletter portrait of Lewellen Georges [see Figure 12-3], the easiest method is to put it in a frame and move it. Note that if you enlarge a graphic in a column in Version 2, even if it has center alignment, the picture will enlarge only to the right. In order to get it in the center of the column, put the picture in a frame, then center the frame and the picture separately.) Note that in Version 6 this last technique is unnecessary.

Figure 12-3: To place a graphic so that it projects beyond a column edge, put it in a frame and move it.

Borders Around Graphics in Tables: You can put separate borders around a table cell and its graphic, if you want to. Just select each individually and format in the Format/Borders and Shading (Format/Border) dialog box.

Creating Space Around a Graphic: The easiest way to do this is to put the graphic in a frame and size the frame to accommodate the needed space and the graphic. Then select the graphic and size it. To format the space, use the Format/Paragraph dialog box alignment and spacing options.

Adding a Caption to a Graphic or Chart: Version 6 provides a new command, Insert/Caption, which makes it a snap to add a caption to any graphic. You can also use the AutoCaption feature to create a series of captions automatically. You can still use the Format/Font and Format/Paragraph commands to make your captions look exactly as you want them. Your chosen formatting can be saved as a Style for easy application. (In Version 2, adding a caption is a bit more complex. If your graphic or chart is in a frame, merely select the frame, put the insertion point to the right of the graphic and press the Enter key. Word will insert an empty paragraph inside the frame below the graphic. Use this space to add your caption. Since the caption will be within the frame, it will automatically move with the graphic or chart. This is the best method. I did this in the Magical and Mystical Symbols paper and the Zoo Resources report [both in Chapter 9]. If your graphic or chart is not in its own frame, you can add the caption just below the graphic or chart as normal text. In this case, be sure to set the graphic's paragraph to Keep With Next in the Format/Paragraph dialog box; otherwise the graphic and caption may become separated.)

Making a Chart into a Graphic: While Microsoft Graph allows you to move parts of a chart to improve its readability and appearance, it will not allow you to move every part. To move these parts, or remove them, you can convert the chart to a drawing tools (or Microsoft Draw) graphic.

Method for Version 6: First, create your chart exactly as you want it, because after you alter it with the drawing tools you won't be able to change it with the charting program—it will become a Word 6 picture. Select the chart and copy it to the Clipboard. Go to Insert/Object and select MS Word 6 Picture (yes, Picture). A picture frame will appear on your page. Next, select Edit/Paste Special, choose Picture. Your chart should now appear in the picture frame. Click on the chart to select it. Next, click the right mouse button and you will see a short menu. In this menu, select Edit Picture. The chart will ungroup and you can move labels and sections where you want.

Method for Version 2: First, make your chart. Be sure it's exactly the way you want it. Once you turn it into a graphic, you won't be able to convert it back to a Microsoft Graph chart again. Select the chart. Cut the chart to the Clipboard, using Ctrl+X. In Word's Edit menu, select Paste Special (because the chart is an embedded object). In the Paste Special list, select Picture. (If Picture does not appear in your list, see the alternate method below.) Your chart will now be pasted back into its position as a picture. Next, double-click on the chart-picture. Microsoft Draw will load automatically. Every label and chart section will be selected as a separate object. Click anywhere in the picture to deselect all. Then proceed as you would to edit any other graphic.

Alternate method for Version 2: If you do not see Picture as an option in the Paste Special dialog box, make your chart as above, but while still in Microsoft Graph, select Copy Chart in the Edit menu. Next, minimize Microsoft Graph. In Word, go directly to the Edit menu and select Paste Special; you should see Picture in the list. Return now to the instructions above at the Paste Special picture selection step.

A Note on Printing Graphics

Word's superior printer interface allows you to print many graphic files—both vector-based from drawing programs and bitmapped from image editors (photos, .TIF files, etc.)—much faster than the programs that originate the drawing and image files. I have found this to be especially significant with color printing. Word can reduce the printing time by two-thirds! Just bring your artwork into Word with the Insert/Picture command and print. Try it, you'll like it.

MOVING ON

Now that you're equipped with the information you need to use Word's graphics capabilities, you're ready to work on your own documents. However, if you're like most of us, you may experience unexpected problems. If you do, don't despair—complex programs often present surprises until we've used them for a while. In the next, and last, chapter, I'll offer you some technique and trouble-shooting tips.

Tips & Trouble-Shooting

In this chapter I'll revisit some of the features already discussed and give you some reminders and tips about using them effectively. I'll also point out some potential pitfalls in creating complex page layouts and give you some suggestions on how to handle them.

I'll start with some tips on establishing a basic page layout.

PAGE SETUP

After I make a sketch of my design on paper, I set up my page using options accessed through the File/Page Setup (Format/Page Setup) command. If columns are to be included, I create them using Format/Columns. If a table structure is required, I set it up next using Table/Insert Table.

Mirror-Image Pages

If you want mirror-image pages, such as those I used for the Damask Lullaby book (Chapter 9) and the Gizmos newsletter (Chapter 8), be sure to click on the Mirror Margins option on the Margins tab in the File/Page Setup dialog box (Page Setup's Facing Pages) option. You'll notice that your left and right page margin labels will now read "Inside" and "Outside." Now when you set up headers and footers with the View/Header and Footer command (headers and footers while in Normal View), you'll be able to select odd and even headers and footers.

To Make Uneven Columns

Word for Windows Version 6 has vastly improved column controls and now allows for uneven columns. These are very easy to create using the Format/Columns dialog box. In the Presets section you can select the unequal Left or Right model closest to your goal. Word will automatically reformat your document, or section, in an unequal manner. Or, you can manually set the number and sizes of unequal columns in the Width and Spacing boxes. Once your columns are established you can also visually alter the column structure using the column markers on the horizontal ruler. Setting them up is so easy, I'd say it's fun. However, designing with unequal columns can be a challenge. Don't use them unless you have a specific purpose for each column.

Version 2 does not provide for automatic uneven column widths. If you want to work with such a design, you'll need to do some planning. Format the page with one extra-wide margin designed to accommodate the odd-size column plus the standard page margin. You can create such a margin on the left or right of a page or on the outside or inside of facing pages. (You could also create an unusual middle column by specifying a large space between columns in the Format/Column dialog box.) Insert a frame the size of the odd-size column. While the text will not flow into or from this column into another column, it will provide you with an excellent space for graphics, notes, etc. Try it, you'll like it. (I used such a margin in the Mystical and Magical Symbols paper—Chapter 9 and Figure 13-1 in this chapter.) Odd-size columns work well for newsletters, advertisements, brochures, etc. But be sure you have a specific reason for the uneven columns.

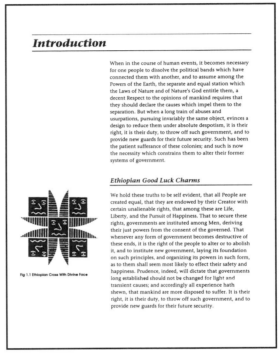

Figure 13-1: An odd-size column provides space for design features.

Margins for Large Text & Graphics

Occasionally you'll find that you can't get a large graphic, frame, table or text (100-point, for example) to fit snugly against your top or bottom page margin. The reason is that Word builds a particular amount of space (leading) into each size of a graphic, text, frame or table. With small text sizes, you don't notice the space; with a large graphic, text, frame or table, however, the leading that's automatically included can become quite noticeable. To eliminate the visual gap created by this effect, you may need to set the page margin larger than your printer can theoretically handle. If you do this, Word warns you that your margins are set outside the printable area when you go to print. Just ignore this message and click on Continue.

When your paragraph has large text or a graphic, you might also fix the problem by using an exact line-spacing setting that's smaller than the text size. I had this difficulty with several documents, especially the Silverado certificate, which uses very large dingbats at the top. Dingbats often cause spacing problems because their actual sizes are disproportionately small in relation to their point sizes.

Figure 13-2: Dingbats require special attention to spacing.

Changing Page Dimensions Inside a Document

In long documents, you might want to have different page margins for a title page, table of contents, first page of a section, etc. You can change margin dimensions part-way through a document by selecting This Point Forward in the File/Page Setup (Format/Page Setup) Apply To list box. When you make a change in your page setup part-way through a document, Word automatically creates a page break.

Test for Paper-Tray "Slop"

Most laser and some other paper-tray-fed printers do not print exactly in the middle of a sheet of paper because of extra space in the paper tray (paper-tray slop). To see if you have this problem, run a few test sheets to determine the amount your paper is off-center, left and right. Once you have exact measurements, you can easily compensate when you set your margins. You can also incorporate this amount into your NORMAL.DOT template.

Headers & Footers

Version 6 has isolated working on headers and footers to a special view. You access this through the View/Header and Footer command. Here you'll find the Header and Footer toolbar for inserting common fields such as page number, date, time, etc., and for positioning headers and footers. Relevant header and footer settings are also available in the File/Page Setup dialog box in the Margins and Layout tabs. The vertical ruler is especially useful for establishing the height and vertical placement of headers and footers. Don't forget that you can format all header and footer information the same way you format all other text in Word with the Format/Font and Format/Paragraph commands.

(In Version 2, setting up headers and footers takes more time and care than some of the other features. However, it's time well spent when you can avoid unpleasant surprises at printout time. To set up headers and footers, you should be in Normal View, then click Header/Footer in the View menu. In the special pane that opens at the bottom of the screen, you can insert field codes for automatic page numbers, date, time, Style references, etc. You can also type in any text that you want to stay the same in all headers or footers.)

Note that you can specify a different first-page header or footer; you can also choose to have different headers and/or footers on odd and even pages. If you selected mirror pages (facing pages) in your page setup, Word then allows you to select these odd and even headers/footers to format in the special pane.

Be sure to set up for facing pages, and hence, for different odd- and even-page headers/footers from the beginning if you're going to use them. If you change your page layout later, you may lose them and have to create them over again. Also, be sure to enter the information for both odd and even headers/footers once you have chosen that option; if you don't, one set of pages will be blank.

If you want mirror-image headers (for instance, the chapter title aligned to the outside of each page) but identical footers (for instance, the page number in the center of each page), you'll still have to format both headers and footers as if they would be totally different for odd and even pages. Once you've filled in the information, you should go into Page Layout View to format the headers and footers so that you can see what they look like.

If you just want to add page numbers, use the Insert/Page Numbers command. Much simpler!

While alignment for headers/footers is handled in the Format/Paragraph dialog box, vertical placement is easily handled with the vertical ruler. (In Version 2, vertical positioning can be done in Print Preview by dragging the header or footer to the desired location or by specifying the From Edge distances in the Header/Footer dialog box via the View menu.)

Space between the regular document text and the header/footer can be formatted with the tools on the Header and Footer toolbar, accessed through the View/Header and Footer command. (In Version 2, use the Format/Paragraph dialog box or alter page margins in the Format/Page Setup dialog box.)

Before tampering with headers and footers, save your work. I have found often that once headers/footers are deleted, it's not possible to retrieve them with the Undo command.

Frames vs. Tables vs. Text Boxes

Typical of most excellent software, Word gives you more than one way to deal with most page layout dilemmas. Frames, tables and Text Boxes all give you the ability to place graphics and text in special locations and to format them in ways that ordinary text can not do. How do you decide which to use? While I can't give you hard and fast rules to suit every case, the following summarizes the important points.

Frames: While frames can be moved virtually anywhere on the page, they are susceptible to numerous problems because they are formatted with the same commands as ordinary text paragraphs. It's easy to accidentally change their paragraph settings, for instance. As noted elsewhere, this makes their behavior somewhat erratic. While you can combine them with text in such a way as to place text over a graphic, as in the Succulent Sandwich Society Survey, for such purposes a Text Box is always preferable. (In Version 2 there are no Text Boxes.) On the other hand, because the frame is text, it integrates well with other text on the page. Other text will automatically flow around it. You can also apply the double borders in the Borders and Shading dialog box available to all paragraphs and table cells. These double borders are not available to Text Boxes. Also, like tables and Text Boxes, frames will occasionally clip the bottom of descends. You need to watch for this and resize the frame if this happens.

Text Box: New with Version 6, Text Boxes can be created while in the drawing tools. Text Boxes are *not* part of the text layer. They can be placed in front of or behind text. Hence, a Text Box makes it easy to place a graphic behind text. But if you need text to flow around a graphic (say an illustration), you'll probably be better off putting the object in a frame or table. Text Boxes are not subject to unpredictable alteration as frames are because they are drawing objects, not paragraphs. While they are infinitely adjustable in size, you must manually size them to fit any text or graphic you place in them. If you're not careful, something can be cut off. While borders can be put around Text Boxes, you must use the selection in the line tool of the drawing tools, not that in the Format/Borders and Shading dialog box. Unlike a frame, a Text Box can hold multiple paragraphs with various indents and alignments and still surround them with a single border.

Tables: While more rigid than frames and Text Boxes, tables offer you the chance to format multiple objects in a consistent and predictable manner quickly and easily. Like frames, each cell of a table can be formatted using the options in the Format/Borders and Shading dialog boxes. Tables are more prone to cutting off descends and lines of text than either frames or Text Boxes. They demand a bit more planning. Like frames, a table is part of the text layer and will cause other text to wrap around it. Like a Text Box, tables can hold paragraphs with differing indents and alignments and still surround them with a single coherent border.

PRINTING TIPS

If you're testing some special formatting and don't need to see the whole page: when you're ready to print, leave the area in question selected and you'll see the selection rather than the current page in the Print dialog box. This allows you to print just the selected item—a big time-saver.

When you're printing multiple copies, if you find that Word re-images the page for each copy, try the following:

If printing a multiple-page document, turn Collate Copies off. If you leave Collate Copies on, the printer must compose *each page* separately. With this feature turned off, the printer can duplicate identical pages quickly.

To facilitate accurate printing, Version 6 provides a good range of view options through the View menu. It's also easy to bring the View/Zoom command onto the Standard toolbar. Word's WYSIWYG has improved greatly, and in Page Layout View you can see typefaces more accurately represented than ever before. The Print Preview Magnifier button on the Standard toolbar lets you quickly toggle to Print Preview. You can now edit in Print Preview, as well. To do this, click the right mouse button while you're in Print Preview or select one of the commands from the main menu. Further, Multi Page View lets you see thumbnails of between 20 and 40 pages of your document. Like other commands, this is easy to place on the toolbar. It is part of the Print Preview toolbar. Also, don't forget that the status bar now has buttons for Normal, Page Layout and Outline views of your document. A most handy addition.

In Version 2, I have made several macros that change my document view to print preview, draft, page layout and zoom 200 percent. You might want to make such macros also. Another option is to reassign one of the View buttons on the Toolbar or create a new one (the magnifying glass makes a good icon choice) with the View/Zoom command. With this command you merely click on the button and a dynamic arrow drops down. By dragging over the arrow with the mouse, you can instantly select any zoom view from 25 percent to 200 percent. This is especially handy for working with landscape orientation and odd-size pages. (To alter the Toolbar icons, see your *User's Guide* for instructions and Chapter 2.)

TROUBLE-SHOOTING

Here are some problems you may encounter while attempting to create complex layouts. You'll be pleased to know that I also suggest solutions to these problems.

Tortured Text

Problem: Descenders of some letters are cut off.

Currently, versions 6 and 2 will truncate the descenders of some letters or cut off the bottom of all letters (if text is subscripted enough) when text is in a table and you're using exact line spacing. Version 2 also often does the same thing when text is placed in a frame with Exact line spacing.

You'll have to be careful when working with any superscripted or subscripted letters, especially in tables.

Solution: For now, here are your choices.

- Find a way to format the material as regular text—not in a frame or table.

- Try formatting the paragraph with Single (Auto) spacing or larger line spacing (leading).

- Use a font with shorter descenders (such as Goudy Old Style).

- Rewrite the text to exclude the letters j, y, g and p.

- If the problem text is at the bottom of a frame or table and if the bottom edge has no visible border (and you don't mind having a gap below the text), you can pull the bottom edge down and away from the text. This will work, especially if combined with using Single or larger line spacing.

- Pray no one will notice. If they do, tell them the printer goofed.

Problem: Lines of text (characters) cut off at the bottom of a table cell.

Currently, in cells with Exactly line spacing, if there is too much text to fit in a cell, Word prints as much text as it can fit in the cell. It doesn't print as many *full lines* as will fit but literally *as much type*. Consequently, you may see a partial line of type with the letters actually cut off at the bottom of the cell. In Appendix A, the Bitstream Amerigo specimen pages show this clearly.

Solution: Until Microsoft rethinks this peculiar situation, you must edit your text to fit your table cell. Or, you must abandon any Exact sizing of cells. *Note that this is not a "bug."*

Toolbar Trials

Problem: Changes you made in the Standard toolbar (Toolbar) icon assignments, menus or macros are not there when you start the program again.

Solution: You forgot to save the global changes the last time you exited Word. You may have saved the changes with the template you were using, so check there first. But if they're gone, I'm sure you won't forget the next time. After all, experience is what lets you make a *different* mistake next time.

Problem: You've made many changes to the Standard toolbar (Toolbar) that you now regret. You'd like to re-store the Standard toolbar to its original settings.

Solution: The simplest way to restore the Standard toolbar is to select Reset All in the Tools/Customize/ Menus Tab (Tools/Options/Toolbar) dialog box. If you are using a template other than the NORMAL.DOT, you must click on Context Global for the reset to work.

Another method is to delete the NORMAL.DOT. Before taking such a drastic step, be sure to save it with a new name because deleting the NORMAL.DOT will remove custom macros and glossaries you've saved globally. You may have custom features in it that you'll need for other projects. When you delete the NORMAL.DOT, Word makes a nice, new shiny one with all the original de-faults, including the Standard toolbar setup. Note that in Version 2 the NORMAL.DOT will not appear in the list box of *.DOCs in the File/Open dialog box until after you have saved it with a change. (It will appear in the list box when you select New from the File menu, however.)

Flying Objects

Problem: After an editing action, a graphic, frame or table appears in an unexpected location or, heavens, it has disappeared all together.

Solution: You've probably deleted a crucial paragraph mark—most likely the one associated with a frame or graphic. Or you've reformatted the frame's paragraph mark. In either case, select Undo immediately. If you're lucky, Undo will work. If not, try reformatting the frame's paragraph settings. Remember, if the frame retains the Normal Style paragraph formatting and you make any change to the Normal Style, the frame will be affected.

You should create a neutral Paragraph Style for your frames and apply it immediately after you make the frame. If you've developed a complex layout with frames, please save it before you begin editing. If you can't recover the original positioning, close the document without saving and load it again. Or load the backup file. (Of course you have a backup file.)

Problem: A frame in a margin with a fixed position moves unexpectedly to the same position on the following page.

Solution: Probably the frame's edge ever so slightly intrudes into the adjacent text area. Note that it doesn't have to be near any actual text. This is most likely to happen if the frame contains a graphic or chart you're trying to size and/or place attractively on the page. If you display your text borders, you'll be able to see that this has happened. If even a tiny smidgen of the frame is in the area of the text, the program treats it as text. If you add enough text above the frame, wham, it moves. If it was specifically positioned, it moves to the same relative location on the next page.

To remedy the situation, press Undo. If it's too late for that, go back and delete the text that caused the frame to move. Reducing the frame size so that it fits within the margin may also induce it to move back where it belongs. After you alter the text or frame, if it doesn't go back to its proper place, drag it back. Once it's in its proper position, adjust its edges so that they don't intrude into the text area.

Frame Frights

Problem: Text appears in a frame unexpectedly after an editing action, often with newly acquired style characteristics.

Solution: This is probably caused by the deletion of the paragraph mark belonging to the text. Immediately select Undo. If it's too late for that (and assuming you saved before the deletion), close the document without saving and open it again. You can also cut and paste the text back into the document in its proper place; or select the paragraph mark of the unwanted text and format it with the proper paragraph settings. It should then separate and go back where it came from.

Problem: You're working with text in a frame when, all of a sudden, the frame appears to split into two frames.

Solution: Version 6 allows different indents for paragraphs within the same frame. However, you still can't put a single border around such a group. Use a table or create a Text Box with the drawing tools to put a frame on top of the group of paragraphs.

(In Version 2, you've changed a crucial paragraph setting for some of the text in the frame. You can alter character settings—including subscript, superscript, typeface and type size—for different paragraphs in a frame and still surround them with a single border. However, indents, line spacing, borders and shading must be consistent inside the frame; otherwise Word will create two or more bordered paragraphs in the same frame. *If you need different paragraph indents inside a single border, use a table.*)

Problem: You click on Insert/Frame and the program boinks at you, or the Insert/Frame option is gray.

Solution: You have a frame currently selected; just deselect it. (It's that easy to fix!)

Problem: You can't seem to get the insertion point out of a frame.

Solution: Several different problems may cause this. If you don't mind losing the formatting in your frame, just select the frame and press Ctrl+Q. This will remove the frame and all of its formatting.

You should be able to add a frame below the current one by choosing Insert/Frame.

Sometimes the problem is caused by the frame overlapping its own paragraph mark. If this is the case, you'll need to temporarily raise the lower edge of the frame to find the paragraph mark under it. This may necessitate major alteration of the frame contents—not a fun task.

You can add a new frame above the frame you're stuck in by pressing Ctrl+Shift+Enter.

Missing Pieces

Problem: You've inserted a chart or graphic into a table, a frame or text, and it's not displaying properly.

Solution: You've set line spacing or dimensions that won't accommodate the new material. If you've inserted directly into the text, select the paragraph mark at the insertion point; format it with Auto line spacing and no indention. To solve the problem with frames or tables, select the table cell or frame and reformat its paragraph settings and dimensions with Auto everything. Once the graphic is displaying properly, you can go back and alter spacing and dimensions as needed.

Problem: It's gone! You've just moved something and started to type again, and now it's disappeared! This frequently happens after you've moved selected text and pressed the Enter key to get to the next line.

Solution: Anything that's selected will be replaced immediately by the next keyboard action, including pressing the Enter key. In this case, pressing Enter deleted all the selected material. Press the Undo icon immediately and all will be well. Or close the document without saving and open it again. Or retrieve your backup. If it's too late for that, you'll have to reconstruct the lost material. Ouch, this hurts.

Stubborn Styles

Problem: You've added so many Styles to your Style sheet and changed them so often that your Standard Styles don't behave properly any longer.

Solution: Restore the NORMAL.DOT. (See "Toolbar Trials" discussed earlier.)

Problem: You've decided to change all the occurrences of Style A to Style B. You select all the A's and click on the B style name in the Style list. But some of the A's stay the same. Or you change the characteristics of a certain Style using Format/Style, but some of the items tagged with that Style don't acquire the new characteristics.

Solution: You undoubtedly changed the recalcitrant items manually. Manual character and paragraph changes take precedence over all other changes. This is actually good, because manual changes take longer and you don't want to have to redo them—for instance, a series of items changed to italic or all-caps. To return your text to its nominal Character Style, select it and press Ctrl+Space bar. To return your text to its nominal Paragraph Style, select it and press Ctrl+Q.

Flighty Fonts

Problem: You've installed new fonts, but they don't show in your Font list box.

Solution: Because Word stores printer information in its own .INI file, each time you add fonts it's a good idea to go into the File menu, choose Print Setup again, click on OK and close the box. Also, check to make sure you're using the printer you installed the fonts in. If these steps don't fix the problem, you may have installed the fonts improperly.

Version 2 Problem: Your fonts don't appear in Microsoft Graph or Microsoft Draw. Sometimes I've found that Microsoft Graph or Microsoft Draw lists the default Windows fonts instead of those of my currently selected printer. I don't know why this happens. (Version 6 has incorporated all fonts into both the drawing and charting functions.)

Solution: Try going back into Word and working for a while. Try setting up the printer again. Then go back and see if the correct set of fonts lists.

Pages Plus

Problem: Every time you print, you get an extra, blank page at the end of your document. You will note that the program shows the extra page. This page has an empty paragraph mark on it, and you can't delete it.

Solution: Word always inserts an empty paragraph at the end of your document. To get the mark back onto the preceding document page, increase the bottom margin of the preceding page to accommodate it. You can also reformat the final paragraph mark with smaller character- and line-space settings to make it fit on the preceding page.

Memory Messages

Problem: All of a sudden you get an Out Of Memory message even though you know you have plenty of memory. (To check available memory, click on About in the Help menu.)

Solution: Don't leave multiple documents open. Word's generous saving of document changes in its Undo function will use up memory. Save your document often to empty the Undo buffer. Try closing Word and Windows. If you have a screen saver or other Windows TSR's, close them as well. Then start again.

You'll have more available system resources (memory) if you limit the number of program groups in the Windows Program Manager. You can also try reducing the number of screen fonts if you are not using a scalable outline font manager.

If Out Of Memory messages continue, another possible answer involves Windows's and Word for Windows's need for plenty of hard disk space to function at their best. Your hard disk may have become too crowded. I leave 10 megabytes clear for Word and Windows to do their work. Find a way to remove material, buy a bigger hard disk or get a program like Stacker, which increases your hard disk space by compressing files. Optimize your hard disk often so that all available space is located in contiguous clusters.

If you can, make a permanent swap file on your hard disk as well as a RAM disk. These options are discussed in detail in your Windows manual.

Problem: All of a sudden, documents don't display or don't print correctly. You get Out Of Memory messages when the system still has plenty of memory. (You can check your available memory and disk space in the Help/About submenu.) The system seems sluggish or exhibits other unusual behavior.

Solution: Save your work; close Word and Windows and begin again. Try closing any and all Windows TSR's, even the screen saver. (I can hardly function without After Dark, but sometimes I find things work better without it.) If this doesn't help, close Word and Windows and turn off your computer and printer for at least one minute. The system is having a nervous attack (my unscientific diagnosis) and needs to clear its memory. You could probably use a break too—these things usually happen when you're stressed or working at a feverish pace.

CONCLUSION

I hope the information and examples in this book have inspired you to explore Word for Windows's vast reservoir of design and page layout capabilities and encouraged you in your pursuit of great-looking pages and fantastic documents.

V

Appendices

A

Type Selection Guide

Ninety percent of your job in designing documents involves selecting and arranging type. Therefore, some knowledge of the history and evolution of typefaces will not only help you identify the differences between them but will also sensitize you to their evocative properties.

Typefaces vary from one another in many ways. In the following sections, I describe the major typeface classifications, their best uses in documents, and some well-known examples and their contemporary offspring. If you're interested in particular typefaces, look in the Index in the back of this book. And be sure to read about Adobe Type Manager, Bitstream FaceLift and TrueType later in this chapter.

TYPE FAMILIES

A type family consists of a group of faces that share common characteristics, such as serifs, stress and basic letter shape. The members of a family vary in weight, width and italic forms. The first true type family, created in the early 1900s by Morris Fuller Benton, was the Century family. Prior to this printers had to search out roman, italic and bold faces that were compatible even though they hadn't been designed specifically to go together.

Now, virtually all roman faces suitable for text are designed in sets that include italic (or oblique), bold and bold italic siblings. Some type families include many more versions. Historic classification schemes rarely use these when classifying a typeface.

Romans

The basic face in any type family is traditionally referred to as the "roman," but you may also see it identified as "normal," "regular," "text" or "book." These faces are all upright and of a moderate weight. The fundamental characteristics of the roman determine the recurring traits of the family.

Italics & Obliques

The first italics imitated a formal handwritten script, known as Chancery Cursive. The publisher who first used them, Aldus Manutius, had the type made because the letterforms were much narrower than standard roman letters, allowing him to squeeze more type on the page, save money on paper and sell books for less. His cheaper books were a big success.

Though Aldus Manutius used italics for long texts, I recommend that you do NOT. Because of their slanted orientation and narrow, uniform shapes, italics are more difficult to read than roman letters. Use them in text when something needs to be set apart: foreign words and phrases, quotations, etc. Use them for invitations or for short texts in brochures, advertisements, etc. Their similarity to handwriting gives all italics a certain informality. The serif italics also possess a graceful decorative quality.

Italics can be distinguished by their slant to the right and by their proportions, which are considerably narrower than their roman counterparts.

Obliques look much like italics but are created differently. A true italic is designed from scratch as a distinct typeface. Obliques are made by simply slanting the roman forms to the right. Consequently, obliques often go unnoticed when they're imbedded in text—the slant alone is not enough to draw attention.

Bolds

Treat bold typefaces as display faces. The thickening and consequent darkening of the roman and italic forms make headings, titles and such stand out on the page and attract attention; but they also make the letterform strokes less distinct and the text consequently harder to read. Many type families include Demibold or Semibold, Black and/or Heavy versions as well as Bold.

Expanded (or Extended)

Expanded faces are widened versions of normal faces. Most of them are upright sans-serif faces, such as Univers Extended, Helvetica Extended, etc. Expanded fonts also serve as display faces. Their oddness attracts attention, but their width and rather uniform shapes often make them difficult to read.

Condensed

Condensed type styles were designed to pack more information into a smaller space. But, like italics, the letterforms display less variety in their shapes, which makes them less legible. Don't use them in long texts. For special situations—on forms, letterheads, business cards, schedules, etc.—condensed faces can work very well. When your reader is highly motivated, he or she will find the information. But if the information is critical—as in warnings, for instance—DON'T use condensed type. My favorite condensed face is in the Frutiger family (it's not called condensed but it is a very narrow upright sans-serif face).

Other Variants

Type styles labeled "light," as in Futura Light, are often excellent text faces. You should evaluate each for its intended purpose. Faces with an "ultra-" prefix should be reserved for display purposes.

SIMPLIFIED TYPE CLASSIFICATIONS

Most type classification schemes reflect the history of type, which goes back to the 1400s. The simplified system I offer here provides only a bare outline of the evolution and diversity of type. (See the Bibliography for a listing of books that will broaden your understanding.)

Letterforms changed over time in response to the same aesthetic and technological forces that influenced other facets of culture. For instance, printers took advantage of improvements in printing and paper quality to produce more delicate letterforms. More recently, other changes occurred due to the increasing use of printing for advertising. The following nutshell profiles will give you an overview.

Following each profile is a list of some available digital typefaces. An initial following the name indicates the exclusive vendor for that face. All other faces are available from several vendors (though the typeface name may be changed). The initial A means Adobe; B means Bitstream; C & G means Casady & Greene; DTC means Digital Typeface Corporation; E means Emigre; L means Linotype-Hell; M means Monotype.

Old Style Romans

Old Style Roman type designs originated in 15th-century Italian printing. These typefaces copied the then popular hand-lettering we call Humanist Bookhand. Printers selected this model because it was eminently readable. The fact that most typefaces in the Western world descend from these faces is testimony to their utility and beauty.

Here are some of the significant characteristics of Old Style Roman:

- All have distinct, full-bodied serifs.

- Capital letters are not as tall as ascenders, which prevents them from overpowering the lowercase letters.

- Letterform proportions reflect the Renaissance passion for geometry. B, E, F, K, L, P, R and S are roughly half the width of O and N. X is half the width of V, and M is the width of two V's.

- Character strokes have angled stress. This can be seen by drawing a line through an O where it thins—at approximately 11 and 5 o'clock.

- Stroke width varies, but the thin-to-thick contrast is not great.

Many of the most popular text faces used today incorporate these characteristics in their designs. The uses for traditional Roman typefaces know no limit. There are no finer book faces. In display work they impart a formal, elegant and classical air.

Popular Old Style Roman faces available: Monotype Bembo (M); Berkeley Old Style; Bookman; Monotype; Centaur (M); ITC Galliard; Garamond; Goudy Old Style; Granjon (L); Palatino; and Trump Mediaeval.

Unusual Romans

Many modern designers have been inspired by the Old Style Romans to create beautiful if somewhat eccentric typefaces. Dramatic shapes and stroke-width variations give these faces strong, distinct personalities. Many communicate an old-world elegance and charm. While they can be used for text, your reader will be acutely aware of the unusual letterforms. Therefore, don't use them for long text passages in books, reports or manuals. All work extremely well as display faces.

Here are some well-known Unusual Romans and their distinguishing characteristics:

- Elegant, old-world feeling: Bernhard Modern (B); ITC Cheltenham; ITC Tiffany.

- Art Nouveau overtones: ITC Benguiat; ITC Korinna; ITC Souvenir. Ed Benguiat (pronounced Bengat) created ITC Benguiat, which, in modern typeface design, has no equal for its unusual sensual shapes. But don't let its beauty seduce you into thinking you can set long text with this typeface! Ed

Benguiat is also responsible for ITC Tiffany as well as the Art Nouveau revivals ITC Korinna and ITC Souvenir.

- Modern, calligraphic quality: Bitstream Amerigo; Hiroshige. These handsome faces can be used for text in specialized art books, for instance, or long brochures. They make distinguished headings, titles and company names.

- The 1920s: Bitstream Copper Light (B); Bernhard Modern (B).

- A special case: Optima. Hermann Zapf's exceptionally successful design is a serif face without serifs. Its simple appearance belies its extreme subtlety and complexity. The subtlety of the design features can't be reproduced by a low-resolution printer, so I recommend against its use on 300 dpi printers.

Transitional Romans

Type styles remained much the same from the late 1400s until the early 1700s. The first typefaces now identified as "transitional" were those of John Baskerville. Baskerville's designs (called simply Baskerville) have become the basis for the most popular of all modern type styles. Transitional Romans have the following characteristics:

- Increased contrast between thick and thin parts of strokes.

- Sharper points on the serifs.

- An almost vertical stress.

- Near equality in width among capital letters—hence, a wider R, S, K, etc., and narrower M.

These design changes were made possible in part by improved printing equipment, which allowed more pressure to be applied without damaging the thin lines of the type, and by better ink, which allowed both thick and thin areas to print well with the same amount of ink. The improved inking capabilities also allowed Baskerville to use a harder, whiter paper.

Also classified with the historical transitional faces are the so-called "legibility" typefaces designed in more recent times for improved reading. These faces were designed to be legible in the small sizes typically used in magazine texts. Century and Times Roman (correctly, Times New Roman) are in this group. Matthew Carter's Bitstream Charter, a contemporary face, was designed to produce legible type even from laser printers. I also put the modern Caslon 540 in this group.

Available Transitional Romans: Adobe Caslon (A); Baskerville; Caslon 540; Bitstream Charter (B); ITC Clearface; Cochin; ITC Stone Serif; New Century Schoolbook.

Modern Romans

Firmin Didot in France and Giambattista Bodoni developed "modern" typefaces at almost the same time in the early 1700s. By the 1780s, these faces had become the most popular in Europe. They inspired the contemporary "Bodoni" faces. Modern typefaces pushed the Transitional type characteristics to their logical conclusions:

◆ The thick/thin stroke-width variation became pronounced, making hairlines of the thinnest parts of the letterforms.

◆ The stress became absolutely vertical.

- Most serifs were reduced to mere hairlines and others became daggerlike finials.

- All capital letters became nearly equal in width.

In contrast with earlier printers who used a soft cream-color paper, Bodoni and Didot printed on very hard, stark-white paper. The effect was formal, cold and exquisite.

Contemporary, digitized Bodoni faces lack the full refinement of the originals, but they still communicate a formal elegance, and Bodoni still looks best on hard, bright-white paper.

Available Modern Romans: various Bodonis, including the very refined Bauer Bodoni (A); Hermann Zapf's Melior.

Sans-Serifs

Sans-serif faces, which most people think of as "modern," actually date from the early 1800s. Their appearance marked the most radical departure from traditional letterforms in the history of type. Two traits distinguish these faces: the absence of serifs and an absolute minimum of stroke-width variation. (Virtually all letterforms show narrowing of stroke width where two strokes join; otherwise the join looks fat and clumsy.) Because of the latter trait sans-serif faces are often called "Linear." Because of their primitive look, the Germans named them "Grotesque," the English called them "Gothic" or "Sans-serif" and the French labeled them "Antique." Sans-serif designs can be loosely divided into two groups—traditional and geometric.

Traditional Sans-Serifs

Traditional sans-serifs derive from those popular in the 1800s. Their basic proportions and shapes evolved from traditional serif faces. Berthold's Akzidenz Grotesk, currently available from Adobe, has been in production since the 1890s! Helvetica, by Max Miedinger, was created in the 1950s and clearly reflected the deliberate sterility of the International Style in architecture. It's surely the most well known, and though I find it cold, its neutral shapes make it acceptable for virtually any business application. Univers, which I regard as the most beautiful traditional sans-serif, works equally well, and its slim, elegant look gives it an urbane quality.

Other popular traditional sans-serifs are: ITC Stone Sans (a remarkably warm sans-serif); Letter Gothic; News Gothic; ITC Eras; Eurostile; Frutiger.

Geometric Sans-Serifs

The popularity of the traditional sans-serifs waned in the 1920s with the appearance of sans-serifs based on true geometric arcs and angles. The most famous of these is Paul Renner's Futura of 1927. This dramatic typeface, one of my personal favorites, epitomizes the Bauhaus era. Whenever possible, Renner constructed his letters of absolutely straight and absolutely circular lines. To me, the original Futura always evokes the avant-garde style of the 1920s. While the original's weight seems a bit heavy for most book work, the modern book versions function well.

Take care when using a geometric sans-serif. Their strong shapes cry for attention, and they're generally more difficult to read than the traditional sans-serifs.

Available geometric sans-serifs: ITC Avant Garde Gothic; Futura; Kabel (Cabel); Avenir.

An Odd Couple

Gill Sans, designed by Eric Gill, uses the proportions and basic letterforms of traditional serif faces. Its weight, like that of Futura, seems a trifle heavy for text, but it is a beautiful sans-serif face. Copper Plate Gothic, designed by the famous Frederic William Goudy, is really a sans-serif face with tiny serifs! Use it as a sans-serif.

Square (Slab) Serifs

The square, or slab, serif faces (known originally as Egyptiennes) achieved prominence in the 19th century. These faces resemble sans-serif types in their even stroke widths. They differ from the sans-serifs in that they have stubby, square-cornered serifs. Since nearly all typewriter faces were modeled after square serif faces, many readers associate square-serif type with the typewriter.

Few of the older square serifs have survived into our time. The Clarendons are among the oldest exceptions. Their proportions are more like traditional sans-serif faces. ITC Lubalin Graph, on the other hand, is a square serif version of the geometric sans-serif Avant Garde.

As a general rule, reserve square serifs for display work. Sophisticated readers will appreciate Lubalin Graph or Serifa as text face in brochures and flyers. My favorite is Serifa, which I use for correspondence.

Popular square serifs: ITC American Typewriter; Clarendon; Courier (monospaced); Glypha; ITC Lubalin Graph; Memphis; Prestige Elite (monospaced); Rockwell and Serifa.

Decorative/Display

Virtually all other Western typefaces belong in this category. Reserve them for short texts and display work. They can be subdivided in many different ways. A simple system would include imitations of handwriting (scripts), mediaeval revivals, chisel-cut letterforms, "poster" faces and dingbats. (Also see listings of poster/display faces and dingbats below.)

Examples of decorative/display faces:

◆ Formal scripts: These faces are based on old-fashioned copperplate engraving. They're often used for invitations and certificates. Examples of formal scripts: Linoscript; Englishe Schreib-schrift (DTC); Kunstler Script; the Shelley variations; Vivaldi.

◆ Informal scripts: These faces work well for personal messages in correspondence and advertising as well. Italics can function in the same capacities, where a less dramatic impact is desired. Examples of informal scripts: ITC Studio Script; Kaufman; Murray Hill; Freestyle Script.

◆ 1930s-style scripts: Coronet; Park Avenue. These will bring back the past.

◆ Brush scripts: These most informal letterforms will add dash and spontaneity to your work: Dom Casual; Cascade Script; Choc; Mistral (my favorite—it mimics cursive handwriting better than any other typeface); and Reporter No. 2.

◆ Imitation pencil printing: Tekton; Jott (C&G). Very neat.

◆ Mediaeval revivals: Among these are imitations of Black Letter and uncial letterforms. These faces bring to mind castles, cathedrals, monks and knights in armor. Mermaid, Bitstream's version of Ondine, is reminiscent of the Arabian Nights. They work well for certificates, greeting cards, Christmas newsletters and the like. They're often used in newspaper nameplates. They also work well as initial caps to introduce long texts in newsletters, magazines and books. Examples of mediaeval revivals: Cloister Black; Ondine (or Mermaid); Fette Fraktur; Omnia; Linotext; several from Casady & Greene, including Dorovar, Meath, Paladin.

◆ Chisel-cut letters: Lithos has the look of ancient Greek stone-carved letters; Trajan imitates the hand-chiseled letters of ancient Rome; Hiroshige has a robust, calligraphic look.

Poster/Display

I've lumped everything else together in this group—faces that suggest machine and computer output; exaggerated versions of traditional faces; faces designed for advertising in past eras such as imitations of wood type; whimsical and absurd faces. All are designed for use in large sizes—for headlines and titles:

Examples of poster/display faces:

◆ Exaggerated Old Style: ITC Tiffany; Cochin.

◆ Art Nouveau: Arnold Böcklin.

◆ 1920s–1930s: Broadway; Hobo; Parisian; Ritz (C&G); Gatsby (C&G); Binner (D); ITC Anna; Bernhard Fashion (D).

◆ Wood Type: P.T. Barnum (B); Juniper; Mesquite; Ironwood; Ponderosa; Desparado; Abiline.

- ◆ Eccentrics: Peignot; BeesKnees; University; ITC Benguiat; Modular Tall (E).

- ◆ Modern/Machine Look: Eurostile; ITC Eras; Britannic (DTC); Serpentine; Variex (E).

Dingbats

Dingbats are collections of typographic ornaments. I find their strong graphic quality works well in almost any text situation because they have the same black/white qualities as type. I frequently prefer them to illustrations. Windows 3.1 includes an excellent set of dingbats, Wingdings, designed by Bigelow and Holmes, who also produce the Lucida family of faces that comes with Windows.

In the last several years a vast array of dingbat, ornament and pi fonts have become available. Excellent fonts from major foundries that have been used in this book include: International Symbol Set; Carta (A); Wood Type Ornaments I & II (A); Adobe Caslon Ornaments; ITC Zapf Dingbats (A, L and others); Vine Leaves (DTC); Linotype Decorative Pi; Linotype Holiday Pi; and Linotype European Pi. In addition to these, I highly recommend Caravan from Linotype and Rococo from Monotype. If you're interested in the historical, unusual and whimsical, please send for the font catalogs of Judith Sutcliffe (2216 Cliff Drive, Santa Barbara, CA 93109, 805-966-7563), Richard Beatty (2312 Laurel Park Highway, Hendersonville, NC 28739, 704-696-8316) and U Design Type Foundry (270 Farmington Avenue, Hartford, CT 06105, 800-945-3648)— you won't be disappointed!

Selecting typefaces is somewhat like choosing a wardrobe. You need basic good-looking outfits for business, dressier things for evening wear and all those fun clothes for leisure time. For business, you probably opt for better-quality, more conservative wear than you choose for personal activities.

By the same token, your everyday typefaces should be of the best quality you can afford. Adobe and Bitstream, Linotype-Hell, Monotype and DTC offer excellent type quality at competitive (with each other) prices. Start your type collection with one serif and one sans-serif type family. Each family should contain at least the four basic faces: regular (normal, book or medium weight), italic, bold and bold italic. If your budget is very tight, buy only the serif faces, then add a sans-serif family. Your italics, bolds and bold italics will work very well for display.

Another basic purchasing criterion is how well a typeface will print on your particular equipment. Not all type designs digitize with equal ease. Some are far too subtle and complex to reproduce well on a 300 dpi laser printer. In the following listing I have indicated with a (1) those I consider the best for 300 dpi. Faces followed by a (2) are slightly less well adapted to 300 dpi but are nevertheless good choices. If you're working with a high-quality dot-matrix or ink-jet printer, you're better off with the class (1) faces.

I have not specified type vendors for the faces below; but, in my experience, faces from Adobe, Bitstream, Digital Typeface Corporation, Linotype-Hell and Monotype are the best current offerings for use in Windows. Casady & Greene and Emigre offer imaginative collections of display faces at very reasonable prices.

Some Serif Typeface Starter Families

Baskerville	Granjon (2)
Berkeley Book	ITC Galliard (2)
Bitstream Charter (1)	ITC Garamond
Caslon 540	ITC Stone Serif (2)
Goudy Old Style	

Some Sans-Serif Typeface Starter Families

Futura (1)	Stone Sans (1)
Gill Sans (1)	Univers (my first choice) (1)
Helvetica (1)	

Typefaces for Special Situations

By now you have some good ideas about how to use typefaces. But the following suggestions may help you make appropriate choices for specific types of documents.

Letterheads and business cards: You can use any face that creates the image you want. For address and phone numbers, a sans-serif is always effective. Condensed sans-serifs are commonly used.

Business correspondence: I don't normally use traditional serif type for correspondence because it looks too impersonal. Instead consider the following: Bitstream Charter; Serifa; ITC Korinna; ITC Stone Sans; ITC Stone Informal; and, in a pinch, good ole Courier.

Forms and surveys: Most users expect to see sans-serif type on this kind of document—it looks businesslike. But legible serif faces will also work.

Promotional materials: Virtually any typeface can be used for brochures and advertisements as long as it conveys the impression you want to make. You need to consider the typeface's historical associations and its visual impact in the context of your product or information.

Newsletter nameplates or banners: Here again, any face might be right. Look for the ones that communicate the image you want to project.

Newsletter text face: Generally, serif faces work best. Review my list of recommended starter faces.

Newsletter headings: Because of their often borderline status between information and advertising, newsletters can often use some of the more exotic display faces for headings, though don't feel obliged. Choose headings for contrast with your text face.

Books, manuals, reports: Serif for text and sans-serif for headings are always the safest choices. Reserve the display faces for initial caps, chapter openings, title page, etc.

CREATE A TYPE SPECIMEN

When you need to select a typeface from your own collection for a specific purpose, it helps to have a set of type specimens already made. I have created specimens like those illustrated here for each of my text and display faces (Bitstream Amerigo, on page 414, is a text face; ITC Anna, on page 415, is a display face). They provide me with a very good idea of how any of the faces will look in a variety of typical settings. I advise you to make a similar set of specimens for yourself. You can make a complete set of alphabetical samples of all your installed fonts using the Font Sample Generator macro in Version 6.

Bitstream Amerigo
ABCDEFGHIJKLMNOPQRSTUVWXYZ
abcdefghijklmnopqrstuvwxyz 1234567890&?!@

11/13 points

The complex relationship between line length, type size and leading determine the readability of your typography. It is virtually impossible to create guidelines which can encompass all these variables accurately. However, I offer a few suggestions. Most readers look at their material from 12 to 14 inches away. Given this, studies show that type between 9 and 12 points is the most legible. Though the trend is toward larger text type, faces over 12 points appear to slow reading down. Line lengths of ten to twelve words (60 to 70 characters) in the suggested point sizes are about as long as possible. (This equates to something between 18 and 24 picas.) Line spacing must increase as the line length increases. Usually, lines set without leading are more difficult to read than those with leading. I always recommend leading unless there is some pressing space problem and the text being set is short and/or

11/15 points

The complex relationship between line length, type size and leading determine the readability of your typography. It is virtually impossible to create guidelines which can encompass all these variables accurately. However, I offer a few suggestions. Most readers look at their material from 12 to 14 inches away. Given this, studies show that type between 9 and 12 points is the most legible. Though the trend is toward larger text type, faces over 12 points appear to slow reading down. Line lengths of ten to twelve words (60 to 70 characters) in the suggested point sizes are about as long as possible. (This equates to something between 18 and 24 picas.) Line spacing must increase as the line length increases. Usually, lines set without leading are more difficult to read

12/14 points

The complex relationship between line length, type size and leading determine the readability of your typography. It is virtually impossible to create guidelines which can encompass all these variables accurately. However, I offer a few suggestions. Most readers look at their material from 12 to 14 inches away. Given this, studies show that type between 9 and 12 points is the most legible. Though the trend is toward larger text type, faces over 12 points appear to slow reading down. Line lengths of ten to twelve words (60 to 70 characters) in the suggested point sizes are about as long as possible. (This equates to something between 18 and 24 picas.) Line spacing must increase as the line length increases. Usually, lines set without leading are more

12/16 points

The complex relationship between line length, type size and leading determine the readability of your typography. It is virtually impossible to create guidelines which can encompass all these variables accurately. However, I offer a few suggestions. Most readers look at their material from 12 to 14 inches away. Given this, studies show that type between 9 and 12 points is the most legible. Though the trend is toward larger text type, faces over 12 points appear to slow reading down. Line lengths of ten to twelve words (60 to 70 characters) in the suggested point sizes are about as long as possible. (This equates to something

2

ITC ANNA (DTC)
ABCDEFGHIJKLMNOPQRSTUVWXYZ
ABCDEFGHIJKLMNOPQRSTUVWXYZ 1234567890&?!@

24 points

MIST

ANEMONE

CHIMES

CERULEAN

MIGNONETTE

AMARYLLIS

ORIOLE

18 points

CLAUDE MONET

ALEXANDER THE GREAT

MARK TWAIN

D.H. LAWRENCE

WINSTON CHURCHILL

VICTOR LAZLO

WILLIAM TURNER

MAURICE RAVEL

J.A.D. INGRES

SHERLOCK HOLMES

36, 54 & 48 points

SCINTILLATING SENSATIONAL SENSUOUS
EXTRAVAGANT

NEWSLETTER

THE DAMASK LULLABY

Below I cover some of the issues involved in producing and using digital typefaces, and I describe the developers of the typefaces used in this book.

This discussion focuses on scalable outline fonts because I find them the easiest to use and because there is an ever-growing selection of high-quality typefaces available in this form. There are many other products you can try, but these are the ones I can recommend without reservation. I have used all the products discussed here, but in the production of this book I used only the LaserMaster Professional printer controller with my now venerable LaserJet II. All final artwork was output on this device at 800 x 800 dpi using the fonts indicated in the illustration descriptions. I can highly recommend this product, which I describe briefly at the end of this Appendix.

Bitmaps Versus Scalable Outlines

Digital fonts come in two forms: bitmap fonts and scalable outline fonts. Both forms can be used to create matching fonts for printer and screen. Matching screen fonts give you a much more accurate picture of what your document will look like when it prints, though no screen will look exactly like the printed output—it has many fewer dots per inch.

Bitmap fonts, which only a few years ago dominated the PC world, create characters by arranging bits (also called pixels or dots) in a fixed image of a character at a specific point size and device resolution. These bitmaps can be highly accurate and can create beautiful fonts, as with the Bitstream Fontware. However, one of the disadvantages is that each font (i.e., one point size of one typeface) must be stored as a separate file. This means that a collection of one typeface in sizes ranging from 6 points to 72 points can consume several megabytes of hard disk space.

Scalable outline fonts, by contrast, use mathematical descriptions to create the outlines of characters. One outline can be used to generate all point sizes of a given typeface for any and all supported printers and screen resolutions. This flexibility and the savings in disk space and installation time make scalable outline fonts the clear choice. In addition, the number of high-quality typefaces available as scalable outlines far exceeds those available as bitmaps.

While bitmap fonts can be used directly by the screen or printer, scalable outline fonts must first be converted to bitmaps, a process more complex than might be thought. In the conversion to bitmap fonts, the best scalable out-line fonts (all those from the developers whose fonts are used in this book, for instance) use a process called *hinting,* which makes sophisticated judgments about the place-ment of the individual dots that form each character. This is especially important in small point sizes where indivi-dual characters are constructed of relatively few dots.

FONT MANAGERS

If you plan to work with scalable outlines, and I highly recommend that you do, you should use a Windows font manager. Font managers install fonts, generate matching screen fonts on the fly and send the properly formatted font information (whether outline or bitmapped) to the printer. Without them, you must perform all these tasks manually. Not fun. While there are other font managers on the market, I recommend Adobe Type Manager, Bit-stream FaceLift and TrueType (incorporated in Windows 3.1 in April 1992). These programs work well, they work easily and they allow you access to thousands of high-quality digital typefaces.

Note: Because scalable outline fonts come in a number of formats, you should find out whether the font manager you're considering will support the scalable outline font formats you will use. The most popular outline formats are PostScript Type 1, Bitstream Speedo and TrueType. Many font developers will soon be making their fonts available in all three formats. At this time, PostScript is certainly the most popular format.

Many graphics professionals use PostScript because their document files can be sent to a service bureau to be output on a high-resolution typesetter using the same fonts used in the original documents. With the introduction of TrueType in Windows 3.1 (also available on the Macintosh in System 7), a new breed of high-resolution imagesetters should be available for that format. If you plan to have your documents printed at higher resolution by a service bureau, be sure to find out about the equipment they use.

Adobe Type Manager

In February 1992, Adobe Type Manager Version 2.0 retailed for about $100. It comes with the 13 most popular Adobe fonts: Times, Helvetica and Courier families, plus Symbol. Adobe is well known for its very successful scalable outline font technology, PostScript. Largely because of Adobe's exorbitant licensing fees, until recently only graphics professionals owned PostScript printers and bought PostScript fonts. But with Microsoft's and Apple's decision to develop a competitor to PostScript (TrueType), all that changed. Since then, Adobe has created such important, and inexpensive, devices as the PostScript cartridge that will turn your LaserJet into a PostScript printer (for about $250, street price). They have also made many fonts available at discount prices.

The Adobe Type Manager works with Type 1 PostScript outlines and virtually all Windows output devices, including LaserJets, DeskJets, PaintJets, IBM laser and dot matrix printers. It makes available to these printers thousands of Type 1 fonts from Adobe and other developers. ATM works quickly, with no fuss or muss. It does not interfere with Windows; you'll never know it's there. The screen and printer fonts match exceptionally well. Printing is somewhat slow—reminiscent of PostScript printers. One advantage of the ATM is that it installs fonts for both itself (which allows Windows the use of any printer) and a PostScript printer as well.

Bitstream FaceLift

Bitstream has always produced high-quality fonts and font-generating software, such as its Fontware program. Its FaceLift Version 2.0, released in spring 1992, offers 13 typefaces (Times and Helvetica families plus exotic display faces). It is able to install and use at the same time not only Type 1 PostScript fonts but Bitstream Speedo and TrueType fonts as well, giving the user access to even more fonts and the ability to mix font formats. Like ATM, FaceLift creates on-the-fly printer and screen fonts for all Windows printers, including LaserJets, Paint-Jets, Desk-Jets, IBM laser, dot matrix, PostScript, TrueType, etc. The new FaceLift also possesses the ability to apply shadows and fills to any installed typeface; it will permit the user to access characters in multiple character sets. Even Post-Script Type 1 users will be able to use characters above the ANSI Windows character set. FaceLift retails for $99.99.

Bitstream currently offers several very reasonable expansion font packs: Value Pak—24 typefaces for $199; PostScript Companion Pack—35 typefaces for $179; and another package of four typefaces for $129. (See the Bitstream, Inc., section that follows.)

TrueType

TrueType, built into Windows 3.1, provides automatic matching screen fonts and printer fonts for all Windows-supported printers. It automatically installs 13 fonts equivalent to those shipped with Adobe Type Manager: Times New Roman, Arial (a version of Helvetica), a Courier family and the Symbol font. The samples of TrueType fonts that I have seen are all of the highest quality. Adding new fonts can be accomplished easily by accessing the Fonts icon in the Control Panel.

Because TrueType is part of the Windows environment, it should work faster than the two font managers mentioned above. Most type foundries, such as Bitstream, Digital Typeface Corporation, Casady & Greene, Emigre and Monotype, will offer their type libraries in this format. Font conversion utilities currently make it possible for you to convert any existing scalable outline fonts to the TrueType format.

Another advantage of TrueType is that its font files can be sent between the PC and the Macintosh (which installed TrueType fonts in its System 7 release) without conversion. If you do not already have a font collection, be sure to explore TrueType in Windows 3.1 before investing in more fonts. I recommend the Microsoft TrueType Font Pack for Windows. It contains 44 fonts to round out the collection that installs with Windows 3.1. Among these you'll find a handsome set of Lucida faces, including script and black-letter versions, as well as the Monotype version of the Zapf Dingbats.

Zenographics SuperPrint

If you work extensively with graphics, Zenographics SuperPrint provides the best and fastest graphics printing from Windows. In fact, files that won't print properly from many other Windows font managers and printer drivers will print perfectly from SuperPrint. SuperPrint provides superior results because it rasterizes the entire page, graphics and text, in the computer and then sends it to the printer. SuperPrint also allows you to use Type 1, Bitstream Speedo, Agfa Intellifonts, Nimbus Q and all other Windows-compatible scalable outline fonts. It comes with 22 typefaces (versions of Times, Helvetica, Century Schoolbook, Futura and Bitstream's Charter families) from Nimbus Q, Agfa and Bitstream. On the down side, SuperPrint is complicated to install, usually takes longer to print text files and, for a number of reasons, often produces a somewhat lower-quality font than the three font managers discussed above. SuperPrint retails for $195; SuperFonts, an additional typeface collection, $195. Zenographics, Inc., 4 Executive Circle, #200, Irvine, CA 92715; 714-851-6352.

RECOMMENDED FONT DEVELOPERS

Adobe Systems, Inc.

Adobe Systems, Inc., offers more than 1,700 typefaces in more than 250 packages, which contain between 1 and 12 typefaces and cost $95 to $375 per package. Adobe offers many specially priced sets, and vendors usually discount the suggested retail prices. Two sets deserve special mention. Adobe's "True Basics" package contains 65 fonts as well as Adobe Type Manager (discussed above). The fonts include full families of text faces as well as script faces, formal display faces and ornaments. This set costs around $150. Adobe's "Wild Type" provides 14 charming and whimsical faces reminiscent of illuminated manuscripts, children's illustrated books and Western motifs of the 1950s. Suggested retail price: $60. Their library is virtually identical with that of Linotype-Hell, with which they have had a long-term licensing agreement. Adobe faces are of the highest quality and come in the PostScript Type 1 format that can be used with Adobe Type Manager as well as Bitstream's FaceLift 2.0 and Zenographics SuperPrint, allowing you to print these faces on any Windows-supported printer. (See previous discussion under "Adobe Type Manager" and "Bitstream FaceLift.") Adobe Systems, Inc., 1585 Charleston Road, P.O. Box 7900, Mountain View, CA 94039-7900; 800-833-6687.

Bitstream, Inc.

Bitstream was the first all-digital type foundry and has remained the most eminent. Bitstream will soon offer its large (1,100 plus), well-rounded typeface library in three formats: its own Speedo, which works specifically with FaceLift; Type 1 PostScript; and TrueType. All three formats will ship with each typeface and all three work with Bitstream FaceLift 2.0. The Bitstream faces used in this book were derived from their earlier scalable format, which works with Fontware, because the LaserMaster can convert these for its use. These faces are among the best available, which is why I used them in this book.

Bitstream's type packages usually come with a family of 4 typefaces and cost about $129; a few collections of 12 faces retail for $199. Bitstream, Inc., 215 1st Street, Cambridge, MA 02142; 800-522-3668.

Best Buys: Bitstream TrueType Font Pack—40 faces lists for $79. It costs about $40 on the street. The TrueType Font Pack II sells for 20 for $20.

Note: CorelDRAW! 4.0 includes 650 Bitstream fonts on CD-ROM. See Chapter 12, "Graphics," for more information.

Casady & Greene, Inc.

Casady & Greene, Inc., offers Fluent Laser Fonts, a collection of 79 PostScript Type 1 fonts, for $189. These fonts make a fine supplement to any basic collection; they contain handsome original display and script faces. (C&G also offers a series of unique mediaeval and Art Nouveau faces as well as Cyrillic fonts on separate disks.) If you're looking for a distinctive face with a hand-drawn quality, be sure to look at these. Casady & Greene, Inc., 22734 Portola Dr., Salinas, CA 93908; 800-359-4920.

Digital Typeface Corporation

Digital Typeface Corporation is part of the LaserMaster family of companies, though its parent, The Company, was founded by the famous type developer Mike Parker. While a few of the over 350-plus typefaces currently available are not of the quality of Adobe, Bitstream, Linotype-Hell and Monotype, the majority are excellent; and DTC offers many faces not available from other vendors, such as Vivaldi, Britannic, ITC Anna, ITC Bees-Knees, Bernhard Fashion, ITC Studio Script, and the Vine

Leaves dingbats. Like some other large vendors, they will soon offer their fonts in TrueType, PostScript Type 1 and their own Nimbus Q format.

DTC offers their faces in a range of collections. The best values, if you're only beginning your typeface collection, are the DTC MasterWorks, Volumes I, II, III and IV. Each contains 100 high-quality fonts for $1,695 retail (the street price should be considerably lower). If you want a good-size, high-quality type library, this is an excellent place to start. Individual families are also available in sets at prices proportional to the number of fonts in each package. Digital Typeface Corporation, 9965 W. 69th Street, Eden Prairie, MN 55344; 612-944-9330.

Linotype-Hell

Linotype-Hell, for most of its history known as Merganthaler Linotype, or just Linotype, changed the history of printing in 1886 with its introduction of the Linotype machine, a mechanical typesetter. This company has produced thousands of typefaces, and it dominates PostScript typeface production today. Most of the Adobe typefaces available were designed and digitized by Linotype. These faces are sold by Linotype in the same sets as Adobe, for the same prices. The ever-growing library currently includes over 1,500 PostScript and over 100 TrueType fonts. Prices are comparable to Adobe's. Linotype's range of type offerings is both wide and deep. They offer the full gamut of display and text faces; multiple variations of the most popular faces, such as Garamond; and large, extended families of popular sans-serifs, like Helvetica (over 30 varieties). They offer recently designed faces and faces from the past, and an extensive selection of dingbats (called pi fonts) and script faces, which I have used throughout this book. All of their faces are of the highest quality. Currently they do not offer keyboard character charts with their fonts of pi characters or expert sets, so you may wish to buy the Adobe type packages, which do contain the charts. Linotype-Hell, 425 Oser Avenue, Hauppauge, NY 11788; 800-633-1900.

Monotype Typography

Monotype Typography, like Linotype, has a venerable place in the history of modern type design. They have produced hundreds of exceptional typefaces, among them some of the most famous of modern times. These remarkable designs include Bembo, Centaur, Plantin, Times New Roman (usually now called Times or Times Roman) and Gill Sans. Monotype's designs are among the most subtle and refined in the business. Like Adobe and Linotype, they offer expert sets to complement the primary fonts. The Monotype Classic Fonts collection comes in more than 100 packages, priced from $90 to $295, with two to eight faces in each. Monotype Typography, 150 S. Wacker Drive, Suite 2630, Chicago, IL 60606, 800-MONOTYPE; 312-855-1440.

Emigre Graphics

Emigre Graphics produces a growing collection of over 92 unusual Type 1 and TrueType display faces. Unlike those of the other, more traditional font developers discussed here, Emigre's fonts reflect a post-modern, avant-garde philosophy toward letter design and typography. This viewpoint is also expounded in the well-known magazine, *Emigre*, published by Emigre. If you want something distinctive and offbeat in your publication, you must see these fonts. Emigre Graphics, 4475 "D" Street, Sacramento, CA 95819, 800-944-9021.

In the following list of type families used in this book, and their developers, please understand that my choice of one version from one developer does not imply that I consider the others inferior. I have deliberately shown a variety of typefaces from a number of developers. Following the developer's name, I give a general type classification for the roman member of the type family. (***Note:*** a few italics are singled out because of their unusual qualities. Display faces, of course, generally have no family; they're classified by themselves.) This will help you find alternate typefaces.

Alternate Typefaces

You may never want to re-create exactly any of the documents in this book, but I hope you'll want to re-create their look. The typefaces I used play an important part in creating the mood of each piece. Since you probably won't have all the faces listed below, look for ones close in feeling. The general classification of the typeface will give you a start.

Reread the description of typeface classifications on the previous pages. In looking for a substitute typeface, analyze and match the qualities of the original: weight (bold, medium, light, etc.), serif or sans-serif, slant (upright like Romans or slanted like a script or an Italic), large or small on the body, tall or short ascenders and/or descenders, the smooth regularity or more dramatic calligraphic quality of the strokes that form each character, and typeface classification. (You can use my simple classification system or refer to a more comprehensive one. See the Bibliography.) Depending on the face itself, several of these qualities will dominate your impression of the design. You may be most impressed with its delicacy, its boldness, its squat proportions, its angularity or whatever.

Above all, attempt to interpret the mood or style evoked by the type. Sometimes a face from a different classification will create a similar mood. Don't be afraid to experiment.

NAME, DEVELOPER & TYPEFACE CLASSIFICATION

Adobe Caslon, Adobe, Transitional Roman

Adobe Caslon Ornaments, Adobe, Dingbats

Arnold Böcklin, Adobe, Display–Art Nouveau

Avant Garde (ITC), Adobe, Geometric Sans-Serif

Bauer Bodoni, Linotype, Modern Roman

Bembo, Monotype, Old Style Roman

Berkeley Oldstyle (ITC), Adobe, Old Style Roman

Bernhard Fashion, Digital Typeface Corporation, Display–1920s

Bernhard Modern, Bitstream, Unusual Roman

Bernhard Modern Italic, Bitstream, Display–Scriptlike

Bitstream Amerigo, Bitstream, Unusual Roman

Bitstream Charter, Bitstream, Transitional Roman

Bodoni, Bitstream, Modern Roman

Britannic, Digital Typeface Corporation, Display

Carta, Adobe, Dingbats

NAME, DEVELOPER & TYPEFACE CLASSIFICATION

Caslon 3, Adobe, Transitional Bold Roman

Caslon 540, Adobe, Transitional Roman

Centaur, Monotype, Old Style Roman

Cochin, Adobe, Transitional Roman or Display

Cochin Italic, Adobe, Display–Scriptlike

Copperplate Gothic 29AB, Linotype, Special Sans-Serif

Copperplate Gothic Bold, Digital Typeface Corporation,
  Special Sans-Serif

Cottonwood, Adobe, Display–Old West

Duc de Berry, Linotype, Display–Mediaeval Revival

Eurostile, Digital Typeface Corporation,
  Display–High Tech

Fette Fraktur, Adobe, Display–Black Letter

Frugal Sans, Digital Typeface Corporation,
  Traditional Sans-Serif

Futura, Bitstream and Linotype, Geometric Sans-Serif

Galliard (ITC), Bitstream, Old Style Roman

Galliard Italic (ITC), Bitstream, Display–Scriptlike

Gatsby, Fluent Laser Fonts, Display–1920s

Goudy Old Style, Bitstream, Old Style Roman

Granjon, Linotype-Hell, Old Style Roman

Granjon, Linotype-Hell, Small Caps

Helvetica, Adobe, Traditional Sans-Serif

Helvetica Inserat, Adobe, Display–High Tech

NAME, DEVELOPER & TYPEFACE CLASSIFICATION

Hiroshige, Adobe, Unusual Roman

Insignia A, Linotype-Hell, Display–Sans-Serif

Ironwood, Adobe, Display–Old West

ITC Anna, Digital Typeface Corporation, Display–1920s–1930s

Juniper, Adobe, Display–Old West

Korinna (ITC), Bitstream, Unusual Roman

Linoscript, Linotype-Hell, Display–Formal Script

Linotype Decoration Pi 1, Linotype-Hell, Dingbats

Linotype Decoration Pi 2, Linotype-Hell, Dingbats

Linotype European Pi 3, Linotype-Hell, Dingbats

Linotype European Pi 4, Linotype-Hell, Dingbats

Linotype Holiday Pi 1, Linotype-Hell, Dingbats

Lithos, an Adobe original, Display–Chisel-Cut

Meath, Fluent Laser Fonts, Display–Mediaeval Revival

Mistral, Adobe, Display–Brush Script

Modula Tall, Emigre, Display–Eccentric

Monotype Bembo, Monotype, Old Style Roman

Ponderosa, Adobe, Display–Wood Type

Reporter Two, Adobe, Display–Brush Script

Serifa, Bitstream, Slab Serif

Shelley Allegro Script, Linotype, Display–Formal Script

Shelly Volante Script, Linotype, Display–Formal Script

NAME, DEVELOPER & TYPEFACE CLASSIFICATION

Stone Sans (ITC), Adobe, Traditional Sans-Serif

Stone Serif (ITC), Adobe, Transitional Roman

Tekton, Adobe, Display–Imitation Pencil-Hand Printing

Trajan, Adobe, Display–Chisel-Cut

Univers, Bitstream's Zurich, Traditional Sans-Serif

Vine Leaves Folio One, Digital Typeface Corporation, Dingbats

Vivaldi, Digital Typeface Corporation, Display–Formal Script

Weiss, Adobe, Old Style Roman

Zapf Chancery (ITC), Bitstream, Display–Chancery Script

Zapf Dingbats (ITC), Bitstream

Zurich, Bitstream's version of Univers

LaserMaster

LaserMaster makes a wide variety of high-speed, high-resolution and printer upgrades. I purchased my first one shortly after I got my LaserJet II, in 1987. Today, I use the LaserMaster WinJet 800, which upgrades the LaserJet 4 into a 1200 dpi printer. For most purposes, 800 and 1200 dpi provide printing quality good enough for camera-ready copy—thus avoiding typesetting costs.

Both LaserMaster's WinJet upgrades feature a host-based design that uses the power of your computer to process print jobs. Not only is this incredibly fast, it means that your printer automatically gets faster every time you upgrade your computer with a faster processor or more

RAM. In addition, both WinJets add PostScript to your printer (though you don't need to use it) and come with 50 TrueType fonts from DTC. The WinJet was easy to install.

If you're interested in the WinJets or any other LaserMaster printing upgrade products, call LaserMaster at 612-944-9330.

Font Library

◆ DECORATIVE

ANNA REGULAR (DTC)

ABCDEFGHIJKLMNOPQRSTUVWXYZ
ABCDEFGHIJKLMNOPQRSTUVWXYZ
0123456789

ARCHITECT REGULAR (DTC)

ABCDEFGHIJKLMNOPQRSTUVWXYZ
abcdefghijklmnopqrstuvwxyz
0123456789

BERNHARD FASHION REGULAR (ADOBE)

ABCDEFGHIJKLMNOPQRSTUVWXYZ
abcdefghijklmnopqrstuvwxyz
0123456789

BRITANNIC REGULAR (DTC)

ABCDEFGHIJKLMNOPQRSTUVWXYZ
abcdefghijklmnopqrstuvwxyz
0123456789

EUROSTILE REGULAR (ADOBE)

ABCDEFGHIJKLMNOPQRSTUVWXYZ
abcdefghijklmnopqrstuvwxyz
0123456789

LITHOS (ADOBE)

ABCDEFGHIJKLMNOPQRSTUVWXYZ
ABCDEFGHIJKLMNOPQRSTUVWXYZ
0123456789

MISTRAL REGULAR (ADOBE)

ABCDEFGHIJKLMNOPQRSTUVWXYZ
abcdefghijklmnopqrstuvwxyz
0123456789

RIALTO REGULAR (DTC)

ABCDEFGHIJKLMNOPQRSTUVWXYZ
abcdefghijklmnopqrstuvwxyz
0123456789

SALTO (IMAGE CLUB)

ABCDEFGHIJKLMNOPQRST
UVWXYZ

abcdefghijklmnopqrstuvwxyz

0123456789

SNELL ROUNDHAND (ADOBE)

ABCDEFGHIJKLMNOPQRSTUVWXYZ
abcdefghijklmnopqrstuvwxyz
0123456789

SWING REGULAR (ADOBE)

ABCDEFGHIJKLMNOPQRSTUVWXYZ
abcdefghijklmnopqrstuvwxyz
0123456789

VIVANTE (DTC)

ABCDEFGHIJKLMNOPQRS
TUVWXYZ
abcdefghijklmnopqrstuvwxyz
0 1 2 3 4 5 6 7 8 9

◆ SANS SERIF

ITC AVANT GARDE REGULAR (ADOBE)

ABCDEFGHIJKLMNOPQRSTUVWXYZ
abcdefghijklmnopqrstuvwxyz
0123456789

ITC AVANT GARDE OBLIQUE (ADOBE)

ABCDEFGHIJKLMNOPQRSTUVWXYZ
abcdefghijklmnopqrstuvwxyz
0123456789

FRUTIGER REGULAR (ADOBE)

ABCDEFGHIJKLMNOPQRSTUVWXYZ
abcdefghijklmnopqrstuvwxyz
0123456789

FRUTIGER OBLIQUE (ADOBE)

ABCDEFGHIJKLMNOPQRSTUVWXYZ
abcdefghijklmnopqrstuvwxyz
0123456789

FUTURA REGULAR (ADOBE)

ABCDEFGHIJKLMNOPQRSTUVWXYZ
abcdefghijklmnopqrstuvwxyz
0123456789

FUTURA OBLIQUE (ADOBE)

ABCDEFGHIJKLMNOPQRSTUVWXYZ
abcdefghijklmnopqrstuvwxyz
0123456789

HELVETICA REGULAR (ADOBE)

ABCDEFGHIJKLMNOPQRSTUVWXYZ
abcdefghijklmnopqrstuvwxyz
0123456789

HELVETICA OBLIQUE (ADOBE)

ABCDEFGHIJKLMNOPQRSTUVWXYZ
abcdefghijklmnopqrstuvwxyz
0123456789

OPTIMA REGULAR (ADOBE)

ABCDEFGHIJKLMNOPQRSTUVWXYZ
abcdefghijklmnopqrstuvwxyz
0123456789

OPTIMA OBLIQUE (ADOBE)

ABCDEFGHIJKLMNOPQRSTUVWXYZ
abcdefghijklmnopqrstuvwxyz
0123456789

SANS EXTENDED REGULAR (DTC)

ABCDEFGHIJKLMNOPQRSTUVWXYZ
abcdefghijklmnopqrstuvwxyz
0123456789

SANS EXTENDED OBLIQUE (DTC)

ABCDEFGHIJKLMNOPQRSTUVWXYZ
abcdefghijklmnopqrstuvwxyz
0123456789

ITC STONE SANS REGULAR (ADOBE)

ABCDEFGHIJKLMNOPQRSTUVWXYZ
abcdefghijklmnopqrstuvwxyz
0123456789

ITC STONE SANS ITALIC (ADOBE)

ABCDEFGHIJKLMNOPQRSTUVWXYZ
abcdefghijklmnopqrstuvwxyz
0123456789

UNIVERS REGULAR (ADOBE)

ABCDEFGHIJKLMNOPQRSTUVWXYZ
abcdefghijklmnopqrstuvwxyz
0123456789

UNIVERS OBLIQUE (ADOBE)

ABCDEFGHIJKLMNOPQRSTUVWXYZ
abcdefghijklmnopqrstuvwxyz
0123456789

SERIF

CASLON REGULAR (ADOBE)

ABCDEFGHIJKLMNOPQRSTUVWXYZ
abcdefghijklmnopqrstuvwxyz
0123456789

CASLON ITALIC (ADOBE)

ABCDEFGHIJKLMNOPQRSTUVWXYZ
abcdefghijklmnopqrstuvwxyz
0123456789

ITC BERKELEY OLDSTYLE REGULAR (ADOBE)

ABCDEFGHIJKLMNOPQRSTUVWXYZ
abcdefghijklmnopqrstuvwxyz
0123456789

ITC BERKELEY OLDSTYLE ITALIC (ADOBE)

ABCDEFGHIJKLMNOPQRSTUVWXYZ
abcdefghijklmnopqrstuvwxyz
0123456789

BODONI ANTIQUA REGULAR (DTC)

ABCDEFGHIJKLMNOPQRSTUVWXYZ
abcdefghijklmnopqrstuvwxyz
0123456789

BODONI ANTIQUA ITALIC (DTC)

ABCDEFGHIJKLMNOPQRSTUVWXYZ
abcdefghijklmnopqrstuvwxyz
0123456789

FRIZ QUADRATA REGULAR (ADOBE)

ABCDEFGHIJKLMNOPQRSTUVWXYZ
abcdefghijklmnopqrstuvwxyz
0123456789

FRIZ QUADRATA ITALIC (ADOBE)

ABCDEFGHIJKLMNOPQRSTUVWXYZ
abcdefghijklmnopqrstuvwxyz
0123456789

ITC GALLIARD REGULAR (ADOBE)

ABCDEFGHIJKLMNOPQRSTUVWXYZ
abcdefghijklmnopqrstuvwxyz
0123456789

ITC GALLIARD ITALIC (ADOBE)

ABCDEFGHIJKLMNOPQRSTUVWXYZ
abcdefghijklmnopqrstuvwxyz
0123456789

ITC GARAMOND REGULAR (ADOBE)

ABCDEFGHIJKLMNOPQRSTUVWXYZ
abcdefghijklmnopqrstuvwxyz
0123456789

ITC GARAMOND ITALIC (ADOBE)

ABCDEFGHIJKLMNOPQRSTUVWXYZ
abcdefghijklmnopqrstuvwxyz
0123456789

GOUDY OLDSTYLE REGULAR (ADOBE)

ABCDEFGHIJKLMNOPQRSTUVWXYZ
abcdefghijklmnopqrstuvwxyz
0123456789

GOUDY OLDSTYLE ITALIC (ADOBE)

ABCDEFGHIJKLMNOPQRSTUVWXYZ
abcdefghijklmnopqrstuvwxyz
0123456789

MERIDIEN REGULAR (ADOBE)

ABCDEFGHIJKLMNOPQRSTUVWXYZ
abcdefghijklmnopqrstuvwxyz
0123456789

MERIDIEN ITALIC (ADOBE)

ABCDEFGHIJKLMNOPQRSTUVWXYZ
abcdefghijklmnopqrstuvwxyz
0123456789

ITC NEW BASKERVILLE REGULAR (ADOBE)

ABCDEFGHIJKLMNOPQRSTUVWXYZ
abcdefghijklmnopqrstuvwxyz
0123456789

ITC NEW BASKERVILLE ITALIC (ADOBE)

ABCDEFGHIJKLMNOPQRSTUVWXYZ
abcdefghijklmnopqrstuvwxyz
0123456789

PALATINO REGULAR (ADOBE)

ABCDEFGHIJKLMNOPQRSTUVWXYZ
abcdefghijklmnopqrstuvwxyz
0123456789

PALATINO ITALIC (ADOBE)

ABCDEFGHIJKLMNOPQRSTUVWXYZ
abcdefghijklmnopqrstuvwxyz
0123456789

ITC SOUVENIR REGULAR (ADOBE)

ABCDEFGHIJKLMNOPQRSTUVWXYZ
abcdefghijklmnopqrstuvwxyz
0123456789

ITC SOUVENIR ITALIC (ADOBE)

ABCDEFGHIJKLMNOPQRSTUVWXYZ
abcdefghijklmnopqrstuvwxyz
0123456789

ITC STONE SERIF REGULAR (ADOBE)

ABCDEFGHIJKLMNOPQRSTUVWXYZ
abcdefghijklmnopqrstuvwxyz
0123456789

ITC STONE SERIF ITALIC (ADOBE)

ABCDEFGHIJKLMNOPQRSTUVWXYZ
abcdefghijklmnopqrstuvwxyz
0123456789

TRUMP REGULAR (ADOBE)

ABCDEFGHIJKLMNOPQRSTUVWXYZ
abcdefghijklmnopqrstuvwxyz
0123456789

TRUMP ITALIC (ADOBE)

ABCDEFGHIJKLMNOPQRSTUVWXYZ
abcdefghijklmnopqrstuvwxyz
0123456789

WALBAUM REGULAR (ADOBE)

ABCDEFGHIJKLMNOPQRSTUVWXYZ
abcdefghijklmnopqrstuvwxyz
0123456789

WALBAUM ITALIC (ADOBE)

ABCDEFGHIJKLMNOPQRSTUVWXYZ
abcdefghijklmnopqrstuvwxyz
0123456789

◆DINGBATS

CARTA (ADOBE)

0123456789

ZAPF DINGBATS (ADOBE)

✡✤✢✣✦✧★☆❂☉✩✪✫✬✭✮✯✰✱✲✳✴✵✶✷✸❀❁❃❄❅❆❇❈❉❊❋●○■□❏❐❑❒▲▼◆❖◗▮▯
✎☞☛✔✓✗✘✕✙

A Few Words on Paper

Reading about paper is like reading about food: it always whets the appetite. Just as you judge a meal by actually tasting it, you learn to appreciate paper by actually handling it. Your choice of paper can be critical in producing a successful document, and there are several factors to weigh in your decision making.

Not only does the paper your document is printed on have an immediate impact on your reader; it creates a subtle and lasting impression as well. People respond to the color, opacity and texture of paper as much as to the quality of the printing. When selecting paper, keep the following considerations in mind.

Your paper's *texture*, *weight* and *substance* (thickness) reveal its quality (or the lack of it); so it's important to consider the purpose of your document. For example, for throwaway flyers you needn't invest in high-quality paper; but your letterhead should use the best, as should brochures that will stay with readers and remind them of your product and company. In general, if the typography and artwork in your piece are of high quality, the paper should be too. Rag content (usually cotton fibers) always improves the look and feel of paper for letterheads. Improving the quality of the paper you use is the cheapest way to upgrade your document.

Paper *color* sends a strong message. When choosing letterhead paper, remember that bright white communicates a stark, no-nonsense feeling; off-whites say sturdy and dependable. Pastels have a "designer" look; grays are friendly yet businesslike; light blues are usually considered masculine yet sensitive; yellows are upbeat and a bit unconventional; lavenders, peaches and pinks have a feminine connotation.

Brochures printed in color almost always get more attention than those printed on white paper. Here, pastel papers work well and color associations are not as specific as they are with letterhead stationery. Peach, for instance, is becoming popular for all types of brochures.

Since all *inks* are transparent, you should consider the effect of paper color on ink color. Also, be sure there's enough contrast between ink color and paper color to set off the text and make it easy to read. The best way to do this is to examine a printed sample before you give your order to the printer.

Many *textures* and surface *finishes* are available, such as felt, linen, parchment, imitation handmade finish, etc., that add personality and character to your document. For example, people associate imitation parchment with formal occasions and awards; hard, smooth (uncoated) paper with elegance; and rough recycled papers with expensive handmade stock. You should consider texture carefully in view of the nature and purpose of the document it will be used for. If it makes too strong a statement, it will dominate the message. Of course, this is perfectly all right if it's what you want; just be aware.

Again, there's no magic formula in matching paper with the type of document you're publishing. For newsletters, you need a paper that takes ink well and reproduces artwork adequately. I don't recommend textured or colored paper for newsletters *unless* your newsletter is also a form of advertising that needs to stand out among the competition. Generally, texture and color get in the way of text and graphics because they have their own story to tell. When printing on both sides of the sheet, as in brochures, newsletters, books and manuals, be careful to select papers with sufficient opacity. If your design is going to back up (that is, if your type will be aligned precisely back to back on both sides of the page), your paper can be thinner and less opaque.

All merchants and most printers have free samples you can use for testing. Collect a stack of these for future reference. While your printer should have a large selection of the most popular papers, you might find something you like better at a stationery, office supply store or a mail-order paper merchant. Selecting a paper that is not commonly used can help your work stand out and be remembered.

Mark Beach's *Papers for Printing* (Coast-to-Coast Books) is an excellent sourcebook, covering all aspects of selecting, using and pricing paper. It includes 44 printed samples that illustrate popular process colors and color simulations, solid ink formulas and simulations, halftone screens, full-color separations, graduated screen tints and laser-printer-type specimens produced at 300 dpi resolution, and higher resolution photo type.

Companion Disk Sneak Preview

Make quick work of duplicating many of the actual documents discussed in the *Word for Windows Design Companion, Second Edition,* with the companion disk! Enjoy using this ready-made collection of attractive and flexible clip art.

The companion disk include:

- One hundred and sixteen pieces of clip art—including all the clip art used in the documents illustrated in the book. The clip art comes from Computer Support Corporation, Micrografx and T Maker.

- Templates for actual documents discussed in the book: the calendar, invitation, invoice, one-column newsletter, two-column newsletter, three-column newsletter, modern style report, task chart and type specimen pages for display and text faces.

- Five macros for increased productivity.

- Monotype's Corsiva TrueType font.

- One PC-compatible disk, with complete and easy-to-follow instructions

Save time and energy by using the illustrations, clip art and tools on this disk to enhance your desktop publishing capabilities and help you achieve your design goals quickly and effectively. If you're not completely satisfied, your money will be returned.

Glossary

A

Alignment   Vertical placement of text elements that orients the lines of type to a left, right or center axis. In Word for Windows, alignment options are Left-aligned, Centered, Right-aligned and Justified.

Ampersand (&)   A wonderfully ornamental letter that means "and." It derives from the word *et*, which means "and" in Latin (and in French as well).

Arm   In type characters, a horizontal or diagonal stroke attached to the stem but not connected at the other end (*e.g.,* E, F, K).

Ascender   The part of a lowercase letter that rises above the x-height, as in d and l. (*See* x-height.)

Asymmetry   A design or layout scheme achieved by using an underlying grid to create informal, visual balance rather than a strict centered arrangement of typographic elements.

B

Banner   The title of a newsletter; it usually extends across the top of the front page. Also called the nameplate.

Baseline   The imaginary line on which the body portions of type characters rest. Descenders of lowercase letters extend below the baseline.

Black Letter   Also known as Old English, a dense, angular type design that dates back to the Middle Ages. Cloister Black is an example.

Body copy (or body type) The main blocks of columnar text that form the document's "body," as opposed to display type used for accents. Body copy type sizes of 8 to 12 points are typical.

Boldface type A heavier, darker version of a typeface—used for emphasis and separation in titles, headings, subheadings, etc.

Bowl In typeface design, a closed curved portion of a letterform, as in P, R, d and p.

Bullets Large dots, squares or other ornaments, used to introduce items in a list or to serve as graphic accents. (*See also* Dingbat.)

Byline Author name or names, usually placed under the title or at the bottom of an article.

C

Caption Descriptive text that accompanies an illustration. It's usually set in a type style and size that distinguish it from other text on the page.

Character Any letter, number, punctuation mark or symbol included in a type font set.

Clip art Preprinted published art usually packaged in collections. It is copyright free; selections include a wide variety of illustration styles. Clip art can be purchased on disk in .TIF, .PCX and other file formats. It can also be purchased in inexpensive printed forms and scanned into your work via the computer.

Colophon A short description, traditionally placed at the end of a book, of the particulars of a book's design, such as typefaces, type sizes, printer, brand of paper, etc.

Column rule A thin, vertical border rule that separates columns of text.

Condensed type A typeface version with narrow, tall characters—suitable for fitting the maximum amount of text into a given horizontal space, as in table listings and chart labels.

Counter The fully or partially enclosed space of a letter, as in C, S and e.

Crossbar   In typeface design, a stroke that crosses the character's stem, as on the f and t.

D

Descender   The part of a letter that extends below the baseline, as in p, q and j.

Dingbat   Ornamental type characters and symbols, sometimes called pi fonts. They're useful as bullets, markers to signal the end of a text segment and decorative accents. One of the most popular collections of dingbats is the Zapf Dingbats series.

Display type   Unusual type designs or very large type sizes of conventional designs used for titles, headings, initial caps and graphic accents. Usually much larger than body-type sizes.

Double-page spread   Left and right facing pages, as in a book. Pages in a "spread" are designed to be viewed as a unit.

Drop cap   An initial cap—usually the first letter of the first word in the opening paragraph of an article or book chapter—that is set into the text block. The first two to four lines of text are indented to accommodate the letter.

E

Em space   Traditional printer's typesetting measure; a space the width of a capital M.

En space   A space approximately half the width of an em space.

End sign   *See* Dingbat.

F

Filler   A short item inserted to plug a hole in a newsletter layout.

Fleuron   Traditional leaf-and-flower ornament design that originated hundreds of years ago. Their modern descendants are called dingbats.

Flush-left   Type aligned to the left-hand margin.

Flush-right   Type aligned to the right-hand margin.

Folio   Most often used to refer to a page number. It also means a single sheet of paper folded once.

Font   Traditionally, a single type style that includes all letters, numbers and punctuation in one point size. However, font and typeface are commonly used interchangeably.

Footer   A line of text, placed at the bottom (foot) of the page. Footers are usually placed on all pages except the first page of a document. They provide reader cues such as page number, chapter title or other information. (*See also* Headers.)

Format   As a verb, to arrange or compose. As a noun, the basic shape of a composition.

G

Gothic   A term Europeans coined to describe sans-serif typefaces (such as Letter Gothic) because they considered them so primitive compared to serif type designs. They also used the terms Antique and Grotesque. Type manufacturers today continue to use these designations.

Graphic   I use this term interchangeably with "illustration." It can also be used to refer to any printed element used in a publication.

Grid   A matrix of horizontal and vertical lines used as guides for the placement of type and graphics in a page layout. "The Grid" refers to a rather rigid grid design approach developed by Swiss typographers. Grids are especially useful for establishing order and proportion in asymmetrical typographic layouts.

Gutter   The empty vertical space between columns or between facing pages in a publication.

H

Hairline rule   A very thin rule.

Hanging indent   An indentation scheme in which the first line of a text block is flush to the left margin (or outdented into the left margin); then all subsequent lines in the text block are indented.

Head   *See* Heading.

Header   Text appearing at the top, or head, of each page (except the first) in a document. The header may include document title, chapter title, page number or any combination of these reader cues. (*See also* Footer.)

Heading   A title or summary line set in large and/or bold type to distinguish it from the body text it introduces.

Hung punctuation   Punctuation placed outside the body copy. (*See also* Hanging indent.)

I

Indent   Space inserted at the beginning of the first line of a paragraph. The traditional paragraph indent is one em space, though this can vary with page design.

Initial cap   An oversized capital letter, usually the first letter of the first word in a text line. It's often used to attract attention at the beginning of a paragraph or a chapter. An initial cap can be raised above, set outside of, or dropped into the paragraph.

Italic type   A slanted version of a typeface design, often simulating handwriting. A true italic font is an individual design, not a slanted adaptation of an upright design. (*See also* Oblique type.)

J

Jumpline   A short text line that indicates where an article resumes when it's continued from one page to another.

Justification   Type aligned both flush-left and flush-right. Justification imparts a formal tone.

Justified type   *See* Justification.

K

Kerning   The practice of fitting certain letter pairs closer together than their normal spacing would allow. Kerning improves the appearance of letter combinations such as AT or LT and makes text easier to read. Kerning should not be used to get more words on a page. (*See also* Letter spacing.)

L

Landscape orientation   Horizontal, rather than vertical, page orientation: the width exceeds the height, e.g., 11 in. x 8 1/2 in.

Layout   The process of placing type and graphic elements on a page.

Lead   *See* Leading.

Leading   The amount of white space between lines of type. The term derives from the strips of lead inserted between lines of type in the early days of printing when metal type was set by hand. Like type sizes, leading is measured in points.

Letter spacing   Adding an equal amount of space between letters in lines of type in order to even out the visual space between letters. Often used with all-caps. I recommend it.

Ligature   Two letters joined by a common type stroke, such as ff, ffi, fl. Not all digitized fonts have ligatures.

Line art   Any art created with black lines; distinguished from artwork containing shaded or colored areas. Pen-and-ink drawings are typical line art.

Logo   Short for logotype. A unique design composed of combinations of letters, words and graphics that serves as an emblem for an organization, corporation, business or product line. Traditional Japanese and European family crests are logos. Modern examples include the blue-and-white-striped IBM logo, the NBC peacock and the Apple apple.

Lowercase   The small letters, as opposed to the capital (uppercase) letters. The term derives from traditional typesetting where lead type was kept in a divided drawer, called a case. Because the noncapital letters were used most, they were kept in the lower case (closest to the typesetter). The capitals were kept in the upper case.

M

Masthead   The listing in a newsletter or magazine of the publication's staff members and contributors, place of publication, subscription information, etc. This information is usually set in small type and enclosed in a box.

Minus leading   In phototypesetting and computer typesetting, a feature that lets you set one line of type over another or over a graphic (something that was impossible in traditional printing). *Note:* Do not confuse this with using a minus sign in front of your line-spacing number.

N **Nameplate**   Sometimes refers to the logo, but more often to the upper front page area where the newsletter's name and subtitle (also called the banner) are placed.

Negative space   *See* White space.

O **Oblique type**   Often mistaken for italics. The difference is that oblique typefaces are created by slanting the roman (normal) type style, not by creating an entirely new typeface. Oblique versions are found mostly in sans-serif type families—rarely in serif families.

Old English   *See* Black Letter.

Orphan   An isolated line of type appearing at the top of a column or page. Should be avoided. Relative of "widow."

P **Pi**   A printer's term that refers to an assortment of type characters. The term also applies to a collection of dingbats.

Pica   A typographic measurement unit that equals 1/6 of an inch, or 12 points. Column widths and line lengths are usually measured in picas. (*See also* Point.)

Point   A typographic measurement unit that equals 1/72 of an inch, or 1/12 of a pica. Type sizes and leading are usually measured in points.

Pull-quotes   A short text segment taken from an article or chapter and set off in some special way. Pull-quotes attract and engage the reader, and provide visual relief on a text-heavy page.

R **Ragged left/ragged right**   Text set flush-left has a ragged right edge; text set flush-right has a ragged left edge; centered text has ragged left and right edges.

Raised cap   A large initial cap that rests on the baseline of the first row of text but extends into the white space above the line. (*See also* Drop cap; Initial cap.)

Recto page   In a multipage document, the right-hand page. Numbering always starts on a recto page; therefore, the recto page always has an odd rather than an even number. (*See also* Verso.)

Reversed type   Type that prints white on a black background. (Some laser printers can't produce reversed type.) Use it with caution as it can be difficult to read.

Roman type   A term with several meanings. It is often used to designate the normal or regular type family member that's used for body text. Roman can also refer to upright as opposed to italic or oblique type. And it can mean an Old Style serif typeface with distinct thick and thin stroke variation.

Rules   Lines used to separate columns and form boxes, frames and borders. Rule thickness is measured in points—the thinnest being a hairline rule.

Running head   A header that remains the same for at least several pages.

S

Sans-serif type   Type with uniform strokes without serifs. Helvetica and Futura are sans-serif typefaces.

Serif type   Type designed with small, ornamental finishing lines at the free ends of strokes. Times Roman and Garamond are serif typefaces.

Sidebar   A short text segment usually enclosed in a box and placed adjacent to a longer, related article.

Slab-serif type   A type design characterized by even stroke widths and square-edged serifs. Serifa and ITC Lubalin Graph are slab-serif typefaces.

Stress   Thick/thin variations in type character strokes.

Strokes   The straight and curved lines that make up a type character.

Subheads Headings that are subordinate to main headings. They are essential for guiding the reader and breaking up long text passages.

Subtitle Usually placed below a newsletter's title and within the nameplate, it often identifies the purpose or focus of the publication.

Symmetry A centered or balanced layout. The term can apply to a single page or to a double-page spread. Symmetry produces a formal, harmonious quality. However, its lack of variety can be boring.

◆ ◆ ◆ ◆ ◆ **T**

Text *See* Body copy.

Thumbnails Small, rough sketches used to test possible page layouts.

Tombstones Headings arranged side by side in adjacent columns. The reader may be misled into reading across columns, mistaking two headings for one. Also, this type of layout looks static.

Type family A group of typefaces that share common design characteristics, such as serifs, stress and basic letter shape. A typical family might include regular, italic, bold, bold italic, book, book italic, light, light italic, heavy, heavy italic, expanded, condensed, etc.

Typeface A type design that includes all letters, numbers and punctuation in all sizes. Times Roman, Futura Bold and Garamond Italic are all typefaces.

Typography The art of designing and printing with type; also the art of type design.

◆ ◆ ◆ ◆ ◆ **U**

Uppercase Capital letters. (*See also* Lowercase.)

◆ ◆ ◆ ◆ ◆ **V**

Verso page The left-hand page, always even-numbered.

W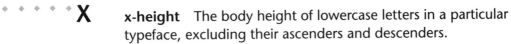

White space   The blank space in a page layout between and around text and graphics. White space plays a critical role in establishing relationships and making publications more interesting and readable.

Widow   A single word as the last line in a paragraph, or a single line isolated from the remainder of its paragraph. To be avoided. (*See also* Orphan.)

WYSIWYG   Acronym for what-you-see-is-what-you-get. This term is used to describe software programs that show you onscreen what your document will look like when it is printed. Word for Windows's Page View and Print Preview are WYSIWYG modes.

X

x-height   The body height of lowercase letters in a particular typeface, excluding their ascenders and descenders.

Bibliography

I love books of all kinds. I look on beautiful printed material the way a child looks at sweets—with joy, wonderment and lust. I've been inspired by far too many books to list them all. Instead, I list below my current favorite sources of inspiration, the works I've used in doing research for this book, and publications that you may find beneficial.

BOOKS

Beach, Mark. *Getting It Printed: How to Work with Printers and Graphic Arts Services to Assure Quality, Stay on Schedule, and Control Costs.* Portland, OR: Coast to Coast Books, 1986.
The title says it all!

Beach, Mark, and Ken Russon. *Papers for Printing: How to Choose the Right Paper at the Right Price for All Your Design and Printing Needs.* 2d ed. Portland, OR: Coast to Coast Books, 1991.
See Appendix C for a description of this book

Beaumont, Michael. *Type: Design, Color, Character & Use.* Cincinnati: North Light Books, 1991.
A fine text complements a wealth of illustrations on how to use type effectively.

Binns, Betty. *Better Type*. New York: Watson-Guptill, 1989.
A detailed look at the interaction of line length, letter spacing, kerning and typeface design. Highly recommended for anyone interested in fine typography.

Carter, Rob, Ben Day, and Philip Meggs. *Typographic Design: Form and Communication*. New York: Van Nostrand Reinhold, 1985.
A thoroughly written and lavishly illustrated introduction to the art of typography.

Collier, David, and Bob Cotton. *Basic Desktop Design & Layout*. Cincinnati: North Light Books, 1989.
A brief but thorough treatment of design principles and techniques that covers all types of document design in the context of desktop publishing. Well illustrated.

Cook, Alton, ed. *Type and Color: A Handbook of Creative Combinations*. Rockport, MA: Rockport Publications, 1989.
A remarkable book constructed with acetate overlays to allow you to preview over 800,000 combinations of type and background color and grayscale. If you plan to work in color, you need this one.

Gosney, Michael, Jim Odam, and Jim Benson. *The Gray Book*. Chapel Hill, NC: Ventana Press, 1993.

This "idea gallery" for desktop publishers offers a lavish variety of the most interesting black, white and gray graphics effects that can be achieved with laser printers, scanners and high-resolution output devices.

Gottschall, Edward M. *Typographic Communications Today*. Cambridge, MA: MIT Press, 1989.
This 14- x 11-inch book contains more than 900 illustrations of modern typographic design. Its author hopes to

develop in those new to publication design a better understanding of typography's power to make information more attractive, legible and memorable.

Hurlburt, Allen. *The Grid*. New York: Van Nostrand Reinhold, 1982.
This is the basic book on grids.

Labuz, Ronald. *Contemporary Graphic Design*. New York: Van Nostrand Reinhold, 1990.
A comprehensive survey of the design innovations of the 1980s. An excellent introduction to current typographic trends.

Lawson, Alexander. *Printing Types: An Introduction*. Boston: Beacon Press, 1974.
A concise, clear introduction to the history of type styles—a classic.

LeBlond, Geoffrey. *Windows 3 Power Tools with Disk*. New York: Bantam Books, 1991.
An excellent source of information on getting the most from Windows 3.0. It comes with a disk of useful Windows utilities.

Martin, Diana, and Mary Cooper. *Fresh Ideas in Letterhead & Business Card Design*. Cincinatti: North Light Books, 1993.
A great collection of contemporary letterheads and business cards from the totally whacky to the understated. Illustrated completely in color, you'll find great inspiration here.

Microsoft Corporation. *Users' Guide for Microsoft Word for Windows*. Redmond, WA: Microsoft Corporation, 1991.
The manual that comes with the Word for Windows software package.

Parker, Roger. *Looking Good in Print: A Guide to Basic Design for Desktop Publishing.* 2d ed. Chapel Hill, NC: Ventana Press, 1990.
A treasure trove of publication design information and illustrations.

———. *The Makeover Book: 101 Design Solutions for Desktop Publishing.* Chapel Hill, NC: Ventana Press, 1989.
Features over a hundred examples of actual publication makeovers using desktop publishing techniques.

Pedersen, B. Martin, ed. *Graphis Letterhead.* New York: Watson-Guptill, 1990.
A sumptuously produced, full-color collection of over 250 stunning letterhead suites (letterheads, business cards, envelopes, etc.). Graphis is a world-renowned magazine dedicated to graphic design.

Perfect, Christopher, and Gordon Rookledge. *Rookledge's International Typefinder: The Essential Handbook of Typeface Recognition & Selection.* New York: Moyer Bell, Ltd., 1991.
This remarkable book belongs in the library of anyone who is interested in type. It uses an ingenious method of type classification to help you identify virtually any typeface. It also presents over 700 full-alphabet type specimens.

Pfeiffer, Katherine Shelly. *The LaserJet Font Book.* Berkeley: Peachpit Press, 1990.
While focused around fonts used with the LaserJet laser printer, this book also discusses how to choose and use type for desktop publishing. It provides extensive notes on the origins and appropriate use of most popular typefaces.

Rand, Paul. *A Designer's Art*. New Haven, CT: Yale University Press, 1985.
A collection of writings, copiously illustrated, by one of America's most well-known graphic designers. I recommend this for its visual inspiration and for those who want to look into the great designer's mind and heart.

Siebert, Lori, and Mary Cooper. *Working with Words and Pictures*. Cincinatti: North Light Books, 1993.
If you need to work with illustrations and/or photographs in your publications, this profusely illustrated book will be a great help. Examples are taken from the work of many of our greatest publication designers. The commentary is concise and inspirational.

Step-By-Step Graphics Staff. *Step-By-Step Graphics: Designers Guide to Typography*. Peoria, IL: Step-By-Step Publishing, a division of Dynamic Graphics, Inc., 1991.
A special issue (Vol. 6, No. 2) of the magazine *Step-By-Step Graphics* (mentioned below under Periodicals) republished in book form. Contains many excellent articles on all aspects of contemporary typography, including: signage, advertising type, typography and corporate identity, dangerous typography (mixing type styles artistically), newspaper typography, producing readable and beautiful type, and evaluating digital typeface quality.

Stone, Sumner, and Brian Wu. *On Stone: The Art and Use of Typography on the Personal Computer*. San Francisco: Bedford Arts, 1991.
While this book does discuss the history of typography and the significance of the current use of the personal computer, its real value lies in its presentation of the beautiful Stone type family in a series of documents shown full size. Stone's succinct commentaries reveal much of the subtleties of good typography.

Strunk, William, Jr., and E. B. White. *The Elements of Style.* 3d ed. New York: Macmillan, 1979.
This classic, entertaining treatise on effective writing includes basic grammar and usage information.

Swann, Alan. *How to Understand and Use Design and Layout.* Cincinnati: North Light Books, 1991.
Profusely illustrated, this volume briskly reviews the theory and practice of page layout.

Tufte, Edward. *Envisioning Information.* Cheshire, CT: Graphics Press, 1990.
See comments following next book.

——— . *The Visual Display of Quantitative Information.* Cheshire, CT: Graphics Press, 1983.
Envisioning Information covers the visual issues involved in the presentation of complex, dense data, as in timetables, scientific diagrams, maps, etc. *The Visual Display of Quantitative Information* covers the creation of visually successful statistical graphics, maps, charts and tables. Tufte's standards of book production are so exacting that he published these books himself. With meticulous typography, color printing and exquisite paper, they are examples of book production at its best.

Type Directors Club Staff. *Typography: The Annual of the Type Directors Club.* New York: Watson-Guptill, date varies.
The title of this annual publication changes each year. These full-color publications present the winning entries of the annual Type Directors Club design contest. Here you will see the work of the world's most respected typographers.

Utvich, Michael. *The Official Arts & Letters Handbook*. New York: Bantam Books, 1990.
An excellent guide to using Computer Support Corporation's Arts & Letters Graphics Editor drawing program. It also comes with an excellent disk of additional clip art. If you use the program you should get the book; if you're interested in what the program can do, this is a first-rate source.

White, Alex. *How to Spec Type*. New York: Watson-Guptill, 1987.
This is one of my favorite books: a concise and witty presentation of solutions to a myriad of typographic problems.

White, Jan. *Graphic Design for the Electronic Age: The Manual for Traditional and Desktop Publishing*. New York: Watson-Guptill, 1988.
Jan White has written a host of fine books on graphic design. This one has much of the best of his advice.

Will-Harris, Daniel. *Dr. Daniel's Windows Diet: A Fast Cure for Your Windows Pains*. Berkeley: Peachpit Press, 1993.
Short and to the point, Daniel Will-Harris helps you cope with those pesky little problems most Windows users experience. As always, Daniel's work is full of humor and good sense. A pleasure and a treasure.

——— . *TypeStyle: How to Choose & Use Type on a Personal Computer, Featuring Bitstream Fonts*. Berkeley: Peachpit Press, 1990.
An excellent source of information on all aspects of using type in desktop publishing. It includes 50 full-page examples of handsome business documents. While the first edition showcases Bitstream fonts, the second edition covers all type developers.

Before & After: How to Design Cool Stuff on Your Computer, PageLab, P.O. Box 418252, Sacramento, CA 95841-9855. Bimonthly.
This exciting, full-color publication is full of tips and techniques—a timeless reference tool and daily workbook for desktop publishers of all levels. Concisely written and profusely illustrated—not an inch of wasted space.

Communication Arts, Coyne & Blanchard, 410 Sherman Ave., Palo Alto, CA 94303. Eight issues a year.
Traditional "required reading" for art directors and graphic designers, now devoting increased space to desktop publishing concerns. Special focus issues showcase samples of the year's best designs in advertising, illustration and photography.

Font & Function, Adobe Systems, P.O. Box 7900, Mountain View, CA 94039-7900. Twice yearly.
This free publication includes articles on new typeface designs, gives samples of Adobe typefaces in use and shows specimens of many available Adobe fonts.

Inside Word for Windows, The Cobb Group, 9420 Bunsen Pkwy., Ste. 300, Louisville, KY 40220. Monthly.
Each thoroughly illustrated issue provides an in-depth look at various aspects of Word for Windows. Every issue will bring you an invaluable tip.

Print: America's Graphic Design Magazine, RC Publications, 3200 Tower Oaks Blvd., Rockville, MD 20852. Bimonthly.
Focuses on techniques and economics of professional graphic design, with an eye on advances in desktop publishing. Its yearly regional design and advertising design issues by themselves justify its subscription price.

Publish, Integrated Media, Inc., 501 Second St., San Francisco, CA 94107. Monthly.
In-depth critiques of the latest publishing hardware and software, along with design- and technique-oriented articles. Of special interest is its monthly typography column.

Step-by-Step Graphics, Dynamic Graphics, 6000 North Forest Park Dr., P.O. Box 1901, Peoria, IL 61656. Bimonthly.
Technique-oriented advice for advanced desktop publishers and others who aspire to greater expertise in layout and design. Its how-to format helps you implement the best traditional and electronic tools and methods of graphic design.

U&lc (Upper and Lower Case, The International Journal of Type and Graphic Design), International Typeface Corporation, 866 Second Ave., New York, NY 10017-2991. Quarterly.
This large-format tabloid contains features written by many of the world's leading typeface designers. It balances a historical perspective with down-to-earth treatment of contemporary publishing issues.

VIDEO

Word for Windows Desktop Publishing Shortcuts and Practical Tips by Daniel Will-Harris. Learnkey.

Notes on Hardware & Software

I use a Nortgate 386, 20 Mhz Super microcomputer with 8mb of RAM; a NEC MultiSync 4D and an ATI VGA Wonder Plus graphics adapter; and a Seagate ST 4144R 120mb hard disk.

The illustrations and documents I created for this book were printed using the LaserMaster Professional Level III printer controller in conjunction with my Hewlett-Packard LaserJet II printer.

Software products used in conjunction with this project:

- ◆ The Desktop Set (Okna Corporation) for scheduling

- ◆ After Dark for Windows screen saver (Berkeley Systems).

- ◆ Arts & Letters Graphics Editor (Computer Support Corporation)

- ◆ CorelDRAW (Corel Corporation)

- ◆ Collage-Complete screen-capture program (Inner Media)

- ◆ Correct Grammar for Windows (The Writing Tools Group)

- ◆ Clip art from Arts & Letters Graphics Editor (Computer Support Corporation) and from the Clip Art Gallery packaged in Artline (Digital Research—artwork originally from T/Maker Company)

- ◆ Typefaces from Adobe, Bitstream, Digital Typeface Corporation, Casady & Greene, Emigre, Linotype-Hell and Monotype

Index

A ◆ ◆ ◆

A–Z Graphics advertisement   174–75
Abrax Inc.   142–43
Adobe Systems, Inc.   421–22
Adobe Type Manager   418–19
Advertisements   168
   examples   182–83
      asymmetry   184–85
      correspondence included   180–81
      frames   174–75
      mixing typefaces   176–77
      newspaper   173, 178–79
      postcards   172
      white space   184–85
Alignment   55–57, 323–25
   choosing   56–57
   flyers   194–97
   frame contents   333
   frames   337
   graphics   369
   letterheads   84–85
   mixed in same line   324–25
   resumes   124–25
   See also Justification
Announcements   92
   examples   126–27
ANSI symbols   310
Appendix
   defined   251
Asia Imports invitation   131
Asia Imports invoice   140–41
Asymmetry   40–41
   advertisements   184–85
   books   254, 266–73
At Least line spacing   320

Athens Estates advertisement   176–77
Attention getters   59–62
Auto Formatting   329
Awards   92
   examples   128–30

B ◆ ◆ ◆

Background Repagination   30
Banners   212
Baseline   49
Baskerville typeface   403–4
Bibliography
   defined   251
Bitmapped images   361, 416–17
Bitstream, Inc.   422–23
Bitstream FaceLift font manager   419–20
Bodoni typeface   404–5
Body copy   214
Bold text   188–89
Bold typefaces   399
Books   247–99
   back matter   251
   covers   273
   examples   258–99
      business reports   266–73
   front matter   248
   graphics   250
   main section   249–50
   modern design   253–54
      examples   274–81
   pagination   254–55
   traditional design   252–53
      examples   258–65
   typefaces   252, 413
   See also Manuals

Borders   19, 77–78, 339–45
    around tables   350–51
    attention-getting   61–62
    combining   341
    creating   340–45
    exotic   343–44
    length   340–41
    mixed-style paragraphs   343
    nonprinting   335, 344
    page   344–45
    between paragraphs   341
    series   341–43
    styles   340
    in tables   349–51, 370
    thick   340
Boxes   77–78
    attention-getting   61
Brochures   169–70
    examples   198–209
        classical   206–9
        graphics   198–209
        symmetry   206–9
        three-fold   202–5
        white space   198–209
Business cards   88–89
    examples   108–9
    typefaces   412
Business letters   91–92
    typefaces   412
    See also Letterheads
Bylines   213

C ◆ ◆ ◆

Calendars   162–63
Captions
    books   250
    graphics   370–71
    newsletters   214
Casady & Greene, Inc.   423
Catalogs   256
    covers   295
    examples   294–99
Cells
    printing problems   385–86
    spacing   352

Changes
    abandoning   23
    global   32
Chapter headings   249, 262
Character dialog box
    See Font dialog box
Characters
    find and replace   308
    formatting   9–12, 18–19, 303–15
        applying   305
        copying   305–7, 327
        find and replace   307–8
        options   304
        undoing   307, 327–28
    nonprinting   30
    raising/lowering   309
Charts   14–15, 361–62
    converting to graphics   371–72
    creating from tables   348–49
    examples   160–61
    inserting   368
Clip art   357–58
Clipboard   366
Cogent Books news release   114–17
Cogent Books order form   148–49
Colophon   251
Columns
    attention-getting   60
    spacing   353
    unequal   376–77
Commands
    author's referral methods   20
    common   18–20
Consistency   69–70
Contacts form   152–53
Contrast   38–39
Copying
    character formatting   305–7, 327
    drop caps   314–15
    paragraph formatting   326–27
Copyright   248
Crowding   79–80
Customizing   29–32
    toolbars   31–32
    views   6–7, 29–30

D ◆ ◆ ◆

Damask Lullaby 258–65
Dashes 311
Dateline 212
David M. Rubin fax cover 109–11
David Rubin Music Services 96–97
Day and Night Security
    advertisement 173
Deleting frames 332–33
Department heads 212–13
Descenders 355, 384–85
Design
    fundamentals 35–64
    preliminary sketches 65–66
    sequence of activities 63
Desktop publishing
    vs. word processing 2
Dialog boxes
    author's referral methods 20
Digital Typeface Corporation 423–24
Dingbats 60–61, 363–64, 410
    defined 60
    examples 445
Disappearing items 25, 387, 390
Double spacing 319
Drag & drop 7
Drawing programs 358–59
Drawing toolbar 12
Drawing tools 360–61
Drop caps 313–15
    copying 314–15
    creating 314
    problems 315
Dunham Industries flyer 194–97

E ◆ ◆ ◆

Em dashes 311
Embedded objects 367–68
Emigre Graphics 425
En dashes 311
End sign 215
Endnotes 251
Estimate forms 154–55
Exactly line spacing 320–21

Exiting
    frames 337–38
    tables 354
Eyebrows 212–13

F ◆ ◆ ◆

Facing pages
    See Mirror images; Spreads
Fax covers 89–90
    examples 109–11
Files
    formats 366–67
    multiple 23–24
Films International 98–99
Films International business card 109
Find and replace
    characters 308
    formatting 307–8
Flyers 168–69
    examples 186–97
        alignment 194–97
        bold letters 188–89
        business 194–97
        graphics 190–93
        text arrangement 186–87
Font dialog box 303–15
    gray/blank 305
    See also Characters—formatting
Font managers 417–21
Fonts 25–27
    bitmap 416–17
    installing 25
    matching screen & printer 26–27
    not displaying in list box 391–92
    scalable outline 416–17
    See also Typefaces
Footnotes 250
Formatting toolbar 4
Forms 133–36
    components 135
    examples 138–55
        contacts 152–53
        estimate 154–55
        inventory 150–51
        invoices 138–41
        order 142–49

matching letterhead   154–55
typefaces   412
See also Surveys
Four Seasons   286–93
Frames   331–38
   advertisements   174–75
   aligning   337
   anchoring to paragraph   335–36
   centering contents   333
   deleting   332–33
   effects on formatting   331–32
   exiting   337–38
   fitting against margin   377–78
   formatting   20
      contents   332
      space around   333–35
      space inside   334
   headers and footers   336
   inserting   18, 389
   margins   335
   moving unexpectedly   387
   overlapping   337
   problems   337–38, 387–89
   repeating   336–37
   selecting contents   333
   splitting   388–89
   stuck in   337–38
   styles   332
   unexpected text appears   388
   vs. tables/text boxes   381–83
Full Deck business card   108

G ◆ ◆ ◆

Gizmos newsletter   238–43
Global changes   32
Glossary
   defined   251
Graphics   12–13, 357–73
   attention-getting   60–62
   books   250
   brochures   198–209
   captions   370–71
   centering   369
   converting charts   371–72
   distorted in tables   355
   fitting against margin   377–78

flyers   190–93
importing   366–67
   problems   366–67
inserting   368
modifying   368–69
newsletters   214
print managers   421
printing   372–73
screen redraw speed   368
space around   370
symbols   363–64
See also Charts
Graphs
   See Charts
Great Videos   144–47
Grids   57–58
   advertisements   175
   brochures   204
   business cards   109
   catalogs   294, 296
   flyers   193, 197
   invoices   140
   newsletters   215
   order forms   142, 147–48
   résumés   120
   table of contents   276

H ◆ ◆ ◆

Hana Hotel advertisement   180–81
Hana Hotel letterhead   94–95
Harmony   38–39
Headers and footers   379–81
   books   249–50
   frames   336
   mirror-image   278–81, 380
   newsletters   212
Headings   71–72
   book chapters   249, 262
   column bottoms   76–77
   manipulating   24–25
   typefaces   413
Headlines   213
Help   8–9
Holes   73–74

I ◆ ◆ ◆

Illustrations
 See Graphics
Imitation   67–68
Importing images   366–67
Indenting   74–75, 323–24
 effect on drop caps   315
 frames' effects   331–32
Index
 defined   251
Initial caps   228, 312–15
Introduction
 examples   271–73
Inventory forms   150–51
Invitations   92
 examples   131
Invoices   138–41
Italics   398–99

J ◆ ◆ ◆

Jasmine Theatre flyer   190–93
Jumplines   214
Justification   55, 73

K ◆ ◆ ◆

Keeping fit brochure   202–5
Kerning   53–55
KSP with Flowers   104–5
KSP Writer/Designer   106–7

L ◆ ◆ ◆

LaserMaster   430–31
Layout   57–62, 375–83
 newsletters   215
Leading   51–52
 determining amount   52–53, 71
 Exactly   320–21
 At Least   320
 options   318–20
Letter spacing   54–55
 advertisements   182–83

Letterheads   83–90
 aligning   84–85
 examples   94–107
  avant-garde   98–99
  classical   102–3
  combined traditional/
   contemporary   106–7
  informal   104–5
  logos   96–97, 100–101
  news releases   114–17
  symmetry   94–95
 functions   83
 logos   86–87
 typefaces   86, 412
Letters (correspondence)
 See Business letters; Fax covers;
  Letterheads
Line styles
 See Borders
Lines
 beyond screen edge   26–27
 creating new   323
 length   52–53, 70–71
 spacing
  See Leading
Linotype-Hell   424–25
Logos
 business cards   108–9
 letterheads   86–87, 96–97, 100–101

M ◆ ◆ ◆

Macros   6, 27–29
 recording   28–29
 supplied with Word   27–28
Manuals   255–56
 covers   287
 examples   286–93
 See also Books
Margins
 inserting frames   335
 part of document   379
 tables   351–52, 354–55
Masthead   212
Measurement units   30–31
Memory problems   392–93

Memos   90
    examples   112–13
Microsoft Draw   360–61
Microsoft Graph   14–15, 361–62
Mijinsky Ballet flyer   186–87
Mirror images
    headers and footers   278–81, 380
    pages   375–76
Money Talks newsletter   222–25
Monotype Typography   425
Multimedia News newsletter   232–37
Mystical Symbols   266–73

N ◆ ◆ ◆

Nameplates   212, 222–25
Negative space
    See White space
News releases   91–92
    examples   114–19
        on letterheads   114–17
Newsletters   211–45
    column formats   216–20
    components   211–15
    examples   222–45
        nameplates   222–25
    five-column   220
    four-column   219–20
        examples   238–43
    front page   233
    graphics   214
    layout   215
    one-column   217–18
    pitfalls   215–16
    three-column   219
        examples   232–37, 244–45
    two-and-a-half columns   220
    two-column   218
        examples   226–31
    typefaces   413
Newspaper advertisements   173, 178–79
NORMAL.DOT file   32, 330

O ◆ ◆ ◆

Obliques   399
Order (design element)   37

Order forms   142–49
Orphans   76
Out of Memory message   392–93
Outdenting   323–24
Outlines   24–25

P ◆ ◆ ◆

Page breaks   354
Page layout
    See Layout
Page numbers
    repaginating   30
Page setup
    See Layout
Pages, mirror-image   375–76
Palos Verdes flower show
    brochure   198–201
Paper selection   447–49
Paragraph dialog box   317–25
    See also Paragraphs—formatting
Paragraph marks   21, 315–16
    displaying   316
    removing   316
    See also Paragraphs
Paragraphs   20–22
    defined   20–21, 315
    formatting   10–11, 19, 315–30
        copying   326–27
        removing   326
        undoing   327–28
    spacing between   321–22
Plagiarizing   67–68
Pleasure Craft News   244–45
Point size   49–50, 52
Positive space   39–40
Postcards
    advertisements   172
Printers
    setting up   26
    upgrades   430–31
Printing
    blank page   392
    cell text cut off   385–86
    graphics   372–73, 421
    middle of paper   379
    tips   383–84

Promotional materials   165–209
    arranging-text   166–67
    attention getting   165–66
    checklist   167–68
    examples   172–209
    typefaces   413
    See also Advertisements; Brochures;
       Flyers
Pull-quotes   214

Q ◆ ◆ ◆

Quotation marks   75, 312
Quotations   250

R ◆ ◆ ◆

Recto   247
Repeat command   306
Repetition   166, 170
Reports
    examples   274–81
       technical   282–83
       title pages   284–85
    See also Books
Respighi résumé   120–25
Résumés   90–91
    examples   120–25
       centered   124–25
       conventional   122–23
       modern   120–21
Reverses   240, 346–47
Ribbon
    See Formatting toolbar
Rivers of white   55, 73
Roman numerals   75
Roman typefaces   398, 401–5
    modern   404–5
    Old Style   401–2
    traditional   403–4
    unusual   402–3
Rows
    height   348
    spacing   352–53
Rulers   4–5

Rules (lines)
    See Borders
Running headers
    See Headers and footers—books
Rx Pharmaceutical fraud   282–83

S ◆ ◆ ◆

Sans-serif typefaces   42–45, 405–7
    defined   42
    examples   436–39
    geometric   406
    traditional   406
Saving
    global changes   32
    recommendations   22
Scanning   362–63, 367
Screen fonts   26–27
Screen redraws   368
Screens, background
    See Shading
Section dividers   249
Selecting   25
    text in frames   333
Sentence spacing   72
Serif typefaces   42–45, 407
    defined   42
    examples   439–44
Shading   78, 345–47
    attention-getting   62
    options   339–40
Signs of the Times   294–99
Silverado Garden Council   128–30
Single spacing   318–19
Sketches   65–66
Ski Books   126–27
Slysbrochure   206–9
Smart Quotes   75, 312
Soft Trix News Release   118–19
Space bar   74–75
Spacing
    cells   352
    columns and rows   352–53
    design elements   78
    frames   333–35
    graphics   370

letters 54–55
    advertisements 182–83
lines 51–53, 71, 318–21
    See also Leading
paragraphs 321–22
sentences 72
vertical 322–23
words 308–9
Spreads 58, 68
    See also Mirror images
Standard toolbar 3
    changes gone 386
    restoring original 386–87
Structure 37
Style 37
Styles 327
    applying
        Auto Formatting 329
    borders 340
    built-in 328
    creating 329
    effects of changing 328
    frames 332
    links 328
        avoiding 329
    problems 390–91
    Standard 329
Subscript 309
Succulent Sandwich Society
  Survey 156–59
Sunshelters estimate form 154–55
Sunshelters letterhead 100–101
Superscript 309
Surveys 136–37
    examples 156–59
    typefaces 412
    See also Forms
Symbols
    ANSI 310
    graphics 363–64
    inserting 310–11
Symmetry 40–41
    brochures 206–9
    letterheads 94–95

T ◆ ◆ ◆

Tab leaders 325
Table of contents
    books 248, 260–61, 268–69, 276–77
    newsletters 212
Tables 294–99, 347–55
    advantage over frames 352
    borders around 350–51
    borders inside 349–51, 370
    converting to charts 348–49
    creating 348–49
    distorted text/graphics 355
    exiting 354
    fitting against margin 377–78
    formatting contents 349
    inserting 18
    inserting text above 354
    margins 351–52, 354–55
    page breaks 354
    problems 354–55
    spacing between columns/
      rows 352–53
    stuck in 354
    uses 347
    vs. frames/text boxes 381–83
Tabs 325
Templates
    See Styles
Text
    bold 188–89
    distorted in tables 355
    fitting against margin 377–78
    flyers 186–87
    formatting 9–12, 230, 305
        See also Characters—formatting;
          Paragraphs—formatting
    problems 384–86
    promotional materials 166–67
    reversing 240, 346–47
    typefaces 45–46
Text boxes
    vs. frames/tables 381–83
Title page 248, 259, 266–67, 284–85
Tombstones 216
Tone 37
Toolbars 3–5

customizing   31–32
    See also Drawing toolbar; Formatting
       toolbar; Standard toolbar
Trouble-shooting   384–93
    cell printing   385–86
    descenders cut off   355, 384–85
    disappearing items   25, 387, 390
    display   390
    fonts   391–92
    frames   337–38, 387–89
    importing images   366–67
    memory   392–93
    printing   392
    Standard toolbar   386–87
    styles   390–91
    tables   354–55
TrueType font manager   420–21
Type families   47–48, 397–400
    defined   397
Typefaces   42–50, 397–447
    advertisements   176–77
    bold   399
    books   252
    buying   411–13
    choosing   45, 412–13, 426–27
    condensed   400
    decorative   433–35
    digital   416–17
    display   46–47, 408–10
       poster size   409–10
    examples   433–44
    expanded   399
    letterheads   86
    ornamental   365
    printing samples   66–67, 413–15
    Roman
       See Roman typefaces
    sans-serif
       See Sans-serif typefaces
    serif
       See Serif typefaces
    size   48–50, 52, 70–71
    sources   421–25
    text   45–46
    used in this book   426–30
    varying   59
    See also Fonts

U ◆ ◆ ◆

Undoing   23
    character formatting   307, 327–28
    paragraph formatting   327–28

V ◆ ◆ ◆

Vector images   359
Verso   247
Victor Lazlo flyer   184–85
Views
    customizing   6–7, 29–30

W ◆ ◆ ◆

White space   39–40, 79–80
    advertisements   184–85
    attention-getting   59
    brochures   198–209
    caused by justification   55, 73
Widows   75–76
Windows
    customizing   29–30
Windows Paint   361
WJR invoice   138–39
WJR letterhead   102–3
Word for Windows
    Desktop publishing features   17–32
    optimizing   22–23
    screen features   3–15
    terms in versions 2 & 6   18
Word processing
    vs. desktop publishing   1–2
WordArt   13–14, 365
Words
    spaces between   308–9
Writer's Hollywood Digest
    newsletter   226–31

Z ◆ ◆ ◆

Zenographics SuperPrint font
    manager   421
Zoo Resources   274–81

Colophon

Word for Windows Design Companion, Second Edition, was produced on a Macintosh Quadra 700, using PageMaker 5.0. Body type is 11 1/2-point ITC Stone Serif set on 14 1/2 points of leading. Chapter titles and heads are set in ITC Stone Sans Semibold.

All the documents discussed and illustrated in Part III were composed in Word for Windows and printed using a LaserMaster Professional Level III controller and an HP LaserJet II.

Page proofs were produced on a LaserWriter IIg and a LaserWriter Pro 630. Film output was produced on a Linotronic 330 imagesetter.

Notes

the
Ventana Press

Desktop Design Series

To order these and other Ventana Press titles, use the form in the back of this book or contact your local bookstore or computer store. Full money-back guarantee!

Return order form to:
Ventana Press, PO Box 2468, Chapel Hill, NC 27515

☎ **919/942-0220; Fax 919/942-1140**

Can't wait? Call toll-free, 800/743-5369 (U.S. only)!

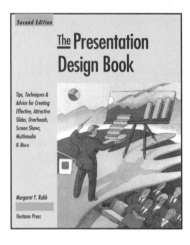

Looking Good in Print, Third Edition
$24.95
424 pages, illustrated
ISBN: 1-56604-047-7
With over 200,000 copies in print, **Looking Good in Print** is looking even better, with a new chapter on working with color, plus new sections on photography and scanning. For use with any software or hardware, this desktop design bible has become the standard among novice and experienced desktop publishers alike.

The Makeover Book: 101 Design Solutions for Desktop Publishing
$17.95
282 pages, illustrated
ISBN: 0-940087-20-0
"Before-and-after" desktop publishing examples demonstrate how basic design revisions can dramatically improve a document.

Advertising From the Desktop
$24.95
464 pages, illustrated
ISBN: 1-56604-064-7
Advertising From the Desktop offers unmatched design advice and helpful how-to instructions for creating persuasive ads. This book is an idea-packed resource for improving the look and effect of your ads.

Newsletters From the Desktop
$23.95
306 pages, illustrated
ISBN: 0-940087-40-5
Now the millions of desktop publishers who produce newsletters can learn how to dramatically improve the design of their publications.

The Presentation Design Book, Second Edition
$24.95
320 pages, illustrated
ISBN: 1-56604-014-0
The Presentation Design Book is filled with thoughtful advice and instructive examples for creating presentation visuals that have the power to communicate and persuade. For use with any software or hardware.

The Gray Book, Second Edition
$24.95
272 pages, illustrated
ISBN: 1-56604-073-6
This "idea gallery" for desktop publishers offers a lavish variety of the most interesting black, white and gray graphics effects that can be achieved with laser printers, scanners and high-resolution output devices.

From Ventana Press...

More Companions For Creative Computing

The Windows Shareware 500
$39.95
417 pages, illustrated
ISBN: 1-56604-045-0
Whether you're a shareware veteran or skeptic, this book is required reading. The only comprehensive guide to 500 of the best Windows shareware programs. Comes with four disks.

Desktop Publishing With Word for Windows, Second Edition
$21.95
328 pages, illustrated
ISBN: 1-56604-074-4
Desktop Publishing With Word for Windows is your key to creating attractive newsletters, brochures, ads, proposals and reports, correspondence and more.

Looking Good With CorelDRAW!, Second Edition
$27.95
328 pages, illustrated
ISBN: 1-56604-061-2
Guidelines and suggestions are given on how to best take advantage of CorelDRAW's powerful new desktop publishing features for Version 4.

Windows, Word & Excel Office Companion, Second Edition
$21.95
600 pages, illustrated
ISBN: 1-56604-083-3
Your Microsoft business bible. This three-in-one reference is organized as a quick course in each program. Chapters contain valuable information on basic commands and features, plus helpful tutorials, tips and shortcuts.

Voodoo Windows
$19.95
282 pages, illustrated
ISBN: 1-56604-005-1
A unique resource, *Voodoo Windows* bypasses the technical information found in many Windows books to bring you an abundance of never-before-published tips, tricks and shortcuts for maximum Windows productivity. A one-of-a-kind reference for beginners and experienced users alike.

The PC Internet Tour Guide
$24.95
275 pages, illustrated
ISBN: 1-56604-084-1
Push your PC to cruising speed on the Internet! Comes complete with software that converts the Internet to an easy graphic interface, along with free trial service and step-by-step instructions.

The Official America Online for Windows Membership Kit & Tour Guide
$34.95
402 pages, illustrated
ISBN: 1-56604-025-6
This book/disk set includes the AOL starter disk, 10 free hours of online time for new and current members, a free month's membership plus your official AOL "tour guide."

Widen Your Word World!

Increase your desktop publishing productivity and creativity with this helpful imaginative companion disk! With art and examples taken directly from the book, *Word for Windows Design Companion Disk, Second Edition,* offers a multitude of valuable, time-saving tools, including

- ◆ 70 images from the Arts & Letter Clip Art Collection, all of which are showcased throughout the book.
- ◆ Two commercial fonts.
- ◆ Templates of various documents, including: three newsletters, an invitation, an invoice, a task chart, a calendar and a report.
- ◆ 45 clip-art files from Micrografx's Windows Draw Collection.
- ◆ Seven productivity-enhancing macros specifically created to facilitate your desktop publishing and graphics tasks.

This innovative disk will provide you with the materials necessary for creating successful documents that have the power to communicate and persuade. Your money returned if not completely satisfied.

___ **YES!** Please send me _____ copy(s) of the *Word for Windows Design Companion Disk, Second Edition,* for just $16.50 each.

Name _____

Street Address (No PO Box) _____

City/State/Zip _____

Phone _____

Please add $3.90 shipping/set for standard shipping, $7.00 for "two-day" or Canadian shipping.

___ Payment enclosed (check or money order; no cash please)

___ VISA/Mastercard _____ Exp. _____

___ disks @ $16.50 + _____ shipping = _____ Total

Return to Ventana Press, PO Box 2468, Chapel Hill, NC 27515.
Fax 919/942-0220

CAN'T WAIT? Order toll-free 800/743-5369 (U.S. only)!

Ventana Press
Attention: Word for Windows Design Companion
PO Box 2468
Chapel Hill, NC 27515

Ventana Press
Attention: Word for Windows
        Design Companion
PO Box 2468
Chapel Hill, NC 27515

Place
Stamp
Here

TO ORDER additional copies of *Word for Windows Design Companion, Second Edition,* or any other Ventana Press title, please fill out this order form and return it to us for quick shipment.

	Quantity	Price	Total
Advertising From the Desktop	_____	x $24.95 =	$_____
Desktop Publishing With Word for Windows, 2nd Edition	_____	x $21.95 =	$_____
The Gray Book, 2nd Edition	_____	x $24.95 =	$_____
Looking Good in Print, 3rd Edition	_____	x $24.95 =	$_____
Looking Good With CorelDRAW!, 2nd Edition	_____	x $27.95 =	$_____
The Makeover Book	_____	x $17.95 =	$_____
Newsletters From the Desktop	_____	x $23.95 =	$_____
The Official America Online for Windows Membership Kit & Tour Guide	_____	x $34.95 =	$_____
The PC Internet Tour Guide	_____	x $24.95 =	$_____
Presentation Design Book, 2nd Edition	_____	x $24.95 =	$_____
Type From the Desktop	_____	x $23.95 =	$_____
Voodoo DOS, 2nd Edition	_____	x $19.95 =	$_____
Voodoo Windows	_____	x $19.95 =	$_____
The Windows Shareware 500	_____	x $39.95 =	$_____
Windows, Word & Excel Office Companion, 2nd Edition	._____	x $21.95 =	$_____

Shipping: Please add $4.50/first book, $1.35/book thereafter; $8.25/book "two-day air," $2.25/book thereafter. For Canada, add $6.50/book.   = $_____

Send C.O.D. (add $4.50 to shipping charges)   = $_____

North Carolina residents add 6% sales tax   = $_____

Total   = $_____

Name _____

Company _____

Address (No PO Box) _____

City_____ State_____ Zip_____

Daytime Telephone _____

___ Payment enclosed ___VISA ___MC Acc't # _____

Expiration Date_____ Interbank # _____

Signature _____

Please mail or fax to: **Ventana Press, PO Box 2468, Chapel Hill, NC 27515**
☎ 919/942-0220, FAX: 919/942-1140

CAN'T WAIT? CALL TOLL-FREE ☎ 800/743-5369 (U.S. only)!